£4.50

D1458204

The Complete Guide
to Herbs

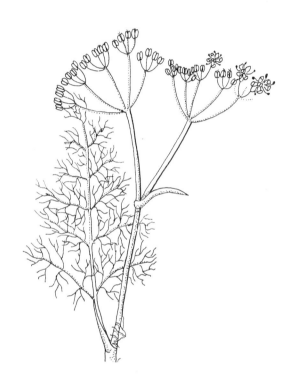

The Complete Guide to Herbs

HOW TO GROW AND USE
NATURE'S MIRACLE PLANTS

EDITED BY

Josie A. Holtom
and
William H. Hylton

WITH CONTRIBUTIONS FROM

John Braun	Josie A. Holtom
Nelson Coon	Louise Hyde
Levon Darlington	William H. Hylton
Bonnie Fisher	Elaine Neilson
Barbara Foust	Patsy Strong
Heinz Grotzke	Marion Wilbur

DRAWINGS BY
Joanne Clark

RODALE PRESS · AYLESBURY

ISBN: 0 87857 262 7

COPYRIGHT © 1979 RODALE PRESS

Typeset by
Glendale Offset Co., Chatham
Printed in Great Britain
by the Anchor Press, Tiptree

Rodale Press, Griffin Lane,
Aylesbury, Bucks. HP19 3AS

2   4   6   8   10   9   7   5   3   1

Contents

Contents

PART II
Encyclopaedia of Herbs

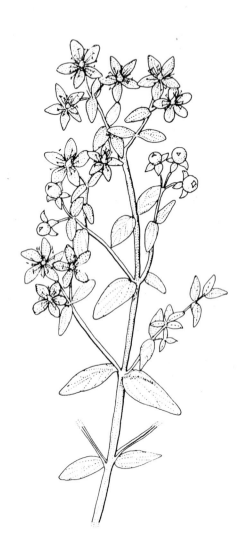

List of Herbs Illustrated

Line Drawings

continued

List of Herbs Illustrated

Photographs

Introduction

Anyone who has walked out into the countryside on a summer's day after a shower of rain and been held by the many scents of the nearby hedgerow will be on the way to discovering the fascination and joy of herbs. But there is no need to travel far to find these plants when you can have them growing in your garden. Besides enjoying their heady fragrance and beautiful colours when you step outside your back door you can have the enormous satisfaction of starting your own herbs, watching them grow and finally harvesting them to use in a myriad different ways: to make a tasty casserole, a delicious cake, or a hot herbal tea on a cold day, to dye your own wool, or to make into delicately perfumed candles.

It is really amazing how easily we take herbs for granted. Have you ever considered how much we depend on herbs in everyday life? For instance do you enjoy eating sage and onion stuffing or mint sauce with your Sunday joint? Have you ever had a headache, a sore throat, or tired eyes? Herbs provide the flavour, the cure and the relief. How many people realise that aspirin is synthesized from willow bark which was used for medicinal purposes by the American Indians? Garlic which is so widely used in French and Italian cooking is also a natural antibiotic useful in combating influenza and other infectious diseases, and grown alongside your raspberry canes it will protect them from aphids and other insect pests.

What is more beautiful than a garden full of sweet smelling roses, and yet the rose itself is a herb. The petals can be candied for cake decoration, or used as a basis for pot-pourri, or fragrant perfume such as attar of roses. Rose water also provides soothing relief for tired eyes.

Our great-grandparents used herbs in everyday life and derived great benefits from them. To keep flies and moths out of the house, tansy was often planted by the kitchen door or bunches of southernwood, sometimes called 'old man' were hung up indoors. They repelled insects just as effectively and far more pleasantly than modern toxic sprays. In the cottage garden how delightful to see lavender, foxgloves and goldenrod making a lovely splash of colour! Yet digitalis, commonly used to treat heart conditions, is derived from foxgloves, and the flowers of goldenrod produce a beautiful yellow dye.

The uses of herbs, quite apart from their pleasing and beneficial presence in the garden, are truly legion. This book is designed to explain in detail everything from identifying the many different herbs found in this country, to their numerous uses in the home. It describes what they look like, and over one hundred plants are illustrated. It explains how to cultivate and harvest them and use them to enhance everyday life making it healthier and happier.

The book is divided into two parts. The first part guides the reader chapter by chapter through the history, cultivation and uses of herbs; culinary, aromatic, dyeing and companion planting, as well as how to lay-out different types of herb gardens. Part two is an encyclopaedia which lists over one hundred and forty different herbs with information on the properties and cultivation of each one.

In the first chapter we have covered the basic principles of Latin nomenclature, so that the reader can become familiar with the Latin names of herbs. This is especially important when using herbs for medicinal purposes or for dyeing, as a common name can refer to two different plants while the Latin name will immediately identify the right plant.

At the back of the book you will find a glossary explaining a lot of the terms used in reference to medicinal herbs, and there is also an extensive bibliography. We have also included a list of suppliers of herbs, together with other useful addresses. There is a general index as well as an index of Latin names and an index of common names which we hope you will find useful.

Many people have been involved in preparing this extensive book, which originated as a project of Rodale's *Organic Gardening* magazine and I would firstly like to extend my sincere thanks to all the contributors: Nelson Coon, John Braun, Bonnie Fisher, Marion Wilbur, Barbara Foust, Louise Hyde, Levon Darlington, Heinz Grotzke, and Patsy Strong; and to William Hylton whom I would particularly like to thank for guiding me through this project and for imparting his knowledge and experience to me.

I am especially grateful to Joanne Clark for the lovely painting of wild herbs which appears on the jacket and for the superb line drawings which appear in the encyclopaedia part of the book. She has put in several hundreds of hours work researching the herbs in order to produce these beautiful and detailed botanical illustrations.

I would also like to thank the people involved in actually putting this book together: Elaine Neilsen for her many hours of work reading and editing the manuscript; Gina Claye for proof-reading the encyclopaedia and for her work on the Herb Suppliers and Useful Addresses, the Glossary and the Bibliography; Katrina Chalke for gallantly re-typing the manuscript and checking illustrations; Skip Knerr for meticulously proof-reading the manuscript; Nancy Lee for checking all the Latin names; Eric Pennell for the index of Latin names and the extensive general index; Jim Hall for the design and production; Peter Holtom for typographical help and advice; and Mr. J.K. Burras, Superintendant of the University Botanic Gardens at Oxford who has patiently answered our botanic queries. Finally I would like to express my appreciation for the help, information and photographs which have been made available to us by: The Herb Society, The Association of British Herb Growers and Producers, The National Book League, The National Trust, The Shakespeare Birthplace Trust, and the Trustees of Beaulieu Abbey.

I hope this book will bring you much enjoyment, by way of new ideas, hobbies and projects as well as serving as a useful herbal reference, for the pleasure of herbs is never-ending.

Josie A. Holtom

PART I

How to Grow and Use
Nature's Miracle Plants

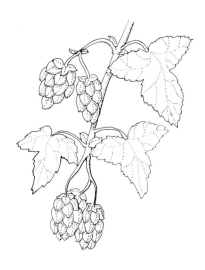

1

Herbal Beginnings

When is a herb not a herb?

A dog is a quadruped, but a quadruped is not necessarily a dog. A herb is herbacous, but a herbaceous border does not necessarily contain herbs.

If, as a herbal beginner, you are confused by this, then a few minutes with a good dictionary should help to dispel what may appear as a paradox.

Herbaceousness, you will find, is a botanical quality, while from the herbalist's point of view, when we speak of herbs we are not necessarily speaking in botanical terms.

The primary definition given the word *herb* by one authoritative dictionary is: "seed-producing annual, biennial, or perennial that does not develop persistent woody tissue but dies down at the end of a growing season." But this is the botanical definition of a herb and would eliminate from the herbal landscape plants that have been traditionally regarded as herbs such as rosemary and thyme, as well as some plants historically regarded as herbs, like poplars and sunflowers.

Tied in with this definition of herbs are such related words as *herbaceous* and *herbage*, which relate to the absence of woody tissue as a plant characteristic. However, the herbaceous character of a plant doesn't make it a herb for our purposes and—since some of the plants we will be considering as herbs do in fact have woody tissues—these terms can only be applied loosely to herbs.

3

These definitions—the ones that do not apply—used as my opening gambit, may seem to be at first sight a rather negative approach. But they enable us to discount them from now on, and so avoid confusion.

The definition we want is; *a plant or plant part valued for its medicinal, savoury, or aromatic qualities.*

The term *herb* as defined here includes a broad spectrum of plants—trees, shrubs, and herbage.

However, this definition is still not universally accepted. The preferred botanical definition is *any plant that may be used for pleasure, fragrance, or physic*—or some variation on that theme.

Different experts have variations on the fundamentally same theme. One of the best is that a herb embraces all plants that can be used for culinary and flavouring purposes, and for medicinal and veterinary uses, and which lend themselves to such practices as dyeing, smoking, and the preparation of cosmetics.

Historically, plants from which a medicinal concoction can be derived from their root, leaf, bark, flower, or fruit have been categorized as herbs. By paging through an old herbal (which, to be exact, is a book dealing with the medicinal aspects of plants), you will find the names of literally hundreds of plants—some of which you may never have heard of before, while others you will have heard of but thought were weeds—and others you considered trees or shrubs. There can't be many people who ever considered a hundred-foot poplar as a herb. Could such a definition, therefore, take in too many plants?

Henry Beston, in his short but delightful book *Herbs and the Earth* suggested just that. He wrote:

> In its essential spirit, in its proper garden meaning, a herb is a garden plant which has been cherished for itself and for a use and has not come down to us as a purely decorative thing. To say that use makes a herb, however, is only one side of the story. Vegetables, quasi-vegetables, herbal what-nots, and medicinal weeds are not herbs and never will be herbs for all the dictionaries. It is not use which has kept the great herbs alive, but beauty and use together. Clumsy food plants, curlicure salad messes, and roots belong in the kitchen garden, in the *jardin potager*, and not with the herbs. They spoil the look of a herb garden, taking from it its inheritance of distinction; they confuse it; they destroy its unique atmosphere . . .

Beston's remarks advance imposing standards, although beauty, in the eye of the beholder, we know can encompass even "vegetables, quasi-vegetables, herbal what-nots, and medicinal weeds".

Euell Gibbons, in his book on wild herbs, *Stalking the Healthful*

Herbs are one of nature's many gifts to man. Throughout history, this gift has continually blessed man with its varied virtues, not the least of which is its beauty.

Herbs, offers a more extensive commentary on using herbs. He suggests that a great utility of herbs stems from the beauty of these plants. "Everyone appreciates the conspicuous and flamboyant beauty of the larger wild flowers," he notes, "but how many have thrilled to the sheer beauty of the thrice-pinnate foliage of the common yarrow that grows by every roadside? How many have ever seen the intricate beauty of the many wild flowers that are so tiny they must be studied under a magnifying glass? Once the eye is trained to see these things, one finds that nature has surrounded us with breathtaking beauty that largely goes unobserved and unappreciated."

Gibbons *does* find beauty and utility in what-nots and weeds, and he cherishes them for themselves. And as our guide to landscaping with herbs will show you in chapter eight, even what-nots and weeds find utility and place in a garden of conscious design. I think Beston is too selective in establishing his standards of bloodlines, breeding, and character, for he is advocating a horticultural aristocracy. We organic gardeners tend to be more homespun, and so we choose to embrace as herbs all sorts of plants with utility, beauty—and with a measure of domesticity.

By what name?

There is yet another vital aspect of defining herbs. I have dealt with them generically and so the next question is what do you call them individually? It is one thing to know what they are termed collectively, but if you can't distinguish each species of plant precisely, then obviously you are at a grave disadvantage.

Botanists have their system of naming plants in Latin, and many herbalists, professionals, and keen amateurs use it. The system may seem confusing in its strangeness—it's like learning a new language. And it is not so easy to find out how these Latin names function. So many written works just assume the reader knows.

However, there are good reasons for knowing the system, not so much to be able to impressively rattle off those double-barrelled Latinate names, but to be able to function with the basics of the system should the need arise. The need could be sooner than you think. Any good local lending or reference library should be able to help you in your studies, and the effort will be well worth while.

At Westbury Court, Westbury-upon-Severn, Gloucestershire, there is a beautiful Dutch style water garden laid out to a late Seventeenth Century design. Here are planted many traditional herbs and medicinal plants, including ancestral roses, pomegranates, rosemary, yuccas, violets, primroses and lavender.
(By Courtesy of The National Trust)

How will this knowledge prove useful? Let us suppose, for example, that you would like to purchase thyme. If you approach a competent herb grower, you will be asked which variety you want. There are dozens, and if you are not specific you will probably end up with *Thymus vulgaris*, the most common variety. Or, suppose you are speaking to someone about herbs; let us suppose you are talking about valerian and that the other party is talking about garden heliotrope. Without the common ground of Latin botanical nomenclature you may never know that you are speaking of one and the same plant, *Valeriana officinalis.*

What the botanists have achieved is really quite remarkable. They have achieved international accord by establishing a uniform system for classifying and naming plants. Botanists, like musicians, speak the same language everywhere. There are disagreements and points of controversy, of course, but in the main, the system is universal and works well.

The classification system includes several levels and ranges of categories, beginning at the top with two basic, tremendously broad divisions and descending with increasing specificity through classes, orders, families, and finally to genera and species—or a particular plant. Occasionally, there can be some slight variation within a species of a plant. Consequently, the Latinate system includes a compensating factor—an extra one, two, or three words, added to the botanical plant name.

A botanist, in classifying a plant, will become more and more specific as he progresses, using its characteristics to move it through the categories and ultimately into the designation of a species. The initial step he takes is to separate plants with flowers from plants without flowers. Plants without flowers are put in Division I and called *cryptogams*; plants with flowers are placed in Division II and are called *phanerogams*.

The phanerogams which interest us, are segregated in accordance with the method of carrying the ovules, or female cells, that will ultimately become the seeds. Plants such as pines, firs, and other cone-bearers which carry their ovules exposed are called *gymnosperms*, Subdivision I, while those that carry their ovules enclosed in a fruit or other protective capsule are called *angiosperms*, Subdivision II.

Next, there are two classes, based on the development of the seed itself at germination. Under Class I are the *monocotyledons*, plants producing a single seed leaf, and Class II, the *dicotyledons*, plants which produce two seed leaves. Distinctions continue, as the plants descend into subclasses, then orders and families, and finally into genera and species. For our purposes, it is only really necessary to understand the designations of genera and species. But it may be of interest to note

Herbs come in all shapes and sizes. Rosemary and lavender make lovely plants for the herbaceous border.

that a large number of the regal herbs fall into five families. These are: Labiatae, Compositae, Umbelliferae, Boraginaceae and Cruciferae.

The common characteristics of the Labiatae (mint) family are square stems and mostly irregular, two-lipped flowers having four stamens. The fruit is small, with four nutlets (seeds). Familiar members of the mint family include peppermint and spearmint. But in addition, there are also basil, lavender, sage, rosemary, and thyme.

All members of the Compositae (Composite or sunflower) family are sun-lovers. These have either a disc flower or a ray flower. The fruits are dry and hard, a type known to botanists as achenes. These often have plumes of hairs to aid dispersal in the wind. Among the family members are the artemisias (southernwood, mugwort, wormwood, tarragon), tansy, calendula, chicory, and santolina.

The Umbelliferae or parsley family members often have hollow stems and flowers in flat-topped clusters called umbels. Caraway, dill, coriander, fennel, lovage, and—of course—parsley, angelica, and chervil are all members of the parsley family.

Members of the Boraginaceae or borage family all that tubular flowers, mostly in curved racemes, and have five stamens attached to the tube. The ovary is superior, usually forming a fruit composed of four nutlets. The name-sake of the family is probably the most famous family member.

The last, and I think least, of our five important herbal families is the Cruciferae or mustard family. Members of this family have flowers with four petals, forming a square cross, with four long stamens and two short ones, and with the ovary superior. Cruciferae may be important, but in the encyclopaedia of significant herbs featured later in this book, compiled somewhat arbitrarily by drawing heavily on the reports of our researchers, only a few herbs of that family are included. Herbs of the Liliaceae family—such as garlic and chives—appear, as well as a number of other families, such as Rutaceae, Rubiaceae, Valerianaceae, Verbanaceae, and Rosaceae. Incidentally, it is interesting to note that there are between 250 and 300 families in the classification system— depending on what source you consult. *Gray's Manual of Botany* lists only 168.

When a variation occurs within a species, the variation is described in a word which is tacked on the binominal name with a *var.* (in Roman type). Thus, a variety of the common yarrow which has red, rather than white, blossoms is named *Achillae Millefolium* var. *rubra*.

Three vagaries of the system that can be puzzling are the variations in some of the common specific names, like *vulgare* and *vulgaris*, or *officinalis* and *officinale*, the only occasional capitalization of a species

Louise Hyde's Herb Farm. The herbs are started in greenhouses and hardened off in a row of cold frames (above) before sale as live plants, or transplanting into the farm's spacious gardens (right).

name, and the appearance, again on occasion, of a letter or apparent abbreviation in Roman type after the binominal, as *Hyssopus officinalis* L. or *Levisticum officinale* Koch or even worse, *Anthriscus cerefolium* L. Hoffm. The first, the difference in species name, is simply a rule of Latin. The two elements of the binominal must agree in gender, and the species element is the one that must agree with the genus element.

It is perhaps worth mentioning at this stage that Latin was originally selected as the standard language for the botanical classification system because, at the time Linnaeus advanced the binominal system, Latin was the language that was almost universally understood by the better-educated classes. Even today, Latin is a basic language of scientific nomenclature.

The generic (for genus) and specific (for species) names are the heart of the binominal system of identifying plants. The system was first proposed by Carl von Linne, a Swedish biologist and botanist, who is better known by the Latinized form of his name, Carolus Linnaeus. In a sense, the binominal system is like the bureaucratic system for handling people's names—last name first, first name last, which means genus name first, species name second.

The generic name of a plant corresponds loosely to the human family name, or surname. Within botanical families—which might be said to correspond loosely with, say, Scottish clans—there are groupings of similar plants, all given a generic name to identify them as to group membership. In the family Compositae, there is the genus *Artemisia*. Just as we tell the Smiths apart by giving them different first names, the botanist tells the *Artemisias* apart by giving them additional names. But these names come second. So we have *Artemisia. vulgaris* (mugwort), *Artemisia Dracunculus* (tarragon), *Artemisia Abrotanum* (southernwood), *Artemisia Absinthium* (wormwood), and so on.

Generic names are more often than not derived from Greek, but other languages are also used. Sometimes the name is representative of the original plant name, of the person who discovered the genus, the place in which it was discovered, some hero of Greek mythology or ancient legend, or whatever else that occurred to the person originally bestowing the name. Thus, we have the *Artemisias* named for Artemis, daughter of Zeus, and the *Achillaes*, named after Achilles. The genus name *Rosmarinus* is constructed of the Latin for dew or spray, *ros*, and for the sea, *marinus*, to denote the seaside habitat of the plant.

Such specific names are supposed to describe the plant, but this ideal is not always achieved. Occasionally, the name commemorates the name of the discoverer or the native area of the plant. Especially

12

A herb garden is a personal thing. It can be a small oasis, such as this tiny circular garden of low-growing varieties or it can be extensive and elaborate.

13

among the herbs, there are many plants with a specific name *officinalis* or *officinale*, which means that the plant had some commercial value—generally to the apothecary. *Vulgaris* or *vulgare* describes the species as being the common or ordinary variety of the genus.

The second puzzle was simply an example of an exception to the accepted rule. The basic rule is that the specific name should never be capitalized except when the species name is a former genus name. The dual capitalization occurs when a botanist reviews a plant's classification and determines that it is in the wrong genus and moves it. He may keep the old generic name as the specific name to go with the new generic name, in which case he capitalizes both elements of the binominal. Specific names derived from a certain location or a person's name used to be capitalized, but that practice is dying out.

The final puzzle turned out to be what journalists might call the by-line. Those few letters spell or abbreviate the name of the botanist who named the plant. The letter "L" is for Linnaeus (also abbreviated Linn.). The L. Hoffm. after *Anthriscus cerefolium* means simply that at some point a botanist named Hoffman reviewed Linnaeus' classification of the plant and confirmed its correctness.

One bit of shorthand that can be seen quite often is the abbreviation of the genus name to the first letter— as in *A. Millefolium*. The abbreviation is only used when it is clear what the genus is and when a complete binominal is being used. One would not talk about the *A. s*, one would talk about *Artemisias*. But in listing the species in a genus, one would spell out the genus only in the first name.

The botanical system of classifying and naming plants in Latin is basically quite simple—which is the major reason it works so well. Perhaps the trouble people have with it stems from the fact that it is based on a language foreign to them. *Armoracia Rusticana* can twist your tongue if you've never seen the words before, but the more you say it and use it, the easier it becomes.

How will you be guided?

Thus you have the basics—the definition of herbs, the system of proper names. Now for specifics and to show the reasons why the bluebloods of the herbal world have that long tradition of being cherished for a variety of uses—and, just for themselves.

This beautiful knot garden has been planted on the foundations of Shakespeare's last home at New Place, Chapel Street, Stratford-upon-Avon.
(By Courtesy of The Shakespeare Birthplace Trust).

It is the purpose of this book to show you how to grow herbs and how to use them. We will start with the healing, cooking, aromatic, and colourful uses of herbs. Once you are convinced sufficiently to want to grow herbs, you will want to know just how and where.

The next chapter tells us that the dried leaves of horehound can be made into a tea or tisane, which has for centuries been known as an expectorant and tonic. The great herbalist Nicholas Culpeper said, "It helps to expectorate tough phlegm from the chest . . ." And if one has other herbs to work with, horehound may be combined with hyssop, rue, liquorice root and marshmallow root as an excellent cough syrup.

Basil is the 'herb of love' and is favoured by many, you will read in chapter three. Its sweet flavour and aroma give it definite uses, whether for main meals or for desserts. Basil is probably best known for its use with tomatoes. It can be sprinkled over sliced tomatoes with oil and vinegar, or used to add piquancy to tomato or spaghetti sauce. For seasoning pizza, basil rivals oregano for first place. Tossed salads, salad dressings, egg and cheese dishes, vegetable dishes, poultry and veal—as well as rolls and breads can be seasoned with basil. When baking apples, sprinkle a few leaves over the apples for a delicious flavour.

Lavender is justly famous for its scent, and the chapter on aromatics explains how to use it for fragrance. To make a sachet: "collect a small bunch of lavender flowers. Lay them in a single layer to dry. When completely dry, grind them to a fine powder. You can use a pestle and mortar, perhaps a blender or, if you have one, a flour mill. One lavender plant should produce enough blossoms to fill 12 two-inch-square (5 cm square) sachets. Place in small cloth bags and sew up the openings."

Later on you read, "If your interest is merely a sweet scent in your bath water, any one of dozens of fragrant herbs will do. Lavender is the favourite of many ladies, as it has been for centuries. It is used to perfume many commercial bath preparations. So, why not use your own garden lavender? Moreover, lavender is reputed to be an excellent palliative for nervousness." There are many other intriguing ways of capturing and using the scent of lavender.

Woad is probably the only herb which measures up to Henry Beston's standards and to the rigours of dyeing. Apart from its fame (or infamy) as an enemy-scaring dye used by the Ancient Britons, woad

The wild beauty of a herb farm, when the
herbs are ready for harvesting.

16

17

was employed later specifically as a dyeing plant, we are told in chapter five.

All these herbs have been cherished for their own beauty, in gardens both formal and informal. Perhaps the purest form in which herbs were used for themselves in the landscape were the elaborate Renaissance gardens. These were mazes and labyrinths framed in herbs.

The famous knot gardens, as they have been called traditionally, are numerous—one of the most famous being at Hampton Court Palace to the west of London. It dates back to the Sixteenth Century when Cardinal Wolsey, who owned the palace originally, gave it to Henry VIII in order to curry favour with his capricious monarch. But Anne Boleyn was not so fortunate in escaping this capriciousness. She lost her head. While she lived, she could often be seen in the charming, but tiny, knot garden at the palace—still intact to this day.

In these gardens herbs of various sizes, densities, textures, and colours were cultivated—all carefully and artfully trimmed and pruned to depict knotted cords.

Today's gardener, however, need not limit himself or herself to these labour-intensive, but traditional forms. Herbs deserve to be a part of your home landscape—even if you restrict them to a border or ground cover. And the bluebloods should be among your prime candidates. These can even find a cherished spot in your vegetable patch—if you have one. As shown later, these herbs and others can benefit your vegetable garden by keeping insect pests at bay. This is a use seldom attributed to herbs, yet the plants commonly regarded as having some insect-repelling qualities are also plants that fall within our definition of herbs.

If, in reading through the following chapters, you feel moved, as I and the other authors hope you will, to buy some herbs or grow them—for teas, seasonings, remedies, scents, or just for beauty—do please be sure to get nothing but the best quality. Organic gardeners use the organic method because we believe it produces the best quality. A tomato grown organically tastes far better than one grown with the help of chemical fertilizers, chemical insecticides, and weed killers. The same is true of herbs; the herb grown organically will be far superior in taste, smell, and insect resistance, to its chemically-stimulated counterpart. Furthermore, you will brew a tea or season a salad with the assurance of knowing that there are no harmful residues present.

To French healer Maurice Messegue this is an important point. For years, Messegue has successfully treated a wide variety of ailments using herbal concoctions. The quality of his herbs, he says in his book *Of Men and Plants*, is vital, as is the moment of harvest and the procedure used in the harvesting, drying, and storage of herbs. All of his herbs are gathered from the wild.

"The first rule," he explains, "is never to pick plants along main roads, where they are poisoned by exhaust fumes, neither pick plants that grow close to cornfields or orchards or vineyards, where they can absorb the harmful spray of chemical fertilizers or insecticides. Plants must be picked as far away as possible from land under cultivation." In an appendix to this book Messegue offers instructions on cultivating certain medicinal herbs and stresses not to use chemical fertilizers and pest killers.

Research by the Henry Doubleday Research Association, Braintree, Essex, substantiates this. David Greenstock of the association has discovered that the quality of garlic, at least, is affected by the growing technique. Lawrence Hills explained in an article in *Organic Gardening* on Greenstock's research:

> David Greenstock has discovered that the active principle of garlic, now called "allicin", is a complex mixture of substances which are mainly allyl sulphides. These are produced by enzyme activity in the bulb, where their balance and effectiveness depend on the presence of assimilable sulphur. This sulphur is produced in the soil by a number of micro-organisms, mainly certain tiny fungi that cannot grow without ample humus.
>
> It is this fact that has produced varied results in the past, with emulsions made from one batch of garlic killing a pest, and then the next one leaving it leering triumphantly at the gardener. Commercial garlic bulbs, or the expensive oil made from them, could have the wrong mixture of allyl sulphides because they were grown with chemical fertilizers and not enough humus to support the fungi, while David Greenstock's own—or those from local peasants—would have plenty. It is possible that measuring the assimilable sulphur in garlic (and probably onions) may be the first definite test to show a clear analytical difference between organically grown and chemically grown produce.

Herbs from the beginning

Historically, the oldest uses of herbs are medicinal. Perhaps this is because much of the lore of herbs is derived from the herbals—the traditional plant medicine books—and it is to these ancient volumes that we tend to turn in determining whether or not a plant may properly be

19

The herb garden at Troy, a fine country farmhouse at Ewelme near Oxford owned by Mr. and Mrs. Ruck Keene. The gardens at Troy are often open to the public. The herb garden, above and left, which was formerly given over to roses and herbaceous flowers, was created a few years ago in response to the public's increasing interest in herb cultivation.

called a herb. There are, of course, other herbal uses explained, but even
the culinary and aromatic qualities seem tied to the curative, salutary,
or hygienic properties of the plants. Sweet-smelling pomander balls and
herbal bags were used not only for the olefactory aesthetics involved,
but for the supposedly hygienic effect of the scents in the midst of
the stench of rotting garbage, putrifying sewage, disease, and death. A
cook used herbs on meat, not so much because the herbal flavour was
appetizing, but rather because the taste of meat going bad was not. At
least psychologically, such culinary and aromatic uses had a salutary
effect.

Probably because so much of the herbal lore is derived from three
Elizabethan herbalists—Nicholas Culpeper, John Gerard, and John
Parkinson—herbs are often associated in history with the Elizabethan
Age. This may be a parochial association for herbs have a far more
wide-ranging part in history. There are some herbs that are native to
England, just as some are uniquely American, but the bluebloods are
almost all of Mediterranean ancestry. And while a rich vein of lore is
found in Sixteenth and Seventeenth Century English herbals, the basis
of that lore is derived from material first recorded by Greek herbalists
and passed through the rise and fall of Rome into the Dark Ages,
emerging in the works of monks.

I have read reports of an ancient record, the *Ebers Papyrus*, which
said that Egypt, two thousand years before Christ, had about two
thousand herb doctors. The Bible, in both Old and New Testaments,
makes repeated references to herbs. These references serve to substantiate that herbs were well known in ancient Egypt.

> And ye shall take a bunch of hyssop, and dip it in the blood that is in
> the basin, and strike the lintel and the two side posts with the blood
> that is in the basin; and none of you shall go out of the door of his
> house until the morning.

The instructions in Exodus 12:22 may stick in your mind, though
the identity of the herbal brush might not (it should be noted that
scholars believe the hyssop of this reference is *Origanum aegyptiacum*
rather than *Hyssopus officinalis*, the latter being today's hyssop).
Similarly, many will recall the story of Manna, Exodus 16:31, but not
its description:

> And the house of Israel called the name thereof Manna; and it was like
> coriander seed; white; and the taste of it was like wafers made with honey.

Other references to herbs appear in the Book of Numbers and the Proverbs.

But other than these Old Testament references and the *Ebers Papyrus*, much of what we know about the herb knowledge of this period is somewhat speculative. We *do* know that in later years the Greeks—as you might expect—studied the herbs and committed their observations and speculations to writing. For them, too, the herbs were well known. Aristotle had a garden of more than three hundred plants reputed to have medicinal qualities, according to Theophrastus, who was a pupil of the great teacher and thinker and had the opportunity to study and write about Aristotle's herbs. Four centuries later, about the time of Christ's birth, Dioscorides, a Greek physician, wrote a justly remembered herbal.

Theophrastus and Dioscorides produced the most remarkable herbals, but information about herbs and references to them appeared in the works of Pliny the Elder, Galen, Virgil, and Homer. New Testament references indicate that herbs continued to be commonplace. The Greek record was passed on to the Romans, who made extensive medicinal and culinary use of herbs. Indeed, the spread of the Roman Empire might be credited with the spread of herbs, for the Roman armies carried them everywhere, planting them inadvertently in some spots, by design in others.

Where the Romans left off, the Christians picked up. In the Dark Ages, the monasteries of Benedictine and Cistercian orders were the centres of herbal activity. Individuals all over Europe had herb gardens, much as they had vegetable gardens, but the monks of these orders collected and cultivated as many varieties as they could find, serving as the most formal vehicle for the perpetuation of the use of herbs for healing. Moreover, the monks developed a record of their lore. Most of their herbals drew heavily on the works of the Greeks, and the illustrations they provided lacked any reasonable semblance to the plant depicted. Nevertheless, the contribution of these pious men was invaluable.

As civilization struggled out of the Middle Ages, the herb garden gained a new respectability and status. It was still a part of the monastery setting, and of the kitchen garden at individual homes and manors. But the garden was being formalized in the Renaissance capitals, and the herbs were a focal point of these elaborate ornaments. As the Renaissance continued, important new contributions were made to the existing body of herbal knowledge, which had simply been regenerating for centuries. In 1475, the first wood cuts known to be used as botanical illustrations appeared. They appeared in a work

23

The Queen's Garden

During the 17th century plants were grown for culinary and medicinal purposes rather than their beauty. They were used in cooking to mask the flavour of tainted meat and strewn either fresh or dry in houses to sweeten the atmosphere in an age when hygiene and cleanliness were not considered important. Flowers were made into nosegays and carried in city streets to disguise unpleasant aromas and ward off the plague. Some plants were credited with supernatural powers and considered more effective when gathered at certain times (a particular phase of the moon) or places (a graveyard). These uses of 300 years ago may amuse us today but old herbal remedies may still be effective and culinary herbs are gaining in popularity. Pot-pourri is a modern counterpart to the strewing herbs and nosegays are still carried by judges in procession at the beginning of the judicial year.

It ſtaies the cough if it be drunke,
    It clénſeth monthly flowres,
If you it ſeethe in water, and
    Thereto put *wine that ſcoures;
Such broth doth ſtaie the belly gripes.
    It helpeth breſt and loong;
It cures the ſicknes of the ſides,
    Cald *Pleurſie in Greeke toong.
The gout and the ſciatica,
    And agues it doth cure,
If it be drunke : and other things,
    As writers do aſſure.

From an account of Rue, Ruta graveolens
Gerard's Herbal 1597.

The Queen's garden at Kew. In the 1950's the area was a wilderness of neglected wartime allotments. Sir George Taylor, Director of the Royal Botanic Gardens, conceived the notion of reconstructing a garden of a style contemporary with the Royal Palace, to which it belongs, and stocking it as far as possible with plants of the time — the Palace was built in 1631. Planting began in 1964, and a sunken garden within the whole was made into the herbal garden shown in our photograph.

called *Das Buch der Natur*, published by Konrad von Meganberg.

Just over one hundred years later, in 1597, the first major new herbal appeared, and it remains one of the best-known of the many the era engendered. The book is commonly known simply as *Gerard's Herball.* It was the work of Englishman John Gerard. Born in 1545 he became a surgeon, but made his mark in society serving as the superintendent of the gardens owned by Queen Elizabeth's Chief Secretary of State, Lord Burleigh, and later as the apothecary to James I.

The next notable herbal of the period was written by another apothecary to James I. This writer's name was John Parkinson, and his herbal *Theatrum Botanicum* was produced in 1640. Only a few years later, sometime between 1649 and 1653, came what is perhaps the most readable of the herbals of this period, the one written by Nicholas Culpeper. His effort was based more in superstition and folk-lore than the works of Gerard and Parkinson. While this did contribute to the readability of the book, it also contributed to an overstatement of the value of many of the plants.

One of the more curious superstitions recorded by Culpeper (and others before him) was the *Doctrine of Signatures.* "And by the icon or image of every herb, man first found out their virtues," he wrote. Modern writers laugh at them for it, but I wonder in my heart how the virtues of herbs first came to be known, if not by the signatures. The moderns have them from the writings of the ancients—the ancients had no writings to have them from.

According to this belief, the medicinal use of a plant could be determined from some element of its appearance. The spotted, lung-shaped leaves of the lungwort indicated to the ancients that it was good for curing diseased, or spotted, lungs. The hollow stalk of the garlic showed it was a remedy for windpipe ailments. Some weeds—like dandelion, plantain, yarrow, and nettles—revealed the broadness of their healing virtues through their abundance.

Equally pervasive in Culpeper's herbal, is his belief in astrology. Invariably, his entries on herbs include some commentary on the influence of the moon, the planets, and the constellations on the plant. (While this is regarded as the rankest form of superstition in some contemporary herb books, it should be remembered that some very successful gardeners and farmers still plant and harvest according to the phases of the moon. And while astrology may be in scientific disrepute, it is hardly in popular disrepute.)

It is perhaps worth noting that most of Culpeper's work is still in print, being available under the title *Culpeper's Complete Herbal*

(Foulsham). Extensive excerpts from *Gerard's Herball* have been published under the title *Leaves from Gerard's Herball* by Marcus Woodward. Selections from many old herbals are included in a number of books written about herbs.

The American Indians formed their herbal lore in much the same way as other peoples formed theirs. The *Doctrine of Signatures* that Culpeper described found practitioners in America. Similarly, the Indians, like their contemporaries around the world, were superstitious, and they based some plant uses in superstition. And, of course, in every age and civilization there are those who experiment. However the uses were determined, the Indians did have some use for almost every one of their native plants.

The first written record of the native American herb lore was made by Juan Badianus, a native Mexican Indian doctor. Badianus had been educated by priests and in 1552 wrote a manuscript, in Latin, recording native medical practices.

The exchange of herbal knowledge between the new and old worlds was begun in the Seventeenth Century by two Englishmen, William Wood and John Josselyn. In 1634, Wood published in London a book titled *New England Prospect*, basically reporting on the new world as he observed it. The book included a chapter, "Of the Hearbes, fruits, woods, waters . . ." Josselyn's book was published in 1672, again in London, and its almost interminable title admirably captured the gist of the texts: *New England's Rarities Discovered: In Birds, Beasts, Fishes, Serpents, and Plants of that Country. Together with The Physical and Chyrurgical Remedies wherewith the Natives constantly use to Cure their Distempers, Wounds and Sores. Also, A perfect Description of an Indian Squa in all her Bravery; with a Poem not improperly conferr'd upon her. Lastly, A Chronological Table of the most remarkable Passages in that Country amongst the English.*

In the early Nineteenth Century, the patenting of medicines to widen their availability provided a major impetus to growers of medicinal herbs.

Among the most interesting of the growers were the religious communities established in various locations throughout the eastern United States by the Church of the United Society of Believers—more commonly known as the Shakers. The first Shaker medicinal herb garden was cultivated in New Lebanon, New York in 1820. Thirty-seven years later, the Shakers were still cultivating medical plants, the New Lebanon community having marketed some 75 tons of plants grown by its members. The Shaker product list included well over three hundred kinds of seeds, flowers, leaves, and barks—as well as a nearly equal

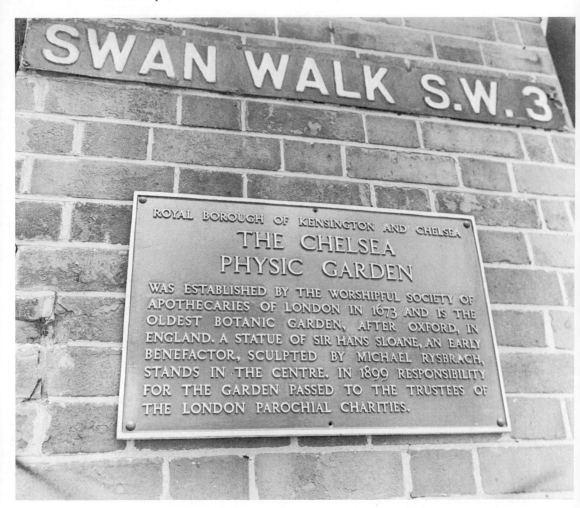

ROYAL BOROUGH OF KENSINGTON AND CHELSEA

THE CHELSEA
PHYSIC GARDEN

WAS ESTABLISHED BY THE WORSHIPFUL SOCIETY OF
APOTHECARIES OF LONDON IN 1673 AND IS THE
OLDEST BOTANIC GARDEN, AFTER OXFORD, IN
ENGLAND. A STATUE OF SIR HANS SLOANE, AN EARLY
BENEFACTOR, SCULPTED BY MICHAEL RYSBRACH,
STANDS IN THE CENTRE. IN 1899 RESPONSIBILITY
FOR THE GARDEN PASSED TO THE TRUSTEES OF
THE LONDON PAROCHIAL CHARITIES.

The Chelsea Physic Garden on the Thames Embankment was presented by Sir Hans Sloane to the Society of Apothecaries on condition that 50 new varieties of plants grown in it should be annually furnished to the Royal Society until the number so presented amounted to 2,000. One area of the garden is set aside for specific herbs, but others are to be found in all parts of the garden which consists entirely of wild and natural flowers, shrubs and trees, and not garden or cultivated plants.
(Photographed by kind permission of the Management Committee).

number of medicinal preparations. The Shakers continued their herb-growing business into the second half of the Twentieth Century, giving it up only when sharply dwindling community membership forced them to.

Scientific and technological developments in the Twentieth Century have led to increasing use of synthetics in pharmaceuticals, but there remains a large proportion of medicinal substances that can reasonably be derived only from plants. Nearly half of all prescriptions contain some drug derived from a plant. Thus, there has been a steady demand for medicinal plants, a demand emphasized during and after the two World Wars—chiefly because of the embargoes and increased needs endemic to war. The wars seemed also to spawn revivals of popular interest in herbs.

One result of the first revival was a two-volume work called *A Modern Herbal.* The English author, Maude Grieve, was a leader in the revival and wrote a number of books. Her Herbal is probably the most thorough and up-to-date book of its type. Undoubtedly, quite a sizable number of the other herbals and herb books of Twentieth Century origin can be traced to one or another of the revivals.

This view of herbal history, of course, reflects a Caucasian view of civilization. But a fabulous load of herbal lore, and the people who are perhaps today's most accomplished herbalists, are to be found in the Orient. If one accepts Oriental, predominantly Chinese, herbal lore at face value, one accepts the Chinese lore as the oldest in the world. The dates traditionally given for the writing of the oldest Chinese herbal would, if true, make it older than the *Ebers Papyrus*, by nearly a millennium.

The oldest of the Chinese pharmacopoeias, *Pen-ts'ao*, or *Herbal*, is reputed to be the work of the Emperor Shen-nung, a great cultural hero who is said to have lived from 3737 to 2697 B.C. Shen-nung is supposed to have compounded and self-tested hundreds of herbal preparations, aided by a transparent abdomen which enabled him to observe the workings of his internal organs. This freakish condition was undoubtedly a gift of legend, rather than of nature. Recorded in the *Pen-ts'ao* are 365 medical preparations—all but 51 of which are herbal.

The emperor who succeeded Shen-nung was also interested in medicine and prepared his own medical text. The book, *Huang-ti Nei-ching*, or *The Yellow Emperor's Classic of Internal Medicine*, is less of a herbal and more of a comprehensive review of the state of medical arts in China. It is presented as a dialogue between the Yellow Emperor, Huang-ti, and his chief minister, Ch'i Po. Huang-ti is said to have ruled from 2697 to 2595 B.C.

The authenticity of both these works is in question, however. The ancient Chinese had a propensity for attributing their writing to older sources in hopes of bolstering their value, and such is probably the case here. Studies have placed the two in the first millennium before Christ, making them not as old as the *Ebers Papyrus*. Despite the discrepancies of the dates, the *Pen-ts'ao* and the *Huang-ti Nei-ching* are valuable and legitimate old herbals.

Some time prior to the birth of Christ, the Chinese and their neighbours in India exchanged medical information, enhancing the knowledge of both peoples. Curiously, though the Eastern and Western civilizations centuries later opened trade, there apparently was never an exchange of medical information to the extent there was in the contacts between the Europeans and the American peoples. Nevertheless, the herbal knowledge developed in China and other Oriental countries is almost completely compatible with that developed by the Westerners.

The first major Chinese medical work to be translated into Western languages was the *Materia Medica of Li-Shih-Chen*, a masterpiece written by Li-Shih-Chen during the Sixteenth Century. A great compendium of remedies, it listed 12 thousand prescriptions and formulas and analysed 1,074 plant substances, 443 animal substances, and 354 mineral substances. The book is still studied by traditional Chinese physicians, who are very important people in Chinese medicine today. For unlike the Western nations, where the typical medical practitioner disdains intuitive folk medicine practices, the Chinese base their research and practice on traditional theories and techniques.

The Chinese, typically, steer their own course. But during the regime of Chiang Kai-shek (1912-1949), the Western influence was officially favoured and traditional medicine fell into disrepute. With the ousting of Chiang in 1949 came a resurgence of Chinese nationalism. The guiding principle today has been articulated by Chairman Mao. "Chinese medicine and pharmacology are a great treasure house. Efforts should be made to explore them and raise them to the highest level," he said.

Joining in the rise to the highest level are the herbal remedies. Herbs are widely cultivated, chiefly for their medicinal qualities. Even military installations have prominent herb gardens, each plant carefully labelled. Soldiers are taught to identify medicinal herbs to enable them to forage for healing plants in the field.

Paramedical personnel work closely with the people, using herbal remedies to a great extent. Moreover, as one Western observer put it, "Everyone in China is a little bit of a herbalist. Housewives, farmers, and even school children grow herbs and learn to recognize them.

Furthermore, herbs, readily available from stores, are extremely cheap and are reasonably safe to use." Coupled with the resurgence on the popular level is the emphasis on clinical and laboratory research on the healing plants. Of course, there is some interest in this work throughout the world, but the Chinese seem to be the leaders.

More and more people are turning to gardening, to part-time farming, to handicrafts and homecrafts, to quieter and simpler pleasures. Certainly, growing and promoting the use of herbs constitutes a quiet, simple pleasure that shouldn't be denied as being too modest. The delight of herbs is a never-ending one, rooted in the fact that herbs have always been and will continue to be a way of life.

The herb garden within the walled botanical garden of the Palace of the Bishop of Fulham. It is geometrically laid out with the beds bordered by miniature box hedges. It has only recently been opened to the public, and can be viewed any weekday. The Palace and garden are a part of the riverside public park on the north bank by Putney Bridge.

33

2

The Healing Herbs

Few indeed are the inhabitants of this world of ours who are not subject to the need, at one time or another, of medicines or of the advice from those who are accepted as knowledgeable either through local or tribal education or who, even without much education, are acknowledged by society to have "powers". Such practitioners have high status. "Medicine men" have always had great influence and in Western civilization the prestige of our medical profession is well known.

Yet, as these words are being written, Western doctors are taking a second look at the ancient skill of acupuncture, and pharmaceutical companies are widely exploring the healing properties of as many as forty thousand different plant species.

The use of herbs for healing must surely date back to the dawn of man's history, when tribes and family groupings gathered selected wild plants for use internally or for application to wounds. This could only have been a process of painful trial and error, and there must have been many a tragedy as a result—a situation not unknown today with people experimenting with sophisticated drugs.

Herbal lore has a long tradition handed down by word of mouth and recorded in ancient books. A great deal has been learned from the Chinese who have an authoritative compilation of over one thousand ancient herbs. For example, the use of rhubarb and castor oil was taken up by the West from China, while the herb *Ma huang*, used in China for at least four thousand years, has had its alkaloid element isolated from the plant—botanically named *Ephedra vulgaris* (or *E. sinica*)—and is now used with good results in the West for the treatment of asthma. Charaka and Sustrata, healers in the Brahmanistic era of Indian medicine (1000 A.D.), knew over seven hundred indigenous medical herbs.

In the early descriptions of herbal plants and remedies, distortions and errors were inevitable. Original drawings were rare before the Sixteenth Century. The Greeks had written accounts and, according to Pliny the Elder, the physician Crateaus (circa 120 B.C.) produced a herbal with coloured illustrations. Later illustrations continued to be highly stylized, copied, and recopied—often being varied in the process. In addition, mythological notions became incorporated, with human figures entwined with plants. Moreover, treatment was associated with the signs of the zodiac.

Otto Brunfels' *Herbarium Vivae Eicones*, Strasburg, (circa 1530) provided a break towards authenticity, with accurate drawings by the wood engraver Hans Wieditz. Nevertheless, superstition and magic still retained a strong influence.

In England, in the Seventeenth Century, Nicholas Culpeper published his *Physicall Directory*. Cures were connected with the planets and, he proclaimed, his *"Compleat Method of Physick* whereby man may preserve his body in health, or cure himself from being sick for a charge of threepence with such things only as grow in England, they being most fit for English bodies." However, the production of his work and the preceding treatises on medicinal herbs from the eminent apothecaries to James I, John Gerard, and John Parkinson, were of lasting interest. By the end of the Seventeenth Century pharmacopoeias were beginning to list herbs of genuine use.

Christianity added another layer of mysticism. While the early monastries cultivated herb gardens and treated the sick, there were times when potions, prayers, and relics are unavailing and the judgement of God, the visitation of illness and death as a divine retribution, became the final diagnosis—a view that added to the awful sense of doom prevalent among the people when the Great Plague of London descended upon them.

Despite being bedevilled by superstition and ignorance about their potency, and debased by the unscrupulous, the use of medicinal herbs continued to flourish and develop throughout the world, from China to Mexico and Canada (with particular Indian influence and skills), through the Middle East, the Mediterranean and Europe, contributing and accumulating experience and knowledge that, once transcontinental travel became established, was to influence modern medicine. In Britain, in the Eighteenth Century, William Withering discovered that country folk were treating dropsy with foxglove *(Digitalis purpurea)* and in experimenting accordingly on his patients with digitalis, he discovered

The foxglove is often cultivated in flower gardens for decorative purposes, but it is an important drug plant, being the source of digitalis, a heart stimulant. A potentially dangerous drug, digitalis should be used only under a doctor's guidance.

37

that it also had striking effects upon the action of the heart—a discovery with great significance for today's treatment of cardiac irregularities.

By the first half of the Nineteenth Century, French and German chemists had begun to isolate active substances like quinine and morphine from their plant sources and so the link between chemistry and botany began to be established. But still the development of an exact scientific method of measurement remained crucial to eliminate the variations of extractions between one batch and another. Willow bark had been used for generations to cure aches and pains; in 1889 a German chemist produced aspirin from it, probably the most popular household cure of all time.

The healing properties of plant material were well known to the American Indians. The Spaniards reported to their emperor that, not only did the Mexicans have a great pharmacopoeia, but also medicinal-plant test gardens, actually the first in the world, which were to become in Europe several centuries later, places now known as botanic gardens. In 1552, in Mexico, the now famed Badianus manuscript was written which illustrates and describes the use of hundreds of local plants, to be followed within a century by more intensive study of such uses by Hernandez.

In Canada, we find considerable early observation of the ways of the Iroquois Indians with native medicines—which then seemed to promote noticeable longevity.

The adoption of American Indian plant remedies into our own medicine was slow. But the value of plants such as sassafras, ginseng, maidenhair fern, and willow bark (containing what we have now synthesized as aspirin), added greatly to our early medicinal knowledge.

The purpose of this chapter is to list the values that have been placed on a selected few of the wild (and some cultivated) herbs, from every part of Europe, which have been used or recommended as medicinal aids. It is the hope that such a listing will encourage the reader to pursue further his study and use of such medicines, and to keep this knowledge from being lost. It is obviously not possible within the limits of just one chapter, to detail the collecting, preparation, and formulae for preparing and taking medicines. To aid the reader in pursuing his interest, an extensive bibliography has been prepared. The use of this or that plant for a particular medicinal need often varies in different parts of the country. The kind of plant used for a disease must, quite naturally, depend on the plants which grow in a district.

Throughout the study of plant life, careful attention should be paid to the scientific nomenclature, even when the plant is well known by a common name or names. For, and especially with medicinal plants, considerable knowledge can be gained by studying the many specific names which have been given to the plant through the years.

For instance, one will find many plants which are named *officinale*, which means that the plant has been known as an official drug plant. Then one will discover a number of plants which bear a common name of "wort" which again indicates that they were used for healing. A common name of "healing-herb" will naturally make one stop to think of a possible use, as would "cancer-root" or "fleabane". Anything with "bane" added is likely to have been used medicinally. And what would one expect from "flux root", "horse balm", or "alum root"?

It should be noted that within the last decade, the medical "experts" are finding deleterious side effects resulting from using chemical compositions which otherwise have demonstrated known values in healing. These effects are not known to occur with the perhaps less fast-working herbal remedies which, again, may have similar but less potent values. It seems unlikely at this point that medicine will turn back to plant sources for all the needed remedies, but it is certain that there is, at present, renewed interest in the natural chemicals which are found in healing herbs. We are, it seems, entering a new period of understanding of the wonders and workings of nature.

In presenting some samples of the many hundreds of plants which have medicinal values, it should be understood that only a selected few of the various values of plants have been listed here. The number of diseases and afflictions of mankind are manifold, and the remedies of botanical origin are truly of a staggering number.

Many family herbal treatments are hereditary and for that reason imperfectly and incorrectly remembered. Quantities and concentrations are important, as are combinations of herbs. In addition, some herbs are imported from countries with totally different plant varieties to those indigenous to Britain. Nowadays, a much more sophisticated and professional use of medicinal herbs has developed as knowledge has accumulated and has been fed by increasing popular interest. For these and other reasons it must be emphasized that except for well-tried remedies for minor ailments, the advice of a qualified herbal practitioner or nature-cure clinic should be sought. Used correctly, herbs are often of inestimable benefit.

No sensible person would dream of treating himself or herself with drugs without medical recommendation. Nor should herbal remedies be used lightly, for many herbs are the basis of potent drugs. Nor should anyone attempt to ride two horses. Dosage prescribed by orthodox practitioners should not be supplemented by herbal experimentation for in that way the proportion may be disturbed.

All this may seem obvious, but there are misguided people who do not fully appreciate the risks of self-treatment. Health disorders seldom come suddenly. What usually happens is that a condition builds up over a period of time and often it is not until there is pain or serious discomfort that relief is sought. For that reason, it is unlikely that a cure can be effected immediately. Herbal treatments often work more slowly, though ultimately more effectively and without the after-effects that can make orthodox medicine suspect.

We know that a healthy diet is composed of a large proportion of naturally grown and raw food by way of salads and fresh fruit, to which may be added some herbs to enhance nutritional values as well as flavours, and that when this is adopted and maintained along with regular exercise, fresh air, rest and other essential elements the body builds up resistance to disease. But we live in a world of noise, bustle, pollution, and contention and these, with other strains, make constant demands on our energy and nervous systems.

It is not surprising, therefore, that sometimes we find we are not coping as well as usual and have to consult a doctor. There are few, if any, health disorders that some herb, or combination of herbs, cannot treat—provided they are applied and administered with knowledge and skill by one well qualified by study and wide experience of medicinal herbs. A great deal of research is constantly being carried out and for this reason varying conclusions about efficacy may arise from time to time, opinions may differ, and new factors emerge.

The following is intended to give some slight indication of the scope of treatment for which herbs have been, and in many cases still are being, used. It must be appreciated that while most medicinal herbs are regarded as safe when properly used, some are poisonous and that is an added reason why self-treatment should not be undertaken.

The preparation and method of using this or that plant is variable and often highly involved. Obviously, detailed instructions on how to prepare concoctions from each and every plant, from simple infusions to complicated salves, cannot be given. Neither would it be wise within the limits of such a discussion to prescribe doses of even the most simple of medicines, as both diagnosis and prescription must be done with some knowledge of immediate circumstances. Thus, readers should be warned not to chew leaves, bark, or roots of plants mentioned, nor "boil them up", without full investigation of how this is done or in what quantity prepared medicines are taken. There are pharmacological

Mullein was known primarily as a remedy for respiratory ailments. Although the leaves were often used, the flowers gathered when fully open, and dried, are just as effective when made into a soothing infusion.

41

books which give this information. Or, do as I do, try to find salves and concoctions which are indicated as being of plant origin, which may come from a herbalist or health store. One can be one's own doctor with plants, but it is rarely wise.

Of course, there are simple things such as knowing that chewing peppermint is likely to aid a digestive disorder or that the eating of blackberries will modify diarrhoea just as too much rhubarb will have the opposite effect. And there are more involved things, such as the following simple instructions on how to prepare some—but not all—of the medicines discussed:

> The simplest of preparations is an infusion which can be mixed with juice and drunk or applied directly, depending on the injury. To make an infusion, bruise the plant and add a quantity of water. The water is usually poured on the herb while hot.
>
> Tinctures which are used only for outside applications are made by taking one or two ounces (28 or 56 g) of the powdered herb or plant and adding one to two pints (568 ml) to 1.13 l) of alcohol. Let stand for two weeks.
>
> Essences used like tinctures are made by dissolving one or two ounces (28 or 56 g) of the essential oil(s) in one to two pints (568 ml to 1.13 l) of alcohol.
>
> Teas can be made to taste by simmering a quantity of herbs on the stove or pouring boiling water over them. Some plants will lose their potency if boiled, though, and these can be mixed with cold water until ready to use—it takes longer but tastes the same.

Naturally, not all medicines can be prepared in these basic ways, and generally, more extensive herbals should be consulted. Complete details can be found in such a standard reference as *A Modern Herbal* by Mrs. M. Grieve. Other valuable and helpful books are those cited in the bibliography.

The listings that now follow are for the purpose of suggesting uses which have been made of many medicinal plants, all of which the reader might explore in one way or another. Some of the plants are found in the lists of pharmaceutical plants, some are plants which once were highly regarded and now have been superseded by synthesized drugs, while a number of plants mentioned may be those which are listed as having "reputed values". Thus, in all of this matter of plant drugs, one might say in the Latin form *Caveat qui utitut* (let the user beware).

In conclusion, it may be of interest to go back some three hundred years and see what was then said about the matter. For, as everyone knows, history repeats itself, in many phases of our lives, and in reading

Ginseng root has been used for centuries. It has excellent tonic properties and is often regarded as an aphrodisiac. It has long been held as a panacea for all ills.

this quotation think of it as something which might truthfully be said today.

The home herbalist

In the knowledge of simples, wherein the manifold wisdom of God is wonderfully to be seen, one thing would be carefully observed . . . which is, to know what herbs may be used instead of drugs of the same nature, and to make the garden the shop; for home-bred medicines are both more easy for the parson's purse, and more familiar for all men's bodies. So, where the apothecary useth either for loosing, rhubarb, or for binding, bolearmena, the parson useth damask or white roses for the one, and plantain, shepherd's-purse, knot-grass for the other, and that with better success. As for spices, he doth not only prefer home-bred things before them, but condemns them for vanities, and so shuts them out of his family, esteeming that there is no spice comparable for herbs

43

to rosemary, thyme, savory, mints; and for seeds to fennel and carraway seeds. Accordingly, for salves, his wife seeks not the city, but prefers her garden and fields, before all outlandish gums. And surely hyssop, made into a salve, and elder, camomile, mallows, comphrey, and smallage made into a poultice, have done great and rare cures—*A Priest to the Temple*; or the *Country Parson, his Character and Rule of Holy Life.* 1652.

Plants and your ears

As with many plants which are discussed in this chapter, a number have been described in the old herbals as being good for almost anything from head to foot, and in many cases, the values attributed to some plants are beyond belief. But in the instance of plants for treating affections of the ear, only one is worth mentioning and that is an ear-oil made with the leaves or flowers of the lovely roadside great mullein. The flowers should be picked and steeped in olive oil and the extract thus made used as ear drops for an earache or discharges from the ear.

Plants and your eyes

There are several plants listed in the old herbals which are said to be good for alleviating eye soreness, improving the sight, or other conditions of the eye. One of the oldest plants used is eyebright *(Euphrasia officinalis)*. *Robinson's New Family Herbal & Botanic Physician*, published in 1886, says:

> If the herb was but as much used as it is neglected, it would half spoil the spectacle-maker's trade. The juice of Eyebright dropped into the eyes, for several days together, relieves infirmities of the eyes that cause dimness of sight. Some make conserve of the flowers to the same effect.

Extracts from the plant salsify *(Tragopogon porrifolius)* have been used for the eyes. Compresses made from the seeds of fennel *(Foeniculum)* or the shredded bark of the oak tree *(Quercus robur)* are said to be good for inflamed eyelids. A hot compress made from the flowers of German camomile *(Matricaria Chamomilla)* helps styes while rose-water is wonderful for soothing tired and over-strained eyes.

Some minor experimenting with such medicines for eyes might be done by the modern herbalist, but in view of the very delicate nature of the eyes, consult your opthalmologist before herbal treatment is undertaken.

Teeth and twigs

In writing these short comments on the use of plant material for improving conditions of the teeth, my mind goes to advertisements which recommend that your dog be given some very hard biscuits as food to *improve his teeth and gums.* The same advice may well be given to man. The sticks of hazelnut are useful to chew on to exercise the gums and to help extract food from the teeth. In the case of "natural" material, there is still no better toothbrush than one made from hard natural bristles.

All authorities on uses of plants for medicine seem to agree that the acid juice of strawberries is of considerable value in dissolving tartar on

The acid juice of strawberries is useful for dissolving tartar on teeth.

the teeth. And everyone knows the value of the oil of cloves in alleviating a sudden toothache, or, in the absence of this, of getting some relief from oil of peppermint. The American Indians used to chew tobacco for this purpose, relying on the sedative value in tobacco. In the case of the child cutting his first teeth, some tribes used to give the children the roots of the marsh mallow plant to chew on.

Among the herbal medicine-makers of the Eighteenth Century, one finds that mouth washes were made of a tincture of arnica, myrrh, German camomile flowers, bilberry berries, the leaves of bayberry, and essence of sassafras.

All these early uses of plants for the care of the teeth are beneficial.

Soap amongst the plants

It may seem strange to talk about soap among the medicinal plants, and yet cleanliness and sanitation head the list of good health. While it may not be necessary for everyone to make soap from wild plants, it is interesting to note the plants containing substances which act in the same way as the household soap.

One of these, in fact, is peculiar in its values and bears the name of soapwort *(Saponaria Ocymoides)*, which is a common and beautiful pink-flowered wild plant. The leaves and roots, gathered when the plant is in flower, are made into suds by pounding in water. It has long been known as a soap and is especially recommended for washing rare silks, as it not only cleans, but imparts a little sheen to the silk, not otherwise obtainable. Plants such as the yucca can be made into a soap by chopping up the roots and crushing them in water. Amole or soap-plant *(Chlorogalum pomeridianum)* provides a lathery soap from the crushed heart of the plant's bulb.

Hence, nature provides plants useful for purposes quite beyond food or medicine.

The roots of the yucca plant can be chopped and soaked in water to extract a soapy substance the American Indians used for washing. The shoots of the plant can be double-boiled to produce a wine-like liquid which was used as a stimulating tonic.

Plants against the itch

However free from many of the diseases discussed in this chapter the reader may be, there are few people who have not had an itch of some kind. And yet here, with all the thousands of plants there are in the world, only a few are recognized as a help for a plain and simple itch.

One plant which grows almost anywhere in England is the curled dock *(Rumex crispus)*, a common narrow-leaf dock which is equally useful as a spring green, or delightful as an ornamental seed stalk for flower arrangers. For use medicinally for the itch the leaves are boiled in vinegar until the fibre is softened and then combined with lard to make a simple ointment.

Two plants which are found in older herbals as being useful for the itch are leaves of the common pansy *(Viola tricolor)* or of the violet *(Viola odorata)*, while the celandine *(Ranunculus Ficaria)*, has astringent properties and was once recommended for itches.

Among the household remedies for the itch is a poultice made of cornflour, while simple fresh lemon juice may be quickly and efficaciously applied to itching spots.

Antiseptics

English Oak *(Quercus robur)*

The bark of oak has long been known to have antiseptic qualities, and it is a powerful astringent.

Garlic *(Allium sativum)*

More and more these days this ancient vegetable is being suggested as a good medicine, and as a delicious flavouring for food. Here it is being offered as an antiseptic, for which purpose it was used in World War I, when the raw juice of garlic was diluted with water and applied with sphagnum moss as a poultice.

Gentian *(Gentiana lutea)*

Extracts of the roots of the yellow gentian have antiseptic properties and have been used for generations.

Moss *(Sphagnum* sp.*)*

The living plant, which having died and been buried for centuries, becomes the peat-moss of gardening, is not only a superior absorbent material, but the acid water in which it grows has definite antiseptic qualities and can be used as an emergency antiseptic.

Plantain *(Plantago major)*

The common plantain is a medicinal plant used as a very milky anti-septic, and recent investigations show that it has some antibiotic properties.

Witch Hazel *(Hamamelis virginiana)*

This tree has long been known and used as an astringent and hemo-static and because of its sharp sting is often listed as an antiseptic.

Astringents

An astringent, according to the dictionary, is a medicine from plants or otherwise, which "contracts the soft organic textures and checks discharges of blood, mucous, etc." It tends to contract external or internal fleshy parts.

Oak bark and galls have this quality. For internal use, a common tea is made from the dried leaves of one of the species of camellia. Blackberry is "astringent" in the intestinal tract, while witch hazel is good externally.

Beyond this, there are many plants which have in their roots, bark, leaves or seeds, similar qualities. A few of them are reviewed below:

Bearberry *(Arctostaphylos Uva-ursi)*

This common, widespread, and attractive ground cover provides, in a tea made of its dried leaves, a long-used disinfectant in urinary disorders.

Black Alder *(Alnus glutinosa)*

The bark of the black alder has astringent qualities used either externally or internally.

49

English Oak *(Quercus robur)*

Oak bark has astringent properties, but here the most valuable medicine is made from the round oak galls (little brown balls which are really a hatchery, growing around an insect egg). They possess peculiar astringent qualities and contain a large quantity of tannin.

Eucalyptus *(Eucalyptus globulus)*

The eucalyptus trees have come to us from Australia, but the oil extracted is found now in many common medicines. It acts as an astringent in throat troubles.

Myrrh *(Myrica cerifera)*

The wax myrtle is mentioned in the Bible and was used for embalming as well as for wax for candles. A useful medicine was made of the dried root bark as an astringent for external ulcers. It was also used as an antiseptic.

Saint John's Wort *(Hypericum perforatum)*

An astringent useful for digestive problems.

Solomon's Seal *(Polygonatum biflorum)*

The root is used to make an internal medicine with astringent properties. It is also a good antiseptic when applied externally to the skin.

Plants for sores

There are, among the wild plants in this country, many plants which, in one way or another, have qualities in their "juices" which may be soothing, or astringent, or have other qualities which tend to reduce soreness in one or another exterior part of the body.

Comfrey, often called knitbone for its value in healing bone fractures, also has a reputation as the "healing herb". The large leaves and the root were beaten and applied as a poultice to sprains, swellings, bruises, and sores. It is reputed to heal all manner of ailments.

In this book a few plants which have been noted in modern herbals as being good for sores, external or internal, are mentioned.

Plants such as the aloe or the houseleeks have juices recommended elsewhere for healing burns, and those also would have some value in other external sores. Another plant, comfrey, is often called the healing herb *(Symphytum officinale)*, indicating it is of value in sores of various kinds. It is used by beating up the whole plant to bring out the juices and then applying the material directly to the inflamed sores.

The crushed seeds of flax, linseeds *(Linum usitatissimum)* have long been used and applied as a poultice for burns and sores as well as the oil (linseed) which is used as a part of many healing medicines.

Another plant, the seeds of which may be substituted for linseed, is the common plantain *(Plantago major)*. One reliable reference notes that: "Rubbed on parts of the body stung by insects, nettles, etc., or as an application to burns and scalds, the leaves will afford relief and will stay the bleeding of minor wounds."

A careful reading of all the literature on plant remedies shows, as here, that there are multiple uses of plants for medicinal purposes and, with all of the present findings of secondary effects of many synthetic drugs, it behoves everyone to know about relying on such simple uses of plants.

Stings and bites

In surveying all the literature relating to the use of plants and plant products for the alleviation of pain and the effects from bites and stings, it would seem that few of the recommendations are reliable.

With minor bites from bees, mosquitoes, and other small insects, one recommendation would be to rub the part with the juice from honeysuckle vines, or such herbs as rue and camomile. Plain vinegar will be of possible help as will rubbing the affected part with a fresh lemon.

We all know the country practice of rubbing a dock leaf on a nettle sting, but the leaves of the houseleek *(Sempervivum tectorum)* are equally effective and so are lotions made from centaury *(Centaurium umbellatum)*, or the flowers of marigold *(Calendula officinalis)*. Sorrel *(Rumex Acetosa)* and milk thistle *(Silybum Marianum)* can also be used. Nettle itself *(Urtica dioica)* is said to be good for bites and stings because of its formic acid content.

Rue has a considerable reputation as an antidote to poisons of all kinds and in China it is still recommended for malarial poisoning. It is also reputed to be good for many female disorders.

The pain of insect stings is also relieved by rubbing the area with a leaf of plantain *(Plantago major)*, or with oil of peppermint. Comfrey *(Symphytum officinale)* makes an excellent ointment for bites, boils, and unidentified spots or "heat lumps".

Robinson's New Family Herbal, 1886, says that pimpernel *(Anagallis arvensis)* will cure the stings and bites of bees and wasps as will the bruised leaves of marsh mallow *(Althaea officinalis)* and the berries of the bay tree.

Plants for healing burns

Possibly the most repeated demand in the world is for a healing agent for the common burn. In the past a number of plants have been used for healing burns and various concoctions have been made.

The aloe, which unfortunately only grows in southern Europe, is a quick and certain cure for any minor burn. The juice of the leaf applied at once, produces amazing results.

Other old-fashioned remedies are: washing with hot tea, applying the sticky juice which is found around quince seeds, or applying a salve of an extract of Irish moss *(Chondrus crispus)* which is actually an alga. Another recommended procedure is the application of some linseed oil from the common flax plant *(Linum usitatissimum)* to which has been added a little lime water—said to be excellent.

The juice of any of the various sorts of houseleeks *(Sempervivum tectorum)* applied quickly to a burn produces good results, as will burdock *(Arctium Lappa)*, lady's bedstraw *(Galium verum)*, and elm bark *(Ulmus procera)*.

Old herbals record that the juice of the leaves of hound's tongue *(Cynoglossum officinale)* or mulberry *(Morus nigra)* was a reasonably good remedy.

A compress made of shredded marsh mallow roots or leaves is reputed to be good for minor burns, while camomile lotion eases and heals sunburn.

Other herbs which have been found useful in treating burns are: onions *(Allium cepa)*, eucalyptus *(Eucalyptus globulus)*, white lilies

(Lilium candidum), St. Peter's wort *(Hypericum stans);* and beetroot *(Beta vulgaris)* when mixed with a little oil and alum.

Wound treatment with plants

It is a little difficult to decide with the word *wounds* where a wound begins and a cut, or a sore, or a bruise ends. Often all of these conditions may be a part of the wound. Thus the reader is advised to consider plants mentioned under such other headings, where treatment is to be applied. A number of plants have been suggested as having wound-healing qualities of which the following are samples:

Adder's Tongue *(Ophiglossum vulgatum)*

It is a fine cooling herb, and an excellent balsam for fresh wounds, ulcers, and inflammations can be made from the leaves as follows:

"Two pounds (907 g) of leaves chopped very fine put into half a pint (284 ml) of oil and one and a half pounds (679 g) of suet melted together. Boil the whole, (but do not burn it), till the herb is rather crisp; strain off from the leaves and the liquid will be, when cool, a beautiful and efficacious ointment."

All-Heal *(Stachys sylvatica)*

The leaves are bruised and applied to stop bleeding and cure wounds.

Bugle *(Ajuga reptans)*

Bugle is reputed to be good for internal wounds.

German Camomile *(Matricaria Chamomilla)*

The blossoms can be used to make a compress to relieve wounds.

Goldenrod *(Solidago var. sp.)*

Some of the many species of goldenrod offer possible value when an antiseptic powder is made from the crushed leaves.

Marigold *(Calendula officinalis)*

> The flower petals and leaves can be made into a salve to soothe open wounds. It is also useful for eczema.

Solomon's Seal *(Polygonatum biflorum)*

> The hairy Solomon's seal offers a poultice for wounds when the powdered root is used.

Witch Hazel *(Hamamelis virginiana)*

> Everyone knows of the use and effects of the common witch hazel, which with its astringent properties, is valuable mainly for easing the flow of blood from a wound. The leaves are used to make a compress.

Yarrow *(Achillea Millefolium)*

> The yarrow is a denizen of many herb gardens. An ointment made from the leaves can be used for wounds, inflammations, and ulcers.

Plants against bleeding

When one talks of bleeding, the question arises as to the source of the bleeding, and one finds in many herbal books all sorts of plants which are reputed to help in curing bleeding from the lungs, or stomach, or other internal organs. However, one should go at once to a doctor of some repute, rather than going to the woods for a remedy.

Even in the matter of external bleeding, one finds that most of the plants which are possibly helpful in such accidental bleedings are found among the plant genera which are rated as astringents, all of which might be of aid. Parts of the oak such as extract of oak bark are very astringent and fleabane *(Erigeron canadensis)* has similar properties.

Other herbs which are astringent and can be used to check bleeding are: cranesbill *(Geranium maculatum)*, bilberry *(Vaccinium Myrtillus)*, nettle *(Urtica dioica)*, and goldenrod *(Solidago Virgaurea)*.

But here the problem is to find the plant at the moment needed.

Another hemostatic, which is not quite in the plant world, is the use of bunched-up pieces of cobwebs for the same sort of effect, but as cobwebs are so often found on plants, perhaps the reader will pardon this suggestion.

Expectorants

To a certain extent, plants which are considered here as expectorants might well be mentioned under those for coughs and colds and the like, since the purpose of expectorants is to cause the discharge of irritating accumulations of mucus and thereby help to cure the basic trouble. Possibly of greatest help as an expectorant is just plain honey. Yet, there are some plant medicines which seem to be particularly suitable for this effect, of which a few are discussed below:

Coltsfoot *(Tussilago farfara)*

A handful of leaves boiled in a quart (1.14 l) of water till reduced to a pint (568 ml) makes a decoction with powerful expectorant qualities. A tea can be made from the blossoms and leaves; sweetening with honey increases its expectorant properties.

Eucalyptus *(Eucalyptus globulus)*

The leaves are used to make a tea which is sweetened with honey and drunk as hot as possible.

Horehound *(Marrubium vulgare)*

The dried leaves are made into a tea or other drinkable form, and this for centuries has been known as an expectorant and tonic.

Storax *(Liquidambar styraciflua)*

The exuded gum from the bark of the storax is made commercially into a thick liquid which, when combined with benzoin, is a stimulating expectorant. However, it would be difficult to produce as a "home medicine".

The sunflower is widely grown for its seeds and the oil they yield. Though not commonly regarded as a medicinal plant, it does have a variety of healing virtues, namely, as an expectorant, diuretic and alleviator of prostate gland troubles.

Sunflower Seed *(Helianthus annuus)*

Medicinally it is said to have good expectorant qualities; two ounces (56 g) of seed boiled down in 32 fluid ounces (909 ml) of water to 12 fluid ounces (340 ml) with gin and some honey added, is to be taken three or four times a day. It is also listed as a diuretic and the raw seeds eaten in quantity are said to alleviate prostate gland troubles.

Plants for coughs

Possibly the most common complaints of mankind are coughs and sore throats, and through the centuries, many plant remedies have been suggested. One of the easiest of the natural remedies to use is honey. It can be taken alone or combined with some of the plants which themselves are valuable. A selection of the most noted follows:

Angelica *(Angelica Archangelica)*

The root is used to make a useful cough medicine.

Horseradish *(Cochlearia Armoracia)*

The grated root is chewed raw or made into an infusion. It is particularly good in bronchial coughs.

Irish Moss, Carragheen *(Chondrus crispus)*

For those who live in sea-coast areas, the dried pieces of the Irish moss are not hard to obtain. By cooking and boiling them down to a jelly-like material, a substance is made which can be used in puddings and is actually found in many of our food products today. It is extremely soothing to the throat, as well as having nutrient values.

Linseed *(Linum usitatissimum)*

Linseed oil has the quality of soothing inflamed membranes, and could well be used in any afflictions of the pulmonary tract.

59

Liquorice *(Glycyrrhiza glabra)*

> The root is the part used and its demulcent properties make it very useful for coughs and bronchial irritation.

Thyme *(Thymus vulgaris)*

> Use the leaves to make a tea or infusion for spasmodic dry coughs. Reputed to be especially good for whooping cough.

Wild Marjoram, Oregano *(Origanum vulgare)*

> Restores appetite and relieves coughs when taken as an infusion.

Colds and fever

Probably most readers know that one of the best ways of ridding oneself of a cold (with or without a fever) is to go to bed for a day or two, drink plenty of water, and/or some hot lemon juice. If the cold is accompanied by a cough or sore throat, a tea may be made of lemon, honey, and some Irish moss, which eases the soreness. While no longer a plant remedy, aspirin can be justified by the nature-user in that it was introduced to us by the American Indians, who found the same properties in willow bark from which it was later synthesized. Beyond these simple things, here are some plants to give additional help.

Blessed Thistle *(Cnicus benedictus)*

> A tea made with one ounce (28 g) of the dried herb to a pint (568 ml) of boiling water is reported to be good for fevers.

Borage *(Borago officinalis)*

> The leaves, seeds, and roots are useful for fevers.

Comfrey *(Symphytum officinale)*

> It is regarded as being good for fevers. The leaves are infused in water for ten to 15 minutes to make a strong tea.

Dogwood *(Cornus var. sp.)*

> The bark of various dogwoods is reputed to be good for colds.

Elder *(Sambucus nigra)*

The juice of the berries is boiled down with a little honey to a treacly substance and is good for sore throats and colds.

Garlic *(Allium sativum)*

Garlic is an excellent medicine prescribed for many things over the centuries. It promotes expectoration and is useful for all kinds of colds and 'flu. One authority says that garlic provides "many marvellous healing powers." It can be taken in capsules of garlic oil, or rubbed on the soles of the feet.

Holly *(Ilex Aquifolium)*

A tea can be made from the leaves which helps to reduce fever.

Horehound *(Marrubium vulgare)*

A plant which is always good for coughs and sore throats and clears the air passages in bronchial catarrh.

Hyssop *(Hyssopus officinalis)*

This is reputed as a good curative agent for colds and fevers.

Summer Savory *(Satureia hortensis)*

Savory is a good expectorant and soothing medicine for colds.

Wormwood *(Artemisia Absinthium)*

This herb is listed as being a cure for feverish conditions and colds, but it should only be taken in small amounts.

Yarrow *(Achillea Millefolium)*

One of the most common plants in the herb garden is yarrow; a tea made from the dried foliage is an old cold remedy.

The following recipe is an old herbal cure for colds:

One handful of yarrow together with half an ounce (14 g) of ginger root, bruised, or a teaspoonful of Cayenne pepper and about three pints (1.7 l) of water. Boil to one pint (568 ml). Add a little honey to taste. Take a good dose at bedtime and your cold will be cured by the next morning; if not, repeat the dose.

61

Horehound is most familiar as an ingredient in cough drops and syrups, but it has also been used as a mild laxative and as a tonic. The leaves and flowers are used to make a decoction, being simmered in boiling water for about ten minutes. Half-cup doses every three hours are recommended.

Bronchial asthma

In reading about the remedies of this distressing condition one finds a variety of cures tried, some of them soothing, some sedative, and varying with the plant material of the locality.

Black Bryony *(Tamus Communis)*

The root is grated and rubbed over the chest, acting as a mild rubefacient; this has been found to help asthmatics.

Cabbage and Coleworts *(Brassica var. sp.)*

The juice of the leaves mixed with honey is good for those troubled with asthma.

Chervil *(Anthriscus Cerefolium)*

It is an expectorant and is reputed to relieve asthma if boiled in whey.

Coltsfoot *(Tussilago farfara)*

The leaves are used to make a syrup sweetened with honey and reputed to be excellent for chronic bronchitis and asthma.

Garlic *(Allium sativum)*

Mrs. Grieve in her book *A Modern Herbal* recommends a "syrup of garlic" as one good remedy.

Honeysuckle *(Lonicera Periclymenum)*

The flowers eaten raw or made into a tea are taken early in the morning.

Horehound *(Marrubium vulgare)*

A decoction of the dried herb with the seed, or the juice of the green herb taken with honey, is a remedy for difficult breathing, coughs, and bronchitis.

Mullein *(Verbascum Thapsus)*

A soothing tea is made from the dried blossoms. It should be drunk hot, sweetened with honey.

Saffron *(Crocus sativa)*

Saffron has been found good for asthma, coughs, and difficulty of breathing.

Sundew *(Drosera rotundifolia)*

Perhaps because it is sort of a magical plant, in that it gets its food by eating insects, sundew has been rated as having a number of medicinal values, including that of being an aphrodisiac. As well as being listed as an asthma cure, it is said to be a "cure for old age".

Thyme *(Thymus vulgaris)*

An infusion of the fresh tops has been found useful for all cases of difficult breathing and asthma.

Catarrh

In discussing a few plants which are reputed to be good for catarrh, it should be noted that catarrhs may well be found not only in the nasal passages as commonly thought, but in internal tracts such as that of the stomach. For that reason, a number of plants which, in some classifications may be said to be useful for inflamed mucous membranes, could well be considered for catarrhal conditions in whatever area. Here are a few plants which have been used for this condition.

Blessed Thistle *(Cnicus benedictus)*

As with so many plants, a number of healing values are given for blessed thistle including the control of fever. A plant long used by the herbalists, a simple infusion may be made of one ounce (28 g) of the dried herb to three-quarters of a pint (426 ml) of boiling water.

Borage *(Borago officinalis)*

A common garden herb, with most lovely blue flowers, which is often planted just to attract the bees to one's garden, borage has been used for centuries for catarrhal conditions. Infusions of it are healing to inflamed membranes, and it is thought that a known saline content provides other aids, as does a salt gargle.

Borage is a demulcent, acting to soften and sooth inflamed mucous membranes. As such, it has been used in catarrh and some respiratory ailments.

Hound's Tongue *(Cynoglossum officinale)*

This lovely blue-flowered member of the borage family is grown as a beautiful garden flower and has, when prepared as a medicine, a number of listed medicinal values, all of them tending to be demulcent or soothing to membranes and an alleviant to coughs.

Ragwort *(Senecio Jacobaea)*

> A decoction of the herb has been found useful for treating catarrh, as has knapweed *(Centaurea Jacea)*.

Digestion

Perhaps this section might better be labelled indigestion, rather than digestion, for the plants discussed here often not only have some curative properties in easing stomach upsets, but also are a stimulant to encourage good eating. It is actually very interesting to note that almost every substance used in *good* cooking is for the stimulation of the appetite and is most usually a plant product. Thus, to list every plant here which is tasty or adds to the joy of eating would take a book in itself.

Here, also, it is notable that plant products made originally as medicines have sometimes come to be purely appetite stimulants, as in the case of the much-used Angustura bitters, or, in raw plants, the eating of parsley, watercress, horseradish, ginger, nutmeg, and sage. But there are other less well known plants which offer an aid to digestion:

Angelica *(Angelica Archangelica)*

> A common denizen of the home herb garden which is known medicinally as a stimulant.

Anise *(Pimpinella Anisum)*

> The seeds are made into a tea which should be sipped warm before meals to aid digestion.

Blessed Thistle *(Cnicus benedictus)*

> This is a very anciently known, stimulating, tonic plant.

To soothe acid stomachs try mint, catnip or fennel teas, sweet and spicy anise seeds, papaya or generous helpings of natural bran.

Blue Gentian *(Gentiana Catesbaei)*

Gentian is excellent for a stomachic tonic.

Caraway *(Carum Carvi)*, **Dill** *(Anethum graveolens)*,
   Fennel *(Foeniculum vulgare)*

The seeds of these herbs can all be made into teas drunk warm
before meals.

Cayenne *(Capsicum annuum)*

Cayenne and similar peppers are stimulating stomachics.

Dill: See Caraway

Fennel: See Caraway

Ginseng *(Panax quinquefolius)*

Here is the famous ginseng which the pharmacist would call only an
aromatic bitter, but which in China is reputed to cure anything.

Mint *(Mentha var. sp.)*

It is hardly necessary to point out here that some of the mint
family such as spearmint and peppermint are good to aid digestion.

Rosemary *(Rosmarinus officinalis)*

A basic plant for all herb gardens which has been known and used
for millennia as a stimulating tonic, but one which, when used for
cooking meats, makes them much more inviting to eat.

Salsify *(Tragopogon porrifolius)*

Salsify or oyster-plant, when chewed, yields a juice which is said to
aid digestion.

Sorrel *(Rumex Acetosa)*

Culpeper says that this herb "quenches thirst and procures an
appetite in fainting or decaying stomachs". The leaves, seeds, and
roots are used.

Sweet Flag *(Acorus calamus)*

The widely growing water-plant, besides being used for rush-seating, is also an aromatic tonic.

Diarrhoea

Many of the complaints of man are uncommon and afflict only a few people, but the difficulty of diarrhoea is something few people miss. One might mention that, among the most common of remedies which are plant-oriented would be the drinking of strong tea, the taking of blackberry brandy, the eating of oatmeal, and always, as for so many troubles, "an apple a day". Beyond this there possibly would be some plants mentioned under astringents, and also, in a long list of "reputed" cures, the ones named below are most often mentioned.

Alum *(Geranium maculatum)*

Alum root or cranesbill is a reputable cure here.

Blackberry *(Rubus var. sp.)*

As mentioned above, blackberry brandy is known as a quick aid for this trouble, as is also the fresh fruit in quantity, or a decoction of the root bark.

English Oak *(Quercus robur)*

A decoction of the bark of English Oak is recommended in cases of chronic diarrhoea. This is likely to be true with other oaks, as the barks of all oaks are astringent.

Grape *(Vitis var. sp.)*

Grape juice taken in quantity, fresh, is often listed as an aid to simple diarrhoea.

Saint John's Wort *(Hypericum perforatum)*

As the name "wort" implies, Saint John's wort is quite an ancient remedy for many conditions, including that of diarrhoea.

Shepherd's Purse *(Capsella Bursa-pastoris)*

> The common wild shepherd's purse is usually found mentioned in old herbals as a simple cure for diarrhoea.

Laxatives and purgatives

From childhood to old age the most common medicine to be administered is one or another of these, and happily for those who dislike the idea of using synthetics or who may be living in the wild, there are a number of good plants which will supply relief from constipation.

There are fruits such as figs, prunes, or pears, while stewed rhubarb in the spring has sure effects in cleaning out the system. Olive oil is a mild laxative, and in the purgative field one could use castor oil.

Wild plants which can be used in one way or another in quantities according to need for mildness or strength, are as follows:

Cascara *(Rhamnus Purschiana)*

> The bark is dried and made into medicine, the well-known purgative cascara, which is also prescribed as a tonic in lesser doses. But in eating fruit from these plants care should be exercised, as the purgative power is very pronounced.

Croton *(Croton Tiglium)*

> This member of the spurge family was once used as the source of a very strong purgative called croton oil. The common name of the plant is chaparral tea. The plant juices, as are the juices of many other members of the spurge family, are poisonous to animals.

Dandelion *(Taraxacum officinale)*

> Reputed to have been used medicinally in Egypt thousands of years ago, the common and wide-spread dandelion has spring tonic and laxative values well indicated by the specific name *officinale*. A fine spring tonic plant.

Horehound *(Marrubium vulgare)*

> Horehound is a well-known wild plant, providing not only sources for candy and cough medicine, but also a simple laxative.

Linseed *(Linum usitatissimum)*

Few do not know the many values to be found in a flaxseed poultice, or of linseed oil, which has good qualities as a laxative.

Magnolia *(Magnolia virginiana)*

A number of medicinal uses are made of extracts from magnolia trees, including laxatives.

Walnut *(Juglans cinerea* and *J. nigra)*

If walnuts of one or another sort are eaten in quantity, laxative effects may be noted.

Tonics

The definition of a tonic is not easy to settle on, as a tonic may be something which is just stimulating to the appetite, something which improves the activity of the organs, or something which produces a healthful feeling. Some herbs have valuable tonic properties to combat that spent feeling after a period of over-work or an illness, or at the end of a long winter. These include anise *(Pimpinella Anisum)*, briar rose *(Rosa* species), gentian *(Gentianella campestris)*, caper *(Capparis spinosa)*, and carrot *(Daucus carota* var. *sativus)*. Dandelion and burdock beer was a refreshing drink much favoured in the north of England as a tonic and a blood purifier. Basil *(Ocimum Basilicum)* has a reputation as a stimulant and powerful tonic.

The plants found here are of various values, but all of them are noted in one book or another as being tonics.

Barberry *(Berberis vulgaris)*

Certain principles in the barberries are said to be useful in liver and digestive disorders.

Camomile *(Matricaria Chamomilla)*

One of the oldest of herbal remedies is camomile, which is often noted as a valuable aromatic bitter (and thus a tonic).

71

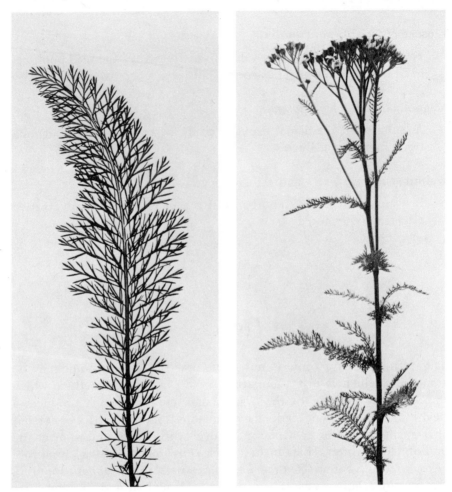

In days of old, yarrow was crushed and applied to the wounds of battle to staunch the flow of blood. The multitudes of tiny flowers on each plant have been used in uterine diseases, catarrh, and as an astringent.

Chicory *(Cichorium Intybus)*

Chicory and especially the related dandelion are both said to be good plants as spring tonics, and have been so used by southern Europeans for centuries.

Horehound *(Marrubium vulgare)*

Horehound is reputed to be of use as a nutritious tonic.

Mint *(Mentha* var. sp.*)*

The mints of many sorts are seemingly all good for aiding digestion, and thus of tonic value.

Self-Heal *(Prunella vulgaris)*

A decoction of the roots and leaves makes an astringent tonic.

Sweet Fern *(Comptonia peregrina)*

Sweet Fern has astringent and tonic properties and is, as well, a good plant to cure poison ivy.

Sweet Flag *(Acorus calamus)*

The water-loving sweet flag is a plant also noted as an aromatic bitter.

Tansy *(Tanacetum vulgare)*

Tansy is an aromatic bitter and thus becomes "tonic".

Watercress *(Nasturtium officinale)*

Watercress has for a long time, been known to stimulate the appetite.

Wormwood *(Artemisia* var. sp.*)*

The wormwoods in one or another species are known as old-time sources for stimulating, aromatic bitters, and as the basis for absinth.

Yarrow *(Achillea* var. sp.*)*

The yarrows are always found in any list of valuable herbs, and can be used as a stimulating or aromatic bitter.

Rheumatism

One reads archeological reports of ancient mummified bodies being dug up in which the condition of the hands, etc., would indicate the presence of what we now call rheumatism or arthritis. Hence one can assume that then, when plants were the only medicine, as well as now, when there are all sorts of scientific knowledge and medicines available, crippling of the body from this disease was a dreaded condition.

One often hears that the only pain-alleviant is synthesized aspirin, which has come down to us from willow bark. Now, more recently, various writers are suggesting that much help can also be obtained by taking vitamin C, which is found in citrus fruits. This is not that new, for a most reliable modern herbal writer said some 40 years ago that "lemon juice is highly recommended in acute rheumatism". Such "medicine" as any of the citrus juices, being harmless and indeed healthful in many other ways, seems to be a first choice here. But there are a number of other plant medicines said to have anti-rheumatic values.

Aconite *(Aconitum Napellus)*

A tincture of aconite is reputed to be a valuable external application for rheumatism, lumbago, and neuralgia.

Angelica *(Angelica Archangelica)*

The distilled water of the powdered root has been used to ease rheumatism.

Bittersweet *(Solanum Dulcamara)*

Bittersweet, which is related to the deadly nightshade, is the climbing plant with the bright red berries, rather than the black berries of the poison form. It is just as well for those not accomplished in nature lore to keep away from using almost any wild plants in the Solanum or potato family as there is a basic poison reserve in all of them. However, in the case of this bittersweet, Mrs. Grieve, in her book, says that for "Chronic rheumatism it has been much employed in the past, an infusion of one ounce (28 g) of the dried herb to half a pint (284 ml) of water, being taken in wineglass doses, two or three times daily."

Black Mustard *(Brassica nigra)*

A very potent poultice can be made from the ground seeds and applied to the painful parts for one minute. Reddened parts of the skin can be soothed with olive oil after the poultice has been removed. It should not be used on sensitive skins.

Dandelion *(Taraxacum officinale)*

The shredded root or root and leaves mixed can be made into a tea which should be taken night and morning during the spring and autumn.

Elderberry *(Sambucus canadensis)*

The juices of the fruit of elderberry in olden times were thought to be a good remedy for rheumatism. Perhaps there is vitamin C here.

Juniper *(Juniperus communis)*

A tea can be made from one teaspoon of the crushed berries with eight fluid ounces (227 ml) of boiling water, left to stand for 20 minutes. This should be taken morning and evening during the spring and autumn for four to six weeks. It is recommended for chronic rheumatism.

Stinging Nettle *(Urtica dioica)*

This is a very old remedy, as the Romans used stinging nettles in their treatment of rheumatism. A tea is made from the dried leaves and taken twice daily for four to six weeks.

Sweet Vernal Grass *(Anthoxanthum odoratum)*

The flowers can be made into a poultice in the following way: Pack the flowers tightly into a cotton or muslin bag and soak in two quarts (2.27 l) of boiling water for 15 minutes. Wring out well and apply to painful area, as hot as possible.

Alternatively, one pound (453 g) of flowers can be boiled in four quarts (4.54 l) of water for one minute and left to stand for 15 minutes. The liquid should be strained and added to the bath water. The patient should bathe in this water for ten to 15 minutes, two or three times a week, resting for half an hour after each bath.

Emetics

There is occasionally in our lives some immediate necessity to cause ourselves or others to vomit, and almost everyone knows that a finger down a throat will usually get the needed reaction. If that is objectionable, then perhaps an overdose of salt will help, or the swallowing of soapsuds. Beyond this, a number of herbal remedies have been known and used in different cultures. These below are a few:

Black Mustard *(Sinapis nigra)*

The use of preparations of the ground seeds of black or white mustard provides every home with not only a good condiment, but, in large doses, a good emetic.

Daffodil *(Narcissus* sp.*)*

The fresh bulb acts as a gentle emetic and purgative.

Groundsel *(Senecio vulgaris)*

A strong infusion of the plant has been used as an emetic as it causes no irritation or pain, and a weak solution has been used as a purgative.

Holly *(Ilex Aquifolium)*

The berries are used as an emetic and diuretic, but should be used with great care as the effect can be quite violent.

Horseradish *(Cochlearia armoracea)*

A strong decoction of the root has been used as an emetic, and is supposed to purify the blood.

Plant stimulants

The casual reader might well ask, why discuss stimulants as far as herbs are concerned, and what function would they play in these days of general over-stimulation?

The plants listed below are those which may stimulate the sense of taste or digestion. They would make a very stimulating herb garden with many uses, medicinal and otherwise.

Angelica *(Angelica Archangelica)*

A well known stimulating herb.

Angelica has several medicinal uses. The root is said to ease rheumatism and is also made into cough medicine. It is a well known general stimulant.

Camomile, Roman *(Anthemis nobilis)*

A common garden herb, camomile has aroma and bitterness.

Elder *(Sambucus canadensis)*

Elderflower tea has a pleasant taste and is useful as a stomach stimulant.

Ginger *(Zingiber officinale)*

A well known stimulant and tonic much valued through the ages.

Horseradish *(Cochlearia armoracia)*

Stimulates the appetite and even causes tears when it is grated.

Lavender *(Lavandula vera)*

A delightful aromatic stimulant. Used for centuries to revive ladies after fainting.

Magnolia *(Magnolia virginiana)*

The foliage of this and other magnolias is an aromatic stimulant.

Mint *(Mentha sp.)*

Who does not know the palate stimulating and gastric correctiveness of almost any of the mint family?

Pennyroyal *(Mentha Pulegium)*

A member of the mint family used as a stimulant, and for all manner of other things, since ancient times.

Pine (Larch) *(Pinus larix)*

The bark is used to make an aromatic stimulant.

Rosemary *(Rosmarinus officinalis)*

Stimulates the brain and nervous system. The oil is used externally as a fragrant rubefacient and linament.

Sassafras *(Sassafras albidum)*

The roots make a stimulating tea and medicine.

Stinging Nettle *(Urtica dioica)*

The leaves can be cooked and eaten as a stimulating tonic.

Storax Gum *(Liquidambar orientalis)*

A first-class stimulating expectorant.

Sweet Flag *(Acorus calamus)*

An aromatic bitter, useful medicinally.

Tansy *(Tanacetum vulgare)*

Common tansy is stimulating, if not especially pleasant.

Wormwood *(Artemisia Absinthium)*

Has been used since earliest times as a stimulating bitter.

Sedatives

In discussing this subject recently with a modern pharmacist, the comment was made that one must be very careful with sedatives recommended, for all too often any substance which may have sedative qualities is likely to be, in larger doses, a harmful or even killing opiate. One could think at once of the relaxing and sedative quality of any form of alcoholic drink, which when recommended by doctors is a useful sedative, but which when abused is a killing drug.

Then there is the presently much-discussed plant called *Cannabis sativa* or marijuana, which has a centuries-old history of use for sedative and religious purposes. A research company in Cambridge, Massachusetts, as reported in *World*, December 19, 1972 says that marijuana may well find application in the treatment of certain forms of psychiatric illness such as depression.

Among other plants which might be mentioned as being highly valuable under proper medical supervision, although all are potent plants, would be: Cowslip *(Primula veris)*, Red Clover *(Trifolium pratense)*, Heather *(Ericas sp.)*, and Opium Poppy *(Papaver somniferum)*.

Beyond these there are a few less potent plants with calmative qualities.

Camomile German *(Matricaria chamomilla)*

One of the most generally useful denizens of the home herb garden is that of camomile, and a tea made from the dry leaves has long been known as a pleasing sedative drink.

Dandelion *(Taraxacum officinale)*

Is reputed to promote rest and sleep.

Hops *(Humulus Lupulus)*

It is hardly likely that the sedative qualities of the seeds of hops are found in ordinary beer, but actually an oil made from this plant is a "reputable" sedative.

Lettuce *(Lactuca Sativa)*

The milky juice which exudes from the plant has mild opiate qualities when allowed to dry in the air and turn brown.

Valerian *(Valeriana officinalis)*

The drug valerian is used for a number of purposes and is one that has survived the onslaught of synthetic and modern chemical medicines. Among its uses is that of a nerve-soothing and calmative drug, but one to be taken under physician's orders. The common name of valerian is "heal-all", which comes from the Latin word *valere*, meaning, to be well.

Plant diuretics

In exploring the field of plant medicine one finds many plants which are reputed primarily or secondarily to have properties which promote the flow of urine. Some of these are well known, such as quantities of water melon or raw onions. Parsley, too, has a strong reputation as a diuretic and is a common food enjoyed by all. Below are a few selected wild plants which reputable books rate as possibly useful diuretics.

Bearberry *(Arctostaphylos Uva-ursi)*

The common acid-soil-loving bearberry has long been known and used as a diuretic.

The milky-white juice of the lettuce stems has sedative properties if allowed to dry and turn brown.

Valerian is an official drug plant still used today. It has calmative and sedative properties and has been used to treat hysteria, epilepsy, migraine and many nervous diseases, but taken in excessive doses or too often it can cause headaches and hallucinations.

81

Campion, Wild *(Lychnis alba)*

> Wild campion is reputed to be an excellent diuretic and is also used for removing stones and obstructions in the kidneys.

Chicory *(Cichorium Intybus)*

> The common chicory with its lovely blue flowers and its usually close-growing neighbour, the dandelion *(Taraxacum officinale)*, have both long been used as diuretics, although they are possibly not very powerful.

Cleavers *(Galium Aparine)*

> A renowned diuretic also useful for urinary complaints and obstructions of the kidney and bladder.

Iris *(Iris virginica* and *I. versicolor)*

> The flags or irises are reputed diuretics.

Juniper *(Juniperus communis)*

> Extracts from bark or berries are listed as stimulating diuretics.

Sarsaparilla *(Smilax* sp.)

> Taken in mild doses, this herb has been found useful for promoting the flow of urine.

Urinary disorders

In this classification would fall such plants as are often considered diuretics and have to do with kidney ailments, bladder disorders, and the like. In no sense is the list below a complete listing of all of the plants in this category, but rather a sampling of botanical medicines, many of which have been known and used for centuries.

Bearberry *(Arctostaphylos Uva-ursi)*

> This plant is usually to be found growing in sunny, acid soils. It, along with other ericaceous plants, has diuretic properties and is a mild disinfectant to the urinary tract. The dried leaves are made into a tea.

82

Burdock is a common wild plant, long regarded as an excellent blood purifier. A decoction of the root, the part usually used, is said to remedy chronic skin diseases. It is also a diuretic and diaphoretic.

83

Couch Grass *(Agropyrum repens)*

The quack or couch grass is a prime pest to the gardener, but the roots of it have constituents which place it among the diuretics.

Cucumber: See Pumpkin

Dandelion *(Taraxacum officinale)*

The fresh or dried root mixed with the leaves can be made into a tea. The tea should stand for 20 minutes, then one cup should be taken three times a day for four to six weeks.

Goldenrod *(Solidago Virgaurea)*

A tea made from the chopped herb is said to be good for all kidney diseases.

Horsetails *(Equisetum hyemale)*

The fresh stems chewed or made into a decoction are not only useful as a diuretic, but are readily available for scouring pots and pans.

Juniper *(Juniperus* var. sp.*)*

The junipers, especially the blue berries of *Juniperus virginiana* and *J. communis*, contain an oil notable as a diuretic and are used to flavour gin. (Gin is a perversion of the French word for juniper, *genievre*).

Kidneywort *(Umbilicus rupestris)*

The juice is reputed to relieve inflamed kidneys and to be good in all urinary complaints when taken inwardly.

Liquorice *(Glycyrrhiza glabra)*

Liquorice is reported to work gently and to be very soothing to ulcerated kidneys and urinary passages.

Medlar *(Mespilus germanica)*

The powdered stones boiled with parsley roots have been effective in removing kidney stones.

Melon: See Pumpkin

The dandelion is an excellent tonic. It is used to relieve rheumatism, promote sleep and also has laxative properties.

Parsley *(Petroselinum crispum)*

This herb is reputed to purify the blood. For kidney diseases a tea made from the fruit should be taken in the morning.

Pumpkin, Melon, and Cucumber *(Cucubita var. sp.)*

In this genus the seeds of both the pumpkin and the cucumber are distinctly diuretic. The seeds are said to contain quantities of vitamin F which is noted for aiding urinary problems, and one authority credits the eating of such seeds with retarding the development of prostate troubles in men.

85

Sunflower *(Helianthus annuus)*

As with members of the cucumber family, the seeds of the common sunflower are strongly recommended for those with urinary or prostate disorders. Two ounces (56 g) of the seeds can be boiled with 32 fluid ounces (909 ml) of water; when 11 ounces (313 ml) are left, add gin.

Yarrow *(Achillea var. sp.)*

The yarrows are well-known herbs which might be useful as minor diuretics.

Female disorders

Perhaps a better title than the above might be "women's problems", for there are circumstances of menstruation and other matters that relate only to women. The home herb gardener in past times, was often a woman who knew about plant values and as might be expected, did a lot of experimenting with concoctions from the plants she knew best, frequently with satisfactory results. Teas made from Solomon's seal roots, parsley, yarrow, and juniper berries were used. There were, indeed, plants suitable for almost any need including that of contraception.

In the book of plant drugs by Fernie called *Herbal Simples*, written at the turn of the century, the listing of "Plants to promote the monthly flow" goes to some 30 names, with a similar list for other special problems in this area. A few of the plants used follow:

Barberry *(Berberis vulgaris)*

Preparations made from the barberry are referred to as reliable anti-periodics.

Lady's Mantle *(Alchemilla vulgaris)*

The leaves can be made into a soothing tea by boiling one or two teaspoonfuls in eight fluid ounces (227 ml) of water for one minute and then letting it stand for 15 minutes. One cup is to be taken morning and evening.

Pennyroyal *(Hedeoma pulegioides)*

Pennyroyal tea was often given for menstrual problems.

Rue *(Ruta graveolens)*

A warm infusion of rue is a remedy that has been used for centuries.

Saint John's Wort *(Hypericum perforatum)*

A decoction can be made by simmering two teaspoonfuls in eight fluid ounces (227 ml) of water. Let it stand for 15 minutes and then take one cupful twice a day.

Shepherd's Purse *(Capsella Bursa-pastoris)*

This was used for excessive menstruation, a tea being made from two teaspoonfuls of the dried herb or four teaspoonfuls of the fresh, boiled in eight fluid ounces (227 ml) of water for one minute, then left to stand for 15 minutes. The dose was one cup, two to four times a day.

Yarrow *(Achilea Millefolium)*

The common yarrow was often used for painful menstruation.

Readers of all the above should understand, as with every other condition discussed here, that the circumstances of recuperation are variable, that detailed instructions for preparing and taking medicines should be carefully studied, and that a trusted physician should be consulted in anything other than very mild disorders. But, just as our modern doctors are now beginning to discover that the Orientals have something not to be overlooked in ancient acupuncture, so, too, must reconsideration often be given to the use of much of the millennia-old knowledge held by the herbalists.

Male disorders

Men, as well as women, have problems which are peculiarly theirs. In the matter of the prostate condition, for instance, the noted authority in this field, John L. Tobe, has proposed in his book that among other cures is the eating of foods which are high in vitamin F, a list of which would include such things as sunflower seeds, pumpkin and melon seeds, wheat germ, and safflower and soybean oils. In one chapter he lists a number of other plant drugs which are used, and generally suggests that there are possible cures for this condition other than an operation. It is pointed out that herbs which assist in urination are also of benefit in this and other conditions.

Rose hips make a fine tea which is an excellent source of vitamin C and thus a fine beverage for cold sufferers.

Odds and ends of health hints

Within the limits of plant medicines, there are a number of miscellaneous plant uses and some little health hints which, while mostly plant-orientated, are not easy to include in a large classification.

Taking food plants as an example, it is likely that most readers would know that the "hips" of almost any rose are very high in vitamin C, actually much higher than oranges. Watercress and parsley both have some valuable chemical constituents, and in addition are valuable as digestants and stimulants to appetite. The tropical papayas, now available in some markets, are excellent as digestants, and the leaves can be used (as is done where they grow) as a tenderizer for any meat dish. For some quick energy there is nothing better than honey, or possibly grape juice. For a real emergency, brandy is always recommended, and of course, it too comes from grapes. Some health food persons object to the use of coffee and tea, but they are indeed both useful stimulants.

There are a few uses of plants which have not otherwise been covered here, such as the eating of quantities of gelatinous foods as a means of reducing the brittle nature of finger nails. If the skin needs softening, then the combined juices of cucumber and Irish moss would be recommended.

Instead of softening, the skin may need stimulation, and here one could rub on leaves of some of the mustards, which are common weeds. An even more stimulating rub would be hot pepper plants.

In 1520, Sir Thomas More, author of the unique book *Utopia*, created a garden in Chelsea that is said to be "one of the first examples of a tradition that has become typically English".

He was a man in many ways ahead of his time and introduced some novel features in garden design. He also used some plants not then considered suitable for private gardens and said:

> There is manie a plant I entertayn in my Garden and Paddock which the Fastidious would cast forthe. I like to teach my children the Uses of Common Things, to know, for instance, the Uses of the Flowers and Weeds that grow in our Fields and Hedges. Manie a poor Knave's Pottage would be improved were he but skilled in the properties of Burdock, of Purple Orchis, Lady's Smock and Brooklime and of Poor Man's Pepper. The roots of Wild Succory and Water Arrowhead might agreeablie change his Lenten diet and Glasswort afford him a Pickle for his mouthful of Salte Meat. Then there are the Cresses and Wood-sorrel for his breakfast, and Salep for his hot evening Mess. For his Medicine there

is Herb Twopence that will cure a hundred Ills, Camomile to soothe a raging Tooth, and the juice of Buttercup to clear his head by sneezing. Vervain cureth the ague and Crowfoot affords the least painfull of Blisters; St Anthony's Turnip is an Emetic; Goosegrasse sweetens the Blood; Woodruffe is good for the Liver; Pimpernell promoteth Laughter and Poppy Sleep; Thyme giveth pleasant Dreams and an Ashen branch driveth evil spirits from the Pillow.

As Sir Thomas indicates, many herbs have considerable value as preventatives as well as cures. Prevention surely is the best approach to maintaining good health. Some herbs have culinary as well as medicinal properties, but for the moment we are concerned primarily with the latter.

There are many wild herbs, valuable in this respect, which would not easily survive if transplanted to our gardens, and others that are often tossed contemptuously onto the compost heap as weeds. Yet groundsel, nettle, daisy, dandelion, bindweed, and sow thistle are among those which might be turned to advantage in harmless remedies, while the following may be cultivated in our own gardens for culinary as well as medicinal purposes: garlic, borage, salad burnet, camomile, horehound, comfrey, lovage, mint, marjoram, mullein, nasturtium, and thyme.

Medicinal herb plants are decorative as well as being useful, and so would contribute handsomely to the garden's general display. Even if you do not go to the extent of a separate bed for herbs, room for some could be found among the vegetables, while rosemary, sage, and lavender would not be out of place, by any means, among the flowering shrubs.

Quite apart from the added interest when the herbs become established, there would be a considerable economy, since the packaged, dried ones are not cheap to buy and often the variety available is limited. But the greater benefits would be that you could gather them at just the right times and that they would always be fresh. When the season is ended for each one, you could then build up your own store of dried herbs.

Many wild indigenous plants are becoming rare as their natural habitats are being polluted or removed due to large-scale farming. Thus, growing some herbs in our gardens can help save them. Another important advantage is that we are much more certain that they will be pollution-free.

3

The Culinary Herbs

Roasts, stews, fish, and even sweets are all enhanced by the addition of that extra flavouring and aroma derived from fresh or dried herbs. In fact, some dishes can be positively tasteless without them. They can also improve bland recipes for people on restricted diets. For example, oregano can replace salt, and sweet cicely can replace sugar.

Fresh herbs are preferable, but when the season or the lack of a garden rule them out, dried herbs are excellent. Provided they are stored in dry and air-tight containers, they will hold their flavour for a very long time. The rule of thumb is to use twice the amount of fresh herbs to the dried ones.

For a hurried scratch meal, or when the cupboard is almost bare and the purse empty, a tin of tomato soup can be transformed into something both fanciful and tasty by adding milk or cream and a generous sprinkle of sweet basil. A few croutons added on serving, and you have a satisfying light meal.

A sample of various herbs and some suggestions for their uses can be found in the succeeding paragraphs.

Angelica *(Angelica Archangelica)*

This sweet-tasting plant is best known for its use in decorating cakes and puddings. It also lessens the need for a sweetener in pies and sauces and, combined with rhubarb and honey, makes a tasty sauce. Angelica can also be used for seasoning fish or cooked and eaten as a fresh vegetable.

Anise *(Pimpinella Anisum)*

Anise has the aroma and flavour of liquorice. The leaves can be chopped and added to cream sauces, salads, and shell fish. The seeds can be crushed and used to flavour cakes and biscuits.

Basil *(Ocimum Basilicum)*

Basil is probably best known for its use with tomatoes, raw or cooked. It can be sprinkled over sliced tomatoes with a French dressing, or used in tomato or spaghetti sauce and pizza. When baking apples, sprinkle a few leaves over the apples for a delicious flavour.

Bay *(Laurus nobilis)*

The leaves are spicy and pungent, and add greatly to the flavour of stews, casseroles, bolognese sauce, and soup stock. Ham is enhanced when boiled with a bay leaf and a few whole cloves.

Borage *(Borago officinalis)*

This is one of the herbs with a cucumber flavour, and in fact the leaves or peeled stalks can replace cucumber in a salad. Borage can also be used in gazpacho and other soups, and to flavour iced tea, fruit drinks, and Pimms No. 1.

Caraway *(Carum Carvi)*

This is most familiar for its seeds in cakes and breads. They can also be added to sauerkraut before it is cooked, and to potatoes for potato salad. Before roasting a pork joint, rub caraway seeds into the meat on all sides before seasoning—it is delicious.

Cheese sandwiches can have a new dimension by spreading a little mustard on one slice of bread, sprinkling caraway seeds on top, adding the cheese and the top slice of bread, and then toasting. The green leaves can be added to potato salads or beet-root salads, cottage or cream cheese, and to soups. The roots, which are similar to carrots, can be eaten as a vegetable.

Chervil *(Scandix Cerefolium)*

Chervil is similar to parsley—except that it is sweeter and slightly anise-flavoured—and can be used in much the same way. It is

Steamed comfrey leaves mixed with lemon juice, seasoning, and vegetable oil make a delicious, nutritious treat.

especially good in salads. In combination with other herbs it brings out their flavour.

Chives *(Allium Schoenoprasum)*

These are most widely used snipped into salads, omelettes, scrambled eggs, and cream or cottage cheese when a subtle onion flavour is wanted. They also add zest to soups and fish sauces.

Comfrey *(Symphytum officinale)*

The young leaves can be used raw as a salad or cooked as spinach.

Coriander *(Coriandrum sativum)*

The dried seeds, which have a pungent flavour, are widely used in curries, chutneys, and spicy dishes. The leaves, which contain vitamin C, are used in salads, cooked with red kidney beans, or used as a garnish in soup. The ground seeds can be added to omlettes.

93

Cumin *(Cuminum cyminum)*

Only the seeds are used, ground or whole, and they are an essential ingredient in many Asian and Mexican dishes. Used sparingly, they combine well with mayonnaise, in salads—green, potato, and cole-slaw—and can be added to many vegetables such as aubergines, leeks, carrots and tomatoes. Other uses are in soups, stews, or on roasting meats and kebabs.

Dandelion *(Taraxacum officinale)*

The young leaves may be eaten alone or combined with other greens to make salads, or cooked like spinach. The older leaves are bitter. The young roots may be peeled and boiled, or fried, as a vegetable. Tea can also be made from the leaves, and wine from the flowers.

Dill *(Peucedanum graveolens)*

This delicately flavoured herb combines with fish—sprinkled over it or in an accompanying sauce—and also goes well with cucumber. It marries well with tomato dishes in the same way as basil. Usually only the seeds are used to flavour salads, and vegetables, particularly white cabbage and marrow.

Fennel *(Foeniculum vulgare)*

A strong-tasting herb that should be used sparingly, fennel is widely favoured for fish sauces, as well as chicken and egg dishes. Florence fennel *(F. dulce)*, which looks like a cross between celery and onion, has a distinctive aniseed flavour and is equally good eaten raw in a salad or quartered and boiled as a vegetable and then tossed in butter.

Fenugreek *(Trigonella Foenum-graecum)*

Mostly used in tea, fenugreek seeds can be sprouted like bean sprouts and used as a vegetable or salad.

Good-King-Henry *(Chenopodium Bonus Henricus)*

Good-King-Henry is a pot herb that is cooked and eaten like spinach. Use the leaves before the plant goes to seed. Wash them and cook in a small amount of water. The leaves can also be used in salads.

Fennel is most commonly known for its use in fish dishes. It has a distinct aniseed flavour and is delicious eaten raw in salads. The leaves can be used to flavour chicken and egg dishes.

Horehound *(Marrubium vulgare)*

Mostly drunk as a tea, it is also a remedy for sore throats, colds, and coughs.

Horseradish *(Cochlearia Armoracia)*

The root is used, peeled and ground, to make horseradish sauce as an accompaniment to roast beef, and is high in vitamin C. It is also good for bronchitis and coughs.

Lamb's-Quarters *(Chenopodium album)*

This weed makes a good spinach substitute. The young tops are nipped off and steamed in a small amount of water. The nutritional value is greater than spinach, and the flavour is similar.

Lemon Balm *(Melissa officinalis)*

Although not often used in cooking, the leaves can be added to dishes where a lemon flavour is wanted, for example, in light soups like gazpacho, casseroles, salad dressings, iced drinks, puddings, souffles, and poultry stuffing. An infusion of fresh or dried leaves makes a refreshing drink.

Lovage *(Levisticum officinale)*

Lovage is a herb with many uses, as the leaves, seeds, young stems, and roots can all be utilized. The leaves and seeds are added to salads, particularly potato and tomato, and the stalks are a celery substitute. The leaves and stems may be cooked as a vegetable and served with butter, or the chopped leaves added to other vegetables to flavour them; the roots, too, can be steamed or boiled. The seeds can be added when baking bread or biscuits, and an infusion can be made from the leaves.

Marjoram, Sweet *(Origanum marjorana)*

Although most often used in stuffings, especially for lamb, sweet marjoram is very good in vegetable soups, salads, and added to a wide variety of vegetables. It goes well in gravies, omelettes, casseroles, and sauces, and baked in breads.

Mint *(Mentha var. sp.)*

Without mint, spring lamb, new potatoes, and the first of the season's peas would not be complete. There are many varieties, but the most commonly used in the kitchen are spearmint and apple-mint (Bowles). A variety of teas can be made from the leaves which not only aid the digestion but are very refreshing. Added to any vegetable during cooking, mint imparts a delicate flavour and creates a wonderful aroma in the kitchen.

Mugwort *(Artemisia vulgaris)*

Rubbed into fatty meat like goose or pork, it makes the fat more digestible as well as adding flavour.

Nasturtium *(Tropaeolum majus)*

The young leaves add a peppery flavour to soups and salads, while the bright petals add interest as a garnish to salads. The young seed pods can be pickled as capers.

Oregano *(Origanum vulgare)*

Oregano is another herb to use with all types of tomato dishes—raw salad, bolognese sauce, tomato sauce, and pizza. It is a flavourful addition to beef or lamb stews and gravies.

Parsley *(Carum Petroselinum)*

It not only tastes good, but it does you good as it has a high vitamin C content. So often it is used merely to garnish a dish, only to be discarded when the meal is over. What a waste of a plant that has such a personality of its own! No salad is really complete without it, and added to egg mayonnaise and fish it gives a delicious flavour. It can be made into parsley jelly, and is one of the ingredients for bouquet garni.

Rosemary *(Rosmarinus officinalis)*

A spray should be added to the roasting tin when cooking lamb or chicken, or alternatively, its needle-like leaves can be rubbed into the meat before it is put in the oven. It has a rather strong flavour so should be used sparingly.

Rue *(Ruta graveolens)*

Rue is the herb of grace. It is not widely used as a culinary herb but can be used sparingly in salads or on pumpernickel bread. Spread the bread with butter and sprinkle with a few chopped rue leaves.

Sage *(Salvia officinalis)*

A very aromatic and pungent herb, it is most often associated with poultry stuffing to give it its characteristic flavour. Crab apple and gooseberry jelly are given added interest by a little sage, as are patés and meat loaves.

Salad Burnet *(Pimpinella saxifraga)*

For digestions that will not tolerate cucumber, this is a useful herb as its leaves impart a cucumber flavour without having any of the upsetting side effects. The young leaves, which have the most

Sage was originally an important healing plant, but it is now most commonly associated with its culinary uses. It is best known as a stuffing mixed with onion for pork or chicken.

flavour, can be used in sauces, soups, cream and cottage cheese; as an infusion; and in fruit drinks.

Salvia Dorisiana

A very aromatic herb that smells like a combination of pineapple and grapefruit, it is used to rub on fish and beef before cooking.

Savory *(Satureia hortensis* and *Satureia montana)*

Savory is to beans as ham is to eggs, and is similar in flavour to marjoram. Any bean or lentil dish, hot or cold, is enhanced by savory—whether the summer or winter variety.

Sorrel, French *(Rumex scutatus)*

This herb is excellent for soups and salads. The young, new leaves are used with lettuce in salads, and the older leaves are better in soups as they are inclined to have a sour flavour.

Sweet Cicely *(Myrrhis odorata)*

As its name implies, this is a sweet, slightly anise-flavoured herb, so is useful for reducing the tartness of fruits like rhubarb and goose-berries, cutting down the amount of sugar needed. The leaves can be added to fruit and vegetable salads, fruit pies and salad dressings, or cooked like spinach, while the roots can be boiled or steamed and served with a creamy sauce.

Tansy *(Tanacetum vulgare)*

Although best known for its medicinal value, it is used in small amounts to flavour pancakes, biscuits, and puddings.

Tarragon *(Artemisia Dracunculus)*

This herb goes particularly well with chicken, egg, and seafood dishes especially crab and lobster, and in stuffed mushrooms. One of its popular uses is in tarragon vinegar.

Thyme *(Thymus vulgaris)*

A strong aromatic herb, it forms part of bouquet garni and is used in all savoury stuffings. It can be added to lamb and beef stews, a wide range of vegetables, and particularly to cole-slaw salad.

Flowers of individual herbs

It is not always the leaves of herbs that are good for cooking. The flowers of some also play an important part, while others make pretty decorations for salads and pastries.

Borage *(Borago officinalis)*

> The star-like flowers are an almost luminous blue. They are used for floating on punches, or candied for decorating cakes and biscuits. When used in drinks they enhance the other flavours as well as decorate.

Chives *(Allium Schoenoprasum)*

> The pale mauve-tinted flowers lend an onion flavour to salads, and add colour when garnishing potato or macaroni salad.

Marigold *(Calendula officinalis)*

> The bright gold and orange petals add colour and a pungent flavour to rice, soups, and stews.

Nasturtium *(Tropaeolum majus)*

> The blossoms give a peppery flavour to lettuce salads, and a bright dash of colour when garnishing fruit salads. For an unusual spread, chop and blend the flowers with butter.

Rose *(Rosa gallica)*

> The petals, apart from their familiar use in syrup and jam, can also be floated on fruit punches or candied to decorate cakes.

Safflower *(Carthamus tinctorius)*

> The petals may be substituted for saffron as a colourant for rice, chicken gravy, and stews.

Saffron *(Crocus sativus)*

> The stigmas of this autumn crocus are the source of the yellow colouring added to rice, noodles, chicken gravy and soup, biscuits,

*Safflower is most prized for its oil,
which is the highest in polyunsatur-
ates of any available oil.*

and pastries. A little goes a long way, so it should be used in very small amounts.

Violet (*Viola odorata*)

The flowers make violet syrup, jam and jelly, and, when candied, very attractive cake decorations.

Recipes

Meat menus

SPICY BEEF STEW

3 lb (1.4 kg) stewing beef
salt and pepper
4 oz (113 g) butter
2 lb (907 g) onions
10 tbsp tomato paste
2½ fl. oz (71 ml) red wine
1½ tbsp red wine vinegar
½ tsp honey
1 clove garlic, crushed
1 bay leaf
1 cinnamon stick
¼ tsp whole cloves
pinch cumin
1½ tbsp raisins

Season meat with salt and pepper. Melt butter, add meat, and arrange onions over meat. Mix tomato paste, wine, vinegar, honey, and garlic. Pour over meat and onions. Add rest of ingredients. Cover and simmer for 3 hours, or until tender, in the oven, 325°F (170°C) Gas 3.

Tarragon has quite a strong flavour and is delicious with vegetables such as carrots and beetroots, but also goes well with shellfish, chicken and eggs. It is often used to flavour vinegar.

BOLOGNESE SAUCE

oil or dripping
2 lb (about 1 kg) minced beef
1 lb (450 g) onions, sliced
1 clove garlic, crushed
1 large 14 oz (397 g) tin tomatoes
1 large green pepper, sliced
½ lb (225 g) mushrooms, sliced
1 tsp sweet basil
1 bay leaf
salt and freshly ground black pepper

Heat oil or dripping in pan and add mince. While it is sealing, brown onions and garlic in a frying pan and then add to mince along with other ingredients. Cover. Simmer gently on top of stove for about 1½ hours. Serve with spaghetti and Parmesan cheese.
As an alternative, the above mix can be prepared in the same way and topped with mashed potatoes. Grate ½ lb (225 g) cheese, cover potatoes liberally with cheese, and put under hot grill until brown and bubbling.

CHICKEN SESAME

1 oz (28 g) whole wheat flour
salt and freshly ground pepper
1 frying chicken, jointed
1 egg, lightly beaten
1 oz (28 g) bread crumbs
1 oz (28 g) sesame seeds
4 oz (113 g) butter

Mix flour, salt, and pepper. Roll chicken in flour, dip in egg, and roll in bread crumbs mixed with sesame seeds. Melt butter in frying pan and sauté chicken until brown. Cover and simmer for 30 minutes, or until done. Remove cover for last 10 minutes.

CHICKEN ROSEMARY

2 roasting chickens, jointed
2 oz (57 g) butter
2½ oz (70 g) chopped onion
1 clove garlic, chopped
4 fl. oz (114 ml) water
1 chicken stock cube
3 tbsp fresh chopped parsley
1 tsp fresh rosemary

Brown chicken pieces on all sides in butter in a frying pan. Remove chicken to baking dish. Fry onion and garlic until brown. Add water and stock cube. Cook and stir until stock cube has dissolved. Add parsley and rosemary. Pour over the chicken. Bake for 45 minutes in a fairly hot oven, 375°F (190°C) Gas 5.

BRAISED SPARE RIBS

4 lb (1.8 kg) beef or pork spare ribs
½ pint (284 ml) beef stock
1¼ oz (35 g) whole wheat flour
1½ oz (42 g) butter
1 tbsp marjoram
1 clove garlic, finely chopped
2 fl. oz (57 ml) sherry
salt and pepper

Brown ribs in shallow pan in oven for 15 minutes at 450°F (230°C) Gas 8. Add stock, cover with foil, lower oven temperature, and cook at 305°F (180°C) Gas 4 for two hours. Brown flour slowly in the butter. Remove stock from pan and add to flour mixture. Stir and cook until thick. Add rest of ingredients. Pour over meat and cook for 15 minutes longer. Serve meat with gravy.

Salsify is a pot herb grown for its root. It is cultivated and cooked like carrots or beetroots.

Vegetable dishes

BUTTERED COURGETTES

1 lb (450 g) courgettes
1 to 2 oz (28 to 56 g) butter
1 tsp rosemary
1 tbsp water
salt and freshly ground black pepper
½ tbsp. chopped fresh parsley

Wash and trim both ends of courgettes. If large, blanch in boiling water for 2 minutes. Slice into half-inch (1.25 cm) sections. Melt butter in pan, add courgettes, rosemary, water, and seasoning. Cover with buttered paper pressed well down and put the lid on. Cook gently on top of stove for 20 to 30 minutes, or until tender. Add parsley at last minute.

JACKET POTATOES

Per person:
1 large potato
1 oz (28 g) grated or cream cheese
1 tbsp fresh, chopped parsley

Allow 1 large potato per person, scrub, dry well, prick with a fork. Bake in a pre-heated oven at 350° F (180°C) Gas 4 until soft when squeezed gently. Remove the top of each potato, scoop out the insides without damaging the skins, and mix in a bowl with grated or cream cheese and a generous amount of fresh, chopped parsley. Pop back into oven to re-heat. Variations on parsley can be any fresh herbs such as chives, salad burnet, or garlic, finely chopped.

CARROTS MARINADE

6 carrots
2 fl. oz (57 ml) oil
4 fl. oz (113 ml) basil vinegar
1 tbsp honey
¼ clove garlic, finely chopped
3 tbsp tarragon, fresh chopped

Slice carrots into 3-inch (7.6 cm) pieces. Cook for 10 minutes until just done, yet still firm. Combine in saucepan oil, basil vinegar, honey, garlic, and tarragon. Heat and pour over drained carrots. Let marinate until ready to serve.

ROSEMARY POTATOES

4 or 5 large potatoes
1½ oz (42 g) butter
1 tsp rosemary

Leave potatoes whole or slice them into ¼-inch (6mm) slices. Fry in a pan with butter and rosemary, until potatoes are brown and crispy.

SPICED BEETROOTS

8 to 10 medium-sized beetroots
1 oz (28 g) butter
4 fl. oz (113 ml) cider vinegar
¾ tbsp cornflour
½ tsp tarragon
3 tbsp honey

Gently boil beetroots until tender. Peel and slice. In a large saucepan, mix rest of ingredients, except tarragon and honey. Cook until thick. Add tarragon, honey, and beetroots and heat through.

Potatoes always taste the most delicious when they have been freshly-dug from the garden.

SUMMER GARDEN CASSEROLE

½ tsp chopped fresh oregano
1 tsp chopped fresh basil
1 clove garlic, chopped
3 tbsp grated Parmesan cheese
6 oz (170 g) grated Cheddar cheese
salt and pepper
2 medium sized courgettes, sliced
4 medium sized tomatoes, sliced
1 small aubergine, peeled and sliced
½ oz (14 g) bread crumbs
1 oz (28 g) butter

Combine oregano, basil, garlic, and cheeses. Season to taste with salt and pepper. Place layer of courgettes, then tomatoes, then aubergine in large greased casserole dish. Sprinkle every third layer with cheese and herb mixture. Continue with layers until all ingredients are used up. Mix bread crumbs and butter and sprinkle over casserole. Bake at 350°F (180°C) Gas 4 for about 50 minutes or until done.

BASIL STUFFED TOMATOES

4 large tomatoes
1½ tbsp bread crumbs
1 tsp grated Parmesan cheese
½ oz (14 g) butter
1 tsp fresh chopped basil

Remove cores and stems from tomatoes, leaving hollows in their centres. Mix rest of ingredients. Fill centre of each tomato with stuffing. Bake for 45 minutes at 350°F (180°C) Gas 4 or until done.

Basil is best known as a companion to tomatoes, both in the garden and in the cooking pot. Basil is also an excellent condiment to use with soups and stews, salads and vegetable dishes.

CUCUMBER IN DILL

1 cucumber, unpeeled and thinly sliced
2 fl. oz (57 ml) cider vinegar
¾ tbsp fresh chopped dill
1 tsp honey
salt and pepper

Combine ingredients and refrigerate for a few hours, before serving.

Salads and salad dressing

CHERVIL-TARRAGON SALAD DRESSING

4 tbsp oil
2 tbsp tarragon vinegar
1 tsp finely chopped onion
½ tsp salt
pinch black pepper
2 tbsp chopped, fresh chervil

Mix all ingredients and serve with green salad.

RED CABBAGE SALAD

1 small red cabbage
1 lb (450 g) crisp apples, sliced
1 tbsp honey
vinaigrette dressing
½ tsp coriander seeds

Finely slice the cabbage, add the sliced apples and honey, then toss in a vinaigrette dressing to which coriander seeds have been added.

POTATO SALAD

4 whole potatoes
1 tsp caraway seed
2 tbsp oil
1 oz (28 g) chopped onion
salt and pepper
1 tbsp fresh chopped tarragon
1 tbsp fresh chopped parsley
½ tbsp fresh chopped basil
2 tbsp vinegar
3 tbsp salad dressing

Boil potatoes with skins on in water with caraway seeds. When done, peel and cut them in cubes. Marinate in oil, onion, salt, and pepper. Meanwhile, chop tarragon, parsley, and basil. Add to potatoes with vinegar and salad dressing. Mix and serve either warm or chilled.

Sauces

HORSERADISH SAUCE

½ pint (284 ml) double cream
salt
2 tbsp grated horseradish root

Whip cream, add sprinkle of salt. Fold in horseradish. Keep refrigerated until use. Serve with roast beef.

MINT SAUCE

1½ tbsp chopped mint leaves
¾ tbsp vinegar
¾ tbsp honey

Mix and serve with roast lamb.

Peppermint is just one of the many varieties of mint. For an unusual salad sprinkle freshly chopped mint leaves over slices of fresh oranges and toss in oil and vinegar.

Desserts

TANSY BISCUITS

3 tbsp honey
4 oz (113 g) butter
1 egg
8 oz (227 g) whole wheat flour
¼ tsp bicarbonate of soda
¼ tsp salt
1 tsp tansy
½ tsp vanilla
¾ tbsp yoghurt

Beat honey and butter, add the egg, then rest of ingredients. Beat until well blended. Roll out to $\frac{1}{8}$-inch thickness (3 mm) on floured pastry board. Cut with biscuit cutter. Sprinkle biscuits with more tansy and bake at 375°F (190°C) Gas 5 for 10 minutes.

ANISEED BARS

1 egg
6 tbsp honey
¼ tsp salt
4 oz (113 g) raw wheat germ
4 fl. oz (114 ml) buttermilk
1 tsp bicarbonate of soda
8 oz (227 g) whole wheat flour
2 tbsp aniseed
2 oz (57 g) hazel nuts

In a large mixing bowl, mix egg, honey, salt, wheat germ, buttermilk, and bicarbonate of soda. Add 4 oz (113 g) of flour, the aniseed and nuts. Mix thoroughly, then add rest of flour. Shape mixture into long rounded bars. Place on greased tin. Bake at 350°F (180°C) Gas 4 for about 30 minutes. Remove from oven, cool, and slice. If desired, toast each slice for 7 minutes or until golden brown.

Rosemary is a versatile culinary herb. It is particularly popular in meat dishes, but is also used in jams, soups and biscuits.

BLACKCURRANT BARS

4 oz (113 g) chopped nuts (pecans or walnuts)
6 tbsp honey
8 oz (227 g) whole wheat flour
4 oz (113 g) butter
¾ lb (340 g) blackcurrants
2 eggs
¼ tsp salt
1 tsp cinnamon
4 tbsp wheat germ (raw)
1 tsp bicarbonate of soda
8 fl. oz (227 ml) buttermilk

Sprinkle a 9 x 13 inch (228 x 329 mm) greased tin with chopped nuts. Mix honey, flour, and butter with fork until crumbly. Pour two-thirds of the mixture over nuts. Pat smooth. Spread blackcurrants over this. In a large mixing bowl, beat eggs, salt, cinnamon, wheat germ, bicarbonate of soda, and buttermilk with left-over flour mix. Pour over blackcurrants and bake at 350°F (180°C) Gas 4 for 35 to 40 minutes or until done. Cool.

CARAWAY FRUIT DESSERT

4 oz (113 g) whole wheat flour
1½ tbsp honey
1 egg
1 oz (28 g) butter
4 fl. oz (114 ml) buttermilk
½ tsp bicarbonate of soda
1¼ lb (567 g) apples, pears, or peaches, sliced
2 oz (56 g) raisins
½ tsp caraway seeds
½ tsp cinnamon
1½ tbsp honey
1 oz (28 g) desiccated coconut

In a large mixing bowl, mix first six ingredients together and spread in greased 9 x 9 inch (228 x 228 mm) tin. Spread fruit and raisins over this. Sprinkle caraway seeds and cinnamon over the fruit, then drizzle honey over them. Top with desiccated coconut. Bake 1 hour, or until fruit is tender, at 325°F (170°C) Gas 3.

Caraway seeds are used to flavour bread and cakes but can also be added to cheese or rubbed on roast pork. The leaves can be chopped and added to salads and soups and the root can be cooked and eaten as a vegetable.

SPICED PEAR SLICES

1¼ lb (567 g) pears, peeled and sliced
12 fl. oz (342 ml) water
3 tbsp honey
2 sticks cinnamon
1 tbsp cloves

Mix all ingredients together and cook slowly until pears are tender, yet firm. Serve as side dish with meals.

117

HONEY FROSTING

6 tbsp honey
2 egg whites
¼ tsp vanilla

Beat ingredients for about 10 minutes while cooking in the top of a double boiler. Remove from heat; continue to beat until mixture is consistency of frosting.

Breads

ANISEED AND BANANA BREAD

1 oz (28 g) butter
6 fl. oz (171 ml) buttermilk
1 egg
9 tbsp honey
2 bananas
12 oz (240 g) whole wheat flour
½ tsp salt
1 tsp bicarbonate of soda
7 oz (196 g) chopped dates
5 oz (140 g) chopped mixed nuts
2 tsp aniseed

Mix butter, buttermilk, the egg, honey and bananas together. Add flour, salt, and bicarbonate of soda. Mix well, then add dates, nuts, and aniseed. Pour into two greased loaf tins. Bake at 350°F (180°C) Gas 4 for 45 to 55 minutes, or until done.

GARLIC BREAD

1 French loaf
6 to 8 oz (170 to 227 g) butter
2 cloves garlic, finely chopped
black pepper

Cut French loaf into slanting slices to within $\frac{1}{8}$-inch (3 mm) of the base; do not cut right through. In a bowl cream the butter with the chopped garlic and black pepper. Spread on both sides of each slice. Press back into shape and smear any remaining butter over top and sides. Secure in cooking foil, and heat through in oven for about 20 minutes at 325°F (170°C) Gas 3. Turn back foil for the last couple of minutes to crisp the bread.

Instead of garlic a tablespoon of mixed herbs can be substituted.

Vinegars

Herb vinegars are cheap and easy to make from your own fresh herbs just before they flower. They are useful for flavouring salad dressings, sauces, mayonnaise, and marinades. Whichever herbs you use, prepare them in the following way.

Pack the herbs into a large jar or bottle and add enough white wine vinegar to cover. Seal tightly—preferably not with a metal cap as this can cause a chemical reaction with the vinegar—and store in a dark place for up to eight weeks. Make sure that no air is trapped under the leaves and that none of them are above the level of the liquid, as this leads to discolouration. Check a couple of days after storing, and top up with vinegar if necessary.

At the end of the storage period strain the liquid into convenient-sized bottles, adding a sprig of the same herb. If the mixture is too strong for your taste, add more wine vinegar. Label.

A favourite herb for vinegar is tarragon. Using four to six ounces (113 to 170 g) of the leaves and the tender stalks, crushed, to two pints (1.14 l) of vinegar, follow the procedure above, storing initially for six to eight weeks before straining.

For mint vinegar the applemint (Bowles) is preferable to other varieties. Use the leaves only. This vinegar needs only three to four weeks before being strained and bottled.

Purple basil is another favourite and it gives the vinegar a rich Burgundy colour. Some sweet basil can be added to give it a sweeter flavour. The purple basil is also very good used in combination with garlic or tarragon.

Dill, either the sprigs or the seed heads, make another interesting vinegar. A dash in tomato juice gives the juice added zest. Beetroot, cabbage, and potato salad are especially tasty when made with dill vinegar.

119

Salad burnet lends a cucumber flavour to vinegar without the digestive upset sometimes caused by fresh cucumber.

Many other herbs or combinations of herbs can be tried when making vinegar. Rosemary, sage, thyme, lovage, oregano, sweet marjoram, parsley, or any of the other cooking herbs can be used. It would be wise, however, to try any combinations in small amounts before making large quantities. A few sprigs of a strong herb and a handful of a milder one would make a better vinegar than two very strong herbs, which can overpower each other. Any of these herb vinegars used with oil will make a good marinade for cheap cuts of meat.

Butters

Herb butter, or green butter as our Victorian ancestors called it when it was commonplace on the table, will enhance and improve the simplest bread snack. It is the easiest thing in the kitchen to make—just cream the butter and mix in the chopped herbs of your choice. If made two or three hours before needed, the flavour will be more pronounced. Large quantities will keep well in the refrigerator—cover it to prevent other food from absorbing the flavour.

Apart from its popular use in herb bread, herb butter can be added to vegetables. After cooking and straining beans, peas, carrots, asparagus, cabbage, or potatoes, toss in a compatible herb butter.

Fish, steak, chicken, and chops can be topped with herb butter before serving. Herb butter can even be used in sauces, casseroles, omelettes, and scrambled eggs. Herbs which lend themselves particularly well for mixing with butter are chives, rosemary, parsley, savory, dill, oregano, mint, tarragon, thyme, and sage.

DILL AND OREGANO BUTTER

4 oz (113 g) butter
1 tsp dillweed or dill seed
1 tsp oregano

Dill seed is a popular condiment, being used to enhance the flavour of pies and pastries, soups and gravies.

SAVORY BUTTER

4 oz (113 g) butter
1 tsp savory
½ tsp dry mustard

ALL-PURPOSE HERB BUTTER

4 oz (113 g) butter
1 small clove garlic, crushed
½ tsp dillweed
½ tbsp tarragon
1½ tbsp chives

LEMON PARSLEY BUTTER

4 oz (113 g) butter
1½ tbsp parsley
1 tsp chives
¼ tsp lemon juice

ZESTY BUTTER

4 oz (113 g) butter
½ tbsp dry mustard
½ tsp horseradish root, grated
¼ tsp salt
dash of pepper

TARRAGON AND THYME BUTTER

4 oz (113 g) butter
¼ tsp tarragon
pinch thyme
2 tbsp parsley

Spinach is a nutritious vegetable, and a valuable source of iron. It is delicious when it is steamed and served with butter and sprinkled with chopped chives, or black pepper.

CHIVE BUTTER

4 oz (113 g) butter
¾ tbsp chopped chives
¾ tbsp parsley
¼ tsp rosemary

Salts

Herb salts are also easy to make. Use sea salt as it is very fine and blends readily with herbs. If using fresh herbs chop the leaves, then crush them with the salt using a pestle and mortar. Spread on a baking sheet and dry in the oven for 40 to 60 minutes at the lowest temperature. Break up any lumps, and rake over frequently during drying. When cool, seal in a glass jar.

If you wish to make herb salt in a hurry, dried herbs may be substituted. Make sure that the herbs are very fine so that they can be poured through the narrow gap of your dispenser. This can be achieved by putting the herbs and salt in a blender. An approximate combination would be four ounces salt to four or five tablespoons of dried herbs.

Teas

Unusual teas may be made from various herbs, either as beverages or for medicinal use. Fresh or dried herbs may be used, but the dried herbs are more concentrated so allow about half the amount that you would of the fresh ones. A rule of thumb is one teaspoon of dried herb to one cup of boiling water.

Make it in a teapot as for normal tea, but allow to steep for five to ten minutes, depending on whether seeds, roots, or leaves are used. The leaves or seeds may be crushed to obtain more flavour. Teas made from some seeds and roots require boiling for five to ten minutes to extract the full flavour. As a sweetener use honey as it blends well with herbal teas. Most teas are best served without milk. Iced herb teas are made in the same manner, but are chilled after straining.

Anise, caraway, fennel, coriander, and cumin seeds used separately or together make refreshing drinks. Dill tea is rich in minerals and makes a good after-dinner tea. Another variety is made from sassafras. Use a few pieces of the bark to two pints (1.1 l) of water; allow to stand for five minutes.

Camomile tea made from the flower-heads is a good aid to digestion and will settle an upset stomach. Angelica leaf tea is used to stimulate the digestion. Herbs with lemon fragrances make pleasant-tasting teas to be served either hot or cold. Lemon verbena and lemon balm are two of these. They are tasty used alone, in combination with each other, or with other herbs. They can replace the slice of lemon often served with tea.

There are few things more pleasurable than a cup of herbal tea. Make a teapotful and share it with a friend.

Some of the most flavoursome herb teas are made with the mints, scented geraniums, sassafras, pennyroyal, lemon verbena, camomile, rosemary, and catnip. A leaf of peppermint, rose, or lemon geranium added to a pot of ordinary tea will lend a characteristic flavour. An unusual combination is lemon herb tea.

LEMON HERB TEA

7 tbsp lemon thyme
2 tbsp lemon basil
¼ tsp lemon balm
3 tbsp mild green tea

Rosemary tea helps cure headaches and colds; it can be used alone or in combination with other herbs. It is very strong so use small amounts. Sage tea is also helpful as a tonic for colds and fevers. Comfrey leaves make a tea which is purported to cure almost any ailment.

Liqueurs

Liqueurs are cordials, flavoured brandies, or gins which are made by mixing distilled spirits with fruit juices or herbs and syrups. The syrup gives the sweetening common to most liqueurs.

When making liqueurs, the alcohol and flavouring ingredients are mixed and allowed to stand at least 24 hours before adding the water syrup. This is to blend the flavour and aroma. After the syrup is added, age the finished product two weeks or more at room temperature to get a full flavour. If wines are used to make liqueur, use a quality aged wine which has a high acetic content. The high acidity of the wine affects the quality of the end product.

The large commercial producers of liqueurs have their own secret list of herbs and spices which they use to produce special blends. Many of these blends are made with the oils extracted from the herbs and spices. For example, one type of Benedictine is made by blending as many as 15 different oils. This makes an especially tasty blend, but for your own use, crushed leaves or seeds of a specific herb make a very flavourful liqueur. Crush the herb with a pestle and mortar, or place the herb with part of the liquid in the blender. For the syrup needed to add to your

126

liqueur, use equal amounts of honey and water. Boil the water for a few minutes, remove from the heat, then add the honey. The amount of honey syrup added to any liqueur can be varied to suit individual preferences.

ANISEED LIQUEUR

3 tbsp aniseed, crushed
1 pint (568 ml) brandy
¼ pint (124 ml) honey syrup

Let mixture stand two to three weeks before straining.

MINT LIQUEUR

3 tbsp peppermint or orange mint leaves, crushed
few peels orange rind
1 pint (568 ml) wine or brandy)
¼ pint (124 ml) honey syrup

Let mixture stand two to three weeks before straining.

Coriander is used to flavour gin, and basil and angelica for chartreuse. Cumin, wild marjoram, peppermint, sage, tarragon, lovage, thyme, vanilla, and angelica can all be used as liqueur flavourings. Other herbs and spices which make interesting liqueurs are yarrow, orris root, centaury, angelica root, cinnamon, cloves, cardamoms or, in fact, any other that appeals to you.

4

The Aromatic Herbs

O how much more doth beauty beauteous seem
By that sweet ornament which truth doth give!
The Rose looks fair, but fairer we it deem
For that sweet odour which doth in it live . . .
                    Sonnet LIV by Shakespeare

To Shakespeare, the sheer beauty and delight that the vision of the rose afforded him was only complete when he could savour its exquisite fragrance.

To most of us there can surely be little more evocative and nostalgic than the fragrant, sweet smell of flowers and herbs, in the countryside in spring or autumn, whatever be your own very personal memory.

The five senses, given us primordially for self-preservation, have in enlightened man become instruments with which to cherish things of beauty. We marvel at the sight of a glorious sunset, are transported by music, delighted by French cuisine, made ecstatic by a lover's touch, and whisked into nostalgia by the merest whiff of lavender a dear one used to wear when we were but children.

The pleasure that one derives through the sense of smell is rooted in nature itself and is as old as man himself. In less urbanized times, this pleasure was more readily enjoyed because people were surrounded by the countryside. They were closer to the earth. Thankfully, we still have much of our countryside left, but we spend little time communing with it. Perhaps though, there are moments when we do find time to *Stand and stare, To stand beneath the boughs and stare as long as sheep or cows* (Leisure by William Henry Davies). And be able to recall as in a "Midsummer Night's Dream"; *I know a bank whereon the wild thyme grows*, and to recall that never-to-be-forgotten fragrance when on that day you stopped hurrying and stood there beneath the bough.

People today still like to smell nature's herbs and flora. But all too often they cannot stop in their city scramble, and so they buy their aromatics in aerosols and the like. Nonetheless, there are those who take the trouble to seek out their perfumes from nature, and more and more people are doing just this. So why not you?

Aromatic herbs arouse different associations in the minds of different people. There is, and always will be, the inherent need in human beings to surround themselves with their favourite country or natural garden odours. And, of course, the beauty of this is that one can do it for one-self—both more beneficially and cheaper than the commercial perfumes.

One of the earliest applications of the use of herbs was the strewing of scented flowers and herbs on the floors of dwellings, especially in mediaeval times. For example, these were laid on the floors of manor houses and churches. When strewn herbs and flowers were crushed under foot they gave off pleasant aromas. This helped to hide the mustiness of damp floors and to camouflage the stench of bad sanitation.

In the distant past, therefore, herbs were used rather out of necessity to "drown" bad odours, rather than for the pleasure of the perfumes they gave off. However, as people became more enlightened and sanitation and ventilation improved, strewing went largely out of practice as an expedient, but nevertheless took on a more picturesque, traditional ritual image—the common image conjured up by most people being young girls scattering rose petals from baskets at festivals.

Strewing herbs was not confined to the rich. Any home that had a herb garden could enjoy the same luxury. That was in the past. As mentioned earlier, it is the easy way out for the modern housewife to use an aerosol deodorant or air-freshener. But with the will, application, and imagination, it is possible for her to use herbs like her grandmother did. After all, with modern facilities it is easier for her. Grandma had a great deal more drudgery to cope with in her day.

So, when you have been bitten by the do-it-yourself aromatics "bug" you will, no doubt, want to progress to making your own sweet-scented soaps, fragrant bathing waters, and aromatic waters, as well as floral-scented powders and perfumed essences.

Pomanders, pot-pourris, and sachets were concocted to perfume

130

The rose is the basis for some of the most exquisite and desired essences in the world.

131

rooms and clothing. The natural aroma of certain herbs was also found to be effective in inhibiting insects. Spice-scented candles and incenses were an important part of ancient rituals and even the breath was sweetened with the use of herbs. All this you, too, can do with the use of your garden and kitchen. Then perhaps you will enjoy the pleasures and experiences of a more leisured bygone age. Take Montaigne, the great French philosopher, for example. He claimed that specific essences could make him happy, excited, contemplative, or just peaceful. Scented herbs are capable of making one more aware as they are able to stir emotions, evoke memories, and inflame love and passion.

By learning which herbs to plant for fragrance and then how to use them, you can enjoy natural scents in your daily life, and discover just how much more pleasurable it is to inhale the natural fresh perfumes, rather than the contrived chemical ones.

There is, of course, no reason why you should not use the real thing. Nature does not change fundamentally and today's herbs are just as fragrant as those of years gone by. The various methods of extracting the scent for use in the home are just as simple as they always were.

Naturally enough, you will want to start simply—which is why I have chosen breath sweeteners to begin with. There is no easier beginning— even for the most lethargic of us.

Then there are pomanders. These are easily put together with ingredients largely obtainable from your local chemist, making them just the thing for people who have the interest, but not the garden in which to grow their own herbs. Then pot-pourris, sachets, herbal baths, and aromatic waters, which can be made with only one type of herb, or with many types. Later, you may wish to try using herbal oils. And you don't have to make the oils yourself, although it is feasible if you decide you would like to. A variety of such oils and exotic herbs is available commercially.

At some stage when dealing with herbal aromatics, you will find the need for fixatives. These are covered in detail a little further on in this chapter. But for the record, a fixative is a vegetable or animal substance used to set and hold herbal fragrances.

Ambergris, civet, and musk, are animal-derived fixatives, while orris root, benzoin, storax, and tonka bean are plant-derived fixatives. Ambergris is a secretion of the sperm whale, civet is extracted from the glands of the African civet cat, and musk was originally taken from the musk deer from Central Asia, which is now sadly almost extinct. Today, most musk is produced synthetically. All three animal substances have a very unpleasant smell in their initial state. But when combined

Sweet woodruff makes an excellent ground cover in the herb garden and is an effective general moth and insect repellent in the house.

with fragrant herbs, the foul odours are lost and the pleasant scent of the latter is enhanced, enriched, and set.

Plant-derived fixatives are more commonly used these days. Benzoin is a gum collected from a tree called *Styrax benzoin*. In Java, Sumatra, and Thailand these trees are grown commercially for the gum benzoin. Storax *(Liquidambar orientalis)* a gum or resin collected in much the same way as rubber, is allowed to harden, after which it is ground down to a powder. Tonka beans are grown in several South American and African countries and in Sri Lanka. However, the most commonly used and readily available fixative is orris root—the root of the Florentine iris. This is dried and stored for at least two years before finally being ground into a powder.

133

Breath sweeteners

If their breath smelt, our ancestors could not do as we do today—suck a mint. To cover their bad breath, they relied on sweet-tasting and sweet-smelling herbs to freshen up orally.

In earlier times, one of the most common means of sweetening one's breath was to suck whole cloves. This has been known for over four thousand years. During the Middle Ages, anise seed was chewed slowly to cover up bad mouth odours. In the Orient and Europe, cardamom seeds have long been used to cover strong mouth odours. Early American settlers used bits of sweet sedge root, while small pieces of dried orris root were chewed by ladies to make their breath "kissing sweet".

To purify your breath naturally in this day and age, place a piece of nutmeg in your mouth and chew on it, or keep a portion of mace in your mouth for several minutes. Small pieces of angelica root may also be chewed to the same effect. Legend has it, incidentally, that users of angelica root will be blessed with angelic qualities!

The most obvious herbal breath sweeteners are, of course, the mints. Chew a leaf or two to take that sour taste from your mouth. One person I know has some mint growing at his front door, so that he can snip off a few leaves and chew them on his way to the office in the morning.

The next time you feel the need to freshen your breath, turn to your herb garden—rather than to the medicine chest.

Pomanders

Pomanders are usually associated these days with oranges "pincushioned" all over with cloves. That is the home-made type of pomander, of course. Lemons, limes, and apples are also used. However, this has not always been the case. As far as records show, pomanders first came to be used in the Middle Ages in France and were carried as protection against plague. At that time they were often worn around the neck or on the belt where they were readily accessible should one want to raise them to the nose when assailed by horrible smells. They were also worn to ward off bad luck. That they were pleasantly scented was only an added benefit. Pomanders were originally made of practically anything and everything that had an agreeable odour.

The herb garden can provide a wide variety of aromatic herbs for pomanders, pot-pourris, sachets, and incense.

When they were first introduced in France, they were called *pomme d'ambre*; literally translated, although not quite accurately, "apple of amber". More accurately, a *pomme d'ambre* was a ball-shaped aggregation of herbs and spices. It used to look like an apple—hence the name. Ambergris was the primary fixative and because of the colour of this substance, was dubbed *d'ambre*. The name "pomander" can also be applied to the container in which the herbs are housed. In bygone days, the pomander was either located somewhere in the home, or worn around the neck, or attached to the belt as mentioned. In fact, it was often worn as a piece of jewellery.

The pomander found its origin, as did many aromatic herbal uses, in the foul conditions of mediaeval society. Held close to the nose it acted as a palliative against the stenches of rotting garbage and open sewers.

The aristocracy believed that their aromatic pomanders not only prevented them from experiencing the unpleasant odours in the streets, but also that these devices protected them against the diseases that were a natural part of the unsanitary conditions. It was this belief, as much as any other, that prompted professional men—doctors, judges, and lawyers on their rounds of the poor areas—to arm themselves with these pomanders.

Thus, the orange/clove pomander, a far cry from the original, is today but an aromatic novelty; something to make the home just that bit sweeter.

Ancient recipes reveal that a wide variety of fixatives and perfumes used to be carefully blended. Resinous ingredients, beeswax, or just plain soil served as binding materials for the herbs. Like most old recipes, the assumption was that the "cook" had an inbuilt sense that told her when enough of each ingredient had been added. Indeed, the pomander maker did add perfumes "to smell", rather like the traditional cook who adds seasoning "to taste".

To arrive at today's pomander of cloves and oranges is a far simpler exercise than it once was. If desired, the finished product can be rolled in ground spices for added aromatic effect. In any case, it should be finally rolled in ground orris root fixative, then set aside for about four weeks to dry thoroughly in air.

It sounds simple enough, and it is, although perhaps a trifle tedious. But the results are rewarding. So, here are a few tips on how to make your first attempt satisfying.

Have a separate bowl for each ingredient—the foundation fruit in one, cloves in another, ground spices and fixative in a third. Be warned: if you place the uncompleted orange pomander in the bowl with the

The most fragrant pot-pourris and sachets are started in the garden. The herbs — in this case mint — are harvested just as the sun chases the dew from their leaves when the plant's natural oils are most volatile and fragrant.

cloves, you will find that the latter become limp and sticky, and you will probably have to throw them out.

You will need about one pound (454 g) of cloves to make pomanders of a dozen oranges. If you dust each pomander with spices, use cinnamon and perhaps a pinch of powdered cloves, nutmeg, and ginger.

To start, hold the fruit firmly enough to ease the job of pushing the cloves through the skin, but not so firmly that you squeeze out the juices. It's a skill that comes with practice. When in place, the heads of the cloves should completely cover the surface of the orange. This should avoid extensive splitting of the orange skin. Some people use a darning needle or meat skewer to puncture the fruit first. Some do not think this is a good idea. You will have to adopt the technique that suits you best. But finish your pomander in one sitting because overnight drying of the foundation fruit may lessen the quality of the finished product. Left any longer, it may be completely spoilt.

When completed and dusted, the pomanders should be left in the spice bowl. Then, continue to roll them around about once a day until completely dry. As stated earlier, the spices will add to the perfume and cut down on shrinkage. They are not absolutely necessary if you want to leave them out. Even the fixative isn't necessary, but these processes will make the fragrance last longer.

When the pomanders are dry, they can be used immediately in the home, office, shop, and even the car. You can simply stack a number of them in a bowl, or thread them on a ribbon and hang them up. You can tie one with a ribbon wrapped in colourful cloth or fancy net—just place it on a square of material, gather the corners, and tie them with a ribbon.

Put pomanders in your cupboards, wardrobes, chest of drawers, and similar places to scent your clothes and blankets, and to keep the moths away. Insects will hate it. You will love it.

Pot-pourris and sachets

Since the beginning of civilization, man has been captivated by the scent of aromatic herbs and has sought methods of introducing their fragrance into his home. Grecian ladies were known to carry perfumed sachets in their gowns. Roman households boasted large urns of dried aromatic herbs used to perfume the air with summertime fragrance and destroy unpleasant odours.

From mediaeval times, on into the Seventeenth and Eighteenth Centuries, fragrant herbs were used in many ways to mask the odours of the primitive sanitation and to ward off concomitant diseases.

But with the relatively recent facility of being able to obtain chemical scents, pot-pourris and sachets lost their popularity. Recently, however, pot-pourris and sachets have gained in popularity as old recipes have come to light—with the result that gift shops now commonly display them on their shelves.

There are two ways of enjoying the luxury of pot-pourris and sachets. You may spend hard-earned money on high-priced pot-pourri jars and decorative sachet bags, or else have the fun of creating your own perfumes.

In a day and age when one tends to become disillusioned with mass production and technology, you can turn back the clock by making blends of herbs to perfume a room or cupboard. The ingredients for pot-pourris and sachets may already be growing in your garden. Such aromatic plants as lilac, roses, lavender, sweet peas, mint, rosemary, and thyme are just a few varieties you can use. And if you don't have any of these already in your garden, you can grow them with a minimum of fuss.

Pot-pourris and sachets are almost identical, except that pot-pourris are composed of coarse, broken pieces of herbs, spices, and flowers; whereas sachets are powdered mixtures. Pot-pourris are kept in pretty glass jars, and whenever a sweet scent is desired, you merely open the lid and allow the fragrance to flood out and fill the room. Sachets, on the other hand, are small decorative fabric bags for perfuming a cupboard or clothing drawer. They can also be slipped into a purse to make the contents smell pleasant.

Here are a few simple rules to follow when concocting your own pot-pourris and sachets. Cut and collect your herbs on a dry morning—after the dew has dried. Collect three to four times the volume you plan to have when finished (drying decreases volume markedly). Cut or pull off flower petals, discarding any that are brown, and lay them to dry in a shallow layer on a clean cloth or paper.

Dry flowers away from the light in an airy place, stirring the petals frequently (fast drying helps retain volatile oils). Cut your annual herbs to the ground, perennials about half-way down. Take a bunch of herbs—all you can comfortably hold in one hand—and tie securely. Label them and hang up in a warm, airy, dark place to dry. An attic is ideal. When the herbs are crumbly dry, strip the leaves from the stem. Don't toss the stems on your compost heap. Instead, sprinkle them on a wood fire to perfume the air. When drying citrus peel, first scrape off

Herbs should be dried away from the light in an airy place. An attic is ideal. They should be tied in bunches and hung up until they are crumbly dry.

all the fruit pulp from the inner skin. Break it into small pieces, and allow them to dry in a warm place until brittle. But remember; make sure your ingredients are perfectly dry, or else mould will develop and ruin your pot-pourri.

With the exception of the knife or scissors with which you cut the herbs, never expose them to metal when drying or preparing. Instead, use wood, enamel, or ceramic utensils. Be sure to use plants which you know to be free of poisonous herbicides and insecticides. After all, you don't want to inhale the stuff!

Use a large wooden spoon to stir the dried ingredients together, taking care to blend them thoroughly. Measure all ingredients exactly. Pour the completed mixture into a large, wide-mouthed jar. Screw the cap on tightly and place the jar in a cool, dark place for several months; under a kitchen sink, for example. About once a week, remove the cap, stir the contents with a wooden spoon, replace the cap, and put away again. After several months your mixture will be ready to make pot-pourris and sachets.

Pungent pot-pourris

For pot-pourris you can search out pretty antique bottles in attics, basements, junk shops, at auctions, or from antique shops. Glass food jars can be washed and recycled as pot-pourri jars. Always make certain your jars are very clean and that they have tight-fitting lids before filling them with pot-pourri blends.

For added glamour, you might glue onto the jars and lids bits of colourful yarn, ribbon, sequins, or felt cutouts. If you are skilled with a paintbrush, try adding designs to the jars with acrylic paints. These are fast-drying and do not wash off.

Besides scenting and beautifying your own home, these pot-pourris make lovely, long-lasting gifts. And you could, perhaps, turn them into an enjoyable and profitable sideline.

Sweet sachets

Sachet bags may be made from any type of pretty fabric. Start collecting pieces and remnants of various multi-coloured cloths; lace, satin, silk, cotton, and muslin. Fringes or frilly lace may be sewn on to make

The herbs are thoroughly dried, by hanging them in bunches in the attic, or in a low heated oven. Then the leaves are stripped from the branches. The branches of many herbs make an aromatic kindling, and can be saved for that use. The leaves can be stored, or immediately mixed with other herbs and a fixative.

Any bowl can be used for the mixing, except a metal one. The ingredients are measured out into the bowl, and stirred with a wooden spoon. If a pot-pourri is the goal, the hard work is finished; if the goal is a sachet, the hard part is yet to come. In either case, the mixture is put in a tightly sealed container (never a metal one) and stored for several months. This will blend, mellow, and fix the various scents.

Finally, the day comes when the herbal mixture is ready to be put to use. A pot-pourri need only be transferred to a decorative container. A sachet is created by grinding the herbal mixture to a powder, pouring the powder into fabric bags or pillows, and stitching them closed. The pot-pourri can be used to perfume the air in a room, the sachet to fill a drawerful of clothing with its fragrance.

143

a decorative scented bag. Sequins, stitched patterns, and small beads may be added. For a "quickie" sachet, simply place your ground ingredients in a frilly handkerchief, bring the corners up, and tie securely with a piece of velvet ribbon.

Traditionally, sachets are rather small. But fragrant bags needn't be tiny; they can be any size you want them to be. Indeed, in bygone days, insomniacs laid their heads on scented pillows, believing they would cure their malady. Grandmother sometimes used sparsely-filled bags—more pads than pillows—between blankets and clothing, partly to perfume the garments and partly to ward off moths.

For your very first sachet, start simply. Collect a small bunch of lavender flowers. Lay them in a single layer to dry and, when completely dry, grind them to a fine powder. You can use a pestle and mortar, perhaps a blender or, if you happen to have one, a flour mill. One lavender plant should produce enough blossoms to fill 12 two inch (5 cm) square sachets. Place in small cloth bags and sew up the openings. You don't have to age the ingredients. The purpose of ageing is to give the scents of the various herbal ingredients time to fuse. If you are using more than one herb in your sachet, grinding isn't done until the mixture has been aged. When this is done, the herbs are ground up and the small bags are filled. And there you have your sachet!

Now try one of these more involved recipes.

Recipes

First, bear in mind that the ingredients are the same for both pot-pourris and sachets, only the consistency of the ingredients is different. For sachets, you must crush all flowers to a fine powder and finely grind the spices and citrus peels. Pot-pourris, on the other hand, are usually made from coarsely broken herbs, spices, and flowers. In the old days salt was used to preserve the fragrance of flowers that would not be injured if bruised. Roses, in particular, will retain their scent for years if preserved with salt. Some of the following ingredients, such as vetiver root and tonka beans which grow in the tropics, will not grow in colder climates. Purchase such herbs from a reputable herbal supplier. And don't forget the fixative.

LEMON VERBENA

1 lb (453 g) lemon verbena leaves
½ lb (226 g) lemon peel
¼ lb (113 g) violets
½ lb (226 g) rose geranium
1 oz (28 g) clary sage (fixative)

Not only is lemon verbena good to smell, it also flowers beautifully and its dried leaves make a refreshing tea.

HERB GARDEN

8 oz (226 g) thyme
4 oz (113 g) rosemary
2 oz (56 g) lavender
4 oz (113 g) mint
1 oz (28 g) tansy
1 oz (28 g) cloves
½ oz (14 g) orris root (fixative)

LAVENDER BLEND

8 oz (226 g) lavender
½ oz (14 g) thyme
½ oz (14 g) mint
¼ oz (7 g) ground cloves
¼ oz (7 g) ground caraway seeds
1 oz (28 g) common salt (well dried)

EXOTIC POT-POURRI

4 oz (113 g) orris root
4 oz (113 g) sweet flag root (bruised)
3 oz (85 g) yellow sandalwood
1 oz (28 g) sweet cedarwood
1 oz (28 g) gum benzoin
1 oz (28 g) storax
½ oz (14 g) cloves
1 oz (28 g) nutmeg
1 oz (28 g) patchouli leaves

WILD FLOWER

8 oz (226 g) sweet flag root
4 oz (113 g) caraway seed
8 oz (226 g) lavender
4 oz (113 g) sweet marjoram
1½ oz (42 g) cloves
8 oz (226 g) Damask rose petals
2 oz (56 g) rosemary
4 oz (113 g) thyme

FOR LINEN

1 lb (454 g) rose leaves (crumbled)
1 oz (28 g) ground cloves
1 oz (28 g) ground caraway seeds
1 oz (28 g) ground allspice
4 oz (113 g) salt (well dried)

Mix well and sew into muslin bags to be placed among the household linen.

SPICY PERFUME FOR SACHETS

1 oz (28 g) cloves
1 oz (28 g) nutmeg (grated)
1 oz (28 g) ground cinnamon
1 oz (28 g) caraway seeds
1 oz (28 g) tonka beans
6 oz (170 g) orris root (fixative)

Mix well and pound in a mortar until a fine powder, then use to fill muslin bags to place or hang among clothes.

WOODY MIXTURE

2 oz (56 g) coriander seeds
2 oz (56 g) cinnamon
2 oz (56 g) rose leaves
2 oz (56 g) lavender
1 lb (454 g) oak shavings

OLD ENGLISH POT-POURRI

1 lb (454 g) Damask rose petals
4 oz (113 g) common salt (well dried)
4 oz (113 g) coarse salt (well dried)
4 oz (113 g) brown sugar
½ oz (14 g) storax
½ oz (14 g) benzoin
½ oz (14 g) ground orris root
½ oz (14 g) ground cinnamon
½ oz (14 g) cloves
1 oz (28 g) lemon verbena

ROSE LILAC

3 cups rose petals
2 cups lilac blossoms
2 cups marjoram
1¼ oz (35 g) orris root (fixative)
(N.B.: 1 cup = 8 fl. oz (227 ml))

Insect repellents from the garden

Great-grandmother was wise in her ways. She knew exactly which green growing things were effective in repelling insects and moths. In her cupboards and drawers you would have found fragrant herbs distasteful to insects, but which imparted a sweet aroma to her clothes.

To prevent moth grubs from eating your clothes, dry some rosemary leaves and sew them into small decorative cloth bags of any shape you wish. Place several such bags among your clothing in a drawer or cupboard. A simple method of keeping the herbs in a drawer is to line the bottom of it with paper, on top of which sprinkle herbs and then cover with a layer of cloth, securing it with drawing pins.

Another moth repellent is a mixture of equal parts of ground camphor wood and wormwood placed in bags among your woollens. Or to sweetly perfume your wardrobe as well as chase away moths, mix equal

Wormwood is particularly useful as an insect repellent, serving in the garden or, harvested and dried, in the home. Sewn in bags, it will protect clothing from moths.

parts of dried southernwood, wormwood, and lavender, and sew it into little bags to hang among your clothes.

Try this simple recipe for keeping moths at bay: Into one ounce (28 g) of melted paraffin wax, stir one tablespoonful of heliotrope oil, ¼ teaspoonful of bergamot oil, and $\frac{1}{8}$ teaspoonful of clove oil. Pour the blended mixture into a flat enamel or wooden dish. When cool, cut into small bars and place in your wardrobe.

For a manly scented moth repellent, sew equal parts of cedar wood shavings and ground sassafras root into small cloth pillows and place among sweaters and woollens.

For general moth and insect control in your home, use woodruff, which smells pleasantly like vanilla. Mix together vetiver root and crushed bay leaves to repel insects of all types. For a repellent to freshen your nose while scaring insects away, try this recipe: Combine equal amounts of lemon peel, crushed cloves, lavender, spearmint, and tansy. Place in bags among your clothing, and give the extras to friends.

A piece of dried calamus root, from the perennial herb more commonly known as sweet-flag, is a good general insect inhibitor. Place a dried rhizome in each of your clothes drawers. Or sprinkle in several tonka beans. For centuries, these have been worn about the neck as good luck and love charms. Patchouli, a herb from the Malay Peninsula, is another effective insect repellent with a lovely perfume.

Dry and powder the aromatic flower-heads of pyrethrum or feverfew to use as a contact poison for all insects and cold-blooded vertebrates. Pyrethrum is harmless to humans and pets and is a good indoor insect repellent. However, it should be borne in mind that, if you grow pyrethrum, beneficial pollinating bees will avoid your garden.

To rid your kitchen of ants, crush some catnip and sprinkle on the ant trails. Ants dislike the smell and will leave your house. To keep flies outside where they belong, combine equal parts of clover flowers, broken bay leaves, crushed cloves, and eucalyptus leaves. Tie this mixture in small mesh bags inside your entrance doors.

Don't let mosquitoes and gnats drive you inside. Make your own insect repellents from herbs which are safe to use. Before encountering these biting insects, apply a little citronella oil to your skin. To extend the oil, add about one part pure ethyl alcohol to two parts of the oil. To attract the man in your life while repelling insects, mix three parts of lavender oil to one part of pure ethyl alcohol. Dab the mixture on your skin. The distinctive aroma of pennyroyal is also effective in keeping biting insects at their distance so rub a small amount on your body for good protection.

Southernwood, like wormwood, is a member of the genus Artemisia. Dried and powdered it is an excellent repellent for moths and much nicer to use than chemical moth balls and insect repellents.

Scents to pacify your pets

Don't neglect the dog or cat in your life. You can make aromatic pillows for your pets' beds that will keep them free from fleas. Cats are attracted to certain herbs and become playful over simple-to-make catnip toys.

To please the most finicky feline, dry equal parts of camomile flowers and pennyroyal. When crumbly dry, grind the herbs coarsely and fill a fabric pillow. The camomile and pennyroyal will rid your cat of fleas. A pillow filled with rue or cedar shavings will also keep your pet free of fleas.

A few catnip plants will supply your cat with toys all year. When the catnip is dry, strip the leaves from the stems and crumble slightly. Fill small bags, about one inch by two inches (2.5 x 5 cm), with the dried herb. The smell of catnip will make your cat a playful kitten again.

Another herb cats enjoy is valerian root. Collect, dry, and coarsely grind the herb before filling small toys or pillows for your pet. Bits of felt or pillow ticking will last longer than finer fabrics.

Herbal baths

At the end of a day, that for one reason or another was too long, one fills the bath brim-full of restfully warm water and climbs in. As the heat and moisture slowly open the pores and float out the dirt, the tensions of the day seep away, relaxing the muscles and the mind. It's a pleasant experience.

But the leisurely bath can be improved—and all it takes is a few of the right herbs. Added to the water, certain herbs can assist in cleansing the body as it soaks, and their fragrance will surely assist the psyche in dispatching tensions. After that hard day, a herbal bath is a tonic your body needs. Moreover, herbal lore has long attached medicinal values to the herbal bath. There are baths for aching muscles and for stimulating the circulation. Herbal footbaths are reputed to be the cure for any number of ailments. In his book *Of Men and Plants*, Maurice Messegue, a French herbal healer, lists dozens of recipes for footbaths he has demonstrated to be effective against everything from dyspepsia to constipation, and from insomnia to varicose veins.

151

Many a great beauty of the past has been reputed to have maintained the loveliness of her skin by bathing in scented waters. Ninon de Lenclos, a famous French beauty, was attractive to young men even when in her seventies. Her secret was put down to this herbal bath: Take a handful each of dried: lavender; rosemary leaves; mint; comfrey roots; and thyme. Mix all together loosely in a muslin bag. Place in your bath, pour on enough boiling water to cover and let soak for ten minutes. Then fill up the bath. Rest 15 minutes in the "magic water", and think virtuous thoughts!

Likewise, most herbal baths are simple to prepare. You can place the herbs to be used in a pan of water, cover, and boil for about ten minutes. Strain them and add the decoction to your bath water. Alternatively, you can tie the herbs at the spout so that the water washes over the herbs on its way to filling the bath. You can put the herbs in a clean nylon stocking or a cheesecloth bag if you like.

Another possibility is to simply stitch up a large muslin "tea bag", which you fill with herbs and hang over the side of the bath in the water. Steep until ready, then hop in.

You'll enjoy your herbal bath more if you first take a quick soap and water bath or shower. Then relax and soak in the herbal water for 15 to 20 minutes before patting yourself dry.

The only question remaining at this point is: "What herbs should be used?" Different herbs have different effects, so your choice should be governed as much by what you wish to accomplish as by what herbs you have available.

If you're interested in merely a sweet scent in your bath water, any one of the dozens of fragrant herbs will do. Lavender is the favourite of many ladies, as it has been for centuries. It's used to scent many commercial bath products, so why not use your own garden lavender? Moreover, lavender is reputed to be an excellent palliative for nervousness. If you are interested in becoming more lovable, try lovage. Herbal lore attributes "lovability" to this herb.

There are a number of recipes for skin tonics. With prolonged usage, comfrey will help regenerate ageing skin. Mix equal parts of comfrey, alfalfa, parsley, and orange peel for a rejuvenating bath, or combine three parts jasmine flowers with one part orange blossoms. This combination smells good, and will help your skin retain its youthful glow. Another bath formula for retaining youthful skin is to combine equal parts of rose petals, orange blossoms, and lavender.

To get pleasant relief from stiff muscles and joints, use a combination of sage and strawberry leaves. Another effective herbal combination to

Lavender is a delightful aromatic herb which has been used for centuries to perfume clothes and bedding, as well as herbal baths and waters.

ease aches and pains consists of employing equal parts of agrimony, camomile, and mugwort. For best results, you should massage aching muscles while soaking in the bath. That comforting glow of warmth is a sign that the therapy is working.

An alternative to lavender for tension relief is valerian. One herbal specialist recommends boiling one pound (453 g) of this herb in water for 30 minutes, then adding it to bath water. Other remedies for tension include the use of a decoction of equal parts of hops and meadowsweet as a rinse during the regular bath, and spiking the bath water with a decoction of a half-pound (227 g) of sweet flag roots and leaves.

A pleasant-smelling herb bath for men can be made by combining equal parts of spearmint and thyme leaves.

Experiment with various combinations of two or more of the following aromatic herbs to invent your own herbal baths—angelica root, marigolds, lovage root, lemon peel, rosemary, lavender, pennyroyal, sandalwood, cloves, cinnamon—or any other aromatic herbs you have access to.

Sweet powders

After partaking of a leisurely herbal bath, pamper your body by smoothing on sweet-scented powders. The ingredients for powders are easily found in your garden and kitchen. Make only a small amount so that the fragrance is not lost with time.

ROSE LAVENDER POWDER

Using a wooden pestle and mortar, grind to a fine powder one ounce (28 g) dried rose petals, one ounce (28 g) dried lavender buds, and one ounce (28 g) orris root. Using a wooden spoon, blend well while adding two ounces (56 g) cornflour. It makes a fine floral-scented powder.

TANGY HERBAL POWDER

Combine half an ounce (14 g) powdered cloves, half an ounce (14 g) powdered sage leaves, and one ounce (28 g) powdered orris root. To make this go further, blend in two ounces (56 g) arrowroot.

SPRING-FRESH POWDER

Combine one ounce (28 g) violet flowers, one ounce (28 g) lilac blossoms, and one ounce (28 g) orris root—all of which have been ground into a very fine powder. Add two ounces (56 g) cornflour, blending thoroughly. Pat on your body with a soft powder puff—and feel great!

It is the leaves of the Scented Geranium which are very aromatic. When rubbed or crushed they give off a delightful perfume often lemon-scented. They are a useful addition for pot-pourris and sachets.

Aromatic waters

After a long day refresh your weary mind and body with aromatic waters; after washing splash some on your face and neck for a fragrant "lift". Aromatic waters are pure waters that have been blended with fragrant herbs and are used as skin toners and tonics, body washes, or hair rinses. Sweet-smelling waters may be stored simply in decorative glass bottles in the bathroom or bedroom. You can be sure that your home-brewed cosmetic waters are free of harmful ingredients. The following combinations are all even good enough to drink.

Never use water containing chlorine or fluoride when concocting aromatic waters (this rules out most tap water). Use pure spring water free of all chemicals. If you are one of the lucky few who have their own pure spring water, use that. Otherwise, purchase a bottle at the health food shop. Distilled water or rain water may also be used. Mix the aromatic waters in glass or ceramic containers—*never* use metal ones.

Mint water is used to refresh and stimulate the skin: Purée fresh spearmint leaves with cold water in a blender. Dab the mixture on your face and neck. Dried mint may also be used: four ounces (113 g) of dried, crushed mint to a pint (568 ml) of pure water in a quart (1.14 l) glass jar with a tight-fitting lid. Put this glass jar in a convenient place and shake once or twice daily for two weeks. Strain and store in small glass vials with tight-fitting lids.

To make old-fashioned rose water, gather rose petals early in the morning, place them in an enamel pan, just cover with water, and slowly bring the mixture to the boil. Simmer for several minutes and strain. Rose water makes an excellent hair rinse, especially for oily hair. Also use as a rinse on oily skin. Rose water is often used to flavour foods in many countries. In India it is used to flavour soft drinks, ice cream, and cakes. Arabs use it as a glaze for roasting fowl.

Clover flowers make an aromatic water which is effective in correcting dry skin. Drop the freshly collected flowers into an enamel pan, barely cover with water, bring to a full boil, and simmer for two minutes. Strain and use. Store extra water in glass jugs with tight-sealing lids to protect the aroma. Camomile water helps firm skin tissue, keeps the skin youthful, and perks you up. Add three parts of camomile to four parts of water; allow to age for two weeks, shaking twice daily. Strain and bottle. Blondes will find camomile water to be a good hair rinse.

Herb vinegars, the same ones you use in cooking, are helpful to both dry and oily complexions and act to refine the skin pores. Vinegar

Rose water is easily made, and works wonders when dabbed on oily skin. Simply cover rose petals with water, bring the mixture to a boil, then cool and strain.

tightens skin pores and re-establishes the skin's natural acid balance. Refer to the recipes for making herb vinegars in chapter three. Start with either apple cider vinegar made from organically grown whole apples or white wine vinegar. Add one part petals or leaves to two parts of vinegar and place on a sunny window-sill in a tightly sealed glass bottle. Shake vigorously daily for two to three weeks. Strain and rebottle.

Such pungent herbs as sweet basil, thyme, sage, rosemary, dill, or marjoram may be aged in vinegar and used either as a facial rinse or in your cooking. For a more delicate floral fragrance, you may select lavender, violet petals, roses, carnations, lemon verbena, honeysuckle, sweet peas, or lilac, or experiment with your own combinations of two or more scents to create exciting new aromatic surprises.

Exotic herb oils

Herb oils are the very essence of the herbs from your garden. The more you use herbs for aromatic and cosmetic purposes, the more likely you are to find a situation where only an oil will do. It is at that point that you will get into a most delightful aspect of herbal aromatics.

Herb oils are usually extracted by distillation. But this is a process that is beyond the scope of most individuals. Given a bit of patience, however, you can extract oils from herbs. (If you haven't the patience, you can purchase a wide variety of herb oils from herbal suppliers).

If there is only one oil you want to make, by all means choose attar of roses. This fine-quality oil takes over two hundred pounds (91 kg) of roses to produce a mere ounce, or 28 g! So, as you can imagine, it is very expensive indeed. To make attar of roses, fill a large, clean ceramic crock with rose petals. Now, lightly press the rose petals down and cover them with pure spring or rain water. Place the crock outside where it will receive, we hope, a full day's sun. Watch the surface of the water for scum to form (this will take four to seven days). This scum is the attar of roses and should be oily with a yellowish colour. With a small piece of cotton wool absorb the oil and squeeze it into a small vessel. Remove the rose oil daily. If rain threatens, cover the crock so the roses aren't flooded and your precious oil lost.

A faster method of extracting attar of roses is to place two pounds (907 g) of freshly picked rose petals on a cloth tied around the edge of

You can make your own attar of roses, the fabulously expensive oil. Submerge the rose petals in water and, after several days, carefully collect the oil that forms on the surface with a ball of cotton wool.

a large enamel pan filled with hot water. Keep the water hot on the stove and place a dish of cold water upon the petals. Keep changing the pan of water on top to keep it cool. Soak up the rose oil with cotton wool and place in glass bottles.

Pure herbal oils may be kept for a long period of time if stored properly. Once the oil is extracted, tie several pieces of cheesecloth over the bottle and allow any water that may be mixed with your oil to evaporate (several days should do). Next, sterilize a one ounce (28 g), or less, amber or green coloured bottle with a tight-fitting lid. Carefully pour your exotic oil into this small vessel for storage.

Oils can be extracted from practically all plants using this technique. Happily, not all herbs are as parsimonious with their oils as roses. You'll use far fewer blossoms and leaves of other plants to collect similar quantities of oil—take heart!

You may make oils from the following flowers: lilac, geranium, honeysuckle, lavender, violets, lemon verbena, sweet peas, and other sweetly scented flowers. Collect only top-quality floral petals early in the morning. Place the petals in a clean ceramic crock and just cover with rain or spring water. Place the crock in a sunny place and watch for the filmy scum (the oil), to appear. Once this begins to collect, carefully absorb it into a small ball of cotton wool and squeeze it into a small jar. Store in tiny, coloured glass vials.

For herbal-scented oils select such aromatic plants as mint, rosemary, sage, marjoram, basil, dill or thyme. Cut only the good quality leaves and proceed as you do with floral oils or attar of roses.

You may also extract the essential oils of fragrant woods such as cedarwood, sandalwood, rosewood; the sweet essence of roots such as sassafras, orris, sweet flag; and the aromatic oils of barks such as cinnamon. First reduce the wood, root, or bark to shavings, using a garden shredder or electric blender, or a wood plane for thick, tough roots and wood. To extract the oils, merely follow one of the recommended methods for producing attar of roses.

To make oil of roses collect half a pound (227 g) of rose buds. Use a pestle and mortar to crush them finely, place them in an earthenware crock, and add 32 fluid ounces (896 ml) of olive oil. Place the crock in a sunny location for three to four weeks, stirring daily. At the end of this period, heat the roses and oil in an enamel bowl until warm, force the warmed mixture through a fine sieve, or use a blender. Filter through four layers of cheesecloth before storage in two ounce (51 g), or less, dark glass bottles.

Once you've collected herb oils, you'll never lack ideas for using them.

Perfume essences

Perfumes have been made for over twenty thousand years since man first learned to extract fragrance from aromatic plants. When kings and queens reigned in every European country, members of the court each had their own "secret" essence. Perfumes are made from aromatic roots, woods, flowers, seeds, and leaves. In the Fourteenth Century, alcohol was first used as a carrier for perfume. Herbal fixatives are used to prevent the volatile plant essences from evaporating.

The nice thing about homemade perfumes is that the ingredients will all be natural, with no chemicals. You don't have to rely on the chemist's test tube to make yourself smell good. If you grow, collect, and make your own perfumes, you will also save a great deal of money.

Perhaps the easiest way to make a herbal perfume is to pack fragrant plants—leaves, blossoms, shavings—with sweet-oil-soaked cotton wool in a glass jar with a tight-fitting lid. Sweet oil is a highly refined olive oil. Just put some cotton wool in your jar, pour on enough oil to saturate it, then add the blossoms, leaves, or shavings and cap the jar. Put it in the sun or in a warm place all day. Next day, change the plants. Do likewise the next day, and the next, and so on. Eventually, the cotton wool will be as saturated with the scent as it is with the oil. At that point, you merely squeeze the oil into a vial—and you have your perfume. As a cautionary measure, pop the oil into the refrigerator to prevent it from going rancid.

Other perfumes can be made by combining herb oils, aromatic waters, and other fragrant ingredients. Directions for making both herb oils and aromatic waters have already been given. Recipes follow for more aromatic delights.

SCENT OF ROSES

8 fl. oz (227 ml) surgical spirit
2 fl. oz (57 ml) rose water
3 tbsp rosemary oil
1½ tbsp rose oil
¾ tbsp storax oil (fixative)

Combine ingredients in a glass bottle. Shake well and wait four weeks before using.

HERB NO. 4 SCENT

8 fl. oz (227 ml) surgical spirit
1 tsp basil oil
1 tsp sage oil
1 tsp dill oil
¾ tbsp sandalwood oil (fixative)

Combine and store three weeks, shaking often, before using.

LAVENDER COLOGNE

1 pint (568 ml) surgical spirit
5 fl. oz (142 ml) lavender water
2 tbsp lavender oil
1 tbsp storax oil (fixative)

Combine—and enjoy after several weeks.

LEMON PERFUME

10 fl. oz (284 ml) surgical spirit
2 tbsp lemon oil
1 tbsp citronella oil
1 tbsp lemon verbena oil
1 tbsp sandalwood oil (fixative)

Place ingredients in a glass bottle, shake well. The mixture gets stronger with age.

SPICY ESSENCE

8 fl. oz (227 ml) surgical spirit
¾ tbsp clove oil
1½ tbsp cinnamon oil
1 oz (28 g) ground orris root (fixative)

Combine above ingredients in a tightly sealed glass vial. Set aside for two months. Filter and store in sterile glass perfume bottles.

Sweetly scented soaps

Most people believe soap-making to be a difficult task and view it as something they wouldn't attempt. Actually, making your own scented soaps is simple and relatively inexpensive—with the added bonus of knowing just what ingredients are in your soap. No chemical dyes, hardening agents, chemical additives, alcohol, or fillers in your home-made soap! You don't have to have an elaborate set up. Homemade soap can be prepared in small amounts in a city flat or in large amounts in country homes using iron kettles.

It is believed that soap was discovered accidently over three thousand years ago in Rome and has been purposely made ever since. The Pakistanis made soap from silkworms, while the American Indians made soap from desert plants. The two essential ingredients for making soap are fat and lye, both of which are easy to obtain.

Here are some general rules that must be remembered for successful soap-making.

1. Never use aluminium utensils. Instead, use enamel or iron (lye reacts with aluminium).
2. Use only clean fat or lard.
3. Never allow ageing soap to get in a cold draft as it turns hard and flinty.
4. Pour soap into moulds of about one and a half inches (3.8 cm); (too thin a soap will curl when drying and soap too thick is difficult to hold).
5. Ageing improves soap.

To render fat, fill a large pan with several inches of hot water and add the finely cut fat. Cook over a medium heat, stirring occasionally, until the fat is completely melted. Strain the melted mixture to remove all impurities. Allow to cool, then lift off lard (from pork) or tallow (from beef).

DR. MAGGIE'S OLD-FASHIONED LYE SOAP

This recipe comes from Dr. Margaret Ballard, a retired American doctor and professor of medicine. Every summer she attends mountain festivals in the USA where she charms old and young alike as she demonstrates soap-making using a large iron kettle.

This is the recipe.

4 lb (1.8 kg) fat (home-made lard preferred)
1 can lye (13 oz or 370 g)
¼ lb (113 g) borax
2 oz (57 g) rosin
6½ quarts (7.2 l) water.

This is what you have to do:
1. Heat water in a large enamelled iron kettle.
2. Add lard and stir until dissolved.
3. Sprinkle in lye, a little at a time, stirring constantly with a wooden spoon.
4. Gradually stir in the rosin and the borax.
5. Bring to a slow boil and allow to simmer until the soap "flakes off" the wooden spoon.
6. Stir often while "cooking".
7. Pour into 2 inch (5 cm) deep greased enamel or glass pans and cool overnight.
8. The next day cut into bars, but do not remove from the pans for two days.
9. Place on waxed paper and allow to dry for three to six weeks before using.

BASIC SOAP

1. Heat 6 lb (2.72 kg) of lard or tallow to 120-130°F (49-54°C) in an enamel kettle.
2. In a separate enamel pan stir together 13 oz (368 g) of lye and 2 pints (1.13 l) cold water and heat to 90-95°F (32-35°C).
3. Slowly pour the lye solution into the melted fat, stiring with a wooden spoon.
4. Simmer and stir until thick enough to hold its shape, about 30 minutes.
5. Pour to a depth of 1 to 1½ inches (2.5 to 3.8 cm) in greased glass or enamel pans.
6. Cool overnight.
7. Cut in bars and remove from the pan after several days.
8. Allow to age for two weeks before using.

*Fresh strawberries make a lovely soap which
is wonderful for the complexion. Just add the
juice to the basic soap recipe. This also colours
the soap a pretty shade of pink.*

Scenting your soap

Just before pouring your soap into moulds, add any of the following oils for a sweet-smelling aroma—lavender, citronella, rose, rose geranium, rosemary, cloves, cinnamon, sassafras, or lemon. To the basic soap recipe add two tablespoons of one of the above oils. To Dr. Maggie's add three tablespoons.

Citronella oil will leave you smelling like a lemon, while making your skin lustrous. Besides smelling delicious, lavender oil is also good for acne. Olive oil is a good addition if your skin is dry; sandalwood oil is an effective astringent and disinfectant. Oils that work as deodorants are thyme and patchouli. Other oils and combinations you may experiment with are palm, mace, peach kernel, and sage.

To colour your soap naturally, add the juice of fresh strawberries. Strawberry soap is a wonderful complexion preparation. To make your soap lather, add soap bark herb—this contains saponin which creates a lather when it comes into contact with water.

To make a good shaving soap, fill a glass mug with finished soap and add a quarter of a teaspoon sage or clove oil, or add one tablespoon powdered sage leaf or powdered cloves. Allow to age for one week before using.

To really pamper yourself, use a loofah sponge as you bathe with your scented soap. The loofah, or sponge gourd, incidentally, is the skeleton of the Japanese bottle loofah *(Luffa aegyptiaca)*. When dry, the loofah is flat, when placed in water, it inflates into a luxurious bathing sponge.

Rose beads

The rose, aristocrat among flowers, is a most versatile plant. Not only is the rose acclaimed for its fragrance and beauty, but it is also cultivated for its "hips", which are rich in natural vitamin C and are brewed into rose hip tea and natural vitamin C supplements. Rose petals, also used in jelly, may be candied or made into rose water. Rose leaves are ingredients for pot-pourris and sachets.

Rose beads, made from rose petals, are a delightful way to enjoy the fragrance of roses all year round. Rose beads have been made and worn by countless women over the centuries, and their fragrance must have played a part in many a romance.

If you have access to any of the old-time perfume roses, such as Damask or cabbage rose, by all means use them in preference to the newer varieties. Deeper coloured roses are more fragrant than the lighter ones. However, any varieties of rose may be used. Collect them early in the morning on a dry day. Pull the petals off and, using a pestle and mortar, crush them very fine. Then spread the mashed petals on a piece of waxed paper to partially dry. Return the petals to the mortar and add a small amount of water to create a fine paste.

Dip your fingers into the rose oil (see the section on oils) and then roll the petal paste into small beads. (Ebony-coloured beads can be made by crushing the roses in an iron mortar or pot—where they will be oxidized by the iron and turn black.)

While still wet, carefully poke a needle through the centres of the beads to make a hole for threading later. Lay the finished beads to dry on clean waxed paper, turning several times, so that drying takes place evenly. When thoroughly dried (it will take two or three days), polish them with a soft cloth.

Now that all of your pretty, sweet-smelling beads are made, you can decide how to use them. Rose beads may be strung on thin nylon thread of varying lengths. In this way, they can be used as a scented necklace. Several threaded strands may be made into a belt. Similarly, you can make scented pendant ear-rings. The ambitious may even attempt to make a room divider or screen divider made out of multi-coloured rose beads.

When your beads begin to lose their sweet smell, merely dip them in rose oil and allow them to dry. This way, your hand-made rose beads will always smell of summer delights.

Fragrant incense

Incense has been used for centuries as part of various pagan and religious rituals. In recent years, burning of incense has become increasingly popular as a method of perfuming a room. Intricate burners and many aromas of incense are available in gift and novelty shops. Incense is easily made and becomes more fragrant if matured over several months.

FRANKINCENSE

Here is a recipe using frankincense: Combine and mix together two tablespoons of powdered frankincense, one tablespoon powdered orris root, and one teaspoon of powdered cloves. Stir one tablespoon of oil of lemon through the mixture. Place in a cool, dark area for two to three months. To use, sprinkle a little on some burning charcoal.

LIGHT FLORAL INCENSE

For a light floral incense, combine two tablespoonfuls of ground rose petals, two tablespoonfuls of ground lavender, and one teaspoonful powdered vetiver. In another small bowl mix half a teaspoonful of oil of lemon and half a teaspoonful of oil of lavender. Blend the oils through the dry mixture. Store several months before using—again, by sprinkling on a piece of burning charcoal.

SPICY INCENSE

A spicy incense may be concocted by mixing together two tablespoonfuls of ground cinnamon, two tablespoonfuls of ground cloves, one tablespoonful of ground cascarilla, and one tablespoonful of powdered orris root. Stir in one tablespoonful of oil of cloves. Sprinkle on smouldering charcoal after ageing.

Candle making

During the last few years there has been a revival in the age-old craft of candle-making. Some craft shops sell candle-making supplies. You need not rush out to buy a lot of fancy candle-making equipment. Your kitchen will provide almost everything you need, with a little help from your herb garden, plus some solid paraffin wax and a length of wick.

The first thing to do is to collect all the materials you will need:

plenty of paraffin wax, wick, an old double boiler to melt the wax in (or a big tin can and a saucepan), and moulds. The latter are fun to hunt for, with many practically under your nose in the kitchen, attic, and basement. Waxed milk cartons make perfect moulds, as do used plastic bottles of all shapes and sizes. For the scent, you will need aromatic herb oils or powdered herbs.

Cut the paraffin wax into pieces and place in the top of a double boiler to melt. Don't use a good cooking utensil because it will be ruined. If you don't have an old double boiler, you can melt the wax in a large tin can placed in a pan of boiling water (never melt wax directly over a flame, it's dangerous). Perfume your wax with aromatic herb oils such as: clove, mint, rose, sage, lavender, or lemon. Various combinations of fragrant oils are often pleasing. Alternatively you may add powdered aromatic herbs to the melted wax.

Use a pestle and mortar to powder the dried herbs. After warming the mould, insert a length of wick to the bottom of the mould, allowing about one inch (2.5 cm) extra above the top of the mould. If you have trouble with the wick moving, tie a small weight on it—a nut or screw— and drop the heavy end of the wick into the mould. For coloured candles, melt a piece of wax crayon in the paraffin wax. Now, slowly pour the scented wax into the slightly warmed moulds. As the wax cools, a depression will form in the centre of the candle. Top up this depression with hot wax until the mould is filled and level.

Allow your candles to dry thoroughly before removing them from their moulds. Tear away waxed cardboard moulds, or moulds with inwardly tapering tops. Plastic will be easy enough to remove. Glass, plastic, and metal moulds with straight sides may be placed very briefly in hot water, enabling the candle to dislodge and slip from its mould.

For a finer quality of candle, add one part pure beeswax to one part of paraffin wax, melt, and pour into moulds. You may also make candles out of beeswax, with no paraffin wax added.

Now you can turn out the lights, light your candles, and enjoy their beauty and aroma.

The possibilities for making practical use of the aromatic qualities of herbs are virtually unending. You are limited only by time, interest, and imagination. Even if you have time for nothing more, a walk through a garden of fragrant herbs is a refreshing experience. And once taken, it may compel you to make time for aromatics.

5

The Colourful Herbs

I can rarely resist the call of a wool shop—even though the walls of my house almost bulge with uncounted skeins. All those textures! All those colours! I have a friend who owns such a shop, and we share the same excitement over the visual and tactile joy of wool and colour. These yarns, to me, have a life and character quite special. They remind me of homespun, vegetable-dyed yarns—to me the most beautiful of all woollen yarns.

Best of all, these subtle, glowing, infinitely varied colours are quite easily available for the making. If your definition of a truly satisfying hobby is like mine—one which involves you in constant adventures, chances to learn, and which produce a unique and practical product— then consider vegetable dyeing.

The scarlet uniforms of the English who fought in the Napoleonic wars got their bright colour from carmine, the pigment made from cochineal. Cochineal is obtained from the dried bodies of the female scale insect which feeds on cacti in Mexico, the West Indies, and the Canary Isles. The Aztecs also used this form of dye. And at one time the blue of our policemen's uniforms owed their colour to woad (*Isatis tinctoria*), a plant belonging to the Cruciferae family.

The term *vegetable dyes* actually encompasses animal, vegetable, and mineral. The "animal" dyes include cochineal; the "vegetable" dyes do sometimes include edible vegetables but also any growing plant materials—leaf, bark, root, nut, fruit, berry, and flower seed; and the "mineral" dyes include rust (iron oxide).

171

I am assuming you are going to find vegetable colours as evocative, lively, and beautiful as I do, but perhaps you are used to commercial dyes and the process of vegetable dyeing sounds rather involved and messy. Why bother?

I agree. Synthetic dyes are inexpensive. Synthetic dyes are easy to use—quick and relatively (some very) permanent. Synthetic dyes come in a wide range of colours. With careful mixing, an infinite range is possible. Quantity is unlimited. With care, they dye evenly to any degree of depth desired. I also agree vegetable dyes are a lot of trouble—picking (sometimes drying), soaking, washing, mordanting, and dyeing, sometimes with less than satisfactory results.

Synthetic dyes are pure colours. They do not readily sit beside each other harmoniously. Vegetable dyes are impure. Because each colour contains elements of many other colours, the skeins harmonize with each other. It is almost impossible to find a "clash" of colours.

Vegetable dyes have a very special life—a subtle character all their own. They blend happily with other earthy handicrafts such as wood and pottery. Vegetable dyes, when they fade eventually, will fade to a softer tone of their original colour, still keeping their original identity (witness old coverlets and tapestries). (You *know* what terrible things can happen to synthetic dyes—fading to sometimes different and ugly colours.) Vegetable dyeing puts one in touch with a fascinating world of history.

And it's even useful, though really it doesn't have to be. It pleases the soul just to see and handle the rainbow of coloured wools, to know that you had a part in the magic of their creation.

Getting started

As with any new hobby, it is as well to experiment initially with small quantities such as skeins of wool, undyed. Tie these in two or three places with strong cotton loosely enough to allow the dye to penetrate all parts, but not so loosely that the wool works free.

After tying, the wool then has to be well washed in mild, soapy water (preferably soft) to eliminate all traces of dirt, oil, or chemicals

The array of dyeing equipment shown opposite, plus the skill, imagination and patience of the dyer are all that's needed to imbue wool with an endless number of beautiful natural colours.

which could repel the dye, and then thoroughly rinsed. If you live in a district where the water is hard, use a water softener or a little vinegar. Either squeeze the skeins gently and hang them to dry, or leave them soaking in clear, lukewarm water until you are ready for the next stage—mordanting.

Apart from substantive dyes like lichens, vegetables dyes require a mordant. This is best described as a "fix" which combines with the colouring agent to prevent fading. Nowadays mordants are chemical, although in days gone by cruder methods were used to "set" the colours—notably stale human urine.

The mordant most often used is alum (potassium aluminium sulphate), and it is usually used with cream of tartar (tartaric acid) to brighten colours. A skein of four ounces (113 g) of wool would require one ounce (28 g) of alum and half an ounce (14 g) of cream of tartar to six and a half pints (3.7 l) of water. If you are working with more than one skein, the quantities for one pound (453 g) of wool would be four ounces (113 g) of alum (three ounces (85 g) for fine wool) and one ounce (28 g) of cream of tartar added to three and a half gallons (15.9 l) of water.

Mordanting with alum is usually done before the dyeing, although it can be done before, or sometimes even after the dye process. To mordant before means the skeins may be dried and stored away until such time as you have the dye plant or plants you want. If this is the case the skeins should be suitably labelled to indicate which mordant was used. They then only have to be re-soaked and rinsed to be ready for dyeing.

The next step is to add the mordant to the warm water, stirring until it has dissolved, add the wool, bring the water *slowly* to a simmer, and hold it at that temperature for an hour. Turn off the heat, and leave it until cool. Provided you have used enough water, the wool will be able to move freely with only an occasional poke or gentle turn from you.

Never, never agitate the wool at any stage of mordanting or dyeing; gently stir, spread, or poke. Neither must you ever subject it to sudden temperature changes. And the pot you use should be large and roomy enough to allow the wool plenty of space.

The wool can now be wrapped in a towel and placed in the dye pot right away, or it can be dried and stored until a later date. This is where labelling becomes necessary, because you may decide to do a batch of mordanting one day, using various chemicals, and do your dyeing some time in the future, and different mordants give different colour results.

You will be able to dye a lot without feeling the need for any mordant other than alum. Eventually, however, you may feel the urge to

Using cotton crocheting cord strung in a figure of eight loop, loosely tie together small skeins of woollen thread for the dyeing process.

experiment more widely—in which case you could start with chrome (potassium dichromate). This requires much the same process as alum, but chrome is both poisonous and light-sensitive so the lid should be kept on the pot during mordanting. The mordanted skeins should also be kept well away from the light until they are ready for dyeing.

Chrome will give the wool a soft, silky quality and add a yellowish-green colour, as well as a new dimension to your experiments. For example, coreopsis with alum produces a bright yellow; with chrome a brick-red. One pound (453 g) of wool would need only half an ounce

The dye process is begun by weighing out both the mordant chemical and the wool.

(14 g) of chrome; four ounces (113 g) of wool would need one-eighth of an ounce (3.54 g) of chrome. It is best to use chrome-mordanted wool at once, as storing can lead to uneven dyeing.

Should you want to grey or "sadden" a colour at the end of the dye process, lift the wool out of the pot, add a *very* little ferrous sulphate (iron)—about two teaspoonfuls or less for one pound (453 g) of wool, allow to dissolve, and then return the wool. As soon as the colour has changed, rinse the wool very carefully. However, iron tends to make wool harsh, and spoils the dye pot for other mordants.

To sharpen reds and yellows you can use stannous chloride (tin), but it tends to make wool brittle. Use it as you would iron, but even less of it, adding cream of tartar or oxalic acid and rinsing the wool afterwards in soapy water. Occasionally you will see copper sulphate called for in a recipe to develop greens.

Besides the mordants, you can either acidify or alkalize the dye pot, thus affecting the colour greatly—say from red to blue. The most easily available acid is vinegar (acetic acid), and the most easily available alkali is the clear variety of ammonia (sodium hydroxide).

Substantives like lichens, tea, and black walnut contain their own mordant, so another mordant would only be used if you wanted to alter the colour.

It is advisable to keep dye pots for that purpose only, chrome (potassium dichromate) and oxalic acid are considered poisonous. Do not use pots that will set up a reaction to the dyes. That rules out aluminium, iron, brass, and copper. Stainless steel is perfect, but enamel is cheaper—provided it is not chipped.

Working in a well-ventilated kitchen with food stored out of the way is the only other precaution to take. Although if you want to protect your hands and nails from staining, you should use rubber gloves.

The wool is then soaked in clean water.

Dyeing

After the preparatory work, all is now set for the actual dyeing. Provided you have mordanted carefully, your skeins will emerge evenly and permanently dyed. But it should be appreciated that final results can vary from one user to another since you are dealing with a living medium—a plant.

The plant's own chemistry is affected by many variables: the season, soil conditions, moisture availability, proportions of sunlight and shade, and varieties within species.

Then there are variables in the dyeing process itself: the plant with all the above variables; whether it is fresh or dry, and which part of the plant is being used; the length of time that elapses between picking and using; the mordanting; the length and heat of soaking; the length and heat of brewing; the type and twist of the wool; the time and heat of the wool in the dye pot; the chemicals added; the method of rinsing; and the type of drying.

If you intend to take dyeing at all seriously, this is where you will find the real usefulness of keeping step-by-step records. For example, when using ripe materials, even a day can make a marked difference in the results achieved.

Fresh plants tend to give brighter colours, but there are many that work just as well whether dried or fresh; goldenrod is an exception. Plants and dyes can both be kept fresh in the freezer.

Flowers are best picked just as they open as opposed to when in full bloom, and should be young and healthy. Leaves should be used as they are ready to mature, and roots are best collected in the autumn. Just-ripe berries are the best, while resinous bark should be taken in the spring and non-resinous in the autumn.

But here a word of warning. Indiscriminate stripping of bark can kill trees, and certainly will if the bark is taken from all round the trunk.

The chemicals are added to water in the mordanting pot (top left).

The wool is gently transferred to the mordant pot, slowly heated and simmered, then cooled (bottom left).

The same sort of restraint should also be shown when collecting any plants from the wild; the survival of species can become seriously threatened by any wide-scale collecting, and even soil erosion can result. One serious example of just this occurred years ago in the Outer Hebrides where the roots of lady's bedstraw were collected for their red dye. The grazing lands became eroded to such an extent that a law was passed forbidding the practice. The penalty was death.

Lichens are easiest to collect in the winter and when they are swollen by the early autumn rain. Incidentally, lichens used to be one of the main sources of dye for tartans in Scotland, and genuine Harris Tweed still owes its familiar browns to a rock-borne lichen.

Into the pot

The first stage of the dyeing proper is to tear, chop, and pound the plant material into small pieces. If you are using bark, roots, or nuts this can be hard work and require some elbow grease. Then put it in tepid water to soak, at least overnight. Tough, fibrous material may need several days.

Now put the pot on the stove and slowly raise the temperature to extract a lot of colour. Too much heat could be harmful, so keep it at a steady simmer. If you have let your mordanted wool dry, this is the time to wet it. In order to get an even dye it is important to thoroughly soak the wool for about an hour in lukewarm water, gently squeezing and working the strands open to allow the water to penetrate.

Now strain the dye liquid, unless you want to follow the school of thought which finds this unnecessary—except where you have sharp seeds and residue which would become permanently embedded in the wool. Or you could avoid all this by tying the dye plants in a muslin bag before "brewing" them.

Before adding the soaked wool to the dye pot, ensure that it goes from one temperature in the water to a like one in the dye; this will probably mean cooling down the dye pot. You can do this by adding cool water without any fear of diluting the dye. The same amount of colour will be present no matter how much you dilute.

Once the wool is in the dye pot keep moving it about very gently but always below the surface, to ensure an even dye. Bearing in mind that wet colours always look darker than dry ones, you can test how the wool is taking up the dye by lifting one small bit and squeezing it between finger and thumb to remove the liquid.

After the dye plant has brewed in water sufficiently, strain off the plant materials.

When the wool has reached the depth of colour you want, remove it from the pot and rinse it in hot water. For greater depth of colour you can leave it in the pot to cool. If you want still more colour you can try another simmering and cooling, but remember that the wool must never be subjected to sudden temperature changes. A bit of ammonia added to the rinsing water brightens flower colours. To eliminate kinks in the wool, hang it up to dry with weights on the end.

Most dyes, even when they have given up a lot of colour to the wool, will still have colour left in them, so they can be used again and

181

Gently place the soaked and mordanted wool in the dye liquid.

•

again: this is called "exhausting" the pot. Each successive skein of wool will take up less colour, but you will end up with a selection of skeins in various shades of the same colour, which can be very attractive for weaving or embroidering.

If, however, you want a supply of matching wool, then it will all have to be dyed together in the same pot. It would be too much to hope for to get the identical colour in a subsequent dye pot. Even commercial dyers cannot guarantee that.

As a rule of thumb, equal weights of plant material and wool to be dyed should be used, but this is very general as some plants yield more dye than others; for example, there is little in sunflower petals but a lot in coreopsis.

182

Step-by-step

An easy recipe to start off with is onion skin dye. The dry, papery, outer skins used with alum-mordanted wool will produce a burnt-orange colour, or used with chrome-mordanted wool, a brass-yellow. A four-ounce (113 g) skein of wool needs two and a half ounces (60 g) of onion skins; one pound (453 g) of wool needs ten ounces (283 g).

Boil the skins for half an hour, or alternatively soak them overnight in lukewarm water and then simmer. After straining, bring the dye pot up to the required volume—six and a half pints (3.7 l) for four ounces (113 g), three and a half gallons (15.9 l) for one pound (453 g) of wool.

The principals of herbal dyeing are wool, water, and one of the colourful herbs. You soak the herb, then the wool, in water.

Expose a length of the finished dyed wool to bright sunlight for several weeks while shielding another length of the same piece to determine the colour's permanence.

If the mordanted wool's rinse water and the dye pot temperatures are equal, you can now transfer the wool to the dye pot. Otherwise, either cool the dye pot or gradually heat the rinse water until they have equalized. Squeeze the wool before transferring it as the weight of the water stretches the fibres.

Simmer the wool in the dye pot for half an hour. If you want the deepest colour possible, allow it to cool in the dye pot, rinse it, and then air-dry it. This heating, cooling, and air-drying can be repeated several times.

If the first simmering has produced the colour you want, remove the wool and thoroughly rinse in water of the same temperature, then dry. Similarly, where it has been allowed to cool, it should be transferred to a cool rinse before drying.

184

If you did not strain the skins before adding the wool, most of the debris will float to the top of the rinse water and the rest can be flicked and shaken out when the wool is dry.

Milkweed is more familiar as a medicinal herb, but it will yield some unique colours.

Which plants?

If you want your first experiment to be easier on time and effort, you could start with a dye plant that needs no added mordant—the black walnut *(Juglans nigra)*. There is dye in all parts of the tree, but it is most concentrated in the nut husks. The longer the soaking, the greater the depth of colour—a tan-brown. Variations on brown can, however, be obtained by adding mordants. Deep blacky shades can be achieved, for instance, by boiling the husks in an iron pot which itself acts as a mordant. If you do try this method, do not simmer the wool for too long as it tends to make it harsh.

Alder *(Alnus glutinosa)*

This tree provides four different dye colours; a tawny red from the bark, a pinky-fawn from the new green wood, green from the catkins, and yellow from the young shoots.

Blackberry *(Rubus fruticosus)*

The young shoots with alum give grey which can be deepened in tone by adding iron.

Coreopsis *(Coreopsis tinctoria)*

This plant above all others will put chrome in your repertoire. With alum you get a nice yellow, with chrome a permanent burnt orange, and with tin and cream of tartar a very bright yellow.

Dandelion *(Taraxacum officinale)*

The long tap-roots will give magenta.

Goldenrod *(Solidago var. sp.)*

The fresh, opening flowers give beautiful golden-yellow shades, but some of them can be dyed in indigo to get a good green, or top-dyed with madder to give brick or rosy brown shades.

Lily-of-the-Valley *(Convallaria majalis)*

The leaves of the lily-of-the-valley picked in the spring give a green dye, while autumn leaves give yellow.

186

*The leaves and flowers of goldenrod
yield beautiful gold and yellow colours
in the dye pot.*

Privet *(Ligustrum sp.)*

The berries give a bluish-green, and the leaves give yellow.

Safflower *(Carthamus tinctorius)*

The tinctorius in a botanical name always denotes lots of dye available. This one, too, yields yellows.

St. John's Wort *(Hypericum perforatum)*

The flowers give yellow with alum, and the leaves yield a green.

Scotch Broom *(Cytisus scoparius)*

This gives a yellow with alum or chrome, and is also good to top-dye with indigo for green.

Sumach *(Rhus coriaria* and *Rhus cotinus)*

These are both substantive plants, so need no additional mordant. The berries of the former will give a black dye, while the root and stem of the latter will give a yellow to orange colour.

Sometimes the most unexpected colours can result from flowers of an entirely different hue. For instance, orange chrysanthemum petals have produced greens, oriental poppies have produced lavender, and the deep royal purple dye from wild violet petals have resulted in icy-green coloured wool! So if you are planning to knit yourself a bright orange sweater to match the chrysanthemums in the garden, you would be well advised to try dyeing only a small quantity of wool first to avoid disappointment.

While there are many plants which produce greens, yellows, and browns, for blue one has to rely on indigo which is not native to Britain—although the seas of blue denim in our towns and cities might make you think otherwise. It is a very permanent dye, but since it is insoluble in water it belongs to a different category of dyes—vat dyes.

The dye powder is extracted from the indigo leaves, which is a complicated process. To be usable, it has to be converted from its insoluble form to a soluble one which involves more complex processes including fermentation in urine. Hardly a chore that the home dyer would want to get involved in. It is now possible to buy a soluble form of indigo which requires no mordanting, unless you plan to top-dye with another colour that does need it.

*To many gardeners purslane is a noxious weed. To some gourmets it is a
delicious salad herb, but to the herbal dyer it is an interesting dye plant.*

If you are determined to have blue and do not mind hard work, you
could try woad, indigo's predecessor for blue dye. Although it is rare to
find this plant growing wild, it can be cultivated. It is a member of the
Cruciferae family, and was used by the ancient Britons as war paint.

The leaves were picked and dried in the sun, after which they were
ground to a paste. This was then heaped on the ground, under cover,
but exposed to air where it was left to ferment. A crust would form
which was not split until fermentation was complete. Then the pulpy
mass was pounded and again left to ferment under a crust. The process
was repeated yet again before it was ready for use as a dye.

A hundredweight (50.8 kg) of leaves was reduced to ten pounds
(4.5 kg) of dye, and the smell was nauseating. It is said that the production of woad dye had to be suspended in any town through which
Queen Elizabeth I was progressing. And this was an age when bad

189

smells were an ever-present feature of life in Britain (hence the habit of carrying nosegays). That custom is perpetuated to this day in the posies carried by High Court judges on the first day of a new term.

When weeding your garden consider those weeds which could provide you with more colours for your dye pot. What sweet revenge you would wreak on that scourge, the dandelion! Nettles, plantain, horsetail, ragweed, purslane, yarrow, and others are all worth experimenting with.

A rich source of a wide range of brown and reddish dyes is found in lichens, but these are a form of plant life which is very sensitive to atmospheric pollution and so is gradually disappearing from urban and industrial areas. They are most abundant in areas where there is plenty of rain and a lack of other plants competing with them, typically in Scotland.

One interesting feature about lichens is the dramatic colour changes that can occur when they are extracted with acids and alkalies. For example, one species, cudbear, when extracted with ammonia will produce a vivid purple; when it is fermented in urine it will give red. And it is some of the *Roccella* species, mainly found in Africa, which have provided every laboratory with the familiar litmus paper dye.

In passing it is worth mentioning the importance that urine has played in dyeing processes down the years. The Scottish dye factories used so much of it during the Nineteenth Century that they employed house-to-house collecting agents who would bring back as much as three thousand gallons (13,638 l) a day. To rule out the possibility of diluted samples being offered to them, each agent carried a hygrometer.

Roots, Nuts and Bark

Roots used for dyeing include dyer's madder *(Rubia tinctorum)*, which can be cultivated in this country although it will not be found in the wild. Mordanted with alum or chrome, the roots give deep reds. Close relatives are wild madder *(Rubia peregrina)* whose roots give a rose-pink with an alum mordant, and lady's bedstraw *(Galium verum)* whose roots give red with alum while the flowers yield yellow with alum or chrome. Lady's bedstraw is one dye that prefers hard water and a minimum of heat. The more heat, the more browny-yellow the resultant dye.

Cedar *(Juniperus virginiana)*
    These roots yield purple.

Dock *(Rumex obtusifolius)*

One-half pound (226 g) of the root for one pound (453 g) of wool, plus alum, yields a dark yellow.

Besides black walnut, try other nut husks and acorns. Horse chestnut with chrome gives a nice gold, and pine-cones (although hardly nuts) give a reddish-yellow.

Most of the colour of bark is in the inner layer. Try apple, alder (tawny red), cherry, plum, and willow.

Some plants can give disappointing results and either lack colour or produce poor or unfast colours. Notable among these are beetroot and turmeric, although as you grow more experienced in dyeing methods you could discover ways of extracting and "fixing" colours that others have not yet found. One lady managed to extract a different shade for every month of the year from rhododendron leaves.

Dye plant colour chart

a = alum and cream of tartar.   c = chrome

Dye Plant	Part	Mordant	Pink	Orange	Yellow	Green	Blue	Tan-Brown	Lavender-Purple	Grey-Black
Agrimony *Agrimonia Eupatoria*	leaves and stalks	a or c			x					
Blackberry *Rubus*, var. sp.	young shoots	a								x
Black Oak *Quercus velutina*	fresh inner bark	a or c			x					
Black Walnut *Juglans nigra*	nuts or hulls	no						x		
Buckwheat *Fagopyrum esculentum*	stalks fermented 5 days	a					x			

Dye Plant	Part	Mordant	Pink	Orange	Yellow	Green	Blue	Tan-Brown	Lavender-Purple	Grey-Black
Camomile *Anthemis tinctoria*	flower	a			x					
Cochineal—an insect; not a herb, but a natural dye	dried insect	var.	x						x	
Coffee *Coffea arabica*	green beans	a						x		
Coreopsis *Coreopsis tinctoria*	flower	tin			x					
		c		x						
Dahlia *Dahlia*, var. sp.	flower (yellow best)	c		x						
Dock *Rumex obtusifolius*	root	a			x					
Dyer's Broom *Genista tinctoria*	flowering tops				x					
Elderberry *Sambucus nigra*	fruits	var.					x			
Goldenrod *Solidago*, var. sp.	flowers and plants	a or c			x					

193

Dye Plant	Part	Mordant	Pink	Orange	Yellow	Green	Blue	Tan-Brown	Lavender-Purple	Grey-Black
Grape *Vitis*, var. sp.	fruits	a					x		x	
Indigo *Indigofera tinctoria*	fermented leaves	no					x			
Lady's Bedstraw *Galium verum*	roots or	a or c	x							
	tops	a or c			x					
Lily-of-the-Valley *Convallaria majalis*	spring leaves	c				x				
	autumn leaves				x					
Madder *Rubia tinctorum*	root	a or c	x							
Marigold *Tagetes*, var. sp.	flower	a / c			x					
Mulberry *Morus*, var. sp.	fruit	var.					x		x	
Onion *Allium cepa*	dry	a		x						
	husks	c			x					

Dye Plant	Part	Mordant	Pink	Orange	Yellow	Green	Blue	Tan-Brown	Lavender-Purple	Grey-Black
Safflower *Carthamus tinctorius*	flowers	var.	x	x	x					
St. John's Wort *Hypericum perforatum*	flowers	a			x					
		tin	x							
Scotch Broom *Cytisus scoparius*	flowering tops	a or c			x					
Sumac *Rhus coriaria Rhus cotinus*	berries, roots, and stem	no		x	x			x		x
Tea *Camellia sinensis*	leaves	a or c						x		
	leaves	a			x				.	
Silver Birch *Betula alba*	inner bark	no						x		
		a			x					
		iron							x	
Zinnia *Zinnia elegans*	flowers, any colour	a			x					

Do not let the chart limit you. It only suggests possibilities and some of the more predictable results.

195

6

Cultivating the Herbs

Herbs have been companions of man for many, many centuries. You have seen the many uses to which herbs can be put, accompanying and serving man through his life. Our interest in, and intensive work with, these loyal companions is nothing but a continued comradeship between beings from different realms of life.

As is well known, herbs are obtainable dried and packeted, but these cannot compare in flavour and food value with those gathered fresh from the garden. So if you want really good herbs you must grow your own. This, fortunately, is just as easy as growing vegetables. There is certainly no mystery about growing them.

Furthermore, they contribute handsomely to the health of the garden, since many are excellent pest-repellents. They enhance the garden with their aromas, and their flowers attract pollinating insects. Herbs do not all have to be grown in the vegetable beds. Some, such as rosemary and sage, for example, could be sited among shrubs, or grown in large pots or tubs. Some may even be grown indoors.

Classification of herbs

There are four broad classifications: tender annuals; hardy annuals; biennials; hardy perennials.

Among the tender annuals are basil, sweet marjoram, fennel, and

197

borage, the seeds of which cannot be sown in the open ground until the end of May, although the latter may be sown in warmer gardens in April.

The hardy annuals are started from seed sown in open ground in March/April, provided that soil and weather conditions are favourable. These include summer savory, camomile, dill, marigold, and nasturtium.

The biennials such as angelica, celery, and mullein seeds are sown every other year, but they could be sown annually to bring more colour to the garden.

By far the largest section are the hardy perennials: chives, dandelion, lemon balm, lovage, marjoram, nettle, mint, salad burnet, sorrel, tarragon, and sweet cicely. You can either buy young plants or start your own from seed in spring. Garlic may be sown in the spring and again in October as it is winter-hardy.

Climatic requirements

Often, when the question of physical requirements for herbs is brought up, people are unable to distinguish between herbs on the one hand and other plants like vegetables and fruits on the other. Herbs throughout the centuries have remained "simple" plants, fully expressing their characteristic individualities simply because man has left them alone and has not subjected them to rigorous selection and breeding programmes. Unlike vegetables, they have not been bred for quantitative growth and hybridization is nearly absent. A visitor from the Egypt of three thousand years ago would still recognize a coriander plant growing today in our garden.

The ability of herb plants to hold and reproduce the original characteristics over thousands of years helps us today in answering questions of physical requirements for these plants. The first step is to find the natural habitat or environment of the specific herb. The more the climate in which we grow it resembles that of its home region, the more ideal are the climatic conditions. Since in general most herbs originate from the areas around the Mediterranean and northern Europe, we are safe to assume that a similar climate would make our herb plants feel at home and grow without much trouble. So the great majority of herbs prefer a climate with a great amount of sunshine, low humidity, seasonal changes, and an even distribution of an average amount of rainfall.

198

Soil requirements

The above approach also works in determining the preferable soil requirements for herbs. We know that the soils to be found around the Mediterranean are not the most fertile and productive. Herbs are modest creatures, quite often pioneering plants which make use of the smallest amounts of nutrients a soil can offer and still thrive well and look healthy. Lavender, camomile and thyme, for example, are able to flourish where other plants would make a very poor showing. Though there are exceptions to this rule, I do not hesitate to say that the majority of herbs feel comfortable in a well-drained soil of sandy, even gravelly, structure. This does not mean, however, that they would not do well on other soils, but drainage remains always an important factor. Herbs like peppermint, tarragon, lovage, and others have to be excluded from this generalization because they want to scoop from full barrels. For the purpose of a home gardener every type of soil can actually be prepared without great effort to accommodate any herb that he or she desires to grow.

Fortunately, herbs, unlike many vegetables, have not been specially bred for intensive cultivation and so have retained their original natural vigour and health. They have a capacity for thriving in indifferent soils (provided these are well-drained), and most will flourish where many vegetables would just give up the ghost. Some may have special soil preferences, of course, but in general a soil fed with garden compost will provide all that is required for healthy growth.

Soil preparation

Obviously, different herbs prefer different types of soil and soil conditions and consequently need specific soil preparation. So particulars are discussed with individual herbs in the Encyclopaedia part of the book. There are, however, some requirements that apply to all herb plants.

Drainage

Drainage is a term in farming and gardening describing the ability of a soil to handle the water from rainfall or irrigation. The ideal type of soil

For those herbs that are encouraged by a well-fertilized soil, the best fertilizers are natural ones. Dried manure, (left), and seaweed and kelp (right), mixtures are good, and they are common commercial varieties.

is expected to absorb any normal amount of rainfall within a reasonably short time without leaving excessive water to run-off. A soil which is able to meet these expectations is said to have good drainage. A soil having problems ingesting all water from rainfall, and thereby causing run-off, is said to have poor drainage.

The reasons for poor drainage are varied. It can be a sign of low organic matter content since the organic matter, especially in the form of humus, can absorb a great amount of water. The home gardener could do worse than to add a high amount of manure compost over a period of years until the organic matter content has been improved.

Some gardening areas never seem to produce impressive growth. Drainage is poor; the rain runs off, and during a dry period the soil becomes a dry powder. Plants even begin to wilt unless artificially watered. Closer investigation will usually reveal a rock formation or layers of shale or rock a foot or more below the top soil. The water-holding capacity of this type of soil is rather limited, and plant roots are confined to the few inches of top soil. Here improvement will be achieved by breaking up the subsoil, removing the rock materials, and replacing them with top soil. Should this be too cumbersome or expensive, the only other solution would be to start a garden in a more ideal location.

Another reason for poor drainage could be a so-called hardpan caused by excessive application of chemical fertilizer over an extended period of time. The water-soluble salts are taken into solution by the rain water and leached into the subsoil where they combine with other elements, often iron, and form a rock-like layer that separates the top soil from the subsoil. Neither water nor plant roots can penetrate the hardpan within a reasonable time. During winter months this can cause herbs to frost-heave, during summer months to drown if the water stands too long on top of the soil. An organic grower should not have to face this problem unless he acquires property with soils that were mistreated by the previous owner. The first correction is, of course, to omit water-soluble chemical fertilizers and replace them with organic substances and compost. The hardpan itself has to be broken up by mechanical or biological means, the first being double-spading or sub-soiling, the second by planting varieties with long tap-roots which are able to penetrate the hardpan. After the seasonal growth these tap-roots decompose, thereby creating channels into the subsoil which can be utilized by successive crops. Pioneering plants of the herb group able to correct the situation would be fennel, root parsley, lovage, angelica, and horseradish.

202

In preparing an area for herbs, another requirement should be kept in mind as an important part of soil preparation. Quite a number of herb seeds are small and slow to germinate, while another group of herbs, especially all the thymes, grow close to the ground and hardly reach a height of more than two inches (5 cm). For both groups the soil should be as weed-free as possible and couch-grass entirely absent. If the future herb garden harbours this nuisance grass, and some of the best soils sometimes do, there is no other choice but to get a fork and rid the soil of the white, vigorously running roots by shaking them out of their element. While doing so, there is no reason to become annoyed at this strong weed. It not only is an indicator of good soil, but is by tradition considered a herb. The white roots may be washed, cut into pieces, dried, and used one teaspoonful per cup as a herb tea.

The other weeds should be discouraged by an early working of the soil. Prior to planting the soil can be hoed, raked, rotary-tilled, or cultivated at weekly intervals, thus preventing the sprouting weed seeds from getting established. Ploughing or digging the garden in late autumn aids in weed control and prepares a fine seed bed for spring planting. The pulverizing power of the frost works well for the fine seeds of thyme, marjoram, and others which can be seeded outside if the soil preparation allows it.

The same line of thought applies to rocks. For ease of gardening, especially rotary-tilling and seeding, all stones larger than a small egg should be picked up and deposited into a "stone-saving box" for future needs. Whatever stones pass through the spaces of a rake may be considered harmless.

Fertilizers

The section on fertilizers for herbs can be kept brief simply because herbs have kept their natural taste for manures and composts and never gain in herbal qualities if treated with water-soluble chemical fertilizers. The amounts of concentrations of essential oils in most herbs determine the quality. The formation of these oils is not so much dependent upon the earth but more so on cosmic factors of light and warmth intensities. All animal manures, used as fertilizing agents, support rather than inhibit the gradual build-up of oils and other ingredients in the herb plants. The most ideal manure in my experience is sheep manure, with cattle manure closely following. Remember that all fertilizers, above all artificial nitrogen, which stimulate and bring about a quantitative growth do so by making intense use of water. The plants are encouraged to absorb an optimum of watery solutions causing the plants to become larger and heavier. A herb grower, however, does not really want this because he has to dry the herbs after harvesting which means he has to pay to get rid of the water. And what remains after drying is actually his crop. Granted herbs are also used fresh and at times sold fresh. Even then a quality difference will be found in fragrance and taste.

Compost

Composting is a controlled decomposition of organic materials. It is usually done above ground and is used to preserve and stabilize plant nutrients. In addition, composting breeds beneficial soil microbes which, after reaching the garden with the scattered compost, continue their activity of digesting and converting crop residues in the soil itself.

Herb plants respond quite well to fertilization with compost; in fact, long experience has shown that compost is the ideal fertilizing agent for all herbs, though the stage of breakdown in the compost pile at time of application can vary with the specific plants. For the home gardener and all-purpose use, the compost should be made from a variety of materials (manures, leaves, weeds, kitchen waste) and should be well decomposed at the time of application. In northern climates it takes about a year to finish a compost, including two turnings. Less time is required in warmer areas. Detailed information on composting can be found in *The Rodale Guide to Composting*, available from Rodale Press.

Compost is a natural product easily made from garden and kitchen wastes and costing very little, as distinct from chemical fertilizers which are expensive. Compost provides food for the soil inhabitants who convert it into humus on which the plant roots feed. Furthermore, it makes the soil more moisture-retentive.

If you do not already make your own compost this would be a suitable time to start. After the initial preparations little is needed and the benefits are considerable.

Making the compost

Mark out an area at the bottom of the garden at least six feet (1.8 m) wide and any length beyond that distance. Drive in stout posts at the corners, leaving them about five to six feet (1.5 to 1.8 m) above ground level, and connect them with boards five inches (13 cm) wide and one inch (2.5 cm) thick, leaving spaces of one inch (2.5 cm) between them to provide ventilation. Lightly fork over the soil in this enclosure and lay down a base of coarse materials such as old brassica stalks and dead herbaceous plants. The object of this is to allow air to get into the heap from the base. Then add a six-inch (15 cm) layer of waste materials. These can include dead plants; bean, pea, and tomato haulms; dead flowers; weeds; soft prunings; discarded seedlings; worn-out cotton and woollen clothing (but not man-made fabrics); and old sacks. The kitchen can provide fruit and vegetable parings, egg shells (broken up), tea leaves, coffee grounds, feathers, and hair. In fact, anything that has lived.

Some fallen leaves may be included in a heap made in the autumn, but any real quantity of these is more useful when made into leaf-mould mulch.

Now, spread on a one-inch (2.5 cm) layer of manure. Farmyard is good and so is poultry, but since the latter is very concentrated, only half as much is needed. Cover this with a one-inch (2.5 cm) layer of soil. Repeat these various layers until the heap is about five feet (1.5 m) high and then top up with two inches (5 cm) of soil.

The heap will heat up to about 150°F (65°C), retain this for a few weeks, and then gradually cool as it matures. To ascertain whether it is working, drive a crow-bar or stout stake down and withdraw it. It should be moist and hot.

Rain will cool the heap and could prevent it from working, so on completion cover it with a sheet of black polythene—not tightly as this would exclude air.

When building the heap, you could stand a stout stake in the cente. On completion the stake should be moved a little from side to side to make a central cavity. It may be withdrawn occasionally for inspection. When building a compost heap, it helps if the coarser materials are shredded as this extends the areas for the microbes to work on.

Another good aid is to sprinkle some diluted liquid seaweed on each separate layer. This is made by adding a tablespoonful to a gallon (4.54 l) of water in the same way as it is used for foliar spraying plants during the summer.

If you cannot obtain any manure this is not a disaster for perfectly good compost can be made with QR compost activator. This is a herbal preparation and the powder is mixed with water. Instead of manure, sprinkle some of the solution on each six-inch (15 cm) layer of waste materials and cover it immediately with another layer. A spring or summer heap made with QR will be ready in about six weeks, whereas one made in the autumn would take up to 12 weeks.

Whichever activator is used, manure or QR, the liquid seaweed is most helpful. Where manure is used the heap will require turning sides to middle after the first month if a fine compost is needed, but with QR turning is not necessary. Depending on the weather, a heap made with manure should be ready in about five months. It is likely that you may not be able to complete a heap in one operation and in that case the partially made heap should be covered with a sheet of black polythene until more material can be added.

This is one way of making garden compost; there are others, but this is the basic principle.

It may be made in smaller receptacles but the larger heap will retain the necessary high temperature for a longer period. No doubt as you become proficient you will adopt your own modifications. The greatest enemies are dryness and excessive moisture but you can guard against the latter by covering the heap as has been indicated. Should it become dry, dismantle it half-way, water it carefully through a fine hose, and then replace the material in layers, watering each one, but don't overdo it.

Do not despair if your first effort is not a complete success. This will come with practice and in any case, the material could very probably be used for mulching.

Apply compost in spring, after digging or ploughing the ground. It should be worked into the soil by cultivation, hoeing, or rototilling within a day. If planting does not immediately follow, it is advisable to rototill or work the soil once more before setting out the herbs, thereby destroying young weeds that have germinated in the meantime and

Compost is at the very heart of the organic method and the base for your herb garden. In its many forms and variations, compost is a substance which gives fertility to soil and thus productivity to plants. If you are a successful compost-maker, you are most likely to be a successful organic gardener and herb grower.

Every shred of organic matter — leaves, vegetable wastes, weeds, manure from whatever animals you have — can go into the compost pile. You build it, turn it a few times, and forget it. Some time later you

spade it over, and it crumbles apart — a rich, humusy, dark-looking substance usually full of earth-worms. Smell it. All that waste and rot has turned magically into the sweetest smelling stuff in the world. The end product has become fertilizer for the next growing season.

The compost pile is the beginning and end of your operation. What happens is that by properly building your pile, you start a ferment in the pile that within two weeks creates up to 150°F (65°C) of heat. This heat kills disease organisms and weed seeds. It comes from the furious action of billions of soil bacteria upon the undigested matter in the pile.

at the same time helping to distribute the compost more uniformly throughout the soil.

Garden compost is undoubtedly the best soil fertilizer. It contains no harmful substances and is easily assimilated by the soil, where it is acted upon by countless micro-organisms and worms, and converted into the humus on which the plants feed.

When preparing a bed for sowing seed or planting, mix compost at two bucketfuls per square yard (metre) into the top six inches (15 cm) of the soil—no deeper than that. Then leave the area for about ten days for the ground to settle before sowing or planting. When planting, drop a spadeful of compost into the hole and mix it lightly into the soil. When sieved, it can be added to soil for seed mixtures and for a lawn dressing.

Mulching

The great benefits of mulching are still not sufficiently appreciated by many home gardeners. In the absence of mulch, the annual weeds grow apace (no self-respecting home gardener is troubled by the perennials as these are all dug out before the beds are used) and frequent hoeing is required to control them. True, these weeds can make a contribution to the compost heap, but the gardener's life is easier without them. This chore is avoided when the beds are kept permanently mulched. Furthermore, heavy rain can compact the soil, making life difficult for the plants, and the hoe has to be used again to loosen it.

In spells of fine weather the soil dries out and considerable watering may well be required to keep the crops moving; these seldom fully recover when seriously affected by lack of soil moisture. Providing this with a watering can is a laborious task and even if a sprinkler is used this has to be continually moved along to other beds. Wind as well as sun can cause loss of soil moisture. This surface evaporation is prevented when the beds are covered by a two-inch (5 cm) layer of mulch. In addition to all this, the mulching material is rotting and being carried into the soil by worms and other soil inhabitants and so its fertility is being maintained.

Indeed, if you are short on compost this could well be reserved for mulching between rows of crops. Winter mulching is also beneficial as it prevents the leaching of plant nutrients caused by rain and snow. The organic gardener never leaves the soil bare. After being cleared of crops at the end of the season it can be forked over, then covered with

209

Mulch is a layer of organic material, placed on the soil surface. It acts in several ways: as protector of the topsoil; conserver of moisture; guardian against weather extremes, and comfortable cushion under ripening produce. It also boosts soil fertility — adding organic materials by decomposing gradually into the earth's top layer and stimulating helpful micro-organisms.

When you set out to mulch a garden of any size, there are three factors to be conisdered: (1) how the material will affect the plants most intimately concerned, (2) how the completed mulch will look, and (3) how easily and inexpensively the mulch may be obtained. Organic gardeners like their mulch to be of old plant matter. Such mulches decompose into the essential life-giving elements of a rich, dark humus.

Plants should be mulched because that's the way they've been able to survive repeated disasters through the ages. Spontaneous mulching has been going on for millions of years. As the leaves fall to the forest floor, forming the basis of nature's mulch protection, they also decompose into a compost that makes up a rich soil-rebuilding programme of nature. Out in the open fields, dead foliage of the annual plants falls to cover the ground and protect it from the rigours of winter.

Composting and mulching go hand-in-hand and are, in many instances, inseparable. The aim is to build and maintain nature's complete soil pattern as far as possible. Mulching alone, cannot completely offset the shortage of fertility in the soil. Conversely, building up the fertility can be all the more reason for mulching also.

Mulch with whatever is cheap and handy. Leaves contain twice as much plant food as farm-yard manure. Sawdust will keep the weeds down and the soil moist, but be sure you add some form of nitrogen if you're going to grow a crop immediately. Try leaves, straw, hay, grass clippings, weeds or crop residues.

a good mulch for the winter. An additional advantage is that the mulch prevents the undue penetration of prolonged frost, and consequently the soil will warm up earlier in the spring.

All these uses of mulches are real benefits in that they not only save time and labour, but do much to maintain the fertility of the soil. Materials that can be used include garden compost, peat, leaf-mould, and sawdust. The last-named is particularly good for winter mulching. Laid down two inches (5 cm) thick, it will have rotted down by the spring, when it may be lightly forked into the top three inches (8 cm) of the soil. Raw sawdust should never be dug into the soil since this robs it of nitrogen.

Do not lay down a mulch on dry ground; always give it a light watering beforehand; and never lay the material up against plants. A good time for mulching is just after seedlings have been thinned out. The bed is always watered after this operation and then is the time to mulch between the rows.

Mulching is an integral part of organic cultivation and its value can hardly be over-emphasised. Incidentally, it is often surprising what good protection even a few thicknesses of newspaper can provide for young crops as an emergency measure when frost is forecast.

Propagation

After all above preparations and considerations are completed, the next step for the practical herb grower is planting. Like all other plants, herbs can be propagated from seeds, cuttings, divisions, and to a lesser degree layering. The chart opposite might help to classify them at a glance by listing only the most successful or possible method of propagation.

Sowing seed

Most herbs can be started from seed sown in the open ground in the spring. Others, the more tender, respond better to a sowing late in May when there is no longer danger from frost. But even these can be started from seed sown in boxes in March/April and planted out in June. The actual time of sowing seed in the open ground will, of course, depend on the location of the garden. Seed that can be sown outdoors in southern gardens would have to be sown under cover further north, although even in these areas there may be gardens well sheltered from cold winds and frost where outdoor sowing can be safely carried out. So, like much else in gardening, it is a matter of knowing your own local climate.

Propagation of herbs

From Seeds	From Cuttings	From Divisions
Anise	Lavender	Beebalm
Basil—*all var.*	Lemon Thyme	Chives
Borage	Oregano	Garlic
*Camomile	Pennyroyal	Horseradish
Caraway	Peppermint	Hyssop
*Catnip	Purple Sage	Lady's Mantle
Chervil	Rosemary	Lemon Balm
Coriander	Santolina	Lovage
Dill	Southernwood	Mugwort
Fennel	Spearmint	Nettle
*Marjoram	Tarragon	Peppermint
*Oregano	Winter Savory	Roman Camomile
Parsley		Spearmint
Pot Marigold		Sweet Woodruff
Sage		Tansy
Salad Burnet		Tarragon
Savory		Yarrow
Sorrel		
*Thyme		

* These seeds should be started indoors; all others do well if seeded directly where they are meant to grow.

The most common propagation technique is to start plants from seed. The seeds of many plants may be sown directly in the garden, but some must be started indoors. These are sown in seed boxes filled with a sterile planting medium. As the seedlings develop their first leaves, they should be transferred to small pots. Peat pots can become expensive, but when the herbs have achieved sufficient size and hardiness to be transplanted into the garden, one merely plants pot and all (opposite). The pot will rot away; the plant, hopefully, will flourish.

Herbs from seeds

All the reputable seedsmen offer herbs, and there are specialist herb farms where plants are grown for sale. A few plants could well be bought in to start you off, but for the most part it is better and much more fun to grow your own from seed. You will not require many of each kind as even a small packet will probably contain more than you will need.

It is not good policy to retain seeds until the following season. To remain viable, seeds have to be kept in controlled conditions and just throwing the partly used packets into a drawer is not the best way. Seeds are not expensive and the small economy in keeping them until the next year is just not worth the risk of possible crop failures. If you are growing herbs for the first time, start with a few and gradually increase the range as you become more experienced.

215

When sowing seed, rake the soil to as fine a tilth as possible and make a shallow drill half an inch (1.5 cm) deep. Sow the seed thinly, fill in the drill, lightly firm the soil, and water. Later, the seedlings are thinned out to growing distances as directed on the seed packets. Water after thinning out and then lay down a two-inch (5 cm) mulch.

Do not sow earlier than the required time since a crop failure due to a lower temperature than the seed can cope with will result in wasted time. The young plants will get away well when growing conditions are favourable.

One of the secrets of growing plants from seed successfully lies in selecting the right time for thinning out the seedlings. However thinly seeds are sown, the seedlings will be seriously over-crowded, and if left they will not be able to develop into good plants. Indeed, the whole crop could be lost. So thin them out to growing spacings as soon as they can be handled by a leaf (never a stem). The thinnings can be put on the compost heap or used to make another row.

Firm the soil around the retained plants and water with a solution of liquid seaweed diluted one tablespoonful to a gallon (4.5 l) of water and applied through a fine hose. Ordinary water will serve, but seaweed is good for all plants.

Aftercare

When the young plants are about four inches (10 cm) high, water the ground if necessary and lay down a two-inch (5 cm) mulch of compost. In the absence of this, use peat but mix a trowelful of bone-meal into each bucketful. This reinforced peat is a good substitute for garden compost. From June to September give all the plants a monthly spraying with the diluted liquid seaweed as mentioned earlier, applying it from a fine syringe.

Basil, although a hardy perennial in hot climates, is grown in Britain as a tender annual. Sow two or three seeds in a peat pot filled with soil and keep them in a warm place indoors. They will germinate in about 14 days and then the two weaker seedlings are discarded. Harden them off and plant out to growing positions early in June.

Fennel, another tender one, can be similarly treated. The annual, chervil, may be sown in spring and again in the autumn. Parsley has a reputation for being a slow germinator, therefore line the drill with peat, water this, sow the seed thinly, fill in the drill, and water again.

Rosemary, a perennial, flourishes better when grown in a spot sheltered from persistent cold winds. Lavender, sage, hyssop, and chives will prosper in any part of the garden.

To start herb seeds indoors is easier than you think. There are just a few rules to follow and steps to take. Above all, the herb gardener should stay cool and not get over excited if the sun through its mere presence seems to predict an early spring. Herbs to be started indoors for later transplanting are best started from seed no earlier than March; otherwise they will get too spindly, weak, or fall prey to insects and diseases. Each variety should be seeded in a separate container to allow for the varying length of time each variety needs to germinate. Garden cress, for example, germinates within 48 hours, while lavender might take three weeks. The choice of container is a personal one; but the chosen container should make it possible to plant the seeds in rows rather than scattering them over the whole surface area. This is, of course, suggested for a reason.

Anyone who has started plants from seeds indoors has probably experienced the decimation of his young seedlings, which suddenly mould away soon after germination. This is called damping-off and is caused by an organism which can come from the rooting medium, from an unclean container, or even from the air. To avoid this problem, the modern commercial florist or greenhouse grower either steams his soil or treats it with some kind of fungicide. Until recently the favourites were mercury compounds, which were sold as liquid solutions, diluted by the florist and then used to saturate the soil.

The organic grower employs other means, one of which is the planting of seeds in rows. Contact between seeds is thereby kept at a minimum, and a pocket of damping-off can be isolated or even removed.

Of course, to see an epidemic break out among the seeds, they must be visible. Seeds are sown in rows *without* covering them; the seeds remain exposed to the air. The rows should be at least one inch (2.5 cm) apart and about a quarter of an inch (6 mm) deep, the growing medium itself one inch (2.5 cm) below the rim of the container. After the seeds have been thinly sown in the row or rows, they are watered with a fine mist of water, the container covered with two sheets of newspaper, then placed in a warm area, preferably 70°F (21°C) or a little warmer. From then on, the seeds need misting with water about three times a day. If damping-off is feared or noticed, the misting should be done with a thin tea of camomile, which will help control the disease.

First choice for a growing medium should be finely milled sphagnum moss straight or mixed with crushed granite, or finely screened, aged

217

One of the easiest and most effective methods of propagating plants is by cuttings. Cuttings are parts of plants — leaves, stems, roots — cut from a parent plant and inserted in water, sand, soil, peat-moss, or some other medium where they form roots and become new plants. Plants identical to the parents are produced which means that cuttings are an excellent method for propagating unique varieties developed through hybridization or mutation. With a sharp knife carefully trim the lower leaves from a stem (left), then sever the stem (below), and insert it into a rooting medium (over the page).

compost mixed with equal parts crushed granite. Bear in mind that seeds started indoors do best in a growing medium which in itself has hardly any plant nutrients.

Once the seeds develop their first leaves, which in most cases should happen in seven to ten days, they need to be transplanted either into three inch (8 cm) pots, one to a pot, or into seedboxes with a minimum spacing of one and a quarter inches (3.7 cm). At this stage the little plant should have a single root, which may be tipped for easier transplanting. Set the plant itself into the soil deeper than it grew in the seedbox. Side-root formation is thereby stimulated. The soil into which these little plants are set can be a regular potting soil or at least a richer medium than that of the seedbox.

After four weeks the plants will be ready for transplanting into larger pots and from there, after another three to four weeks, may be planted outside any time depending on variety and weather.

Cuttings

As well as from seed, new stock is obtainable from established plants by taking cuttings from them. A cutting is part of a plant and will grow and flourish as easily as its parent does. It has the same characteristics and requires similar soil and the same cultural treatment. A cutting is very much a "chip off the old block".

Taking cuttings not only enables you to replace plants that are past their best at little or no cost, but is itself an interesting and useful operation. Plants from which you propose to take cuttings should be selected with some care. They must be healthy, growing well, and have given good service.

Fill some three-inch (8 cm) pots with a mixture of two-thirds soil and one-third sand to about one-half inch (1.3 cm) of their tops. Cut off lengths of about five inches (13 cm) from shoots of the current year's growth, cutting just below a leaf. Remove all leaves up to about one and a half inches (4 cm) from the top, make a hole in the sandy mixture, and insert the prepared cutting to leave the lowest leaf well clear of the surface. Firm round the cutting, water, and keep the pots in a frame or under a cloche.

Give them an occasional foliar spraying with liquid seaweed diluted one tablespoonful to a gallon (4.5 l) of water. Give them ventilation on mild days, but close up the frame or cloche at sundown or during heavy rain. They may take up to three weeks to root when, after being hardened off, they can be planted in their growing position. Although not absolutely necessary, it sometimes helps if the cuttings are dipped into hormone rooting powder before being inserted into the pots.

Divisions

Dividing older plants as a means of propagation and also rejuvenation is an old practice which can be used for herbs. It is the easiest way of plant propagation and the most foolproof one, mainly because it is done right in the garden within a relatively short time. The individual plant is dug, the soil shaken off, and the clump either pulled apart (chives, and garlic), cut into sections (hyssop, woodruff, tansy), or carefully separated (lady's mantle, all mints, roman camomile). Each section of plant with a good amount of roots is then treated and planted

221

as an individual plant. Sometimes one clump will give up to a dozen new plants. The spring is the time to do this so that the plants can become established before the winter.

Root division is a method of multiplying the number of plants by splitting mature plants into two or more smaller plants. Of course not all herbs lend themselves to division, but chives, for example, do. Simply grasp a bundle of stalks in each hand and pull them apart. Or, using a sharp knife, cut a large plant clump into several smaller ones.

223

Herbs from commercial growers

The novice herb gardener cannot avoid purchasing a variety of plants from a commercial herb garden or nurseries, especially those that cannot be started from seed, like tarragon and santolina, or others which are rather hard to grow from seeds, like rosemary, oregano, and lavender. Most nurseries will be able to supply at least the more common varieties of herb plants. A few growers also deliver plants to people who have no access to nearby herb gardens. The best and safest time to plant all varieties outdoors is May or early June, with the exception of a few hardy plants which may be planted in April or even earlier.

Customers of local herb gardens and nurseries have the real advantage of having freshly-dug plants, carrying them straight home, and planting them. These plants will need the least care because their growth will be in harmony with the season and accustomed to the weather.

Late summer is the time to pot herbs you want to bring indoors for the winter. A simple potting mixture is made by combining ordinary top soil with peat (above right), various rock powders (below), and gravel (below right).

Herbs on patios

Should there not be enough room in the garden for all the herbs you wish to grow, some could be grown in tubs on the patio.

Prepare the tubs by covering the drainage holes with a layer of crocks or stones and cover this with some coarse material. Fill the tubs to within about two inches (5 cm) of the rims with a mixture of soil and peat reinforced with a trowelful of bonemeal to each bucket of peat; water and leave them for a few days to settle. A tub will hold one of the herbs that grows to about two feet (60 cm) or a number of a lower-growing variety, but keep to one kind of herb. When the patio is not open to the sky some attention to watering will be needed.

If at all possible, room should be found for a bay tree. Although it could exceed 25 feet (7.5 m) in height, it may be kept much lower by judicious pruning.

Cover the drainage holes in your pots with small stones, then a layer of the potting mixture.

Indoor culture

For flat-dwellers and those with small gardens some herbs may be grown indoors. Although some could be grown in four inch (10 cm) clay pots, better plants would be produced in larger ones. Most herbs do like direct sun, and the window that gets at least five hours of direct sun each day is the best for your indoor herb garden. In the warmer environment, the soil will become exhausted sooner than in the open ground and a special mixture will be required. Make one up of four parts top soil, two parts sieved compost or peat, and one part each of sand and bone meal. The common rule of thumb is to use a pot with a diameter of one-third to one-half the ultimate height of the plant.

The main handicap of all indoor plants is lack of local humidity and some provision should be made for this. Place the pots in saucers containing a thick layer of pebbles and add water to just below the level of these. The water will gradually evaporate and so provide the necessary humidity. The water will, of course, require topping up from time to time. The pots are placed on the pebbles and must always be clear of the water. You'll do well to water the plants frequently and spray their foliage. These humidity measures will keep the herbs healthy and pest-free. Should pests invade, you can hand-pick the pests or spray them with soapy water. An occasional taste of a weak manure tea will keep the herbs well nourished.

Herbs can be simply transplanted from the garden to the pot, or they can be started from a cutting or from seed. Probably the most foolproof technique is to transplant a healthy plant from the garden.

Select a proper-size pot. The drain-hole in the bottom should be covered by stones, a bit of broken crockery, or a layer of sphagnum moss to prevent the soil from blocking the drainage area. Partially fill the pot with potting soil. Hold the plant in position with the roots spread naturally. Add more potting soil, tamping it firmly with the fingers. When you are finished, the surface of the soil should be about half an inch (1.3 cm) below the rim in small pots, and about an inch (2.5 cm) from the rim in large, six inches (15.2 cm) in diameter and up pots. If you put too much soil in the pot, your herbs won't get enough moisture when you water; too little soil and your herbs may drown.

When the plant is in the pot, thoroughly water it and leave it outside for several days, permitting it to establish itself. Do move the potted

Carefully arrange the roots of the herb in the pot, making sure you don't try to put too big a plant in too little a pot.

Cover the roots with potting mixture, tamping it firmly.

plant indoors before the first frost. Avoid any sudden temperature changes.

The plants will need the same treatment as all other house plants. They should be given as much light as possible, be situated away from draughts, and meticulous attention to watering should be given. On very warm days they could be put out of doors for a few hours to give them a breath of fresh air. During frosty weather move them away from the windows—especially at night.

229

Finally, give the newly potted plants a thorough soaking.

Growing herbs indoors obviates the necessity for storing them for winter use, and they will always be fresh. Of course, they will not grow as vigorously as in the open ground, but they will give a year-round supply of fresh herbs.

With the herbs established in your home, adding their fragrance and colour to your living environment, don't fail to add them to your meals too. Their foliage will only be fresh and ever-burgeoning if you keep cutting and trimming.

Insects and diseases

Up to this point insects were only mentioned as being necessary for pollination, and this is actually their main function in herb growing. All individual species of herb plants still have strong genetic resistance to insects; the less the variety has been tampered with, the less prone it is to insect attack.

Of the other insects, aphids could possibly attack camomile or sometimes dill, though by observation, I noticed that only a small percentage of individual plants are attacked. I never attempted to control aphids outside. It seemed that each time aphids tried to get established, the population of ladybirds somehow exploded and cleaned up the entire aphid colony. I bypass plants that still show aphids at time of harvest.

In growing herbs for culinary or beverage purposes, it should be remembered that *any* substance which would cause a residue on the leaves, will alter the flavour of the finished product and diminish the purity. So keep away from even rotenone or pyrethrum.

The above applies in a similar way to the treatment of plant diseases which are rare to begin with, in organic herb growing that is. Timely harvest is very important in order to avoid over-aging of leaves. As the leaves grow older, they show less resistance to disease and occasionally become host to mildew, especially if cloudy, moist weather persists for more than three days. For a small area it is preventive disease control to pick up yellow leaves from the ground after harvest or cover them with an inch (2.5 cm) of good compost. Furthermore, it is important to plant sun-loving herbs actually in a sunny spot, and, above all, keep good drainage in mind.

Harvest and storage

Don't wait until the last days of summer to think about how you are going to preserve your herbs. Not only will you work yourself into a dither trying to get them all dried or frozen before the first killing frost, but you'll have missed the prime harvesting time for most herbs. A little planning and thought at the season's beginning will enable you to make the best use of your herbs.

There are several ways to preserve herbs, but take into account what you want to use them for and when they'll be ready for harvest. Most herbs you'll want to dry; but some can be frozen or refrigerated. If you move your favourite culinary herbs to an indoor windowsill in winter, you'll have fresh herbs all the year round.

Most herbs for culinary use are ready to harvest just before the flowers appear on the plant. At this time, the plant contains the most oils and therefore the greatest flavour and fragrance. A good example of this is the nasturtium. Before the plant blooms, the leaves of the nasturtiums are a storehouse of vitamin C. The leaves should be cut at this time since the vitamin C diminishes as the plant blooms.

The herbs for drying should be harvested early in the season so that successive cuttings can be made. Harvesting perennial herbs late in the season not only causes a lessening of flavour, but the possibility of plant loss as well. Plants need the chance for regrowth in order to survive the winter. Do not cut annuals such as basil and borage too closely to the ground. This lower foliage is necessary for continued plant growth. At the end of the growing season for annuals, the entire plant can be harvested.

Herbs should be harvested in the early morning, just as the sun dries the dew from the leaves, since the oils are the strongest in the plants at this time. A chemical change takes place in the plants as the sun becomes more intense and the oils diminish. It is best to do this harvesting on a good clear day.

As soon as the herbs have been cut, waste no time in getting them ready for drying. If the foliage is dirty, wash the leaves, then shake off the excess water. If the plants have been mulched, it is not usually necessary to wash the plants before drying. This is especially important for basil which bruises easily from too much handling. The tops and leaves can be picked off the heavier-stemmed herbs such as lovage and basil. The reason for removing the leaves from the stems is to shorten the drying time—thus getting better flavour and colour. For herbs like parsley, leave most of the stems on until after drying.

Drying

Probably the most commonly mentioned method of drying herbs is the most picturesque. The mention of herb drying inevitably conjures up visions of crispy-dry bunches of herbs hanging from some convenient nail.

To dry herbs this way, one simply gathers the herbs and ties them in small bunches. These bunches are then hung in a warm, dark place for about two weeks until they are dry. One drawback to this method is that the herbs sometimes get dusty. Each bunch of herbs can be put in a paper bag, then hung up to dry, but this variation extends the drying time by several weeks.

This latter variation is good, however, for drying seed heads, such as fennel, coriander, dill, cumin, caraway, and aniseed. Care must be taken to avoid shattering the heads and scattering the seeds everywhere but where you want them. The care begins with the harvest. The seed heads should be gathered in the early stages of ripening, just as the seeds turn from green to grey or brown. It should be done in the morning, just as

The screen rack is excellent for drying herbs on a small-scale.

Herbs can be dried satisfactorily by hanging bunches around the kitchen which is both fragrant and picturesque.

the dew leaves the plants. Manoeuvre the seed heads into a large paper bag or paperlined basket, then clip the stems. When tying the stems, be sure to tie them into the neck of the sack so that they hang freely. Make certain that the seeds are perfectly dry before storing them since it takes seed longer to dry than foliage; give them two to three weeks.

Another variation on the air-drying theme is to disassemble the herb plants and spread the parts on screens to dry. You can use a window screen or one constructed especially for the task. Prop it up in some way to permit the air to freely circulate through the screen. Place it neither in the direct sun nor in some damp spot.

The fastest drying method is oven drying. The oven temperature should be 150°F (65°C) or lower. Herbs are placed on sheets of brown paper. The paper should have slits cut in it to allow for the passage of air. The oven door is left ajar to allow the moisture to escape. With this method it takes from three to six hours to dry the foliage. After a few hours the leaves can be easily removed from the stems, then dried further if necessary to ensure complete drying before storing. Basil and chervil are very sensitive to heat and a temperature of about 90°F (32°C) is best to dry these to retain their colour and prevent browning.

In storing the herbs dried by either of these two methods, an air-tight container such as a glass jar should be used. The herb must be thoroughly dry before sealing in your jars. Check after a few hours and then again after a few days to make sure that there is no moisture present on the inside of the bottle. The moisture indicates that there is still water present in the herb. If not dry, remove from the bottle and re-dry. The herb should crumble easily and be crispy when it is dry.

Leave the herb foliage whole when storing. The flavour is retained longer when whole leaves are stored. Crumble the leaves as you use them. Keep the dried herbs in a dark place to preserve the natural colour. Sunlight will fade the leaves and destroy some of the flavour. Label all containers before storage to alleviate later confusion.

Freezing

Freezing is a very simple way to store the culinary herbs for winter use. Gather the herbs at the specific times previously mentioned for drying, wash them if necessary, shake dry, and then place in plastic boxes or bags, properly labelled. Place these immediately in the freezer. The herbs can be chopped or left whole. They can also be blanched before freezing, although it is not necessary.

Do not defrost the frozen herbs before using. If the recipe calls for chopped herbs, it is easier to chop them while they are still frozen, since they break apart so readily. Chives, sorrel, parsley, dill, oregano, sweet marjoram, lovage, tarragon, and mint leaves freeze well.

Another method is to place the chopped herbs into ice cube trays filled with water. After freezing, place the tubes in a plastic bag, label, and store in the freezer. When needed just pop an ice cube with herbs into soup, stew, or casserole.

Fresh storage

When storing the fresh herbs in the refrigerator, harvest them as usual, place in plastic bags or special crisper boxes, and refrigerate. Herb foliage lasts longer if washed just prior to use rather than before it is stored. This method is especially suitable in the late autumn, just before frost.

Herbs can be your year-round companions. Get to know them; use them for their fragrance, their colour, and their flavour. Travel the road to herbal delights in your own garden and home.

7

The Companionable Herbs

Up to this point, the book has dealt largely with the traditional uses of herbs, but it has not mentioned the companionship most herbs provide for the other plants in the garden.

Herbs have special qualities that make them extremely useful in the garden. Just as they have both healing and culinary properties, they can be used in several ways to improve the garden.

The next, and final, chapter explains how herbs can be used to landscape the garden and how they can constitute an exciting, challenging, and beautiful garden by themselves. But herbs can improve the existing or planned flower or vegetable garden in a number of ways. That is what this chapter is about.

Using herbs and plants to repel or destroy insect pests seems to be part of nature's design. The conscious use of nature's design is largely based in folklore, since no one has yet sufficiently documented and stringently tested this part of the design to suit the scientists and academics in the field.

Herbs and plants which control insect pests are part of nature's varied tapestry. A few plants consume the pests, some simply repel them. By recognizing these qualities in different plants it is possible to put them to good use in the garden in more than one way. A common use is to companion-plant them. Another is to make liquid sprays from them for the benefit of other plants, and yet another is to make mulches for the same purpose.

Companion planting is a traditional gardening practice of placing plants that "like" each other in close proximity, while placing those that "dislike" each other far apart. The idea is to capitalize on plant symbiosis to bolster plant health, control insects, and boost yields.

Controlling pests and diseases

Wherever companion planting is practised, herbs usually feature. For example, in some countries where roses are grown for the perfume industry, garlic is planted amongst them. Not only is the scent of the roses intensified, but they are not so prone to black spot disease.

Very often no explanation is given for much of the practice, just a bald statement like "carrots and dill dislike each other". But any gardener who has seen a plant fail to thrive when it has all it needs in the soil, and has moved it away from its neighbours to flourish elsewhere, will know that there must be a reason—even if it cannot be explained scientifically.

That certainly was borne out in the fairly recent case of the Mexican marigold *(Tagetes minuta)*. Having cleared his land of daffodil bulbs, a Dutch nurseryman planted African marigolds *(T. erecta)* in their place, only to find that they destroyed the narcissus eelworm. He passed on this information to a research station which conducted tests on various species of the *Tagetes* genus.

Although all species proved to be lethal to destructive eelworms, it was the Mexican variety which was the most potent. Experiments were carried out internationally, and it was English researchers who found that its range of destruction was three feet (91 cm) and encompassed such persistent weeds as couch grass, thistles, ground ivy, horsetail, and convolvulus as well as fungus spores and root-eating pests—but it did not attack worms and other beneficial underground creatures.

Another bonus was enriched and clean soil. The research workers identified some of the active chemicals secreted by the roots, and these have since been synthesized to provide a natural pesticide.

As the *Tagetes* is a member of the daisy (Compositae) family, it is likely that other members also produce some of the same excretions although they will not have the quality or the quantity of *T. minuta*. But its close relative, pyrethrum, has long provided the basis for a natural, commercially produced insecticide.

It will be interesting to see if more discoveries are made along the same lines. The greatest activity of any plant's life-cycle goes on under-

Dwarf French marigolds and African marigolds are among the most popular companion plants, valued as deterrents to nematodes.

239

ground; there it is coping with predators, taking in food, and spreading its roots in search of that food, as well as influencing the chemical content of the soil by its own excretions. This is where the bulk of its self-defence mechanism operates.

By using home-made liquid sprays and mulches you not only save money, but you can be absolutely sure that there are no chemical additives in them. It is also a way of giving back to nature what you have taken. Even when you have made yourself a pot of herbal tea, rather than throw away the remains you can put them on the compost heap, use them as a mulch for pot plants, or add more water and feed that to your plants.

Nothing need ever be wasted. If your garden supplies more than your requirements of dandelions for their culinary and medicinal use, they can be composted and will return to the ground their valuable iron, copper, and other minerals. Alternatively, they can be infused and made into liquid fertilizers or folia-feeds.

Plants that trap insects

As in the animal kingdom, plants, too, have their predators. Nature deemed that some should have their own in-built protection, and an additional source of food. Small creatures and insects are trapped by various forms of tentacles, valves, and bristles and are subsequently digested and absorbed by enzymes in the plants.

One of the most widely known species of these insectivorous, or carnivorous, plants is Venus's fly trap *(Dionaea muscipula)*. This rather exotic plant grows in the peat bogs of North Carolina, although the only one I ever saw was growing in a low-lying garden in North Wales. Its hinged leaves close over any insects which alight on them, and are "sealed" by spiky bristles which fringe the outer edges. The aldrovanda, a European water plant, has similar leaves.

The sundew *(Drosera rotundifolia)* has leaves which are covered with tentacles which discharge a viscid acid secretion. As an insect comes into contact with the tentacles it is caught in the sticky secretion; in its efforts to escape it becomes more firmly entangled. The rest of the tentacles are stimulated and curve in over the victim, while the blade of the leaf becomes concave, so escape is impossible. The sticky secretion then turns acid and digests the insect.

Bladderwort *(Utricularia vulgaris)*, frequently to be found in stagnant

The Venus's fly-trap, a curious plant that does have herbal virtues, can do a small part to eliminate some plant pests. Any curious creature who

241

ventures into the fly-trap's jaws, triggers the botanical systems that close the jaws and begin the digestive process. The plant does eat insects.

242

water, although reared in pools and aquaria, has a different method of catching insects. Its leaves harbour small green bladders (metamorphosed leaf segments), and in each bladder is a small opening which operates on a non-return valve system. Insects can get inside, but are prevented from getting out by the elastic trap-like action of the valve. Pronged hairs then emerge from the bladder walls to absorb their prey—and there can be up to a dozen insects trapped at one time.

Yet another form of insect trap is provided by the pitcher plants, *(Nepenthes distillatoria)* and *(Sarracenia purpurea)* which have pitcher-shaped leaves. The *Nepenthes distillatoria* has a lid on the top of its leaf until it reaches maturity, when it opens. The base of the leaf then expands and its hollow partially fills with a fluid excretion. A honey excretion around the rim entices insects which then slip on an extremely smooth patch below the rim and fall, via downward-growing hairs, into the fluid.

Butterworts *(Pinguicula* sp.*)* are small, stemless plants with sticky leaves which attract insects that adhere to their surface. The leaf margins fold over their prey which are trapped by minute epidermal glands.

Companion planting

Aromatic plants play an important role in determining the presence or absence of certain insects. It is well established that insects are attracted to, or repelled by the scent of plants more than anything else. Some of those that attract insects do it for the protection of other species which do not excrete the oils which contribute the scent.

Other aromatic herbs, especially pyrethrum flowers, repel insects by their scent. Early repellents of mosquitoes, for instance, were oil of citronella, eucalyptus, pennyroyal, rose geranium, cedarwood, thyme, cassia, and aniseed.

No one knows why tomatoes, asparagus, and parsley are supposed to make a companionate threesome. But companion planting does work; yet very little formal research is being done on the phenomenon.

There is some scientific evidence for companion planting's value. Men are now working in related fields, especially the area of allelochemics, which is the study of plant excretions on one another.

Allelochemical effects may be a clue to why companion planting works. If plants excrete substances that hinder germination, help dissolve soil so roots can push through, and perform other functions, it is reasonable to assume that other plants can enhance the growth of certain plants nearby.

The late Dr. Ehrenfried E. Pfeiffer of the Bio-Dynamic Association and his associate, Erica Sabarth, conducted extensive tests on companion plants using paper chromatography, which is a relatively simple method of measuring the biological value of any product. Plant solutions are placed in a shallow dish, passed up through a special wick, and precipitated out in a circular pattern on suitable filter paper treated with a photo-reactive substance. The resulting colours and patterns give a "picture" of a single substance or substances in combination. The colour variations and the overall pattern show not only the quantity of chemicals involved, but the quality of a plant or plants as a whole. The results are amazing.

Companion planters believe that cucumbers like beans and that beans dislike fennel. Extracts from these plants were mixed and chromatograms made on them individually and in combination. The cucumbers, beans, and fennel alone each yielded a chromatogram of fine detail, good shape, and colour. When the companions—the beans and cucumbers—were tested, the resulting composite chromatogram showed an enhancement of the features of both. The peculiar bean design was still there, and so was the peculiar cucumber design, but both were enhanced, made stronger and more viable. But when the beans and fennel were tested together, the resulting chromatogram was muddy, dull, ill-defined.

Though these Bio-Dynamic researchers don't say why companion planting works, they do give credence to those who believe that it *does work*. It is still a mystery, but one thing is sure; everything is interrelated in nature.

When planting a companion garden it is important to get the companions close to each other. One way is to plant zig-zag rows, with the zigs and zags of, say, beetroots and onions tucked into one another. Another method is to intercrop, planting several companions in the same row, or certain combinations like fast and slow growing plants, shallow and deep rooted ones. You will find that your companion garden divides into loosely defined sections. The sweet corn, courgettes, and cucumbers might be in one section, and the strawberries, spinach, and beans in another.

Paths are best made between these sections, rather than between companions. Borders of wormwood, yarrow, and marigolds might be planted. They could also be interspersed, along with other insect-repellent herbs and flowers, amongst the vegetables.

Just remember that while cucumbers like peas, and peas like beans, and beans like potatoes, potatoes do not like cucumbers. The onion plants—garlic, chives and shallots—are well liked in the vegetable garden, except by peas and beans. Peas and beans prefer to be near carrots and turnips; carrots and leeks grow well together as leeks discourage the carrot fly. Tomatoes, asparagus, and parsley are a companionable trio as they fight each other's soil pests.

In her book *How to Enjoy Your Weeds*, Audrey Wynne Hatfield states:

> Lettuce and carrots are mates, as are lettuce and strawberries. Long ago an affinity was experienced by some old gardeners who recorded that strawberries had a curious liking for pine and spruce that was not shared by other plants, and when pine needles were given to them as a mulch, with token twigs and cones placed on their beds, the strawberry plants were more vigorous and their fruits had an excellent flavour. This observation is quite true, and these plants have another sympathetic companion in borage, which gives them an extra fillip. Borage is a helpful plant anywhere in the garden and is a generous source of potassium, calcium, and mineral salts in the soil and in the compost.
>
> The worst villains in any garden are the buttercup family, the Ranunculaceae, which give nothing and take all the good things available, and seriously deplete the ground of potassium and other elements. The secretions from their roots poison the precious nitrogen bacteria in the soil so that other plants suffer from their deficiency.
>
> It must be obvious that weeds react in the same ways as cultivated plants, secreting, excreting, and exhaling their characteristic substances which make them good or bad neighbours.

There are many examples of plants whose good neighbourliness is well established. Many, many years ago it was found that a sickly plant would rally when camomile was planted next to it; hence it earned the name "plant's physician".

The aromatic herbs are probably the most effective as they not only repel destructive insects in the soil and in the air, but have a marked beneficial effect on plants in their vicinity. The cabbage fly is one pest that is deterred by such aromatics as sage, rosemary, thyme, mint, and lavender in the cabbage patch.

But there are a few herbs which do not like each other. Sweet basil, rue, and sage should be planted well away from each other if they are to survive, and fennel is disliked by most plants in the garden.

245

Repellent herbs

The largest group of herbs fall into the category of insect-repellent plants. The second group are those which attract insects. Then there are herbs which can be used in crop rotations. Finally, there are herbs which can be made into pest-fighting sprays and dusts. Some herbs fall into more than one category.

Anise *(Pimpinella Anisum)*

See Coriander.

Basil *(Ocimum basilicum)*

Some herbs have an affinity for specific crops, and basil has it for tomatoes. It seems appropriate that a vegetable (or fruit, if you prefer) that tastes better when accompanied by basil, should also benefit from its presence in the garden. As they do not grow nearly as tall as tomato plants and would be dwarfed in amongst them, they could encircle them. As basil is a good fly repellent, it is useful in the house when grown in a pot.

Borage *(Borago officinalis)*

A two to three foot (60 to 90 cm) annual, borage grows from seed sown in spring, self-sows the same season and usually for years after, and flowers continuously up to frost with bright blue or pink blossoms. This is one of those kindly herbs that does good wherever it is planted: it attracts bees and is a pest repellent. Strawberries, tomatoes, and courgettes in particular seem to benefit from its proximity.

Coriander *(Coriandrum sativum)* and **Anise** *(Pimpinella Anisum)*

A pair of annual herbs that have a reputation for repelling aphids. These herbs seem immune themselves, and no pests seem to bother plants nearby.

Many herbs are worthy companions in the vegetable garden. Borage (opposite) is not only beautiful, it deters the tomato eelworm and improves the growth and flavour of neighbouring tomatoes, marrows and strawberries.

246

Feverfew *(Chrysanthemum Parthenium)*

This herb is disliked by many insects, even bees. It grows about one and a half feet (45 cm) tall, has yellow-green ferny foliage, masses of small, white, daisy-like flowers, and self-sows readily.

Garlic *(Allium sativum)*

Garlic is a valuable pest repellent. Although this spindly plant may not be the most attractive one, it has sufficient virtues to compensate. It is most cooks' ally, it is easy to grow, and it does not take up much space in the garden. It will be hardly noticed when planted amongst the raspberry canes or close to the vegetables. But if aesthetic appeal is important, the ornamental *Alliums* could be planted instead, like the golden garlic *(A. Moly)* or giant chives *(A. Schoenoprasum* var. *sibiricum).*

Plant cloves of garlic near fruit trees, cabbages, raspberry, loganberry, and blackberry canes or other susceptible crops to repel aphids, cabbage fly, and other pests. A pound (or half a kilo) of garlic bulbs, separated into cloves and set thickly in early spring here and there amongst your plants, will keep insects away during the following summer; they seem to create an immune area.

For year-round protection, so that grubs will not live and hatch out in the mulch under blackcurrant or gooseberry bushes or in the earth nearby, leave the garlic in the ground. It will self propagate. Some can be picked in the summer; the rest can be left to live on through the winter, to reappear the following spring.

Lavender *(Lavandula vera)*

The strong scent of lavender will protect cabbages from cabbage fly.

Marigold *(Calendula officinalis)*

As we have seen, certain marigolds, namely dwarf French marigolds *(Tagetes patula)* and African marigolds *(T. erecta)* kill nematodes, but only the pot marigold *(Calendula officinalis)* is strictly a herb. The flowers have a strong smell and taste which repels the asparagos beetle and, to some degree, nematodes.

Mint *(Mentha* var. sp.*)*

The mints are particularly good at protecting cabbages from pests; these include peppermint, apple mint, lemon mint, and spearmint.

Mint is a deterrent to the white cabbage moth in the garden and a tasty condiment after the harvest.

Mints are hardy perennials. Most have vigorous growth and spreading habits. A few rooted runners set near cabbage or broccoli should be enough to repel pests. Or grow a single large plant like Brussels sprouts in the vicinity (not too close) of an established clump of spearmint. One gardener I know tried this latter approach. Despite unfavourable growing conditions that year—a severe summer drought occurred—no pests came near the Brussels sprouts, whereas a half-dozen purple cauliflowers in another part of the garden, not near to mints (or any strong-smelling plant), were attacked by aphids. Apparently the spearmint protected the sprouts. You can also plant mint near the barn and henhouse door. Flies don't like mint, nor do rats.

The smallest member of the family, pennyroyal *(Mentha Pulegium)*, was widely used in the days when it grew freely in London. Gerard wrote of it being sold in the Mile End to get rid of fleas, and the royal households used it for strewing on the floor.

Oregano *(Origanum vulgare)*

Oregano is especially effective near cucumber, and marrow.

Rue *(Ruta graveolens)*

Rue is a hardy perennial about two feet (60 cm) in height, very attractive to look at, and very offensive to pests. Rue has powerful properties and very bitter, blue-green leaves. Start rue from seed or make new plants from root divisions. Rue spreads readily, and will help dispel insect trouble-makers amongst vegetables, flowers, and fruit. But do remember to plant it well away from sweet basil; they are not good neighbours. It is at its most useful next to raspberries and roses. This hardy perennial is not to be confused with meadow rue, of the crowfoot family, which grows wild.

Sage *(Salvia officinalis)*

The perennial herb commonly used for poultry seasoning, is about two to three feet (60 to 90 cm) in height, has pebbly, green leaves, and purplish-blue flower spikes in spring. It's a handsome plant that is visible in winter, and deters many troublesome insects, particularly from crops of the cabbage family.

Summer Savory *(Satureia hortensis)*

Although not as easy to grow as basil, and not as effective as a pest repellent, summer savory can control bean beetles. If you grow the savory from seeds, when you put down your beans you can then plant the savory seedlings at intervals in the same furrows. The mature savory plant is slightly shorter than bush beans.

Of course, in addition to interplanting summer savory, go over the bean bushes regularly, wiping off any of the eggs or fuzzy yellow larvae that appear on the undersides of the leaves. Later, clean up any of the beetles that might appear. It helps, too, to make small successive sowings of quick-growing beans, each in a different location. Probably this combination of controls will get rid of any bean beetles. Even though it is not a total repellent, savory is worth growing because it goes well with bean dishes.

Tansy *(Chrysanthemum vulgare)*

Tansy is a tall, hardy perennial that reaches four feet or more in height. It is coarsely handsome, with jagged leaves and clusters of yellow-orange, button-like flowers which dry dark gold and are attractive in winter bouquets. The old herbals always mention tansy. It was used for strewing on the floors of houses. In *Five Hundred Points of Good Husbandrie*, 1573, Thomas Tusser tells us which plants were most commonly used—basil, balm, camomile, costmary, cowslips, daisies of all sorts, sweet fennel, germander, hop, lavender, marjoram, pennyroyal, roses of all sorts, mints, sage, tansy, violets, and winter savory. The dried leaves of tansy sprinkled about—in cellar or attic—are a harmless indoor insecticide. Tansy also discourages ants; planted by the door, it should keep ants and flies out of the house.

Thyme *(Thymus vulgaris)*

In mediaeval times, before sugar was known, honey was the only sweetener and thyme was cultivated for bees. There are a number of varieties and they are effective as pest repellents, although probably not as potent as rue.

Many flowers regarded as merely pretty have valuable pest-repellent qualities. Almost without exception, these flowers are strong smelling but not sweet smelling, and insects find them overpowering and so keep out of their range. Nearby fruit and vegetables that might be subject to attack by these pests are thus protected.

251

Pyrethrum, often called painted ladies or painted daisies, is a perennial related to the chrysanthemum, but a more effective pest repellent. It has big, daisy-like flowers of various colours. One variety, golden feather *(Chrysanthemum Parthenium* 'Aureum') is grown for its chartreuse foliage; the clusters of small, white "daisies" can be kept sheared, if desired. Golden feather makes a good edging, eight to ten inches (20 to 25 cm) high for a path in the vegetable garden. No pest will come near it. One gardener reports having sown seed a few years back and now having dozens of plants that must regularly be divided and reset.

An insecticide of the same name is made from the dried flowers of pyrethrums. If you want to bother, a home-made spray can be prepared from the ground flowers mixed with water. Pyrethrum is toxic to many soft-bodied pests, but not to plants. In my opinion, its presence here and there in the garden is enough.

Attractant herbs

There are some plants which attract, or lure, pests to themselves for the protection of other plants, and many of these are herbs. They all play a part in successful companion planting. The idea is to plant the "lure" near the plant you want to protect so that the pests will gather on it. But the whole point of this strategy is lost if the pests are not then collected and destroyed.

Hyssop planted near cabbage will attract the cabbage butterfly. It will also increase the quality and quantity of the fruit if it is planted under grapevines. Nasturtiums and scotch broom will both lure aphids.

All this can become a little confusing, but the Companionate Herbal at the end of this chapter can be used as a reference when planning a garden. Meanwhile, there are some antagonistic combinations to be avoided.

Anise *(Pimpinella anisum)*
See wormwood.

Basil *(Ocimum basilicum)*
Basil, rue, and sage do not get along.

Pyrethrum flowers are decorative as well as useful. They are pretty in the garden and deadly to the insect invader. They can be planted next to plants you want to protect, or ground into an insecticidal dust that is harmless to humans and animals.

253

Camomile *(Matricaria chamomilla)*

Camomile in large quantities may be detrimental to the growth of wheat and onions, although it is helpful in small amounts. When grown near mint it will have a higher content of volatile oils, while the mint's content is reduced.

Caraway *(Carum carvi)*

See fennel and wormwood.

Coriander *(Coriandrum sativum)*

See fennel.

Dandelion *(Taraxacum officinalis)*

Dandelions exhale ethylene gas which stunts neighbouring plants and causes premature fruiting and flowering. It also absorbs from the soil up to three times more iron than other plants.

Dill *(Anethum graveolens)*

Dill, allowed to bloom, can reduce the carrot crop.

Fennel *(Foeniculum vulgare)*

Fennel is anti-social and disliked by most plants. It inhibits the growth of caraway, beans, tomatoes, and kohlrabi. Its own growth and germination, however, are inhibited by wormwood and coriander.

Garlic *(Allium sativum)*

Garlic, onions, and chives will stunt peas and beans.

Hyssop *(Hyssopus officinalis)*

Hyssop should not be planted too closely to radishes.

Onion *(Allium cepa)*

See garlic.

Rue *(Ruta graveolens)*

See basil.

Dill is a companion for cabbage, improving its growth and flavour.

Sage *(Salvia officinalis)*

See basil and wormwood.

Wormwood *(Artemisia absinthium)*

Wormwood can inhibit the growth of some plants including fennel, sage, caraway, and anise; it should not be planted near young plants or seedlings.

255

Herbal crop rotation

Including herbs in crop rotation is another way in which your garden will benefit. Unhealthy or problem soil can be conditioned or corrected with plants and herbs. The soil-benefitting plant should be planted, then cut and composted or dug under before planting the garden.

Marigolds, soapwort, and other saponin-rich plants like primroses and mullein can all be used as soil conditioners prior to planting. Clover and lupins will increase the available nitrogen. Stinging nettles make a rich contribution to the compost heap. Left to grow, they will encourage nitrogen bacteria while themselves accumulating nitrogen, iron, and other vital minerals.

Lupins also improve sandy soils. Some plants add humus, and loosen heavy clay soils and make them friable. These include camomile, stinging nettles, caraway, and flax. Scotch broom also supplies calcium. Dandelions will attract earthworms, create a humus where they grow, and contribute a wealth of minerals and nutrients to the compost heap. Valerian also is attractive to earthworms and stimulates the phosphorus activity in the soil area. A spray of its juice improves the health and resistance of other growing plants.

Mustard, radish, and turnip are considered "antiseptic" crops, and when turned under, are said to improve the soil and rid it of harmful organisms.

After the harvest

After you have gathered your pest repellent herbs, you can still put them to work in the garden. They can be dried, crushed, and then sprinkled amongst other plants, or they can be soaked and made into liquid sprays.

Powdered, dried pyrethrum flowers can be dusted on plants, or watered down for a spray. Oak leaves, oak bark, dry wormwood, rosemary leaves, and stinging nettles can be sprinkled around to repel snails and slugs. Dried tansy and southernwood leaves will drive away ants.

A mixture of aromatic herbs can also be successful, like rosemary, catmint, feverfew, and rue. The dried, chopped up herbs can be sprinkled around problem areas. Or they can be scalded with boiling water to release the volatile oils and the liquid used, after cooling. The dampened

Feverfew is another attractive herb that the garden pests avoid. It is a hardy perennial, surviving the coldest winters and the closest prunings. It can be grown in full sun or in the shade of other plants.

257

Wormwood can inhibit the growth of some plants so it should not be planted near seedlings. The dried leaves sprinkled on the ground will repel snails and slugs, while an infusion can be used as a spray to deter insects of all kinds.

258

herb mixture can be added to the planting mix when potting out other plants. Excess water is drained off, and can be diluted to water or spray on plants and seedlings. This combination is effective for repelling or eliminating aphids, ants, and other insects. Plants are healthier and sturdier and damp-off problems are eliminated.

The debris of herbs has equal value. For example, when cutting back such rapid growers as mint, use the cuttings to dig in under any plants that are particularly prone to pests. Even in the kitchen you will find food for the garden; the skins of onions make excellent mulch.

Sprays

Liquid sprays are as easy to make as a pot of tea. Put a handful of fresh herbs or a tablespoonful of dried ones in a pan, cover with about a pint (568 ml) of water, and bring it to the boil. Remove the pan from the heat, and allow the infusion to cool with the lid on. Strain the liquid and then dilute it with about four parts water. If it is to be used as a folia-feed rather than a root fertilizer it is a good idea to add a generous squirt of washing-up liquid, as this helps it to cling to the leaves.

Thyme can be made into a spray for flies. Rosemary and catmint are effective as general insect sprays, while garlic, onions, and chives make good sprays to control caterpillars and tomato and cabbage worms. A combination of several aromatic herbs, like tansy, southernwood, wormwood, and sage, can be made into a spray which will both protect plants from pests and benefit their growth.

The flowers of pyrethrum and feverfew make effective insect sprays, and camomile flowers make a useful liquid feed. The infused stems of horsetail, which are rich in cobalt, calcium, and silica, make an effective fungicide against mildew, mint rust, and black spot on roses.

Stinging nettles also make a spray to be used against mildew, black fly, aphis, and plant lice. They also make a good folia-feed. A stronger brew can be made by soaking the nettles for a few weeks until they have virtually rotted. The high content of iron, vitamins, and minerals released into the liquid make a complete plant food.

Old-time gardeners swore by flowers belonging to the Compositae family—daisies, marigolds, calendulas, pyrethrum—to rid their gardens of pests; they grew them amongst vegetables and flowers, and made sprays from them.

One of the best of all sprays is made with garlic, and this has been used for many years to control all manner of garden pests. In a report entitled "Garlic as an Insecticide", the Henry Doubleday Research Association, Braintree, Essex, recommends the following recipe for a spray:

> Take three ounces (85 g) of chopped garlic bulbs and let them soak in about two teaspoonfuls (50 cc) of liquid paraffin for 24 hours. Then slowly add a pint (568 ml) of water in which a quarter-ounce (7 g) of oil-based soap (Palmolive is a good one) has been dissolved, and stir well. Strain the liquid through fine gauze, and store it in a china or glass container because it reacts with metals.
> Try it against your worst pests, starting with a dilution of one part to 20 parts of water, then going down to one to 100, so you use as little as possible . . .

Lawrence Hills, founder of the Henry Doubleday Research Association, suggested the garlic spray could be the "new insect control the whole world needs". His article in *Organic Gardening and Farming* (September 1972) stated:

> David Greenstock, a researcher with the Henry Doubleday Research Association, describes a number of solvents and emulsifiers for garlic, including some that will keep the substances active on the leaves for up to 30 days. Others enable weak solutions to be watered on the land to kill underground pests. The emulsions were highly effective against cabbage, white, and ermine moth caterpillars, scoring 98 per cent kills, and without passing any undesirable flavour to the crop, for the insecticidal principle has nothing to do with the smell, which is gone in four days.
> In a laboratory experiment, the garlic solution killed 87 per cent of the pea weevils . . . At the same time, it spared the Colorado beetle, however, and this quality of hitting weevils and missing beetles appears to be near to that of nicotine, which is harmless to ladybirds and their larvae. But there is scope for a great deal of research to find the emulsifiers and solution strengths that will be safe for as many of our friends as possible.
> By feeding it to chickens, mice, and rabbits, Greenstock has established that all the garlic sprays are harmless to birds, livestock, and wild life. In fact, they improved the health of the experimental animals compared with the non-garlic-receiving controls, and an accidental outbreak of myxamatosis in the rabbits showed they had gained greater resistance.

The qualities of garlic that Greenstock has uncovered might surprise people not familiar with herbs and herb lore, but its effectiveness as a pest spray and a repellent companion plant has been presaged by the

Nasturtium is a pot-herb which does double-duty in the vegetable garden. Its leaves and flowers are tasty salad ingredients. It attracts aphids and other garden pests.

261

lore that has surrounded it for centuries. Horace called it "more poison-ous than hemlock", Homer said yellow garlic saved Ulysses from being changed by Circe into a pig, and a European superstition suggested that a runner could prevent competitors from getting in front of him by eating garlic. And even the lore of companion planting, a relatively recent body of knowledge, presages the discovery of garlic's insecticidal qualities.

As we have seen, of course, garlic isn't the only herb with such qualities. And such qualities, when added to all the other, more tradi-tional, qualities of herbs can mean only that you have more reason than ever to grow herbs in your garden.

A companionate herbal for the organic garden

A list of herbs, their companions, their uses, including some beneficial weeds and flowers.

Basil *(Ocimum basilicum)*

Companion to tomatoes. Dislikes rue intensely. Improves growth and flavour. Repels flies and mosquitoes.

Beebalm *(Monarda didyma)*

Companion to tomatoes; improves growth and flavour.

Borage *(Borago officinalis)*

Companion to tomatoes, and strawberries, deters tomato worm; improves growth and flavour.

Caraway *(Carum carvi)*

Plant here and there; loosens soil.

Catmint *(Nepeta cataria)*

Plant in borders; deters flea beetle.

Camomile *(Matricaria chamomilla)*

Companion to cabbages and onions; improves growth and flavour.

Chervil *(Myrrhis odorata)*

Companion to radishes; improves growth and flavour.

Chives *(Allium schoenoprasum)*

Companion to carrots; improves growth and flavour.

Dead Nettle *(Lamium var. sp.)*

Companion to potatoes; deters potato bug; improves growth and flavour.

Dill *(Anethum graveolens)*

Companion to cabbage; dislikes carrots; improves growth and health of cabbage.

Fennel *(Foeniculum vulgare)*

Plant away from gardens; most plants dislike it.

Garlic *(Allium sativum)*

Plant near roses and raspberries; deters raspberry beetle; improves growth and health.

Horseradish *(Cochlearia Armoracia)*

Plant at corners of potato patch to deter potato root eelworm.

Hyssop *(Hyssopus officinalis)*

Deters cabbage moth; companion to cabbage and grapes. Keep away from radishes.

Lovage *(Levisticum officinalis)*

Improves flavour and health of plants if planted here and there.

Marigold *(Tagetes var. sp.)*

The workhorse of the pest deterrents. Plant throughout the garden; it discourages bean weevils, asparagus beetle, tomato worm, nematodes, and other insects, as well as fungus spores and persistent

263

Horse-radish should be planted with the potatoes to deter the potato bug and to produce a healthy crop of roots to be made into horse-radish sauce at the season's end.

weeds such as convolvulus and couch grass. It also makes a pretty splash of colour wherever it is planted.

Marjoram, Sweet *(Origanum marjorana)*

Plant here and there in the garden as it improves flavours.

264

Mint *(Mentha var. sp.)*

Companion to cabbage and tomatoes; improves health and flavour; deters white cabbage moth.

Nasturtium *(Tropaeolum majus)*

Companion to radishes, cabbages; plant under fruit trees. Attracts aphids. Improves growth and flavour.

Purslane

This edible weed makes good ground cover.

Peppermint *(Mentha piperita)*

Planted among cabbages it repels the white cabbage butterfly.

Pot Marigold *(Calendula officinalis)*

Companion to tomatoes but plant throughout the garden. Deters asparagus beetle and other insects.

Rosemary *(Rosmarinus officinalis)*

Companion to cabbage, bean, carrot and sage; deters cabbage butterfly, bean weevils and carrot fly.

Rue *(Ruta graveolens)*

Keep it away from basil and sage, plant near roses and raspberries.

Sage *(Salvia officinalis)*

Keep it away from rue and sweet basil. Plant with rosemary, cabbage and carrots; but keep away from cucumbers. Deters cabbage butterfly and carrot fly.

Southernwood *(Artemisia abrotanum and A. campestris)*

Plant here and there in garden; companion to cabbage; improves growth and flavour; deters cabbage moth.

Sow-thistle *(Sonchus oleraceus)*

This weed in moderate amounts can help tomatoes, onions, and sweet corn.

265

Tansy is a handsome border plant and an insect repellent too, and is particularly good for deterring ants and house flies.

Summer Savory *(Satureia hortensis)*

Plant with beans and onions; improves growth and flavour. Deters bean weevils.

Tansy *(Chrysanthemum vulgare)*

Plant under fruit trees; companion to roses and raspberries. Deters flying insects, cucumber beetles, and ants.

Tarragon *(Artemisia Dracunculus)*

Good throughout the garden.

Thyme *(Thymus vulgare)*

Plant here and there in garden; deters cabbage worm.

Wormwood *(Artemisia absinthium)*

As a border, it keeps animals from the garden.

Yarrow *(Achillea millefolium)*

Plant along borders, paths, near aromatic herbs; enhances essential oil production.

8

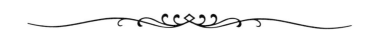

Landscaping with Herbs

Many people have a very limited concept of herbs as landscaping plants. They picture herbs as belonging on the window-sill in pots or in some corner of the vegetable garden. There are some, of course, who recall the intricate, formal gardens of days past, but most people fail to appreciate herbs for themselves. The problem with such a limited concept is that it robs one of the pleasure and beauty of herbs in the landscape.

Herbs are generally very easily grown and require less watering and attention than most other plants. The natural, internal chemistry that produces volatile and aromatic oils, resins, and tannins also renders them relatively immune to insect attack, and provides protection for other plants in their vicinity. Use of chemical fertilizers and sprays can upset this chemical balance and destroy those qualities for which they are valued.

The added pleasure of the fragrance they provide must not be overlooked. The hovering sweetness of lavender seems to float over and around other scents in the garden. Rosemary's spicy aroma makes the air fresh and clean. Few things are more delightful than a creeping thyme trodden under foot, or the fresh, cooling fragrance of mint or lemon balm brushed against in passing.

Herbs found their way into gardens in the first place because of their useful qualities. The mediaeval housewife often had a semi-wild kitchen or medicinal garden beside the door. The landed gentry had the stiffly formal gardens many people associate with herbs. However, the herb-

An English cottage garden with a beautiful herbaceous border in full bloom.

alist often gathered his medicinal plants from the wild. The point of this chapter is not to delineate a history of the traditional formal herb garden or to tell you what others have done, but rather to demonstrate to you that your home can be landscaped in a variety of ways—formal, informal, wild—using herbs and only herbs.

The herb garden can be formal or informal, contemporary or naturalistic, it may be on level ground or a hilly terrain, large or small, but the basic principles of garden design should be observed in order to achieve the desired effect.

The garden must be in harmony with the architecture. In planning a garden, the first consideration must be the house itself. There must be a one-ness with the dwelling, from which the garden design should proceed. A layout or plan should be made, designating the features or divisions that may be required.

Foundation planting designates the material required or desired to cover foundations and footings where needed, and to frame the building, tie it into the site, and make it an intrinsic part of the landscape. Generally, the outside corners of the structure form the starting point. The foundation planting should never be made in straight rows along the foundation, but should form a triangular or curving line, with the wider part at the outside, narrowing towards the entry or walkway. Taller shrubs are used in the corner itself, and against this would be placed lower shrubs with even smaller ones here and there to bring the mass towards the ground as it moves outwards from the building. The natural irregularity, varying shapes, and masses of the shrubs will overcome any tendency towards a stiff, regular descent and will be suggestive of a natural thicket, terminating at the edge of a lawn or ground cover area.

The size of the garden will, to some extent, influence its general layout, and only the larger areas will provide sufficient space for trees. The evergreen bay tree can attain a height of 30 feet (9 m) when allowed its freedom, and so could dominate a small garden. Large and small are relative terms, and for our purposes it has been assumed that the gardens described in this chapter are for suburban houses.

The garden area may incorporate a terrace or other level space to unite house and garden, an expanse of lawn, or ground cover, with beds or borders, or a series of multi-level terraces and slopes on a hilly plot.

Contrast is an important element in garden design. It may be achieved through size of divisions and material used, through colour, light, and shadow. Proportion, mass, and perspective are just as important in a harmonious and beautiful garden design as they are in a painting.

271

The knot garden at Old Mosely Hall, near Wolverhampton is a copy of a knot garden designed by the Reverend Walter Stonehouse in 1640. The garden is outlined with dwarf box hedges.
(By Courtesy of Graham Stuart Thomas).

Every garden has a mood, either by design or by accident. Be it ever so subtle, an emotional response is evoked by the vista presented to the viewer. The formal garden presents a mood of stately dignity, an expanse of low growing plants or lawn, framed with a precise hedge, bordered by tall trees or shrubs arranged in perfect symmetry and balance. The beautiful geometric patterns of Renaissance herb gardens are a classic example of formality in garden design.

Gracefully drooping willow boughs reflected in a quiet pool, surrounded by a delicate green carpeting of sweet woodruff, create a mood of quiet tranquility. This is a very different herb garden.

Flowering herbs in a sunny border, with their bright splashes of colour, create a mood of gaiety, while the deep shaded greenery, with sounds of water spilling over rocks, can provide the peace and coolness of the deep forest within the garden boundary. And a boundary there must be, whether wall, fence, or hedge. Whether large or small, there

Marigolds make a bright splash of colour in the garden and are an ideal border plant. Here they have been planted around a bed of thyme and caraway.

273

The herb garden pictured above is situated at Sissinghurst Castle in Kent. It is enclosed by formal yew hedges. The garden contains many unusual herbs such as orris root, clary and woad. The paths and garden seat are covered with aromatic plants, and nearby is a small lawn composed entirely of thyme. (By Courtesy of The National Trust)

can really be no garden in the true sense until the garden limits are defined. The word "garden" means a place apart, protected or enclosed. Rather than a separation, the boundary should be considered a union between home, earth, and sky. The treasures of the garden are displayed against a background of upward growth, carrying the vision skyward.

You may want to landscape your entire garden with herbs, or you may wish to plant herbs only in a selected area. One should consider the borders, the ground cover, the trees and shrubs; you may begin your landscaping experience with any one or all of these elements. Also, you must decide, before you go too far, whether you want an overall design that is formal or informal, contemporary or traditional. You may even want to consider a rock garden or a wild garden.

In the pages which follow, you'll find information on each of the landscape elements and on creating a design suited to you and your home. Hopefully, your eyes will be opened to some new and exciting ways in which herbs can complement your home.

In planning the herb garden there is some advantage when the area is virgin, as then you start with a clean canvas. First, draw up a plan to scale, marking out the various beds and paths. Then put it away for a day or two, after which you can take a fresh look at it, confirming or altering the plan according to your final decision. The interval will well repay any extra time this procedure may demand, for possible later alterations will cause disruption besides additional work.

You are now ready for siting the plants and here is where special care is required as many factors have to be taken into consideration. All the particular qualities of the plants must be borne in mind when planting or sowing seed to create an environment not only beneficial to the plants, but also one that is pleasant and peaceful to the beholder.

The perennial border

The herbaceous bed or border is a flexible feature and can be used to beautify a variety of areas in the garden: a space between hedges and lawn, a corner between garage and wall, or any other location that would benefit by a decorative planting.

For an attractive border, flowering from spring to autumn, materials should be carefully planned. Consideration must be given to decorative effect, size, habit, colour, texture, blossoming season, and fragrance. Hardiness and adaptability to soil conditions are important. Plants

275

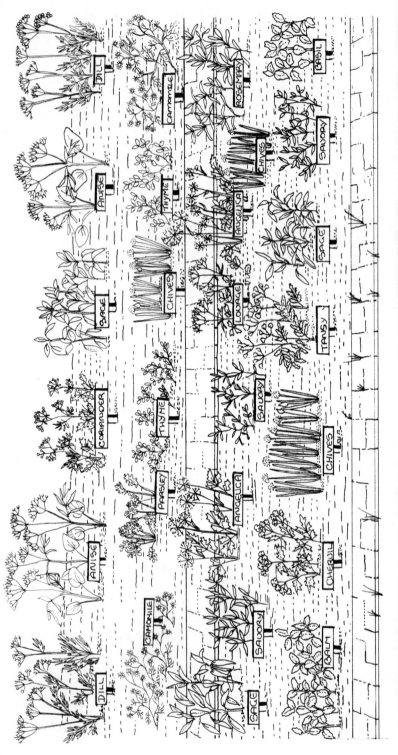

one interested in herbs. Relatively few homes are without some spot suitable for a border garden. A herb garden can be an unusual, beautiful, and striking perimeter for any size lawn, or a useful border for walks and drives. Its limited scale makes it easy to start and maintain. It should be in a sunny spot, preferably with good soil fertility and drainage.

Sketch a plan of the border and select the herbs you would like to include. In planting the garden, remember to put the sun-lovers in the sun, the tall plants at the back, and the low creepers in the foreground.

Perhaps the best overall approach is to start with small block plots for individual herbs, setting the whole off with low-growing edging plants. While the border gardens depicted here are all decorative, they contain many culinary herbs, making them suitable kitchen gardens too.

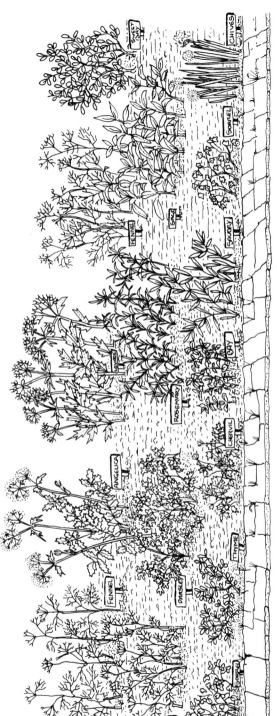

requiring moist shade cannot be planted alongside those sun-loving varieties if they are to thrive.

Taller plants should be placed to the back, the dwarfs in the foreground, and the intermediate ones distributed throughout the rest of the area. Arrange for interesting contrasts in foliage and pleasing combinations of colour. Intersperse the insect-repelling plants in the border to give protection to the others, and by all means have a few fragrant ones within easy reach for a pinch of their scented leaves as you go by.

Here is where we find many of the favourite herbs of long ago: tall mullein in purple, red, or yellow; veronica in shades of pink, lavender, or blue; climbing nasturtiums with their long season of scarlet and orange flowers; tall clumps of white, daisy-like feverfew; the little yellow button-like flowers of tansy; rue with its blue-green foliage, daisy-flowered arnica; and silvery cinquefoil. And no herb garden could be complete without lavender.

An edging may be desired, especially in the more formal designs. Silvery-fringed wormwood and dark opal basil are good for foliage contrast. Germander can be clipped into a neat hedge, and patches of fragrant thymes are always welcome.

Culture and care

The perennial border or bed has been called the "lazy man's garden" because if carefully prepared, it requires a minimum of attention for a beautiful display. Perennials can be expected to last for many years, and the bed should be well prepared prior to planting. If drainage could be a problem, the area should be dug out and a layer of coarse gravel and sand should be placed at least two feet (60 cm) below the soil surface. The planting soil must contain a good amount of humus, well-rotted manure, and about one pound (453 g) of bone-meal for every ten square feet (929 sq. cm), all thoroughly mixed.

A well-prepared bed which has been mulched requires a minimum amount of watering and weeding. Proper watering is important. Too

A kitchen garden includes only herbs of culinary value. The plot sketched opposite provides space for a variety of fragrant, lovely, and useful herbs in easily maintained rectangular beds.

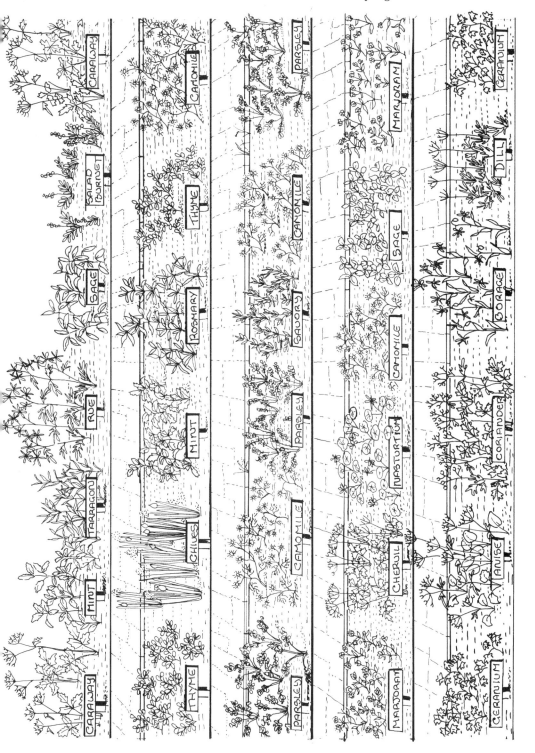

Santolina makes a lovely ground cover plant and is often used in knot gardens.

much water will produce leggy plants, lacking aroma and flavour. Spraying the surface is not desirable as it will have a tendency to bring roots upwards and keep them close to the surface, where they can easily dry out. Watering must be thorough to reach deeper roots. Give the plants enough water to stand in puddles on the surface, then don't water again until it is really needed. With a deeply developed root system, plants can stand long dry periods without suffering any damage. Morning watering is best, especially during warm, close weather, since damp foliage overnight may encourage and spread fungus diseases. A mulch in winter is usually adequate protection, and for lusty spring growth, a top-dressing of compost is beneficial.

280

Ground covers

The use of ground covers provides many interesting possibilities in creating pleasant little garden scenes within the landscape design. They can be used to define various areas by contrast of form and colour. A ground cover may be the best solution for an area too small for the lawn mower, or too shaded for a satisfactory lawn. Ground covers can be used to make dry banks or steep slopes more attractive and help prevent erosion.

Although lawns may be of any size, those in relatively small areas may not allow for the use of a mower to keep them short. A herb that would be a more than adequate substitute for grass is camomile, which is a dense, prostrate perennial with branching stems that can grow to nine inches (23 cm) if left untrimmed. When suitably planted, camomile will make a dense and decorative mat. When trodden on, its flowers and leaves give off a scent rather reminiscent of apples. Indeed, walking over a camomile lawn can be quite a heady experience.

Plants can be purchased, but they are easily and more cheaply grown from seed. Sow in seedboxes and thin out the seedlings to three inches (8 cm) apart. Camomile requires a rather sandy soil, so prepare the growing area accordingly.

In the spring, transplant the young plants four inches (10 cm) apart in rows at the same distance, staggering them at alternate spacings. Camomile can be cut with shears when the plants are about four inches (10 cm) high when grown in small patches, and with the mower blades set high on larger areas.

Other plants suitable for ground cover, serving a double purpose, include creeping thyme, lesser periwinkle, and sweet woodruff. These could well be grown between paving stones and other places where something is needed to soften a hard area.

Trees and shrubs

Trees and shrubs are divided into two main types, the deciduous and the evergreens. Deciduous trees and shrubs lose their foliage in the autumn. Many leaves go through a brilliant change in colouring before dropping to the ground.

The Rose Garden and part of the Rondel at Sissinghurst Castle. The garden is divided by walls and hedges of yew. The roses are mostly the true old-fashioned varieties interspersed with flowering shrubs, irises, peonies, some yuccas and as many pansies as can be crammed in. Also planted among the rose-beds are delphiniums, foxgloves and lilies. (By Courtesy of The National Trust).

Deciduous trees and shrubs can easily be transplanted in their dormant season without taking soil with the roots. Bare root plants can be obtained in nurseries, usually from January until about March. The roots are generally wrapped with peat moss or shavings and kept damp until planted. Many of the ornamental shrubs and most fruit-bearing trees are in this classification.

Evergreens hold their foliage from season to season. The leaves are shed eventually and replaced by new ones, but so gradually that the loss is not noticed. They include some of the most valuable plants used in landscape work, and are used for windbreaks, boundaries, backgrounds, as specimens and hedges. They vary in form from dwarf trailing ground covers to tall, towering conifers. Evergreens serve as a quiet green frame in the garden design to set off the contrasting texture of deciduous trees and shrubs and the bright colouring of smaller annuals and perennials.

Conifers require very little pruning, except in situations where they are used as formal hedges. If the soil is properly prepared when they are planted, very little care is required, perhaps an occasional application of compost, well-rotted manure, or bone-meal. Many are well adapted to poor, sandy soil. They are best moved in early spring before new growth starts, or early autumn after new growth has developed. Care must be taken to prevent injury to the roots, and plants obtained from nurseries will be in containers or balled and burlapped.

Trees

Because of their size and permanent nature, trees and large shrubs should be the first materials selected for the garden plan. Trees play an important role by providing shade, cooling comfort, and background material. Flowering trees provide beauty and pleasure with their colour and fragrance, and the fruits of some varieties are an added attraction. The sounds of leaves rustling in the breeze and birds singing in the branches, provide still another form of garden pleasure.

It is most important that selections be made carefully, to insure their suitability to the site and purpose. Trees generally are not readily transplanted from one spot to another. In a new planting, it may be very desirable to select one or two of the rapid-growing species to provide quick shade or screening. In a very wet or moist area, willows or alders will thrive, improving the drainage, while the silver birch can add beauty to the lawn area.

283

Shrubs

Shrubs are selected for placement in borders, background, and foundation plantings. Size, form, and texture must be considered in relation to placement. An occasional evergreen conifer in a shrub border can provide a pleasing focal point. Sun-loving plants, such as the juniper and rosemary, should not be placed where shading of larger varieties would be detrimental.

Low, muggy areas where drip from overhang causes dampness, should be reserved for plants that will thrive or at least tolerate these conditions. An alder or creeping barberry might be placed in such an area.

When young shrubs are set out, ample space should be provided for their ultimate growth. These gaps can be filled in with perennial plants, which can be relocated when maturing growth begins to crowd them.

Planting and care

Plants may be purchased from nurseries in containers, balled and burlapped or bare-root. Container plants can be set out at any time. Transplants should always be protected against wind and sun for a period of

An attractive garden all year round is a joy to behold. The following varieties are beautiful for months on end and are edible or fragrant, too. In the grey group are English or French thyme, lavender, southernwood, and other artemisias, rue, horehound, and sage. The herbs which give greenery to the winter scene are on a par with the grey types. Beginning with edging material, the gardener has the creeping thymes and bedstraw. Other evergreen herbs include burnet, germander, green santolina, hyssop, and rosemary.

A picturesque combination of the grey and the green herbs, will give effectiveness with the varied shades and textures of their foliage.

Use winter herbs for rock gardens or on difficult slopes, especially if the terrace is in full view of a window. Do not overlook the possibilities of planting herbs near the door, or by the side of rear steps down an embankment.

284

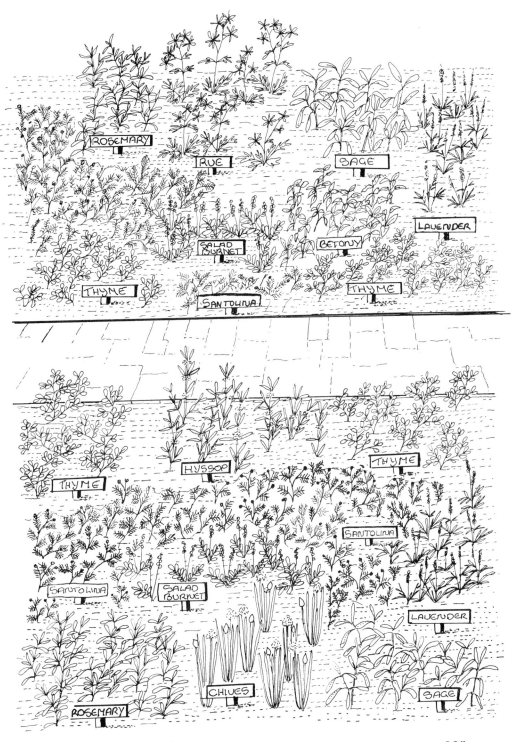

285

Traditional knot and herb gardens surround a perfect example of a moated, timbered Sixteenth Century

time. Bare-root plants should be kept moist until they are put in the ground. Roots and soil of burlapped plants should also be kept moist. These are best planted during the dormant period.

Dig a hole large enough for the roots to spread out without bending or crowding. Check the drainage. To do this, fill the hole with water. If it seeps out fairly fast, drainage is good. If it remains for any length of time, steps will have to be taken to improve the drainage. Dig much deeper, removing sub-soil and replacing it with sharp sand or gravel. In any case, prepare the planting soil according to the needs of the individual plant. Organic materials, composted leaf-mould, and well-rotted manure should be mixed into the soil at the bottom of the hole. Chemical fertilizers should never be used on herbs. Add sand or humus, according to the type of soil. It is better and easier to properly prepare soil before planting than to try to correct it later.

Set the tree or shrub at the same level that it was growing before. Burlap need not be removed or loosened; it will rot away quickly. Fill around roots with prepared soil until it is about three-quarters full. Flood with water to settle any air pockets, then fill level with the surface of the ground. A depression may be made in the soil in a ring at the outer edge to help hold water, but it should drain away from the trunk or stem. Thoroughly saturate the soil, then provide temporary shading or shelter for the newly transplanted material.

During the first growing season, water with extra care. Do not allow the plants to dry out during the spring and summer growing season. Less watering is required in early autumn to help harden the plants for winter. Evergreens should not go into a winter with dry soil around their roots.

The formal garden

This is the easiest of the herb gardens to lay out. It is made up of squares, rectangles, and other quite intricately designed beds. Some take the form of mazes, labyrinths, or knots, but all are precise and wholly symmetrical.

The plants used for these beds are mainly the lower-growing ones, sometimes surrounded by low trimmed hedges. All of these are pruned so as not to mar the general setting.

A circular pattern may be used with walks radiating from the centre

One of the most curious garden forms is the labyrinth or maze. Plants are arranged as hedges to create a long, winding path or passage. Perhaps the simplest form would be a spiral from the outer perimeter of the garden to the centre. The idea is to offer the opportunity for a long, interesting stroll in a limited area. The form had its greatest popularity in the Fifteenth and Sixteenth Centuries, but still survives today.

There is some question as to the difference between labyrinths and mazes. Some people say that the maze is planted with low bushes, while the labyrinth is planted with hedges, taller than a man; another says that the maze forces the stroller to make choices at intersections and risk cul-de-sacs, while the labyrinth offers no choice, just a single route. Whether or not the latter distinction was recognized by the early landscape designers is questionable, since both of the old designs above were labelled labyrinths.

The most interesting of these gardens always included some herbs and was often completely composed of herbal plants.

like spokes of a wheel. Designs may be adapted from some of the early renaissance gardens where the geometrics used formed a knot design as the focal point in the pattern.

For the formal garden, symmetry and perfect balance are essential. Elements of equal size and weight balance each other. They must be neat, trimmed, and precise. Plants are grown within the beds formed by the walks. Lower growing plants are placed adjacent to the central walk, with taller varieties radiating outwards. The varied symmetrical forms of coniferous evergreens make them adaptable to the formal garden, as backgrounds, and borders. Shrubs and plants with irregular growth habits will need pruning or symmetrical arrangement.

The variety of texture, mass, and colour available with herbs creates interesting contrasts and gives definition to the overall design. These elements must also be considered in producing the symmetry and balance required. The formal garden is usually bordered by a trimmed hedge. Individual beds may be defined by neatly trimmed, low-growing plants.

Herbs for the formal garden

The choice of plant material is governed by individual taste or preference, climate, and availability.

Traditionally, those used for these formal beds included basil, balm, sweet marjoram, hyssop, bergamot, mint, rue, sage, lovage, and lavender, but there is nothing to prevent you from substituting others of your own preference. Also recommended are those plants with grey and silver foliage, such as betony, woolly thyme, and antennaria. Dwarf sage and French thyme could also be grown there. For deep green, there is winter savory and English thyme to add variety of colours and foliage.

For year-round beauty, the perennial herbs must form the framework of the garden, allowing areas for the annuals desired to be planted in their season. Plan carefully the arrangement of plant materials according to size, texture or mass, and colour. Arrange foliage colours to provide interesting contrasts, silver-grey against red or bronze, dark greens to accentuate variegated or golden-green colours.

Among the tall, grey-green plants, we find the lavenders, wormwood, mugwort, horehound, sage, and marjoram. Deep greens can be found in winter savory, English thyme, white yarrow, green santolina, germander, and rosemary. Rue has a definite blue-green colouring.

A "parterre" is the name given to a very large knot garden. This superb example is at Oxburgh Hall, Swaffham, Norfolk. It is a copy of a French garden circa 1845, and thousands of plants are needed to fill it. Some of the beds are planted with silvery cotton lavender and others with blue rue. (By Courtesy of The National Trust)

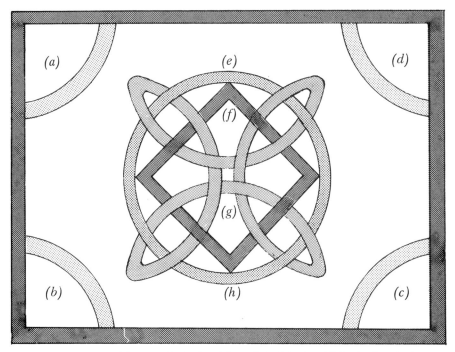

*(a) culinary corner, (b) aromatic herbs, (c) medicinal herbs, (d) herbs for dyeing,
(e) grey santolina, (f) green santolina, (g) lavender, (h) white thyme.*

*The knot garden is an old European ornamental garden form which was
extremely popular in the Sixteenth Century. The idea was to arrange
textures and colours of foliage in a manner that produced the appearance of cords looping over and under one another. Many of the plants
used were herbs. Today, the knot garden is largely a curiosity, cultivated
in botanic gardens and the gardens of stately homes.*

*During mediaeval times, the garden was utilitarian. The beauty of
the garden was the function of the plants, not the form. But as the
Renaissance swept Europe, it touched and shaped landscape architecture as it did other facets of life. The French, especially, developed
palatial estates with elaborate and ornate gardens. A notable quality of
the new garden form was that it was viewed to its best advantage from
a terrace or second-floor window.*

*The knot garden, plotted above, is a Sixteenth Century design,
planted with lavender, and green and grey santolinas. The corners are
planted with scented, culinary, and medicinal herbs.*

*The knot form spread, evolved, and became more elaborate. There
was the open knot, a loosely stitched creation with floral herbs spotted
in the open loops. There was the closed knot, a winter and summer*

garden formed of closely planted evergreen herbs. As the form reached its zenith, the typical knot gardens were plotted in groups of four, either marking the corners of a larger and more varied garden, or forming the quarters of a larger square.

In designing and plotting a knot garden, it is vital to plan every sweep to scale, colouring in each different herb so you see the over-and-under effects. Plotting the design on graph paper and on a corresponding grid on the planting site will ease the task of tracing the design (using sand or lime) for actual planting. Set out actual plants for your knot garden rather than trying to start from seeds. Suggested plants include germander, hyssop, wormwood, winter savory, and boxwood. The low hedges of herbs should be trimmed regularly.

Variegated leaves can be found among the scented geraniums. Dwarf variegated sage leaves are grey-green and white with accents of purple. Variegated mint leaves are green and yellow, with a reddish stem. Golden thyme has gold-tinged leaves in winter and spring; silver thyme leaves are green, edged in silvery white. Both of these are low, upright thymes. Golden lemon thyme is a creeper with golden-green leaves. Most of the other culinary herbs are in the medium green colour ranges.

Plants that lend themselves to clipping into hedges include germander, grey and green santolina, hyssop, lavender, and southernwood. By careful selection the garden can be as colourful and harmoniously designed as a Persian carpet.

Contemporary garden design

Home gardens usually consist of a rectangular lawn bordered on two sides by beds of hardy herbaceous perennial plants and/or rose bushes, and possibly a shrub bed. Vegetables and fruit, where grown, are sited at the end of the area away from the purely decorative garden. As a rule few herbs are grown.

Without altering the general design, this garden may be much improved by the introduction of suitable herbs. They are themselves decorative, so would not bring a discordant note to the environment and, when in flower, would add to the general display. But they have additional qualities none the less valuable. They have an aroma which brings quite another feature to the area.

Rosemary, the thymes, lavender, sweet marjoram, basil, and bergamot all contribute aromas that float in the air to make a stroll around an even more pleasurable experience. Many herbs are excellent pest repellents and in that way help to keep the garden healthy. For this reason, they have an important place in the vegetable bed. And not only there. Chives grown among the rose bushes will deter black spot. Garlic is an excellent pest repellent and may also be grown with the roses to advantage. Sweet marjoram should be grown in all the beds. A hedge of rosemary or lavender will provide a pleasantly scented and productive barrier to screen off the vegetable growing area.

Areas for outdoor living and dining flow out from the dwelling, becoming an integral part of the house itself. Shade here might be provided by the wide-branching silver birch.

293

The herb garden at Hardwick Hall, Chesterfield, Derbyshire, shown above, contains hyssop, valerian, mercury, adder's tongue, yarrow, camomile, comfrey, elder and many other interesting and unusual herbs. (By Courtesy of The National Trust)

This secluded garden shows the qualities of the informal herb garden. The herbs are harmoniously arranged without being rigidly structured. It is a pleasant retreat.

The informal garden

All things that are found in formal gardens are suitable for use in informal design, the difference being in the manner in which they are arranged. Rather than the symmetrical relationship seen in the formal plan, the informal garden is casual in effect, yet by no means does it come into existence accidentally. It must be carefully ordered and planned, bringing into mutual relationship the various characteristics of the garden situation. It does not imply a naturalistic handling of existing materials in the sense of unkempt wilderness or jungle conditions.

The formal garden can be designed with compass and ruler, but the art in informal design is one that conceals the design. It requires strict discipline applied in such a manner that the resulting effect is graceful charm and ease. It might be likened to milady's coiffure; they fussed and worked with her hair for three hours, so it would look casual!

The individual peculiarity of each garden situation will suggest the manner in which it can best be incorporated into the design. Existing trees and shrubs, irregularities in land contours, a rock wall, or rustic fence can all be used to create a design of unique beauty. The transition from house to garden must be a uniting link; all elements are related to the whole.

In the informal garden, there exists the fascination of the unexpected, apparently unplanned feature. It might be an enchanting rockery arranged with tiny creepers, delightfully scented lavenders and delicate blossoms, or perhaps a small pool reflecting light, airy branches, with bright green arbutus trailing over the banks. A small stepping-stone path may lead to a wild garden of natural plants in a shady, woody area.

Straight rows of border plants, precise beds, and trimmed hedges have no place here. Arrangement of plant material must allow for the natural plant forms to complement and contrast with each other.

The informal garden does not of itself mean less work, but it will provide a much more natural environment. It is much less obviously contrived, and furnishing it calls for knowledge and skill.

This may not be easy for the beginner, but in time much will be learned about the nature and characteristics of the plants and experience will bring more understanding of them. Order and discipline are just as important as in the formal garden; the significant difference is that they are not so apparent.

Rock gardens

Rock gardens are primarily used for the growing of alpines and other small plants and herbs which cannot be properly grown in the herbaceous border. It is important, therefore, to create the growing conditions required in a pleasing and natural arrangement. As with other features,

Rocks and herbs go together, whether as a consequence of naturally rocky terrain or of the gardener's contrivance.

There is always a place to grow herbs. Here they have been planted in beds against the cloisters of Beaulieu Abbey, and some of the harder species are growing out of the old walls, themselves.

the rock garden must be an integral part of the landscape, in harmony with the surroundings.

A naturally uneven, rocky terrain creates a perfect setting for a rock garden. Slopes and banks are ideal for arrangements of rocks and plants. A terraced rock garden between two levels can be most attractive. Rocks and rock-loving plants blend and contrast with each other in a beautiful, natural way, each emphasizing the best qualities of the other.

A pathway leading to informal stone steps, up and over a sloping bank, can be a perfect setting for clusters of small plants set among rocks on either side. A dwarf sage or clumps of dark green savory can contrast with silvery, silky wormwood trailing over a step. Creeping mats of thyme and Corsican mint planted in crevices and between the stepping stones give off their delightful scents underfoot, while the fragrance of lavender pervades the air.

In the formal landscape

Generally, most rock gardens are considered informal or naturalistic in design. With careful planning and arrangement, they can, however, be included in the formal landscape. The outer edge of a small lawn area, with a background or boundary planting of shrubs and trees, could be an appropriate location.

A low semi-circular formation of rocks can be arranged, with a small deciduous tree behind to cast light shadows over the rockery. Perhaps a hawthorn could be used here. A group of nicely spaced, low-growing junipers could frame the crescent of rocks. Well-chosen alpines and rock plants could be set neatly among the rocks. Careful placement and balance is needed to produce an arrangement that will be in harmony with the rest of the garden design.

Building the rockery

The rockery should be in proportion to the remainder of the garden so that it does not mar the balance of the general design. The range of plants that it can grow is limited, but for all that it can be an attractive and productive area.

To be of lasting use it must be properly erected. It should face east so that the plants are not exposed to direct afternoon sun. Good drainage

is vital as the plants are grown in separate pockets of soil, and if these lie wet after periods of rain there is a decided risk that some of the plants will rot.

If you do not have a natural mound in the garden, make one. Dig out an area to a depth of about one foot (30 cm) and half-fill the hole with brick or stone rubble, plus some sand, and put the hose on this foundation to wash in the sand. Then throw a good layer of soil on it, watering this again to get rid of any air pockets.

Repeat this until the mound is the required size, mixing plenty of compost into the top six inches (15 cm). Leave it for a time to settle before putting in the rocks. If you can possibly obtain any local ones, these will contribute a more natural effect. Do not use small pieces of rock. In nature, the greater part of rocks is below ground level and this arrangement must be observed when you place your rocks. They should slope downwards and inwards, otherwise they could become displaced by heavy continuous rain. This also allows rain to drain off into the soil. Leave spaces between them for the plants. When all the rocks have been placed, leave the completed mound to settle and for the soil and rocks to become a whole unit.

You could plant an evergreen shrub on the top. Not only will this do well in the full sun, but it will provide some shade.

Low-growing herbs for the rockery include lady's mantle, woodruff, thyme and lemon thyme, winter savory, Roman camomile, dandelion, horsetail, and dwarf nasturtiums. All these are perennial. You could also include some annuals, but these would have to be re-sown each year.

Provided they would marry with the general garden design, the rockery could be flanked with a few taller growing perennials such as rosemary, sage, goldenrod, and sorrel.

The wild garden

Suitable materials for a wild garden are dependent upon the area in which the garden is located. In its truest sense, it is a collection of ecologically correct plants, native to the area.

Flowering thyme (opposite) tumbling over rocks makes a very pretty and aromatic plant for the rock garden.

With a wild garden, all seems right, for in spite of the apparent disarray there is a harmony and balance that brings a feeling of peace and serenity. This may appear a strange contradiction, but go for a walk in the wild countryside and experience it for yourself. Fundamentally, man is a creature of nature.

The wild garden differs from the informal one in that while there may be paths, there are no separate beds. The whole area is a unit containing various kinds of herbs, all flourishing and benefiting from the proximity of their neighbours. Plants are grouped in colonies of like species; varieties and colours are not mixed.

Hence, do likewise. Draw up a plan, marking the positions of the plants you intend using. Regard should be given to appropriate plant associations and reference to the chapter on *The Companionable Herbs* and the section on *The Informal Garden* in this chapter will help.

Only perennial herbs should be grown, so as not to disturb the general display. The plants will assume their natural habits and over-crowding will be controlled when various herbs are cut for use or for drying and storage. The great thing is to let them develop freely.

Herbs originated in the wild and when cultivated in home gardens will not be robbed of their natural vigour by intensive breeding. They should settle down in your wild garden fairly quickly.

Your object should be to establish a piece of natural country, and you will find the operation one of absorbing interest. Remember, you may always make improvements if you eventually find that in spite of your care some of the plants have been wrongly sited.

Obtaining plant material

Many herbs and native plants can be purchased at nurseries. In most areas, there is at least one grower who specializes in collecting and propagating the native plants that can be adapted to the garden environment. Be sure to have the proper botanical name for the plant you desire. There may be several common names for one plant, and several different plants may have the same or very similar common names, but there is one proper botanical name for each plant. Seeds may be available from various speciality seed suppliers by mail.

Arboretums, botanic gardens, and wild-life preserves have many outstanding collections of native shrubs, trees, and wild flowers, either in a natural setting or landscaped, Books, pamphlets, and leaflets on native plants can be studied to help identify plants found in the wild.

A beautiful wild garden using a natural stream, with herbs and other plants planted in amongst the rocks and on the banks.

Collecting wild plant material can become a fascinating hobby. A few basic preparations can turn an ordinary trip into an interesting adventure. A supply of small sandwich bags, staples, notebook, pencil, and clippers are the tools required. When an interesting plant is encountered on a country roadside, or nearby wood, a few notes or sketches should be

The circular herb garden is a popular traditional form. For a small garden, an old wagon wheel can be used to delineate the beds. A larger garden could have gravel paths segmenting it and leading to a central statue or sundial.

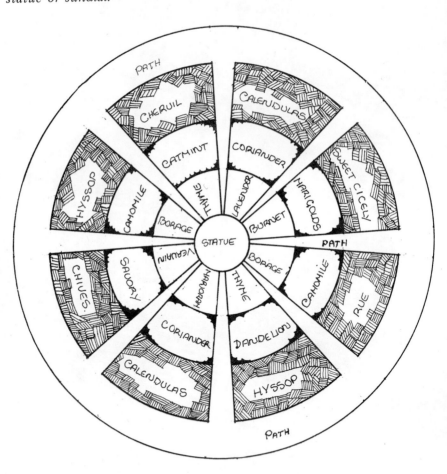

(Opposite) This simple garden is a good design for the beginner. The plot is relatively small, but includes plants which are both useful and pretty, and is suitable for a spot with full sun.

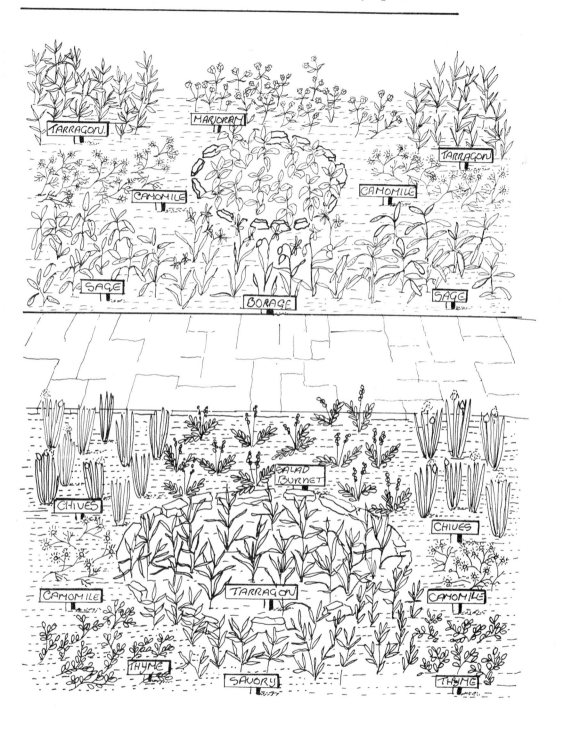

Colour chart of herb flowers

BLUE	Aconite Borage Chicory	Hyssop Rosemary Sage
GREY	Santolina Tarragon	Wormwood
MAUVE PURPLE	Chives Foxglove Lavender Lemon Verbena Marjoram	Mint Savory Thyme Verbascum Violet
PINK	Centaury Soapwort	Valerian
RED	Bergamot Germander	Nasturtium Salad Burnet
WHITE	Sweet Basil Camomile Caraway Sweet Cicely Chervil Elder	Horsechestnut Horseradish Lemon Balm Lily-of-the-Valley Sweet Woodruff Yarrow
YELLOW	Arnica Barberry Lady's Bedstraw Broom Celandine Dandelion Dill	Goldenrod Juniper Black Mustard Rue St. John's Wort Sunflower Tansy

Colour chart of herb flowers

YELLOWISH GREEN	Angelica Lady's Mantle	Lovage
YELLOW TO ORANGE-RED	Marigold	Nasturtium
EVERGREEN	Burnet Germander Green Santolina	Hyssop Rosemary
GREY LEAVES	Artemisia Horehound Lavender Rue	Sage Southernwood Thyme

made in the notebook. Include date and location, brief description, height, colouring, and outstanding features. Observe the area to decide on its suitability for the garden. Does it seek sun or shade? Is it located on a dry hillside, or in a moist, shady location? These items should also be noted in your book. Into one of the little bags, place a leaf or twig, blossom or seed pod, then staple to the page of notes. Sometimes more than one trip is required for positive identification. You may want to see the bloom or seed before you can be certain of the species. The notes and specimen can then be compared to descriptive literature or actual plants displayed in the botanic gardens.

Once identified, we need to know how the plant is propagated; whether cuttings can be taken in spring or autumn, or is it easier to plant the seeds. A few of the woodland plants can be transplanted into the garden, but in most cases digging up the plant is not advised. It is most unlikely that the transplant would be successful. Moreover, many wild plants are protected by law and their removal is prohibited. Seeds may be gathered, or cuttings taken at the proper season, without injury

The herb garden can be a small square surrounded by lawn, as this pretty oasis is. The herbs are interspersed with

to the wild life, and even in protected areas permission may usually be obtained to gather seeds.

It is best to obtain plants by seeds, cuttings, or division of the wild plant. As a point of ecology and conservation, the wild life is being increased, and by starting this way the plants are accustomed to the environment and conditions you have provided from their infancy and do not have difficult adjustments to make. Starting plants from seeds, from cuttings, or by division is covered in Chapter Six.

The end and the beginning

The formal tour of our herb garden is all but completed. There are still individual herbs to meet, books about herbs to discover, and places to visit or write for herb products. But the story has been told. Hopefully, you'll stop by this vista again and again, for the herbal landscape is one that seldom tires or bores.

While this seemingly is the end, it is really only the beginning, for the simplest herbal garden and the most elaborate herbal landscape, the most casual acquaintance with herbs and the deepest, fondest love of them all begin at the same place. One can purchase a packet of powder that once was a living plant, and one can use it to alleviate or remedy some personal ailment, or to enhance the flavour of a favourite dish, or to colour a wool, or for any of the myriad of uses that herbs have. But the beginning is the plant. Herbs are, after all, plants first and foremost.

The herbal landscape is the beginning. Whether contrived or discovered, the herbal landscape should be experienced, and not simply through the pages of a book. If you have the space, do plant a herb garden, even if one of only a few common varieties and of limited space. Put a pot of herbs in your sunniest window.

Then use your herbs for their fragrance, their taste, their colour, or for themselves. Enjoy them, but put them to work. Beginning is the hardest past, but it is only as difficult as planting a seed.

PART II
A Herbal Encyclopaedia

Aconite

Monkshood, Friar's Cap, Blue Rocket
Aconitum Napellus
Ranunculaceae

Aconite is a lovely plant to behold in the garden, but it is also a dangerous one. It is a deadly poison. True, it does have some medicinal value, but an overdose can kill, so do not experiment.

A hardy perennial, aconite will grow to four feet (1.2 m) in height or more, making it a suitable plant for the back row of a border where it can be seen above the flowers in front. Because its flowers have a curious shape resembling a monk's hood, the plant earned the popular name "monkshood" during the Middle Ages. They are quite pretty in cut-flower arrangements. The common variety produces blue flowers, while others produce white and mauve flowers.

Root division is the most practical method of propagation for aconite. It takes two to three years to flower if started from seed. Root division procedure is out of the ordinary, for aconite is not an ordinary plant. Each year, the roots develop small "daughter" roots, then die off. It is these daughter roots that are re-planted to propagate the plant. In the autumn of every third or fourth year, aconite should be dug up and divided. But wear stout gloves,

Aconite
(Aconitum Napellus)

313

especially if you have a cut, or you could suffer from poisoning.

Aconite likes rich, somewhat moist soil. Use lots of well-rotted manure and compost. Its location should be partially shaded. Individual plants should be about 18 inches (46 cm) apart.

Aconite is primarily a garden plant, but it has been cultivated for its medicinal properties. The dried root has the effect of a sedative or depressant, with, it has been said, the ability to reduce pain and fever. It should be stressed, of course, that professional medical advice should be sought first. But in any event, doses must always be small and very carefully controlled. And don't forget, aconite is a poison!

Historically, it is aconite's poisonous properties which stand out. The generic name is said to be derived from *akontion*, a dart, because it was used to poison arrows. It has also been suggested that *Aconitum* is derived from *akone*, cliffy or rocky, because the plant is sometimes found in rocky areas. The ancient herbalists listed the poisonous nature of aconite; most noted its usefulness against venomous creatures, and one, Gerard, pointed out that its power is "so forceable that the herb only thrown before the scorpion or any other venomous beast, causeth them to be without force or strength to hurt, insomuch that they cannot move or stirre untill the herbe be taken away". And stories of aconite poisonings, deliberate and accidental, abound.

Aconite has had widespread use. Europeans knew and used it. The Chinese also used it, and it remains one of the principal drug plants used in Chinese medicine today. In America, the Indians discovered the beneficial and dangerous properties of the herb and used it in early phases of pneumonia and in erysipelas (a fever) and rheumatism.

Agrimony

Church Steeples, Cockebur,
Agrimonia Eupatoria
Rosaceae

Agrimony is a yellow-flowered, spiky plant that grows between one and three feet (30 cm and 1 m) in height. It has few branches. Its flowers blossom profusely along the stem. Its leaves are narrow and about five inches long (13 cm) with saw-tooth edges. The whole plant is a deep green and covered with soft hairs.

Agrimonia Eupatoria is good as a rock-garden plant or in a wild flower border. It is easily propagated from seed and once established, is self-propagating, thriving in a dry, lightly shaded location, although some direct sunlight won't hurt it.

Agrimony
(Agrimonia Eupatoria)

The old herbalists always listed agrimony as an astringent, tonic, and diuretic, and had especial regard for it as a jaundice remedy; Dioscorides called it "A remedy for them that have bad livers". Agrimony was also regarded as a remedy for skin blemishes and diseases. Infusions of the plant are still valued for sore throats:

mix an ounce (28 g) of the dried plant with three-quarters of a pint (426 ml) of boiling water, sweeten with honey, and drink a half-cup as frequently as you like.

Agrimony is also a valuable dye plant, generally yielding a yellow colour, with plants gathered in September giving a light hue, and those gathered later in the year yielding a darker colour.

Alder

Common Alder, English Alder
Alnus glutinosa
Betulaceae

Members of the birch family, alders grow in cool, moist, even wet soils. They can be used effectively along garden boundaries, in groups, and combine well with birch and hazelnuts. On the banks of streams or ponds, the dense root system will help to consolidate them and to drain wet soil. Alder logs can be used to build walks or retaining edges in wet soil as they will not decay easily, even when continuously wet.

They are decorative with attractive foliage and flowers. The green, hang-

315

ing catkins blossom in early spring. Pistillate catkins are woody, resembling small pine-cones. Some alders will reach a height of 70 feet (21 m). Propagation is by seeds gathered in the autumn and kept dry, then sown in moist, shady soil in the spring. The shrubby varieties grow from hardwood cuttings and suckers.

The bark and berries are cathartic, similar to cascara in its purgative action. The astringent bark, prepared as a decoction, is used as a gargle for sore throats, to promote circulation, check diarrhoea and for eye drops. The leaves are glutinous and used as a cure for inflammation. Fresh leaves applied to the bare feet are said to be excellent for soothing burning and aching feet. They can also be used as a footbath when made into a solution prepared in the same way as a strong tea brew.

The bark and cones were once widely used for tanning leather and a yellow-brown dye was made from bark peeled in the spring.

Leaves, with morning dew on them, can be placed where fleas are a problem. They will gather the fleas and can then be quickly disposed of. It has also been reported that insects are repelled by freshly picked leaves.

Angelica

Garden Angelica
Angelica Archangelica
Umbelliferae

Angelica is a veritable giant in the herb world. The towering plant is widely travelled and has a background rich in herbal lore. Use has been made of leaves, stems, roots, and seeds in cooking and in medicine.

Believed to be originally a native of Syria, angelica has spread across the world, growing abundantly in Iceland and Lapland. It likes cool, moist places. Angelica is neither a true annual nor a true perennial. It dies off after flowering, but since the plants often take more than two years to achieve the bloom of maturity, they aren't really biennials. The gardener can play on this quality of angelica and maintain the plant as a perennial simply by pruning the flower stalks and preventing the setting of seeds, thus developing and maintaining the plant as a seven to eight foot (2 to 2.5 m) member of the garden. But the garden will also miss out on the spectacular yellow-green or white-green blossoms.

These blossoms make their appearance early in May, and by July the plant goes to seed. It is the date of blooming that has, in some quarters, been regarded as the source of the plant's name. The day of Michael the Archangel used to be May 8, and angelica quite often blooms on that date—hence, *Angelica Archangelica.* There is more of angelica in the folk-lore, for example, the legend that an archangel revealed in a vision that angelica would cure the Plague. In time, angelica came to be regarded simply as an angelic plant, and to be widely known as "The Root of the Holy Ghost".

But the history of the plant is rooted in prehistoric times and even the passage of centuries did not shake from the Christian mind the associa-tions between angelica and pagan beliefs. It is altogether possible, there-fore, that the plant acquired its angelic stature in folklore because of the pagan regard for the plant as an infallible guard against witches, evil spirits, their spells and enchantments. Peasants tied angelica leaves around the necks of children to protect them from harm, and even uttering the name was supposed to be helpful when a person was in a difficult situation.

An interesting story repeated in a number of herb books supports the antiquity of angelican lore. It is alleged that it is the custom in the lake district of what was once Latvia for country peasants to take part in an annual procession, carrying angelica stems to sell in the towns. Part of the procession chants a chorus with words so old that no one knows what they mean. The ritual is simply an early summer custom and the words of the chorus have been passed from generation to generation. Certainly the rite is pre-Christian.

Country folk had good reason for dealing in angelica beyond the religious or superstitious aspects. This was undoubtedly the popular taste, for angelica is a culinary herb of no small repute. Perhaps best known are the confections made by combining the angelica stems with a large amount of sugar. But you would be better off trying angelica in some other dish. For example, the stems can be cut and prepared like asparagus. Also, the leaves, fresh or dried, may be added to soups and stews. Use about a dessertspoonful of the leaves to a quantity that will serve four, adding it in the last minutes of cooking.

Angelica, understandably, is most used in the countries where it is most abundant. In Iceland, both the stems and roots are eaten raw, with butter. The Norwegians make a bread of the roots. In Lapland, the stalks are regarded as a delicacy. A popular tea, tasting much like China tea, is infused from fresh or dried leaves.

Angelica has long had commercial value as a flavouring in wines and liqueurs, and occasionally as an ingredient in perfumes. The entire plant is aromatic, including the root. The fresh root, when cut, will weep a resinous gum resembling the fixative benzoin. In fact, the gum is used as a substitute for benzoin in perfumes. Not all the commercial uses of angelica are obvious. It is believed, for example, that certain Rhine wines owe their fine flavour to secret recipes using angelica. French absinthe has as an ingredient a blend of herbs, including angelica and wormwood. Both seeds and roots are used in chartreuse. The seeds help flavour gin and vermouth, and the leaves are used in preparing bitters.

You can brew your own bitters by combining one ounce (28 g) of dried angelica, one ounce of dried holy thistle, and half an ounce (14 g) of dried hops, infusing the herbs in two and a quarter pints (1.3 l) of boiling water, and straining them off after the brew has cooled. A wineglassful of the bitters taken before meals is supposed to be a good appetizer.

It should be clear that not all of these uses are strictly culinary. The bitters obviously are a tonic. Eating angelica stalks is said to relieve flatulence and soothe "a feeble stomach". It is true with angelica, as with other herbs, that the medicinal and the culinary overlap. It is said to possess carminative, stimulant, diaphoretic, tonic, and expectorant properties. It is supposed to be good for colds, coughs, pleurisy, flatulence, colic, rheumatism, and urinary troubles. It should be noted, however, that angelica has a tendency to increase the sugar in the urine, so those with a tendency to diabetes should avoid it.

The old herbalists expressed a high regard for angelica in their writings. Parkinson wrote: "It is of especial use . . . in swounings . . . tremblings and passions of the heart, to expel any windy or noysome vapours from it. The green stalks or the young rootes being preserved or candied are very effectual to comfort and warm a

cold and weake stomacke; and in the time of infection is of excellent good use to preserve the spirits and heart from infection." He wrote that it would sweeten the breath, and claimed that taking the dried, powdered root in wine or other drink would "abate the rage of lust in young persons".

Culpeper, too, viewed angelica as being "of admirable use". He enumerated the various uses and included some no one else had (or has). He said angelica's juices, if dropped into the eyes or ears, would remedy dimness of sight and deafness. It would work similarly for toothaches. Powdered root, mixed with a little pitch and "laid on the biting of mad dogs or any other venomous creature, doth wonderfully help". So too, with open wounds, it "doth cleanse and cause them to heal quickly".

According to Culpeper: "angelica is a herb of Leo; let it be gathered when he is there, the Moon applying to his good aspect; let it be gathered either in his hour or in the hour of Jupiter; let Sol be angular; observe the like in gathering the herbs of other planets, and you may happen to do wonders. In all epidemical diseases caused by Saturn, that is as good a preservative as grows."

You can make a good tonic simply by infusing angelica leaves. This is a stimulating and aromatic tea, and if you take it for several days in succession, you will experience the beneficial effect.

An infusion made by pouring three-quarters of a pint (426 ml) of boiling water on an ounce (28 g) of the bruised root, when taken in one tablespoon doses three to four times daily, is said to relieve flatulence. It is also a bronchial tonic and an emmenagogue.

Another bronchial tonic from an old herbal is made by boiling a handful of angelica root in a quart (1.3 l) of water for three hours, straining off the fluid and adding sufficient honey to make a syrup. One tablespoonful should be taken at night and several times during the day.

And here's a herbal curiosity. Tuck a couple of fingers full of ground angelica between lip and gum or in the cheek. Swallow the juice. It's reputed to be an excellent stomach tonic and remedy for the nervousness that comes from too much smoking.

Angelica's size keeps it outdoors, but if you have the space, it is a nice garden plant, for itself and for the uses to which it can be put. Only the first seeds need be purchased, for the plant is readily self-propagating. Indeed, the seeds should be gathered soon after formation in early July, if they are going to be gathered at all, since they fall easily to the ground and germinate. The seeds themselves are fairly large and coated with a straw-like substance.

The seed germinates in light in 21 to 28 days at a temperature of 70°F (21°C). Because it germinates in light, the seed must not be covered. Rather, it should be pressed lightly into the soil and kept moist until germination is evident. The seeds do lose vitality rapidly, so the best time for sowing is in late July or early August, immediately after harvesting. The seed will remain viable for at most two years.

For best results, the seeds should be nurtured indoors. Transplant them at the appropriate time to a spot with very rich, moist soil, preferably with some shade. Angelica doesn't mind being cultivated under trees at all. The best alternative to propagating them indoors is to start them outdoors in their favourite sort of place. In any case, fertilization should be high, using well-rotted manure and compost. Frequent mulching is suggested because the places where the best growth occurs lend themselves to a condition where weeds can easily grow underneath the angelica. Mulching or planting thickly means that no weeds are able to come up.

Harvesting times for angelica depend on the part of the herb required. The leaves can be harvested at any time of the year, in fact whenever they are large enough to handle. And this can be continued from that stage on until the end of the growing season. The seeds should be harvested as they turn from green to yellow.

Since the seeds fall easily upon ripening (recognizable by the change in colour), it is best to be prompt and to lean the seed heads into a bag or lined basket so they will drop into the container when clipped from the plant. In this way there should be no loss of seeds. The stem should be cut in June or early July. The root should be dug up in the autumn of the first year.

Drying is simple. For best results, the angelica leaves should be chopped, then scattered on screens or on paper for drying in the shade. The seeds can be cured in the sun until dry. The root tends to be thick and juicy, so incisions made in the thickest segments of the roots will speed the drying process.

There is, incidentally, another angelica; wild angelica *(A. sylvestris)*. This has been used as a dye plant, yielding a yellow colour.

Anise

Aniseed
Pimpinella Anisum
Umbelliferae

Most people don't think of anise in terms of its popularity with mice, but in the Sixteenth Century, in fact, anise did find wide application as a mouse-trap bait. According to several old herbals, the mice found it irresistible. Of course, many humans find anise irresistible too, for it has a wide variety of applications in cooking and medicine.

Anise is an annual which grows from 18 to 24 inches (46 to 61 cm) in height. The first leaves to develop are fairly large and wide, while the secondary leaves are feather-like. It is these secondary leaves which prompted the ascription of the generic name *Pimpinella* to anise. *Pimpinella* is said to be derived from *dipinella* or twice-pinnate (pinnate meaning feather-like). By midsummer, two-inch (5 cm) clusters of tiny yellow-white flowers appear, followed in late summer by the grey-brown seeds for which the plant is generally cultivated. Each plant will have one to six umbrella-like clusters, each bearing six to ten seeds.

The seeds are the most useful part of the plant, although the leaves can be used in cooking. The so-called aniseed is actually the fruit of the plant, and the seed is actually contained within the eight inch long (20 cm), crescent-shaped, ribbed kernel. Usually a bit of the stem clings to the fruit after harvesting. The aniseed is easily dried by spreading it on paper or cloth in the sun or half-shade, or indoors by placing it in a moderate heat. Once dried, the seeds store well in tightly sealed containers.

The taste of the aniseed is sweet and spicy. Indeed it is one of the four great hot seeds. It has a wholly agreeable aroma. These characteristics of the seed are those which have dictated its use: it has contributed its liquorice-like flavour to cakes, soups, beverages, and medicines, and its aroma to all these and sachets and pot-pourris besides. It has been valued as a diuretic, carminative, aphrodisiac, and a remedy for halitosis.

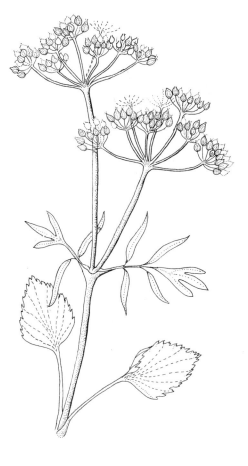

Anise
(Pimpinella Anisum)

Gerard reported that: "the seed wasteth and consumeth winde, and is good against belchings, and upbraidings of the stomacke, allayeth gripings of the belly, provoketh urine gently, maketh abundance of milke, and stirreth up bodily lust . . . Being chewed it maketh the breath sweet and is good for them that are short-winded, and quencheth thirst, and therefore it is fit for such as have the dropsie: it helpeth the yeoxing or hicket [hiccups], both when it is drunken or eaten dry; the smel thereof doth also prevail very much. The same being dried by the fire and taken with honey clenseth the brest very much from flegmaticke superfluities; and if it be eaten with bitter almonds it doth helpe the old cough. It is to be given to young children and infants to eat which are like to have the falling sickness (epilepsy) or to such as have it by patrimonie or succession. It takes away the Squinancie or Quincie (a swelling in the throat) being gargled with honey, vinegar, and a little Hyssop gently boiled together."

The virtues enumerated by Gerard had been recognized for centuries. The plant is indigenous to Egypt, Greece, and Asia Minor, and the peoples of those countries were making use of it long before the birth of Christ. In the Sixth Century B.C., Pythagoras listed anise for epilepsy, suggesting that merely holding an anise plant would ward off epileptic attack. Hippocrates, a century later, recommended anise for coughs. Pliny the Elder noted that anise "has the effect of sweetening the breath and removing all bad odours from the mouth, if chewed in the morning." He also said, "This plant imparts a youthful look to the features, and if suspended to the pillow, so as to be smelt by a person when asleep, it will prevent disagreeable dreams." The Romans cultivated anise on a large scale for these virtues and its uses in flavouring foods and in perfumes.

A most prominent piece of culinary lore from anise's past ties it to the tradition of the wedding cake. The Romans liked to finish off a big meal with a cake called *mustacae*, which was simply a mixture of meal and a number of savoury seeds, including anise. The intention of the *mustacae* was to ease digestion and prevent flatulence. Since it was a custom to conclude really big feasts, like a wedding feast, with a serving of *mustacae*, it has been regarded as the forerunner of today's wedding cake.

Perhaps a better measure of the value of anise to the Romans was the fact that it, along with cumin and other spices and savoury seeds, was a negotiable commodity used to pay taxes. "Woe unto you, scribes and Pharisees," said Jesus in Matthew 23:23, "hypocrites! for ye pay tithe of Mint and Anise and Cumin, and have omitted the weightier matters of the law." A famous herbal quotation, but unfortunately a mistranslation in the eyes of some scholars, who contend that the original Greek was *anethon* or dill (*Antheum graveolens* to some botanists, *Peucedanum graveolens* to others), not anise.

The Chinese, too, put anise to good use—although there is some confusion among anise, star anise, and fennel in the Orient. Star anise *(Illicium verum)* has properties very similar to anise and the two are virtually interchangeable. The Chinese use the seed as a condiment and believe it to be carminative and diuretic, and a tonic.

None of these properties have been diminished with the passage of time, of course. Anise still enjoys a reputation as a cough remedy. Anise tea is also helpful in cases of infantile catarrh. Pour half a pint (284 ml) of boiling water on two teaspoonfuls of bruised aniseed. Sweetened, this should be given frequently in doses of one to three teaspoonfuls.

Anise is a stimulating condiment. It adds piquancy to many a soup. Just add a few seeds to the liquid. Or try substituting aniseed for the cinnamon or nutmeg you add to apple sauce. Mix aniseed with cream cheese and spread on biscuits for an interesting party or evening snack. Aniseed can also be added to almost any basic recipe for bread or cake.

All this omits the uses to which anise leaves may be put, largely because it is the seeds that have built up tradition and reputation. However, the leaves do add a fine aroma to salads and dishes such as carrots, if they are finely chopped and sprinkled sparingly over the food. An excellent tea can be made from the leaves, and this is reputed to be an excellent remedy for colds.

Moreover, anise is a lovely garden plant. It is easily grown, although the seed needs to be kept warm for germination—about 70° F (21° C). Similarly, the plant once growing needs the same warmth in order for the growth cycle to continue and the new seed to ripen. A cool, damp summer can prevent you from getting a crop. It is, however, a short-season plant, and if you plant in May, the anise will probably finish by August.

Since its long tap-root makes transplanting a risky proposition, anise should be seeded wherever it is to grow. The seed should be sown in rows, rather than broadcast. This will ease the task of weeding, which will be necessary in the early weeks of growth. Cover the seeds with an eighth to a quarter inch (3 to 6 mm) of soil. The seeds should sprout in four to six days. Again, germination calls for warmth, so don't plant too early in the year.

Anise is modest in its demands. In fact, it doesn't like too much fertilization. It is best-grown in annual rotations, following a herb such as basil. Mulching may not be necessary, for anise's growing season is short and it grows tall enough to keep its leaves and flowers out of the dirt.

As the seeds ripen, turning from green to grey-brown, harvest them. The best time is in the morning while the dew is still on them. As with other umbelliferous plants, clip the seed clusters into a bag or container of some kind so that the seeds are not scattered and lost. The leaves can be gathered throughout the growing season.

Arbor Vitae

Yellow Cedar
Thuja occidentalis
Cupressaceae

This, the tallest of the species of conifer, grows to a maximum height of some 30 feet (9.1 m). Suitable as a high hedge when grown in numbers, the tree can be clipped to a variety of shapes, but grows naturally to a conical form. Although the natural habitat is North America, arbor vitae grows well in Britain on western seaboard hills. The wood is soft, of fine grain, and light in texture.

The name arbor vitae was given by Clusius on seeing the royal gardens at Fontainebleau, for which it had been brought over from Canada. Yellow cedar was imported into England in the mid Sixteenth Century. The name *thuja* was derived from the Greek word *thuo* "to sacrifice", because the ancients used to burn the wood with their sacrificial offerings and the fragrance given off was, no doubt, to both their liking and the liking of the gods.

In addition to yellow cedar, there are many other similar varieties all over the world.

The leaves and tops are used for chronic cough, fever, and gout. An infusion made of one ounce (28 g) of the tender leaves to three-quarters of a pint (426 ml) of boiling water may be taken half a tablespoonful at a time as a diuretic, emmenagogue, and uterine stimulant. Applied externally, is it said to remove warts and fungoid growths. As a counter-irritant, it is useful for relief of muscular aches and pains. A salve for external application can be made by boiling a quantity of the leaves in lard.

Most of these uses were discovered by the American Indians and passed along to the white settlers. For many years, arbor vitae leaves and twigs were officially accepted drug herbs used for stimulant, diuretic, emmenagogue, and irritant purposes. Later, these plant parts were superceded by the distilled oil in the official pharmacopoeia, the oil being used as a heart and uterine stimulant, as well as a general stimulant, irritant, and antiseptic. The oil has also been used as an aromatic ingredient in soap liniment. Arbor vitae oil may be home-distilled and used as an insect repellent. The odour of the essential oil is pungent, almost overpowering. It is matched by a strong bitter taste. Taken in excess, the oil can produce unpleasant results; it was officially listed as an abortifacient and convulsant in overdose.

Arbutus, Trailing

Ground Laurel, Winter Pink,
May Flower
Epigaea repens
Ericaceae

Trailing arbutus, cultivated in Britain since 1736, is a flat, evergreen creeper with hairy stems and bright green, oval leaves. In early spring, it has white or pink fragrant flowers. It requires moist, well-fertilized, acid soil and thrives in damp, sandy peat in shady places. It can be propagated by divisions and layers, but the best plants are obtained from seeds, which should be planted as soon as ripe in a mixture of peatmoss and sand and covered with a shaded pane of glass. Seedlings emerge in about four weeks.

Known as an astringent, trailing arbutus has the effect of contracting and hardening tissues and deterring secretions by the mucus membranes. It has been used generally as a cure for urinary disorders, but it is said to be particularly useful in cases of gall-stones.

It is commonly suggested that an infusion be made by adding one ounce (28 g) of the leaves to three-quarters of a pint (426 ml) of boiling water, and that it be taken freely several times a day.

This herb is said to be harmful to cattle if eaten by them.

Arnica

Mountain Tobacco, Leopard's Bane
Arnica montana
Compositae

Arnica, native of central Europe, but found in England and Scotland, is a herb noted chiefly for its medicinal properties. A popular folk remedy, it is seldom used internally, although it has stimulant and diuretic properties, since it is something of an irritant to the stomach and cases of fatal poisoning are on record. It is most often used externally on bruises, swellings, and sprains.

Arnica has slightly hairy basal leaves and a long stalk, one to two feet (30 to 60 cm) tall with large heads of yellow ray and disc flowers. There are three to four of these daisy-like flowers to a cluster.

It is easily grown in any good garden soil. Arnica spreads rapidly by division and is very effective in the woodland garden, border, or rock garden. It can also be grown from seed, which should be sown in a cold frame in early spring. The flowers are collected and dried as they bloom, and the roots may be dried in autumn.

It can be painted on unbroken chilblains, sprains, wounds, and bruises, to soothe them. But repeated applications may produce inflammation. A salve made with an ounce (28 g) of lard heated briefly with an ounce (28 g) of arnica flowers, may be similarly used.

A tincture can be made by steeping two heaped teaspoonfuls of the flowers in a pint (568 ml) of boiling water—applying this, once cooled. A slightly different salve is made by mixing equal parts of vaseline or liquid paraffin and powdered arnica. Adding half an ounce (14 g) of the tincture to a hot-water footbath is said to provide relief for tender feet.

In Europe, arnica remained the official drug plant until shortly after World War II. Pharmaceutical preparations of arnica have been used orally, intravenously, and externally.

Balm

Sweet Balm, Garden Balm,
Honey Plant, Lemon Balm
Melissa officinalis
Labiatae

Balm, also named lemon balm because its crushed foliage smells like lemons, has a venerable history of use as both a healing herb and as part of a drink to ensure longevity. Shakespeare mentions it in *The Merry Wives of Windsor* as a strewing herb, used to make the house smell more festive and inviting to one's guests.

Long before Shakespeare's time, however, the Greeks used balm in their own way. In the *Materia Medica* of Dioscorides, we find that balm was

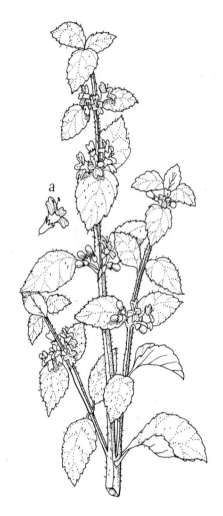

Lemon Balm
(Melissa officinalis)
(a) flower

says, "balm, being applied, doth close up wounds without any perill of inflammation."

Balm is not only fragrant and useful, but it is also very prolific and can be grown easily. A native of southern Europe, it can sometimes be found growing wild.

It is a fairly hardy perennial. The root system is short, but dense, and the stem square and branching. The plant seldom grows more than a foot (30 cm) tall indoors, but may reach three or four feet (90 cm or 1.2 m) outside.

Leaves are heart-shaped or broadly ovate, yellowish-green, and generally one to three inches (2.5 to 7.5 cm) long, growing smaller towards the top of the plant. They are covered with stiff hairs on the top surface. The flowers grow in loose, small bunches from the axils of the leaves, and are bluish-white or yellow. Balm flowers from May until October. After pollination, long, oval, dark brown-black seeds appear.

It can be started easily from seed. If left alone, the plant will re-seed itself in the garden. It can also be propagated in a greenhouse or in pots in the house. To start the seeds in a greenhouse, press them into fine, friable soil in a seedbox. When the seedlings are an inch (2.5 cm) tall, they should be thinned to two inches (5 cm) apart. When they have reached four inches (10 cm) they can be set out. Allow two feet (60 cm) on all sides, since they tend to spread sideways.

Cuttings and root divisions are also

used against scorpion stings, and insect and dog bites. Pliny believed that the power of balm was so great that "though it be tied to his sword that hath given the wound, it stauncheth the blood". Gerard, summing up the opinions of Pliny and Dioscorides,

simple methods of starting balm. Root divisions can be made in spring or autumn by dividing the roots into small pieces with three or four buds on each. Plant the pieces two feet (60 cm) apart. If you are making your root divisions in the autumn allow plenty of time for the plants to become established before the first heavy frosts.

Balm should be planted in fairly fertile, friable soil in partial shade. Although the plants will grow in sunlight, they do much better in the shade. Weed until the plants are well established. An early mulching with hay or straw will prevent the herb from becoming too soiled.

Water during dry periods to maintain continued growth of the plants and prevent yellowing of the leaves. In the autumn, cut off all decayed growth from the roots. Although the roots are hardy, mulching with pine branches or leaves during the winter will greatly improve chances of survival.

Harvesting balm is a relatively simple matter. It is possible—in fertile, well-watered locations—to obtain as many as three cuttings a season. The herb should be harvested before it flowers for optimum fragrance, although a good deal of its odour will be lost in even the most careful drying. To harvest, cut off the entire plant two inches (5 cm) above the ground. Be careful to avoid pressure of any kind if packing the herb in boxes or cartons, and try to avoid bruising either the stem or the leaves.

Balm should be carefully dried within two days of picking, but it has a tendency to turn black if it is dried too quickly. Drying is best done slowly in the shade or indoors at temperatures between 90° to 110° F (32° to 38° C). It is best to use trays or sieves for drying the herb, rather than tying it in bunches on a string. If you plan to use balm for tea, dry both leaves and stems.

Balm is an attractive plant to bees, as the early Greeks recognized. In fact, its present scientific name derives from the Greek word for "bee". Gerard recommended planting balm around bee hives, and also suggested rubbing the inside of the hive with balm to prevent swarming and to encourage other bees to join the hive. A Spaniard, Ibn Al Awam, suggested that a mixture of balm and honey or sugar be smeared over the inside of a hive to make it an attractive home for a new swarm, but he quotes other writers who say that it will have the exact opposite effect.

Cows are also supposed to like balm. If planted in pastures, it is said to promote the flow of their milk.

Many remedies have been ascribed to balm. Gerard says, "Bawme drunk in wine is good against the bitings of venomous beasts, comforts the heart, and driveth away all melancholy and sadness."

Dioscorides suggested drinking an infusion of wine and balm and, applying the leaves to an infected part of the body, such as an insect bite or the bite of a mad dog. Balm is also a component of a drink given to sufferers of fever: "Put two sprigs of balm, and a little wood sorrel, into a stone-jug, having first washed and dried them; peel thinly a small lemon, and clear from the white; slice it and put a bit of peel in; then pour in two and a half pints (1.4 l) of boiling water, sweeten, and cover it close."

Balm is also an ingredient in claret cup: "Take one bottle of claret, one pint (568 ml) of German seltzer-water, a small bunch of balm, ditto of burrage, one orange cut in slices, half a cucumber sliced thick, a liqueur glass of cognac, and one ounce (28 g) of bruised sugar-candy; place these ingredients in a covered jug well immersed in rough ice, stir all together with a silver spoon, and when the cup has been iced for about an hour, strain or decant it free from the herbs, etc."

Balm tea can be made by pouring three-quarters of a pint (426 ml) of boiling water on one ounce (28 g) of the herb. Infuse for 15 minutes, cool, strain, and drink freely. You may wish to add honey or lemon peel. In fact, a balm-honey tea has had amazing powers of longevity ascribed to it.

The tea is generally used to induce perspiration and cool patients who have fevers. It was also used with salt to heal sores and ease the pains of gout.

Balm has its culinary uses as well. Its leaves can be added to salads or to fruit for a pleasant, subtle flavour. A few leaves can improve the taste of a cup of ordinary Indian tea.

Homemade wine can be made from the leaves. According to an old recipe from *The Recipe Book of Richard Briggs*, a cook at the Globe Tavern, the White Hart Tavern, and the Temple Coffee House in London, balm wine can be made in the following way: "Take twenty pounds (9 kg) of lump sugar and four gallons and a half (20.5 l) of water, boil it gently for one hour, and pour it into a tub to cool; take two pounds (907 g) of the tops of green balm, and bruise them, put them into a barrel with a little new yeast, and when the liquor is nearly cold, pour it on the balm; stir it well together; and let it stand twenty-four hours, stirring it often; then bung it tight, and the longer you keep it the better it will be."

Barberry, Common

Berbery, Pipperidge Bush, Berberis Dumetorum, Holy Thorn
Berberis vulgaris
Berberidaceae

An erect, quickly growing shrub, common barberry tops eight to ten feet (2.5 to 3 m) in height and has holly-like leaves, and fragrant, pale yellow flowers in racemes which are followed by drooping clusters of red berries. There are about 175 different species in the genus *Berberis*, and they are considered among the most useful and ornamental shrubs of good growth habit. The many evergreen varieties are not entirely hardy in the north, but will survive given a sheltered position.

All are lovely garden shrubs, many with bronze-crimson autumn leaves. Barberry is easily grown and adapted to various soils and situations. All of the species grow well under trees, especially in moist soils. Propagation is by seeds, cuttings, suckers, and layers. Growing from seed may produce interesting results and some very beautiful forms have originated in this way. True reproductions can be obtained only by vegetative means.

The wood is a beautiful yellow colour, used frequently to make crucifixes. The Italians call barberry "Holy Thorn" because it is believed to have formed part of Christ's crown of thorns.

An excellent wine and jelly is made from the fruit. The berries, boiled in soup, add flavour. The bark and roots can be used as a yellow dye.

While the bark of the root was the source of the official drug "berberis," the berries, leaves, and stem bark have also been used. The leaves were chewed for acne. Some American Indians used the roots and bark for ulcers, as a tonic, and for heartburn and rheumatism. A root decoction was used for coughs, kidney and liver ailments, and as a wash for cuts and bruises. Herbals list barberry as an astringent bitter, a tonic, and a stomach aid when administered in small doses. Large doses have a cathartic effect, causing watery diarrhoea and abdominal pain.

Very effective in shrubbery borders, grown in masses under trees, barberries are available at many nurseries.

Basil

Sweet Basil, Common Basil, Garden Basil
Ocimum Basilicum
Labiatae

Probably nowhere else in the herb world is there a plant with such a split personality as basil. Although a favourite culinary herb in today's kitchens, it stands in the midst of a centuries-old controversy that, on one hand, attributes awful and evil powers to it, while on the other, regards it as an object of sacred worship.

Culpeper wrote; "This is the herb that all the authors are together by the ears about, and rail at one another, like lawyers." While acknowledging that several ancient Greek physicians "hold it not fittingly to be taken inwardly", and another "rails at it with downright Billingsgate rhetoric", Culpeper also reported that other ancient herbal masters defended its salutary effects on health.

He himself reserved judgment on basil's virtues, although his writings on basil are tinged with dread. Being one who always sought to divine a herb's astrological character, Culpeper examined basil and found it to be "a herb of Mars and under the Scorpion, and therefore called *basilicon*, it is no marvel if it carry a virulent quality with it. Being applied to the place bitten by venomous beasts, or stung by a wasp or hornet," he continued, "it speedily draws the poison to it. Every like draws its like."

He added that a French physician "affirms of his own knowledge that an acquaintance of his, by common smelling to it, had a scorpion bred in his brain. Something is the matter; this herb and Rue will never grow together, no, nor near one another; and we know Rue is as great an enemy to poison as any that grows."

Culpeper typified one Western attitude toward basil. Many European herbalists said basil had an affinity for poison, that scorpions were drawn to it and even bred mysteriously by it.

Early Greek and Roman physicians believed that basil would thrive only if it were sown amid vile shouts and curses. That tradition gave rise to the contemporary French idiom *semer le basilic*, sowing the basil, for raving.

The Eastern sentiment toward basil is one of unequivocal reverence. In India, particularly among Hindus, the herb is hailed as a protector. Sprigs of the Indian variety, *Ocimum sanctum*, are placed on the breasts of the dead to protect them from other worldly evil. Pots of the herb are grown in temples, and it is believed that a home built where basil flourishes will be safe from all harm.

One of basil's more pleasant connotations, for example, is in Italy where basil is a sign of courtship. A

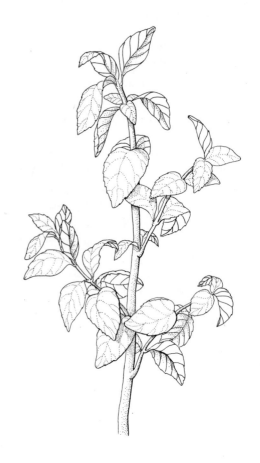

Basil
(Ocimum Basilicum)

young man can guarantee the love of his girl-friend by offering her a sprig of basil. A pot of basil on the balcony is a tacit sign that the lady within is ready to receive her suitor.

And despite the rancorous French idiom spawned by basil, the French name for it is *herbe royale*.

One of England's great romantics, Percy Bysshe Shelley, hailed basil as a symbol of love itself. He wrote:

330

Madonna, wherefore hast thou sent
  to me
Sweet basil and mignonette?
Embleming love and health, which
  never yet
In the same wreath might be.

Western ambivalence toward basil seems to be crystallized in the old herbalists' belief that it was useful both as an aphrodisiac and an abortifacient.

"It expelleth both birth and afterbirth," advised the wary Culpeper. "As it helps the deficiency of Venus in one kind, so it spoils all her actions in another. I dare write no more of it," he concluded.

Whatever basil's true mystical nature, it is one of the most widely known and used herbs in modern cookery. It exists in a bewildering profusion of varieties, the most common being sweet basil, or garden basil.

A similar dwarf bush that rarely exceeds six inches (15 cm) is *O. minimum*. More suitable for indoor cultivation because of its size, it was a common favour bestowed by English farmers on their guests in Tudor times.

O. Basilicum, enshrined in the works of such diverse authors as Boccaccio, Keats, Shelley, and Drayton, is an annual that needs insect pollination for seed formation. Leaves are eggshaped to oval, curled inward along the spine as if they had turned their backs on the world and, depending on soil fertility, are yellow-green to dark green. White flowers form in whorls around the end of each stem. Seeds are very small. On contact with water, they develop a greyish gelatin around them, through which sprouts appear after four or five days at 70°F (21°C). Only the leaves are used for seasoning.

Start basil from seeds each year, since the herb is very sensitive to frost. As soon as that danger has passed, seed in rows not more than a quarter-inch (6 mm) deep. Or, if basil is started indoors, transplant the young shoots only after the danger of overnight frost is over. Keep them 12 inches (30 cm) apart.

Because basil likes a rich, weed-free, well-aerated soil, its bed should be cultivated thoroughly and treated with well-rotted manure or manure compost before planting. After shoots appear, mulch well to hold soil warmth and moisture and to discourage weeds. If basil's leaves curl downwards during a dry spell, sprinkle the plant with tepid water.

Basil grows best if it's harvested before the stems go to flower. The first cutting takes the main stem—a ridged and hairy growth—out from the top, although at least one node with two young shoots should be left intact.

The remaining growth will branch out to be ready for another trimming within two to three weeks. Harvesting can continue until the first frost, which will turn the leaves dark and halt all growth.

To prepare the leaves for storage, pinch them off at the stem and dry them in a well-ventilated, shady area. If they are not dry within three days,

331

finish the process in a low oven or the leaves will turn brown and black.

Gardeners could take a tip from an ancient Chinese herbal that recommends the extensive planting of basil in back gardens to keep down the malodours of fertilizers.

Peptic, aromatic, and carminative properties are ascribed to it, and traditionally it has been used as a treatment for mild nervous disorders such as headaches and nausea. The golden-yellow oil of basil seems to have little use except as an ingredient of perfumes.

In the kitchen, basil imparts a delicious clove-like flavour to bland vegetables and soups, salad dressings, and egg dishes. For an interesting sandwich spread, add chopped basil to creamery butter. Use basil on grilled tomatoes and even in onion dishes. The French find it indispensable in turtle and mock turtle soups, and also use it widely in ragouts and sauces.

Basil can also be preserved for winter use by soaking a few fresh leaves in vinegar. Fill a pint (568 ml) jar one-third full with basil leaves, then pour white vinegar over it, close the jar, and let it stand in the sun for three weeks. Or macerate a double handful of fresh leaves in a two-gallon (9 l) crock of ceramic or stainless steel, then add a gallon (4.5 l) of white or malt vinegar. Bringing the mixture to a boil will cut a week off the steeping time.

Fresh basil leaves, boiled and eaten spinach-style, serve as an aromatic vegetable dish, while basil tea is a most refreshing drink, believed by some people to be a good tonic against rheumatism.

Bay

Sweet Bay, Laurel, True Laurel
Laurus nobilis
Lauraceae

Nothing is too much trouble to keep a bay tree alive and well in your herb collection, some herb lovers will tell you. A well-chronicled medicinal and culinary herb, the bay tree is probably most familiar as a plant grown for its looks, usually in big wooden tubs. It is indeed worth a special place in landscape design.

Left in its natural form, it is a lovely evergreen, aromatic shrub, with elliptical, shiny, dark green leaves. Flowers are inconspicuous, greenish-yellow in small umbels in the axils of stems, followed by dark purple berries. It can be grown as a single-trunk tree by pruning side growth and suckers as they appear. It is slow-growing, and when pruned and shaped as a tub-planted showpiece, the bay seldom exceeds ten feet (3 m) in height. But in Mediterranean areas, the bay tree has been known to top 60 feet (18 m) in height. It is, however, very

Sweet Bay (Laurus nobilis)
(a) fruit

frustrating to grow bay from seed and even to use cuttings, the most popular method of propagation. It will try your patience.

Theoretically, it can be started from either seed or cuttings, but we have planted seeds almost every year and have never been able to germinate one. For some reason they always mould. The seeds are about the size of a pea and are a dark brown colour. They are said to germinate at a temperature of 70°F (21°C) within four weeks. The most reliable starting technique is to use a cutting, selecting a fresh, green stem. One should use standard practices, but exercise more patience, since the cuttings may take as long as six months to root. As a permanent growing medium, a moderate soil with good drainage will suffice. Bay likes the sun and this makes it difficult to maintain as a houseplant. However, bay does do better in a greenhouse. It also needs protection from frost and icy winds.

Bay leaves can be picked and dried all year round. The leaves have a delightful fragrance and are commonly used as seasoning for soups, stews, meat and fish, puddings, custards, and the like.

The leaves have been used to drive away fleas and lice and, placed in canisters, will prevent moths and bugs in flour and cereals. One advantage of the tree is that it is highly resistant to pests and diseases and also protects other nearby plants against insects.

Bay leaves and berries have been used in medicine, having both excitant and narcotic properties. The leaves have been regarded as diaphoretic and, in large doses, as emetic generally being infused and administered as a tea. The berries also serve many of the same purposes. An oil can be distilled from the leaves and berries for use externally on sprains and bruises. This oil was also dropped into the ears to relieve pain.

The old herbalists saw bay as a virtuous tree. "They serve both for pleasure and profit, both for ornament and use, both for honest civil uses and for physic, yea both for the sick and for the sound, both for the living and the dead," wrote Parkinson. Galen, the Greek physician, was quoted as recommending the leaves, berries, and bark as a diuretic and for liver ailments, And Culpeper wrote:

The berries are very effectual against all poisons of venomous creatures, and the sting of wasps and bees, as also against the pestilence, or other infectious diseases, and therefore put into sundry treacles for that purposes. . . A bath of a decoction of the leaves and berries, is singular good for women to sit in that are troubled with the mother, or the diseases thereof, or the stoppings of their courses, or for the diseases of the bladder, pains in the bowels by wind and stopping of urine. A decoction likewise of equal parts of bay berries, cumin-seed, hyssop, origanum, and euphorbium, with some honey, and the head bathed therewith, doth wonderfully help distillations and rheums, and settleth the palate of the mouth into its place.

Culpeper also wrote of some of the superstitions surrounding bay: "It is a tree of the Sun, and under the celestial sign Leo, and resisteth witchcraft very potently, as also all the evils of old Saturn can do the body of man . . ."

Any time protection was needed bay was used; it was always a part of weddings and funerals. Shakespeare wrote in *Richard II*: "'Tis thought the King is dead: we will not stay, the Bay trees in our country are all wither'd."

The Greeks, too, had a superstitious regard for bay. They dedicated the tree to Apollo, and as such viewed it as emblematic of the Sun God's powers. It provided protection against evil and guarded man's social well-being. Moreover, it was related to cultural activities: music and song, poetry and drama. The Greeks also related bay with prophesies; the Delphic priestesses, oracles of Apollo, held bay leaves between their lips as they made their prophesies. It is supposed that they were drugged with bay as a part of the ritual.

Still another famous use of bay developed from the Apollonian symbol for the bay tree: victors, heroes, and artistic figures were given the laurels, crowns of bay. It is suggested that this practice gave rise to the term *baccalaureate*, derived from baccalaureus or laurel-berry, associated with academics.

"Neither witch nor devil, nor thunder or lightning will hurt a man in a place where a Bay Tree is", said Culpeper. He may have overstated the case, but protective or not, the bay tree is worth the effort it takes to have, if only for its culinary and visual appeal.

Bedstraw, Lady's

Cleaver's Vine, Maid's Hair,
Cheese Rennet
Galium verum
Rubiaceae

A good rock and bank plant, lady's bedstraw has leaves from one to two inches (2.5 to 5 cm) long in rings of six around a squarish stem, and abundant clusters of small yellow flowers. Native plants grow in moist thickets and banks of streams and flower from June to September.

Bedstraw is most easily established by dividing the roots. Obtain a first plant or several plants, and, each spring after the plant has taken hold, divide the roots. A spreading plant, it will crowd out weeds. It does well in full sun or partial shade, is not particular as to soil, but does require a well-drained location.

The name was derived from the practice of stuffing mattresses with the mown bedstraw. Indeed, this would suggest that the plant can be cut back sharply, and in fact it can. Bedstraw may be cut before or after blooming. Christian legend has it that it was used to provide a bed for the Christ child in the manger in Bethlehem.

In the days of Henry VII the herb was used as a hair dye, and hence, obtained the popular name "maid's hair". Gerard said that "the people of

Lady's Bedstraw
(Galium verum)

335

Thuscane do use it to turne their milkes and cheese, which they make of sheepes and goates milke, might be the sweeter and more pleasant to taste. The people of Cheshire especially about Nantwich, where the best cheese is made, do use it in their rennet, esteeming greatly of that cheese above other made without it." Hence the popular name "cheese rennet".

In America, the Indians once used it as a healing agent for burns and wounds. The Elizabethan herbalists suggested bedstraw for nosebleeds, for internal bleeding, and for anointing the feet of weary travellers. There is later mention of bedstraw as a remedy for "kidney stone and urinary diseases".

A relative of madder, a famous dye plant, bedstraw does yield a dye, although fairly large quantities of it have to be used. The leaves and stems yield a yellow colour, while the roots yield a red.

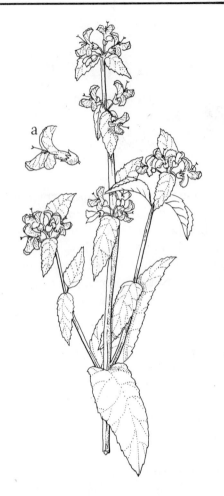

Wood Betony
(Betonica officinalis)
(a) flower

Betony, Wood

Bishopswort
Stachys officinalis
(syn. *Betonica officinalis*)
Labiatae

This herb is a native of Europe, being found in woodlands and open heathlands from as far north as Scotland and as far south as the Mediterranean.

It is also to be found in Spain and as far east as the Caucasus.

There are other plants of the species; *S. arvensis, S. germanica, S. palustris,* and *S. sylvatica.* These are similarly distributed geographically. In America, there is to be found another species, *S. hyssopifolia,* known as hedge nettle, or hyssop hedge nettle.

Betony tea, made with an infusion of the dried leaves and water just off the boil, is a popular remedy for nervousness, tension, and headaches.

The history of betony goes back to the ancient Greeks who extolled the herb in much of their literature. Betony was also praised in many other countries especially Spain and Italy, where it was generally regarded as a panacea for all ills.

Betony is a perennial growing to a height of between one and two feet (30 and 60 cm); stems are slender, square, and furrowed; leaves not too close together, about two to three inches (5 to 8 cm) long, and anything up to one inch (2.5 cm) wide. The majority of the leaves are to be found at the base of the plant and these tend to be larger and of an elongated heart shape. The upper leaves are more of an oblong shape.

Birch, Common

Silver Birch, White Birch
Betula alba
Betulaceae

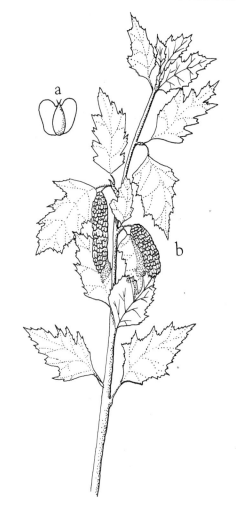

Silver Birch
(Betula alba)
(a) seed (b) catkin

Various species of birch can be used effectively in a garden landscape. They will add a distinctive charm in the dormant season with their delicate branches and conspicuous barks. They blend well into a naturalistic or wood-land type of setting, or near a rocky pool where the autumn gold of the leaves reflects in the water.

Young birches have dark bark and do not develop their characteristic colour until they are several years old. The silver birch grows to 60 feet (18 m), has drooping branches and white bark that peels easily. The branches produce catkins containing both male and female flowers.

Sweet or cherry birch, one of the many varieties chosen at random, is wide-branching with a high head, making good shade but allowing for sun and air underneath. The bark is dark, clean, and smooth, similar to cherry. Several varieties have orange or reddish bark, and a very hardy dwarf species lies flat against the ground. A very slow grower, it is suitable for a cool rockery.

Most birches thrive in moist, sandy loam. They are propagated by seed sown or stratified in sandy soil, also by green wood cuttings under glass.

Beer is often made from the sap of sweet birch. A type of oil of wintergreen is distilled from the inner bark and twigs. This is used for remedies believed by some to purify the blood, to cure rheumatism, and to expel worms. Applied externally, it is said to be beneficial for boils and sores.

The bark and stems of the white birch are bitter and astringent. These are distilled into birch tar oil which used to be employed for preparing Russian leather. The oil was also used as an insect repellent, and as an ointment. Juice extracted from the leaves was used as a treatment for kidney and bladder (gall) stones and as a mouthwash. Birches improve soil, restore fertility to barren soil, and, planted near the compost area, encourage fermentation. Leaves should be added to the compost.

Borage

Burrage, Bee Bread
Borago officinalis
Boraginaceae

Borage is such a cheerful plant to have in your garden or potted by a sunny window that it isn't surprising to learn that it was prescribed four hundred years ago for melancholy. It is, moreover, inextricably aligned with courage in the minds of herbalists everywhere, to the point that it is the inevitable introduction to the herb.

In the garden, borage is almost constantly in bloom, and surrounded by interested bees, who alone can pollinate it. Hence one popular name "bee bread". It grows quite rapidly, spreading over a fairly broad area and self-seeding proficiently.

It is classified as a hardy annual. It grows about 12 to 18 inches (30 to 46 cm) tall, but it isn't an erect plant, and a single healthy plant will spread over an area of roughly four square feet (371 sq.cm), covering it with hairy stems and leaves, brightening it with strikingly blue star-shaped flowers. Occasionally, a borage plant will bear both blue and pink flowers; the capacity to bear more than one colour of flower at a time is characteristic of the Boraginaceae family.

There is some controversy over the source of the borage name. Some say the Latin *borago* is a corruption of

Borage
(Borago officinalis)

connection between the Celtic term, *barrach*, which means "a man of courage", and the herb's character. The wide range of speculation is interesting, if inconclusive.

Not in contention is the history of the plant as a source of emotional strength and courage. The Welsh named it *llanwenlys*, or "herb of gladness". Sir Francis Bacon noted that "the leaf of Burrage hath an excellent spirit to repress the fuliginous vapour of disky melancholie."

Even earlier writers viewed borage in the same general terms. Dioscorides declared borage to be the nepenthe of Homer, the legendary tonic which brought absolute forgetfulness; ". . . if wife and children, father and mother, brother and sister, and all thy dearest friends shouldst die before thy face, thou couldst not grieve, or shed a tear for them." Pliny echoed Dioscorides' assertion, and it has been re-echoed throughout herbal literature.

John Gerard recorded in his herbal centuries later:

Pliny calls it Euphrosinum, because "it maketh a man merry and joyfull: which thing also the old verse concerning Borage doth testifie: Ego Borago Gaudia semper ago. I, Borage Bring alwaies courage." Those of our time do use the flowers in sallads to exhilerate and make the mind glad. There be also many things made of these used everywhere for the comfort of the heart, for the driving away of sorrow and increasing the joy of the mind . . . The leaves and floures of Borage put into wine make men and women glad and merry and drive away all sadnesse, dulnesse and melancholy, as Dioscorides and Pliny affirme. Syrup made of the floures of Borage comforteth the

corago, from *cor,* the heart, and *ago,* I bring, an obvious reference to the long-standing association between the plant and the effect. Others point out that a connection is apparent between the plant's name, its hairy appearance, and the low Latin term for a flock of wool, *burra,* and its derivatives, *borra* (Italian) and *bourra* (French), both of which mean much the same thing. Still a third opinion suggests that a derivation stems from the apparent

heart, purgeth melancholy and quieteth the phrenticke and lunaticke person. The leaves eaten raw ingender good bloud, especially in those that have been lately sicke.

Borage is believed to have originated in Aleppo, a city in north-western Syria. An independent plant, it spread throughout Europe, and it remains a fairly common wild plant on the Continent.

As noted by Gerard, borage is a salad herb and was widely cultivated as a pot-herb. The young leaves are excellent in salads, as the taste of borage is suggestive of cucumbers. The leaves may also be cooked and served as spinach. The leaves should be boiled with only a little water, then chopped fine and served with butter. The flowers are edible, as Gerard said, and their brilliant colour makes them particularly decorative in the salad bowl. The flowers are often served crystallized. Dip them in egg white, then sugar, and dry.

One of the oldest uses of borage blossoms is as a flavour-enhancing decoration in beverages. The Greeks and Romans floated the blossoms in their wine cups, but you can add them to cider, punch, lemonade, or other beverages. The leaves can be used to make their own beverage. Steeped in boiling water, borage makes a tea that stimulates the circulation and soothes the throat. The tea may be served hot or cold.

Culpeper contended in his day that borage was chiefly used fresh, "yet the ashes thereof boiled in mead or honied water is available against the inflammations and ulcers in the mouth or throat, to gargle it therewith . . . the dried herb is never used, but the green," he maintained. Today, though, borage is dried, chiefly for use in making tea. The leaves gathered for this purpose must be selected carefully, after the dew is off the plants, then chopped and dried in an even heat. The dried herb must be stored in tightly sealed containers, for it absorbs moisture readily.

While Culpeper and other early herbalists emphasized the cheering, stimulating effects of borage, it is also listed in herbals as a diuretic, demulcent, and emollient. Because of saline constituents, borage is an effective diuretic and has been used to carry off feverish catarrhs. A drink suggested for fever sufferers is made by pouring a pint (568 ml) of boiling water over a sliced lemon and half a dozen sprigs of borage. The brew is cooled, strained, and served freely. Another suggested infusion is made of an ounce (28 g) of leaves to three-quarters of a pint (426 ml) of boiling water. This tea is taken in wineglass doses. Externally, a poultice of borage leaves is good for inflamed swellings.

The gardener will find borage quite easy to cultivate. If he or she has strawberries, the borage plant will make an excellent companion for them. The two plants are said to be mutually beneficial, if the borage is kept to a relatively small proportion. Borage is also said to strengthen resistance to insects and disease of neighbouring plants.

Borage can be grown from seed either indoors or in the garden. Whether seeded directly or transplanted, the plant should be given sufficient garden space to develop properly. It should be about two feet (60 cm) from any neighbours. Once established, borage will self-seed, and offspring may well sprout around the parent plant before the growing season is through. Although borage is relatively hardy, it shouldn't be seeded or set out-doors until the danger of frost is past.

Borage requires a fairly rich soil. A manure compost is the best fertilizer. The soil should be loose, well aerated, and hoed regularly to eliminate weeds. A mulch is a good idea, for borage likes a moist environment.

Borage is simple to maintain in an indoor garden. It will easily survive a pot-bound existence, given sufficient root space, a fertile potting medium, sunlight, and moisture.

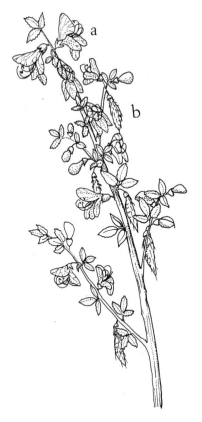

Broom
(Cytisus scoparius)
(a) flower (b) seed pod

Broom

Broom tops, Irish tops, Bizzom, Brum
Cytisus scoparius
Leguminosae

This attractive, evergreen shrub of the pea family, native of Europe, Asia, and Africa, has bright green, almost leaf-less stems with yellow flowers in June. The height ranges from three to ten feet (90 cm to 3 m) and can be trimmed back after flowering to a more compact shape.

Broom requires full exposure to sun and wind, and prefers poor soil, provided that it has good drainage. It is useful for planting on dry, gravelly banks and can also be used in borders, background plantings, or standing alone as an attractive "point-of-interest" shrub. The bright green

341

stems and yellow flowers make a good display.

Small plants are easier to establish than large ones. They are easily started and grow quickly from seed, but may be propagated by cuttings or layers.

Fresh green tops are picked just before flowering. They contain an active principal, sparteine sulphate, which is used as a cardiac depressant to quieten an over-active heart. The plant is rich in potash and has been used as a cure for many ailments including dropsy, toothache, problems of spleen, kidneys, and bladder. It makes a good ointment for guarding against lice or vermin.

Like nasturtium, broom may be used as a bait plant for aphids, attracting them away from other plants, yet seemingly suffering no ill effects from their presence. One of the legumes, it also increases available nitrogen in soil, benefiting plants growing around it, and is a collector of calcium.

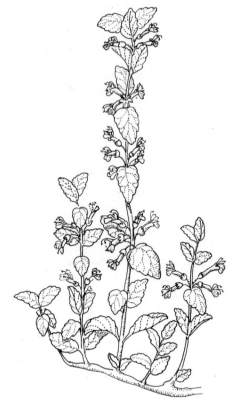

Bugle
(Ajuga reptans)

Bugle, Common

Sicklewort, Carpenter's Herb,
Middle Comfrey
Ajuga reptans
Labiatae

There are three bugles in Britain: the common creeping strain *Ajuga reptans*; erect bugle, a rare highland species,

A. pyramidalis; and yellow bugle or ground pine, *A. chamaepitys*. They are perennials flowering from the end of April to the beginning of July.

Common bugle is easily grown in damp, shady soil and can be propagated by seed and division. It is a popular ground cover, edging, and rock garden plant. It is a prostrate variety whose stems root as they creep. The flowers are pale blue or purplish. In addition to the species mentioned, others include: *A. reptans* var. *atropurpurea* (bronze ajuga), which has blue flowers and bronze leaves; var. *multi-colour* with red, brown, and yellow foliage; var. *rubra*, which has dark purple foliage with pink flowers; and var. *variegata* with leaves splotched and bordered, and cream and blue flowers. *A. pyramidalis* has blue flowers slightly larger than others, stays neat and small, and is less likely to spread.

This herb has several medicinal applications. The bruised leaves may be applied as a poultice for cuts and wounds or bruises. It is also made into an ointment. A decoction of leaves and flowers can be used as a remedy for coughs, and also for hangovers. It is bitter, astringent, and aromatic.

Burdock

**Great Burdock, Thorny Burr,
Beggar's Buttons**
Arctium Lappa
Compositae

Burdock is a weed quite popular with foraging animals, and has a notable past as a medicinal plant. It is a tall, large-leaved plant commonly found on waste grounds with a profusion of burrs in the autumn. It is certainly a plant to know, but few find it really worth cultivating.

A native of Europe, burdock was reported by Parkinson to be "a helpful

Burdock
(Arctium Lappa)
(a) flower

343

remedy for venomous bites". Culpeper said the leaves were "cooling and moderately drying, whereby good for old ulcers and sores. The seed being drunk in wine 40 days together doth wonderfully help the sciatica . . . The root may be preserved with sugar for consumption, stone, and the lax. The seed is much commended to break the stone." Such commendations notwithstanding, burdock was never listed in the European pharmacopoeias of the Seventeenth and Eighteenth Centuries.

Most herbals list its diuretic and diaphoretic properties and many quote burdock as being one of the best blood purifiers. The dried root is the most commonly used plant part, although the leaves and seeds (properly called the fruits) are also useful medicinally. The root, a plant without a flower stalk, must be dug up the autumn of the plant's first year. Generally, the roots are difficult to excavate; a posthole digger or slender spade being helpful in the task. The roots may extend twelve inches (30 cm) or more and be an inch (2.5 cm) in diameter, about a quarter of which is usually a grey-brown bark with the remainder being a whitish pith. The leaves should be collected when they are still young, the seeds as they ripen.

The common prescription is a decoction of the dried root. Add an ounce (28 g) of the root to a pint and a quarter (710 ml) of water, boil down to three-quarters of a pint (426 ml) and take a wineglassful three or four times daily. This same decoction has been used as a wash for ulcers and scaly skin disorders. In any case, the use of the decoction must be continued over a relatively long time for it to be effective.

An infusion of the leaves is said to be useful as a stomachic. The leaves have also been used as a poultice for bruises, swellings, and tumours. A tincture of the seeds is of service as a remedy for certain skin diseases.

The wild food forager relishes burdock for its root particularly, but also for its leaves and stem. The Japanese, who cultivate burdock to some extent, consider it a source of strength and endurance, and something of an aphrodisiac as well. The first-year roots should be peeled, sliced crosswise, cooked for about 30 minutes in water to which a pinch of bicarbonate of soda has previously been added, then cooked another ten minutes or so in very little water. For the best eating, the roots should be gathered in June or early July. The flower stalks should be gathered just as the flowers are forming. These should be carefully peeled of the bitter rind and cooked as you would the roots, using two separate amounts of water, with a pinch of bicarbonate of soda in the first. The young leaves, so cooked, can be used as a vegetable.

Burdock is a quick-growing biennial with large, wavy, egg-shaped leaves and, in its second year, globular purple (and very occasionally white) flowers. The flowers appear on a stalk which reaches three and sometimes four feet (roughly 1 to 1.25 m) in height. They are followed by the burrs, which have been a distinguishing characteristic of the plant throughout its history. Its botanical name, *Arctium Lappa*, is derived from the Greek *arktos*, a bear, an allusion to the roughness of the burrs, and from a word meaning "to seize". The burrs have prompted a number of common names over the years and earned a place in Shakespeare's literature. "How full of briers is this working-day world!" exclaims Rosalind in *As You Like It*. Celia responds: "They are but burrs, cousin, thrown upon thee in holiday foolery. If we walk not in the trodden paths, our very petticoats will catch them." And so they will, even today.

Burnet, Salad

Burnet Saxifrage,
Pimpinella Sanquisorba
Sanguisorba minor
(syn. *Poterium Sanguisorba*)
Rosaceae

Burnet is a bushy perennial that grows 12 to 24 inches (30 to 60 cm) tall and produces nearly evergreen, fern-like foliage. The bruised leaves taste and smell somewhat like cucumbers.

The flowers in each head bear crimson-tufted stigmas with long, drooping filaments. Burnet flowers in June and July. Both the flower and

Salad Burnet
(Sanguisorba minor)
(a) flower head (b) flower enlargement

leaf stalks are a deep crimson colour. Turner in his *Newe Herball* in 1551, describes the plant as follows:

It has two little leives like unto the wings of birdes, standing out as the bird setteth her wings out when she intendeth to flye. Ye Dutchmen call it Hergottes berdlen, that is God's little berde, because of the colour that it hath in the top.

Salad burnet was formerly used as a fodder plant in Britain, but it has fallen out of use now. Its ability to

345

remain green on poor soil throughout the winter adds to its value in the salad garden; it is a long-lasting source of fresh greens. It is easily grown from seed.

Burnet needs full sun and does best in soil with a pH value of between 6 and 8. Sow the seeds one-half inch (13 mm) deep outdoors in late autumn or early spring. When the seedlings are about two inches (5 cm) high, remove smaller ones. Allow 12 to 15 inches (30 to 38 cm) between plants.

Burnet begins growing in March and can be harvested until after the first autumn frost. The leaves should be picked when young and tender. Remove flower stalks to encourage the development of new leaf growth. Burnet often grows spontaneously from seeds dropped by mature plants, and these plants can be transplanted in your garden.

The leaves are used fresh, but can be dried. When dried, they lose some of their cucumber flavour and are a bit more nut-like. They should be dried rapidly in the shade to retain as much of their colour as possible.

Burnet always had its place in the herb gardens of former times. The famous Elizabethan playwright Francis Bacon recommends it to be set in walkways together with wild thyme and water mint to "perfume the air most delightfully, being trodden on and crushed."

It was much used in salads and in wines, being the "pimpernella" essential in the best French and Italian salads. It was also used in drinking cups, like borage, to slightly flavour the drinks; one generic name, *Poterium*, comes from the name of a Greek drinking cup, the *poterion*. Gerard spoke of this use of salad burnet when he said; "It is thought to make the hart merry and glad, as also being put into wine, to which it yeeldeth a certaine grace in the drinking."

The older herbalists recommended burnet for a number of complaints. Pliny suggested a decoction of the plant with honey for several disorders, and it was said to protect against the Plague and other contagious diseases. Burnet had a reputation as a healer of internal and external wounds either as a drink or in an ointment, and it was used by the Tudors to cure gout and rheumatism.

One ancient herbalist, Dodoens, recommended this use of the herb:

Made into powder and dronke with wine, wherein from hath bene often quenched, and so doth the herb alone, being but only holden in a man's hande as some have written. The leaves stiped in wine and dronken, doth comfort and rejoice the hart, and are good against the trembling and shaking of the same.

Gerard suggested the juice of burnet taken in a drink as "A speciall helpe to defend the heart from noysome vapours and from the infection of the Plague or Pestilence, and all other contagious diseases for which purpose it is of great effect. . ."

It is still regarded as a styptic, and an infusion of the whole herb is employed as an astringent. It is also

346

a cordial and promotes perspiration.

The fresh leaves may be used in salads, vinegars, cream cheese, drinks, and as a garnish.

Burning Bush

Fraxinella, False or White Dittany, Gas Plant
Dictamnus albus
Rutaceae

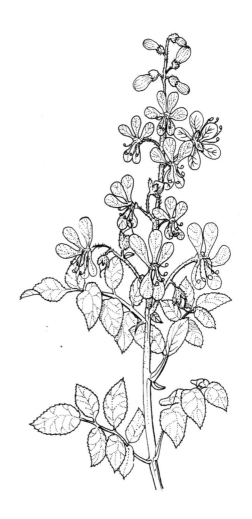

Burning bush is not common to Britain. Its habitat is Germany, France, Spain, Austria, Italy, and Asia Minor. However, it is an interesting plant, if only for its novel pyrotechnic abilities.

A notably long-lived perennial, it resents transplanting. Sow seeds in open ground as soon as ripe in autumn, to sprout in spring. It is a frost germinator. Burning bush has dark green, shining compound leaves, and showy flowers in loose terminal spires. A volatile oil from the flowers is emitted as a vapour on sultry summer evenings. Indeed, if a lighted match is held to this vapour it will flash. The white flowering variety has a lemon fragrance; the pink is more fragrant, but less lemony and has the added scent of almond and vanilla. According to Parkinson, it was used against contagious diseases and pestilence.

*Burning Bush
(Dictamnus albus)*

347

Buttercup, Bulbous

Crowfoot, St. Anthony's Turnip, Frogsfoot, Gold Cup
Ranunculus bulbosus
Ranunculaceae

Truly, buttercup must be one of the most predominant and best-loved flowers of the English pastoral scene. That golden-yellow set against a back-cloth of verdant green, makes for the basis of the traditional Maytime picture of our countryside.

The bulbous buttercup, or crow-foot, one of the most common members of the Ranunculaceae family, is so named in Latin because of its bulbous swelling at the base of the stem, which looks like a small turnip. Hence its other common name. This "bulb", however, is not a true bulb.

On the face of it, the buttercup resembles upright crowfoot and creep-ing crowfoot, but it differs from them by having this bulbous shape. It does not have runners and its sepals are turn-ed back in the fully expanded blossom, touching the flower's supporting stem.

One of the medicinal uses of butter-cup is as a remedy for gout. The juice of this plant applied to the nostrils is said to provoke sneezing and to cure certain cases of headaches. The leaves have been used to produce blisters on the wrists where rheumatism exists. A tincture made with spirits of wine will cure shingles and pimples, and sharp pains between the ribs.

Bulbous Buttercup
(Ranunculus bulbosus)

Camomile, Common

Physician's Plant, Roman Camomile, Mayhen, Mayweed
Anthemis nobilis
Compositae

Camomile, German

Wild Chamomile
Matricaria Chamomilla
Compositae

German camomile and Roman camomile are two distinct plants with similar characteristics, but people familiar with one tend to think of that as the only one. Even variations in spelling add to the confusion; camomile is often spelt chamomile; either is correct.

The camomiles are perhaps best known for their apple-like fragrance and flavour, qualities which always come as a surprise to the uninitiated, for neither camomile has any visual resemblance to an apple or apple tree. The apple-like qualities, however, have been strong enough throughout man's acquaintance to have earned the plants the name "camomile", which is derived from the Greek *kamai*, on the ground, and *melon*, apple, for ground apple.

Although the plants are generically different, their common characteristics are sufficient to confuse them in the minds of many. Both have daisy-like blossoms, the apple-like fragrance, and foliage that could be characterized as feathery. Moreover, the genus *Matricaria* is not as clear-cut as some botanists would like it to be, being difficult to distinguish from *Anthemis* and *Chrysanthemum*, and perhaps from *Pyrethrum*. Nevertheless, there are some distinguishing characteristics.

Anthemis nobilis is a low-growing perennial, seldom topping more than nine inches (23 cm) in height. It has finely divided leaves. The flowers have a large, solid central disc of a deep yellow colour and creamy rays. The variety with double flowers has the best medicinal value. The entire herb is strongly scented.

Matricaria Chamomilla is an annual with fine-cut foliage (though somewhat more coarse than *A. nobilis*) and a single daisy-like flower with a yellow, hollow disc and white rays. The flowers are smaller than those of *A. nobilis* and less strongly scented. The plant is erect, growing two to three feet (60 to 90 cm) tall. The plant has medicinal properties similar to those of *A. nobilis*, but of a lesser quality.

The most obvious difference between the two plants—at least theoretically—is that one is an annual, while the other is a perennial. Such information is not much practical use for making identifications, however. Perhaps the most useful and pronounced distinction is the stature:

349

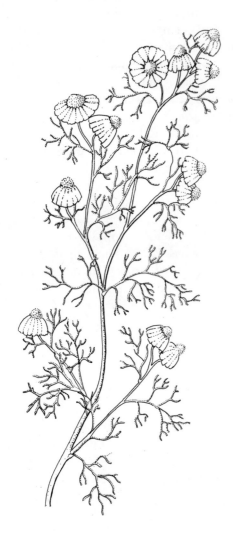

German Camomile
(Matricaria Chamomilla)

A. nobilis is nearly prostrate, while *M. Chamomilla* is erect. The flower size and structure are different.

These differences haven't been sufficient to prevent some confusing of the two plants throughout history.

In general, Germanic-speaking peoples have considered *M. Chamomilla* to be *the* camomile, hence the name "German camomile", while the English-speaking peoples have considered *A. nobilis* to be *the* camomile. But the uses, at least, are so similar that confusion is bound to develop when camomile is discussed.

Of course, the dogmatism of some herbalists contributes further to the confusion and leads to denigration. In English herbals, *M. Chamomilla* is often labelled a weed, but the name-calling cuts both ways. A gardening book of Germanic orientation notes, for example; "The more commonly found Camomile called Mayweed and others of the genus *Anthemis* often become obnoxious weeds; they are not cultivated as a rule."

The fact of the matter is that both plants are cultivated, but both escape cultivation at every opportunity and are occasionally found in the wild. As to which plant is the true camomile, one might speculate that *A. nobilis* is the true camomile and that Linnaeus, who classified and named both plants, chose the specific name *Chamomilla* for German camomile; simply because it closely resembled the plant commonly called camomile, *A. nobilis*.

Both German and Roman camomiles have been held in considerable esteem as medicinal herbs. Both are particularly useful as tonics. The usual infusion is made of a half to one ounce (14 to 28 g) of the dried blossoms and a pint (568 ml) of boiling water.

Roman camomile is said to have, in addition to its tonic effect, stomachic, anodyne, and antispasmodic properties. The plant has also been used in instances where a diuretic or diaphoretic effect was desired. An infusion of an ounce (28 g) of the blossoms to three-quarters of a pint (426 ml) of boiling water is said to have a "wonderfully soothing, sedative, and absolutely harmless effect", and has been used to calm the nerves, remedy delirium tremens, and prevent nightmares.

Equal amounts of camomile flowers and poppy-heads were combined and crushed to produce a poultice of fomentation for external swellings, inflammations, and the like. Muslin bags were filled with the flowers, boiled, then applied to the painful spot. Infusing the two kinds of flowers—a half-ounce (14 g) of each to three-quarters of a pint (426 ml) of boiling water—yields a liquid that has been used as a facial wash to sooth neuralgia and toothaches.

Roman camomile was held in esteem throughout history for these medicinal qualities. The Egyptians consecrated it to their gods. The Romans didn't go that far, but they did make extensive use of it for its medicinal properties. Throughout the Middle Ages, it was so widely used that when, as civilization moved into a new age, Culpeper began his record of plant medicines, he didn't bother to describe the plant, saying: "It is so well-known everywhere that it is but lost time and labour to describe it." He remarked on its history; "Nechessor saith the Egyptians dedicated it to the Sun, because it cured agues, and they were like enough to do it, for they were the arrantest apes in their religion I ever read of." And he included a lengthy list of the reputed virtues of the herb.

Gerard and Parkinson generally echoed Culpeper's view of camomile. And Turner wrote:

It hath floures wonderfully shynynge yellow and resemblynge the appell of an eye . . . the herbe may be called in English, golden floure. It will restore a man to hys color shortly yf a man after the longe use of the bathe drynke of it after he is come forthe oute of the bathe. This herb is scarce in Germany but in England it is so plenteous that it growth not only in gardynes but also VIII mile above London, it groweth in the wylde felde, in Rychmonde grene, in Brantfurde grene . . . Thys herbe was consecrated by the wyse men of Egypt unto the Sonne and was rekened to be the only remedy of all agues.

Turner's remark that camomile was little seen in Germany doesn't make clear whether the German's regard for German camomile was the cause or the effect. But the fact remains that to the German herbalist, German camomile was the true camomile. Heinz Grotzke, one such herbalist, traces the origins of German camomile to southern Europe and the Near East, noting that "the Germanic tribes considered the camomile sacred in ancient times and dedicated it to their sun god Baldur because to them the camomile's yellow centre and white petals

Common Camomile (Anthemis nobilis)

around it seemed to convey sun forces."
Dioscorides and Pliny recommended
a camomile poultice or bath as the
cure for headaches and illnesses affecting the liver, kidneys, and bladder.

The English herbalists were not so
kind towards German camomile. Culpeper called it "a hateful weed",
modifying that a bit by adding that
"it possess virtues that may recom-

pense all the damage it can do among
the corn". Of those virtues, he merely
reported; "These have the virtues of
the flowers of camomile, but with
more cordial warmth. For those who
have cold and weak stomachs, scarcely
any thing equals them. They are best
taken by way of infusion like tea."

Curiously enough, Culpeper refers
to German camomile as feverfew and

352

labels it both *M. Chamomilla* and *Pyrethrum chamomilla*. Parkinson, for his part, likened camomile to feverfew, too. Feverfew's botanical name is *Chrysanthemum Parthenium*, but it has been called *P. parthenium* and *M. parthenium*. All of this serves to point up the relatively unclear distinctions among the members of the genera *Matricaria, Chrysanthemum,* and *Pyrethrum*.

A more contemporary English herbalist, Maude Grieve, commented in her herbal that German camomile "is not ranked among the true Chamomiles by botanists . . . " She, too, acknowledges the value of the herb, however, listing its medicinal properties as carminative, sedative, and tonic. As with most herbals, the uses listed in Grieve's book are very similar to those listed for Roman camomile.

Both camomiles, of course, have served in more than a healing capacity. Camomile tea, made from either herb, is a soothing beverage, an excellent rinse for blonde hair, and is reputed to be an effective insect repellent. For the latter, sponge the tea over the body, leaving it to dry, and it will deter insect bites. Camomile tea was also used as a marinade for meat in the days before refrigeration, to eliminate or mask the odours of the meat. In Spain, where the camomiles are called manzanilla, the flowers are used to flavour the finest dry sherries.

Both Roman and German camomiles are fine additions to the garden, but the latter in particular can serve the gardener in more than an ornamental capacity. The versatile camomile tea can be used as a greenhouse spray, to stem or prevent a number of plant diseases. Followers of the bio-dynamic method have long used a strong tea allowed to brew a day or more to spray on seedlings to protect them from damping-off.

Bio-dynamic gardeners also use German camomile as a principal ingredient in their special compost preparation, a powder which is mixed with water, then poured over the compost heap just after it is made. The reason for this is a mysterious affinity which exists between camomile and calcium in nature. Since bio-dynamic gardeners regard calcium as vital to plant health, they are particularly interested in this herb which, they say, "guides the calcium formative forces in the breakdown of the raw materials" in the compost heap.

For the companion planter, Roman camomile is also a beneficial herb. Nothing contributes so much to the health of a garden as a number of camomile herbs dispersed about it. If a plant is drooping and apparently dying, in nine cases out of ten it will recover if you place camomile near it. This quality earned the herb the common name "physician's plant".

Roman camomile can be cultivated in a number of ways. It can be propagated from seed, but the plants often turn out to be the less desirable single-flowered variety. The seeds should be sown after the last danger of frost has passed.

353

A more reliable method of getting the variety you want is to purchase a plant (or several plants) and propagate by runners or root division. In moist climates such as ours it can be planted as an aromatic lawn. The spreading nature of the herb together with its hardiness makes this possible. The plants are set about six inches (15 cm) apart and watered regularly until they fill the gaps between them. The first and second cuttings should be done with hand shears, but when the roots have established themselves, the camomile lawn may be mowed with a lawnmower, with the blades set fairly high. The herb should be mowed regularly, to prevent blooming.

German camomile, being an annual, has to be started from seed. The seeds are very tiny and unstable. They have a germination rate of about 70 per cent the first year and, unless they are planted and subjected to freezes and thaws, rapidly lose their viability. Camomile seed is one of the rare seeds that needs light for germination.

The most practical and successful method of starting the plants is to broadcast the seeds in early August, pack the soil lightly, and water until the seedlings appear. By early September, the plants will have developed enough to transplant them if you wish. Winter cover is not needed as the plants are extremely hardy.

For spring planting the seeds can be started indoors in March and transplanted outside when large enough to handle. After this they gradually harden off, which entails exposing them to cold temperatures over a period of time. Alternatively, they may be seeded directly in the garden, after the danger of frost is passed. The seeds should be sown in rows rather than broadcast.

There are several other members of the *Anthemis* genus which have the appearance and some of the characteristics of the camomiles. *A. arvensis* is a wild plant generally called corn camomile. In France, it was considered an excellent febrifuge. *A. tinctoria* is the yellow or ox-eye camomile, which also is a wild plant. As its specific name implies, it yields a yellow dye. *A. Cotula* and *M. inodora* are wild camomiles which are also known as mayweeds.

A. Cotula is known as stinking camomile, foetid camomile, stinking mayweed, dog fennel, and a wide variety of other names, all of which indicate in one or another way that it is not a plant you will love to have around. It has an unpleasant smell and a reputation of blistering the hand when touched. But it shares the medicinal properties of the more well-known varieties.

M. inodora is known as the scentless mayweed, or corn feverfew. Although it shares the medicinal properties of the camomiles, it is almost totally without smell.

Caraway

Caraway Seed
Carum Carvi
Umbelliferae

Caraway is a plant so pleasant and useful that it is among the best-known and most widely used herbs in almost all parts of the modern world.

It is used to flavour rye breads and cheeses, and is the base for kummel, the German liqueur. Although it is only of marginal medicinal use, caraway has an enjoyable and distinctive liquorice-flavoured tang, very popular with many cuisines.

Old herbal legends associated the quality of retention with caraway. As a result, caraway was an ingredient in love potions as well as an additive to the feed of homing fowl. And true believers held that any object that contained a few caraway seeds would be safe from theft; that, indeed, if any thief tried to steal such an object, the staying power of the caraway would sieze and root him to the spot until the owner reached the scene.

The plant has feathery leaves similar to those of fennel and coriander, although caraway does not like to grow near fennel. It should be seeded directly into the beds where it will grow; it does not tolerate transplanting well. Because it is a biennial, plant a new crop each year for a steady supply.

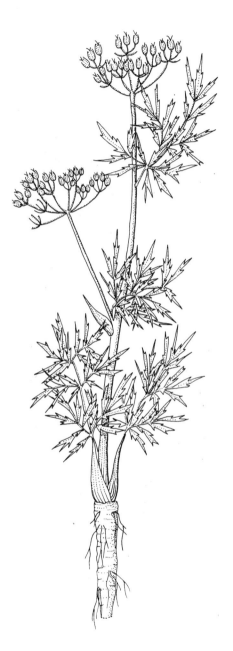

Caraway
(Carum Carvi)

355

Seeding should be done in early spring for the full biennial cycle of the plant. Spring plantings will produce bushy green foliage, about eight inches (20 cm) high, during the first summer. The foliage will retain its verdancy during the winter. During the second summer, two foot (60 cm) stalks topped by clusters of white flowers will develop. Seeds will form by mid-summer and ripen by the autumn. Harvesting time can be shortened if seeds are sown as soon as they're ripe in the autumn. In the latter case, some seeds will be produced late the following summer.

Caraway should be harvested as soon as the seeds ripen and darken. Usually they can be separated from the umbel stems by threshing. Dry them in hot sun or in a low oven heat.

Pay particular attention to weed control during caraway's early months. When the new shoots are about two inches (5 cm) tall pinch out the smaller ones and allow the remaining plants six to 12 inches (15 to 30 cm) of room.

Fertilization is not critical, although caraway seems to prefer a fairly heavy soil on the dry side. Some herbalists recommend a planting of caraway to break up and aerate heavy soils. Other gardeners plant peas and caraway in the same row. The peas come up first, and harrowing them in the normal way simultaneously controls weeds which hinder caraway's early growth.

Roots of the mature caraway plant are a delicacy which can be prepared and eaten much like carrots or parsnips. Parkinson also ascribed medicinal value to them. This Seventeenth Century herbalist advised:

The roots of Caraway, being boiled, may be eaten as Carrots and by reason of the spicie taste doth warme and comfort a cold weak Stomache, helping to dissolve Wind and to provoke Urine, and is a very welcome and delightful Dish to many.

The leaves, too, can be chopped and added to stews and soups and goulashes to impart the tang of caraway. The herb is also said to aid the digestion of heavy starches such as cabbage, turnips, and potatoes. It has aromatic, stimulant, and carminative properties, according to Maude Grieve, who adds that caraway "possesses some tonic property and forms a pleasant stomachic". Caraway seeds are high in protein and fat content and are used, after the distillation of their oil for commercial products for cattle feed supplements.

Culpeper pointed out that caraway seeds, "once only dipped in sugar, and a spoonful of them eaten in the morning fasting, and as many after each meal, is a most admirable remedy for those that are troubled with wind." A similar-acting remedy is made by eating one to four drops of caraway oil on a lump of sugar, or in a teaspoonful of water. For a gripe water for infants, try a caraway julep made by bruising an ounce (28 g) of seeds and infusing them for six hours in three-quarters of a pint (426 ml) of cold water. Give one to three teaspoonfuls at a time.

Caraway makes several tasty confectionery treats, among them comfits of sugar-encrusted seeds. Served sometimes as a side dish with dessert fruits, the seeds also can be added to cakes and puddings. Use the seeds in apple dishes of almost every kind and in rye and black breads.

Caraway can also be used in savoury dishes. Bacon drippings and caraway seeds added to boiled cabbage give an unusual flavour. Try using caraway in the vinegar when pickling beetroots.

Castor Oil Plant

Castor Oil Bush, Palma Christi
Ricinus communis
Euphorbiaceae

A tropical ornamental shrub, the castor oil plant is grown under certain conditions in this country as a branched, annual herb not reaching more than five feet (just over 4.5 m) high. It has large divided leaves of three to five lobes up to three feet (1 m) across. It can be used as a background screen, or as a foliage specimen. In northern areas, it is treated as an annual and will seldom exceed ten or 12 feet (3.7 m) in height. Because it is fast-growing, it can be useful in new plantings, providing cover while slower plants are getting started.

The flowers do not have petals, and grow in upright panicles covered with dark brown spines. The fruit that follows is a capsule containing three large seeds, the source of commercial castor oil. The dark, shiny seeds are extremely poisonous if swallowed, but can easily be removed from the plant when they first begin to form.

The castor oil plant has long enjoyed a reputation as a fly and mosquito repellent and will also rid the garden of moles and plant-nibbling insects. There are several forms which vary greatly in appearance: *Ricinus africanus* has very large green leaves; *R. macrocarpus* has purple-red foliage; *R. communis* 'Cambodgensis' has blackish-purple stems and leaves; *R. communis* 'Sanguineus' is red-leaved; and *R. communis* 'Gibsonii', a lovely dwarf, has dark red leaves with a metallic lustre.

It is a very decorative garden plant, easily grown from seed, which may be reared indoors, then transplanted to its growing location when the weather is settled. Castor oil plants like clay or sandy loam and good drainage.

The oil obtained from the seeds is one of the best-known laxatives, although perhaps one of the least liked. It is particularly suitable for children and the aged because it has a gentle action. The drawback is its flavour and odour, both of which are unpleasant. The oil is also known to have been used externally for skin ailments such as ringworm and itches. The Chinese value castor oil as a laxative, but also use it in cases of difficult childbirth, facial deformities, and stomach cancer.

Castor oil also has a variety of

357

industrial uses, including the manufacture of soap, furniture polish, flypaper, artificial leather and artificial rubber, some types of cellulose, and candles.

Catmint

Catnep, Catnip
Nepeta Cataria
Labiatae

Long a source of mysterious and frenzied ecstasy in the feline world, catmint, a wild English plant, has also served the human race over the centuries as a minor herbal medicine and a major herbal delight. Before European trade with China began bringing great quantities of fine Eastern tea to the West, catnip tea was a domestic favourite.

As a medicine, an infusion of catmint is useful as a tonic, a mild stimulant, nervine, antispasmodic, and emmenagogue. But, of course, this herb is best known for its strange and often hilarious effect on cats. Nearly all members of the feline species, from the randiest alley cat to the fiercest mountain lion, are known to have a passionate affinity for catmint. What they crave, in fact, is the oil that is expressed from a bruised or drying plant.

Maude Grieve advises gardeners to sow catmint directly in its growing bed, and to take care not to injure developing plants. With those precautions, neighbourhood cats are unlikely to "tune in, turn on and tear up" your catmint patch. Her advice is embodied in this old ditty:

If you set it, the cats will eat it;
If you sow it, the cats won't know it.

If you have a cat and the two of you have never been on a catmint high together, be sure to include a row for your next planting. The fun begins when you toss a sprig or a few dried leaves to your whiskered friend. Cats delight in rubbing against catmint, as if trying to coat themselves with it. They roll on it, toss it about with their paws, and rub their faces in it in a comic orgy of delight.

The universal liking that cats have for *Nepeta Cataria* is brought out by the herb's common name, which in every western language contains some variation of the word "cat".

The culinary uses of catmint seem to begin and end with tea garnished with a slice of lemon and served at the end of large meals as a carminative aid. A variation of this after-dinner treat is crystallized catmint leaves, made by sprinkling sugar on catmint leaves coated with a glaze of equal parts of egg white and lemon juice. Allow the coated leaves to dry for at least one day before serving them.

Fortified with honey, catmint tea is used by many as an old-fashioned

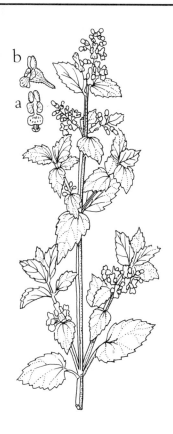

Catmint
(Nepeta Cataria)
(a) flower front (b) flower side)

be two or three tablespoonfuls at a time, as needed; although, taken in large quantities, the tea can act as an emetic. Childrens' doses are two to three teaspoonfuls of the infusion, made with one ounce (28 g) of leaves to three-quarters of a pint (426 ml) of hot water. For an emmenagogue, it is better to use the oil of catmint expressed from fresh leaves. Take one dessertspoonful three times daily.

An English herbalist gave the sobering advice that the root of catmint "when chewed is said to make the most gentle person fierce and quarrelsome, and there is a legend of a certain hangman who could never screw up his courage to the point of hanging anybody till he had partaken of it." As rats are supposed to be repelled by catmint it could protect grain crops.

The plant is a perennial with leaves that are almost heart-shaped and grey-green in colour. The stems are squarish and two to three feet (60 to 90 cm) high. Both stems and leaves are coated with downy hairs that give an overall dustblown appearance to the plant. Flowers ranging from pale lavender to pale pink appear in the leaf axis at the top of the plant from July to September. Insect pollination is needed for seed development. The seeds, which closely resemble basil seeds, can be identified by a little white speck on one side.

Either seeds or root division in autumn or spring can be used to propagate catmint. Planting can be done outdoors in late April or early May, or earlier indoors, if you are

cough remedy. Medicinally, catmint's main use is that of a diaphoretic to induce free perspiration without increasing body heat. Such action is useful in breaking a fever, inducing sleep, and even as a cooler on a hot summer's day.

The herb infused, also soothes nervousness and nervous headaches. Catmint should not be boiled, because too much of its highly volatile oil would be lost.

An adult dose of catmint tea would

359

prepared to risk bruising the plants and attracting cats while transplanting.

In seeding, rows should be 18 inches (46 cm) apart and plants thinned to 12 inches (30 cm) in the rows. Catmint develops quickly and is easy to grow, but it should have a mulch of hay or straw. It prefers a rich soil, but will do fairly well almost anywhere.

Root division can produce up to four new plants from a single growth. The best time to do this is early spring, before the plants get too large.

Harvesting has to be done as soon as the plants are mature, but before they start to turn yellow. Leaves can be stripped off the plant or the entire plant can be cut and dried. In either case, dry catmint in the shade or in a low oven, not in the sun, in order that its volatile oils will not be lost. Two or three days is necessary for drying. Cared for, a catmint plant will last for several years.

Celery, Wild

Smallage
Apium graveolens
Umbelliferae

Wild celery is a native of southern Europe, but it is cultivated in Great Britain. It is a carminative, stimulant, diuretic, tonic, nervine, and useful in hysteria. It is reputed to promote restfulness and sleep.

It is recommended that the roots of cultivated plants be eaten, as well as the oil or fluid extract taken. Wild celery is said to be a very good remedy for rheumatism.

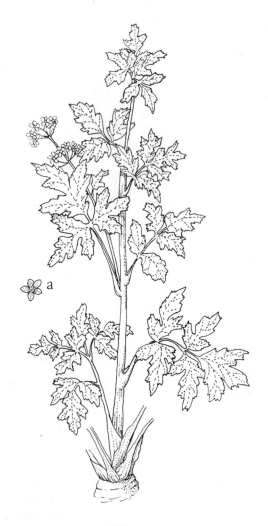

Wild Celery
(Apium graveolens)
(a) flower

Chervil

Anthriscus Cerefolium
Umbelliferae

Brought to Europe from the Levant and the shores of the Mediterranean, chervil is well known to gourmets as the basis of any herbal salad. For centuries, this tasty herb has been an essential part of most English gardens, where it is said to have been introduced by the Romans. In southern Europe, it flourishes in the wild although it is native to Asia.

Many people call it "the gourmet parsley", since it has a more delicate flavour than parsley. It is used mostly to add zest to a salad, but the herb has a rich folklore.

Pliny said that chervil was a fine herb "to comfort the cold stomach of the aged", and the boiled roots were used as a preventive against Plague. In the Middle Ages, people used its leaves to soothe the pain of rheumatism and bruises, and some still eat it today as a cure for hiccups. Chervil is also supposed to have great qualities of rejuvenation.

The herb is best known for its use in salads, but it enhances soups, especially sorrel or spinach soup, and adds flavour to fish, eggs, meats, or vegetables. It is often served with oysters.

John Evelyn, the English herbalist of the Eighteenth Century, instructed that chervil should never be missing from a salad, since "it is exceedingly wholesome and chearing the spirits".

Culpeper cites a host of medicinal qualities of the herb; chervil, he said, "is a certain remedy (saith Tragus) to dissolve congealed or clotted blood in the body, or that which is clotted by bruises, falls, etc.: the juice or distilled water thereof being drunk, and the bruised leaves laid to the place, being taken in either meat or drink, it is good to provoke urine, or expel the stone in the kidneys, to send down women's courses and to help the pleurisy and prickling of the sides."

But Gerard warns; "It has a certain windiness, by meanes whereof it provoketh lust." Inwardly or outwardly, he adds, it affects the bladder.

There are two main varieties of chervil, plain and curly. The plants grow to about two feet (60 cm) in height, with small flowers arranged in umbels. The seeds look like tiny sticks, thin and about one-quarter inch (6.4 mm) in length. Germination takes ten days or longer in the presence of light. The odour is similar to anise or tarragon, and the leaves are somewhat like parsley, but finer.

Gardeners can start chervil from seed, either indoors or directly outside, as soon as the soil can be worked. Since the seeds require light for germination, they should not be covered with soil. However, too much light could dry out the sprouting seed and kill it.

The best method is to make a furrow an inch (2.5 cm) deep. Scatter the seeds evenly, and press them into the ground with the tines of a rake held vertically. Water and keep moist until the young plants are visible.

It is also possible to scatter the seeds freely in a small area. Tap them into the ground with a shovel and cover them with cheesecloth. It will probably be necessary to continue watering the seeds through the cheesecloth until the seeds establish their roots. Then the cheesecloth can be removed. But the soil should still be watered after sunset for another couple of days. Because of the harmful effects of direct sunlight, chervil should be grown in a shaded area. Moreover, because the plant grows so quickly, indoor germination is not as important as with other plants. Chervil is more difficult to transplant than most herbs.

Chervil should be sown in March or early April and after July for an autumn harvest. It should self-sow generously. If some seedlings are lifted in late summer and put into a cold frame they will survive the winter there, and in the spring, when the glass is removed, grow to more than two feet (60 cm) and become covered with blossoms. By putting it in a cold frame, fresh leaves can be obtained all year. Its roots are thin and long.

Chervil grows much better in cool weather, and thus does better early in the year and towards the end of summer again. In the middle of the summer it goes to seed without a real leaf formation. It is possible to cut the leaves six to eight weeks after

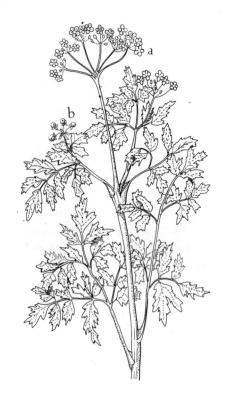

Chervil
(Anthriscus Cerefolium)
(a) flowers (b) buds

seeding. For a continuous supply of leaves, it is best to seed the plant regularly throughout the summer, preferably in the shade.

The herb doesn't require much in the way of nutrients and can easily follow a crop that was fertilized with compost the previous year. Mulching with chopped hay or straw helps keep the soil cool and the plants clean.

The older leaves gradually obtain a horizontal position, stop growing, then start to age. For this reason, cut off these leaves first, prior to their turning yellow. More leaves will develop from the centre until the stalk pushes up, developing into a structure of flowering umbels.

Many gardeners allow one or two plants to fulfil their natural cycle just for the pleasure of watching them grow. Drying chervil is not as important a procedure as with other herbs, because the herb is best fresh. Although it dries quickly, it is better to control drying in order to retain full flavour.

Dried chervil should be stored away from light, since it will turn yellow or greyish in a short time if exposed to light. It will also pick up the slightest moisture above normal humidity and become stale.

Chicory

Succory, Blue Dandelion, Hendibeh
Cichorium Intybus
Compositae

Chicory is that blue-flowered weed that hems the roadside throughout much of the country. The blue flowers are always closed by noon. The leaves resemble those of dandelion sufficiently to have earned it the nickname "blue dandelion". Like dandelion, the plant is the bane of lawn fanatics, for it spreads quickly by sending out runners, and it is hard to eradicate.

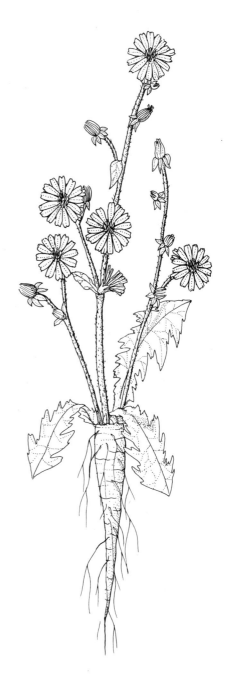

Chicory
(Cichorium Intybus)

But chicory grows taller than dandelion and loses much of the resemblance in maturity.

Because of its tendency to get out of hand, chicory is a plant that must be used cautiously in the garden. It isn't particular about soil, although it does like the sun. It is easily started from seed.

Perhaps the best-known use of chicory is as an additive in coffee. The French are particularly fond of it in coffee. The root is used for this purpose and also makes an interesting beverage on its own.

Chicory was ascribed a variety of medicinal uses including as a tonic, laxative, and diuretic. Ancient herbals suggest bruised chicory leaves as a poultice for swellings, inflammations, and inflamed eyes. A decoction of one ounce (28 g) of dried, powdered root to three-quarters of a pint (426 ml) of water was recommended for jaundice and general liver ailments. Blanched, the leaves can be used in salads.

Chives

Allium Schoenoprasum
Liliaceae

The compactness of this delicate onion-related herb make it an ideal candidate for winter kitchen gardens.

Hardy perennials, chives grow in clumps of small white bulbous roots that send off fine, hollow, green spears. The tender young spears are harvested and chopped to grace a wide variety of dishes.

Because chives are difficult to store, many gardeners choose to maintain a fresh supply through indoor gardening. They can be started from seed or purchased in young clumps. Seed should be drilled into quarter-inch (6.4 mm) rows as early as the soil can be worked, then covered with fine compost or sifted soil. Tap the covering lightly to assure good soil contact. The plants need rich soil, a fair amount of water, and full sun. Chives develop pretty bluish-pink to lavender flowers, and make an attractive border to the garden.

Mulch early to retain moisture and discourage grass and weeds. A fish fertilizer should be used to replace nutrients, especially nitrogen, after repeated cuttings.

Chives are an encouraging project for a new herb grower because they develop quickly and produce in profusion. A bed frequently produces more than a family can use. The tender green spears should be snipped close to the ground regularly to prevent the plants from becoming tough and to help the bulblets develop. Unless there are plans to let the plants flower or seed, cutting should always be done before the round balls begin to develop at the tops of the spears.

The root bulbs develop in clusters, which should be dug up, divided, and

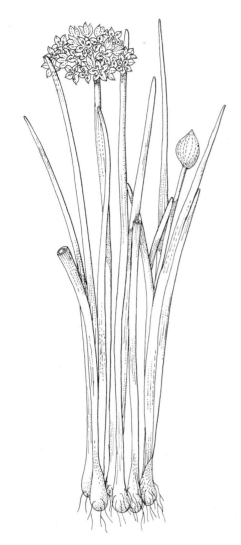

Chives
(Allium Schoenoprasum)

inch (13 cm) pot in late summer and sink the pot into the ground. After the first severe frost, mulch the pot or put it into a cold frame for about 90 days. Chives need this rest period to rejuvenate. Then bring the pot into the house, put it in a sunny location, and water regularly. By January, there will be a fresh supply of chives for harvesting.

If chives are desired between the seasons, chop the spears after harvesting and dry them immediately and completely. Try hanging them in a basket over the stove. Put them in airtight containers immediately, since any trace of moisture will be absorbed by them and they will lose their colour and flavour. A safer way of preserving chopped chives is to freeze a small quantity at a time.

Native to the Orient, chives have been known for almost five thousand years, chiefly as a culinary nicety. No extensive medicinal uses were ever developed, although chives are said to aid the digestion of fatty foods. Gypsies used chives in their fortune-telling rites, and clumps of chives were suspended from ceilings and bedposts in chambers to drive away diseases and evil influences.

Sprinkle chives in green salads and on tomatoes. Add them to sour cream or melted butter as a fine dressing for potatoes, or sprinkle them on soups, sausage dishes, and croquettes.

replanted every two or three years. Keep the new clusters eight inches (20 cm) apart. Six bulbs to a cluster is about right when dividing.

To bring a cluster of chives inside for the winter, transplant it into a five-

365

Cicely, Sweet

Sweet Chervil, Sweet Fern,
Great Chervil, Cow Chervil,
Shepherd's Needle
Myrrhis odorata
Umbelliferae

Sweet cicely is a herb that has been used for centuries and the old herbalists describe it as "so harmless you cannot use it amiss". It is a native of Great Britain, and has very aromatic foliage, but in looks it resembles many plants such as chervil, ferns, hemlock, and anise. Despite its difficulty to cultivate, it is pleasant to have in the garden.

Sweet cicely is a thick-rooted perennial, a hardy plant that develops to a height of about three feet (90 cm), although in isolated cases to a height of five feet (1.5 m). The first shoots are almost triangular, lacy leaves, but as the herb slowly develops it bears many branching stems of feathery leaves, downy and white-spotted on the undersides, smelling strongly of lovage. In the early summer, usually late May to early June, flat-topped umbels of white flowers appear, followed by unusually large fruits called the "seeds". These are about an inch (2.5 cm) long and, when ripe, a dark brown to black colour.

The seeds are spicy and the leaves have a sweet, liquorice and aniseed flavour. All parts of the plant, which is strongly scented, have been used in cooking and folk medicine. Curiously enough, the plant has no recorded history of use for its scent although its botanical name, *Myrrhis odorata*, is derived from the Greek for perfume.

Sweet cicely has a variety of uses in cookery. The French grant it some importance, often combining it with tarragon. While it was once popular in this country, it seems to have fallen from favour here. Nevertheless, when used in cooking, the results are tasty. The leaves are used fresh in salads, soups, and stews. The seeds go into salads when green and into spicy herb mixtures when ripe. The roots may be eaten raw or boiled.

Most of the old herbalists made note of sweet cicely's ability to enhance a salad, with Gerard calling the leaves "exceeding good, wholesome, and pleasant among other sallad herbs, giving the taste of Annise-seed unto the rest". Gerard pointed out that the seeds were also excellent salad ingredients, "dressed as the cunning Cooke knoweth how", but added that he preferred them boiled and served with oil and vinegar. The latter dish he considered "very good for old people that are dull and without courage; it rejoiceth and comforteth the heart and increaseth their lust and strength."

In theory, the seed is brought to germination through a process of alternate freezing and thawing, but the theory is more often than not a failure. Perhaps the best method of propagating sweet cicely is to buy a plant from a grower. Failing this, the

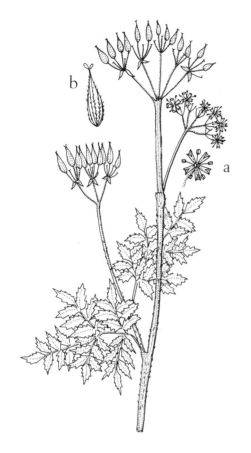

Sweet Cicely
(Myrrhis odorata)
(a) flower (b) fruit

In terms of garden environment, sweet cicely prefers shaded, rich, moist, crumbly soil, which should be enriched with compost or manure. Mulching, however, is seldom a benefit and sometimes a detriment, since it can harbour moulds when coupled with the damp shade the plant prefers.

The leaves can be harvested throughout the growing season. Since they remain green from early spring to late autumn, they are available fresh over an extended period. The seeds should be harvested green or ripe, depending, of course, upon the intended use. The roots should be harvested only after the plant has matured sufficiently for the yield to make the harvest effort worthwhile.

While this gardening effort will yield a lovely garden plant and a tasty pot-herb, it will also provide a useful plant for folk medicine. Sweet cicely is listed as an aromatic, stomachic, carminative, and expectorant. The roots seem to be most useful medicinally. Eaten fresh, the root is said to be a gentle stimulant for debilitated stomachs and good for coughs and flatulence. Similar benefits arise from taking an infusion of the root in brandy or water.

These qualities are not unlike those listed by the early herbalists, of course. Parkinson recommended candied sweet cicely roots as of "singular good use to warm and comfort a cold flegmaticke stomack", adding that the confection was "thought to be a good preservative in the time of the Plague". Culpeper

seed should be sown in the autumn. Though the germination rate will be poor, at least a few seeds should sprout and plants develop. The seeds from these plants may be harvested upon ripening and immediately replanted at the base of the mother plant. Or the plants may be divided in the spring. The process will require several years of persistent effort, but the results are rewarding.

echoed the reports of his fellow herbalists: "The roots boiled and eaten with oil and vinegar, or without oil, do much to please and warm old and cold stomachs oppressed with wind and phlegm, or those that have the phthisis or consumption of the lungs; the same drank with wine is a preservation from the Plague: it provoketh women's courses and expelleth the afterbirth; procureth an appetite to meat, and expelleth wind: the juice is good to heal the ulcers of the head and face . . ."

Gerard, as well as the other early herbalists, lumped sweet cicely with chervil, often calling it sweet chervil or great chervil. While some confusion has since been generated by the association, the descriptions are clear enough. Culpeper wrote:

It groweth very like the great hemlock, having large spread leaves cut into divers parts, but of a fresher green colour than the hemlock, tasting as sweet as the aniseed. The stalks rise up a yard high, or better, being crossed or hollow, having leaves at the joints, but lesser; and at the tops of the branched stalks, umbels or tufts of white flowers; after which come large and long crested black shining seed, pointed at both ends, tasting quick, yet sweet and pleasant. The root is great and white, growing deep in the ground, and spreading sundry long branches therein, in taste and smell stronger than the leaves or seeds, and continuing many years.

While the confusion seems to be in name only, sweet cicely does seem to have suffered from lack of clear-cut identity.

368

Cinquefoil

Five-Fingers, Five-Leaf Grass, Silverweed
Potentilla var. sp.
Rosaceae

This hardy little herb of the rose family can be found in a variety of forms and colours. Generally, from six to 18 inches (15 to 46 cm) high, it is commonly found growing on meadow banks, hillsides, and open grounds. It thrives in a sunny location and prefers a sandy soil, but will grow in most garden soils. It is easily increased by seeds or root division. Cinquefoil can be grown in beds and borders; some species are useful for bare banks and in the rockery.

Silvery cinquefoil is a lovely species growing from five to 12 inches (13 to 30 cm) high. Flowering between May and September, it produces little yellow flowers which cluster at the ends of the branches. The underside of the fern-like leaves are covered with fine silvery wool, contrasting with the dark green of their upper side. In the past, a red dye was made from the root.

Cinquefoil or Five-leaf Grass, as it is sometimes called, has a slender creeping stem with leafstalks one to two inches (2.5 to 5 cm) long, five leaflets joined near the base, about two inches (5 cm) across with prominent veins below, and scattered hairs on the veins and margins. It spreads by runners.

For medicinal purposes the root is usually used, a decoction of which is a useful astringent and febrifuge. It can also be used as a mouth wash. Mixed with honey it relieves coughs, hoarseness, and sore throats. It has also been found useful for piles and diarrhoea.

Clematis

Upright virgin's bower,
Flammula Jovis
Clematis recta
Ranunculaceae

This is a perennial with a stem about three feet (90 cm) high. It is leafy, striated, and herbaceous and the leaves, green to red, are large and opposite.

When bruised, the leaves and flowers give off a vapour that brings tears to the eyes and causes coughing, and when applied to the skin, the juice causes inflammation and vesication; hence the name Flammula Jovis. The leaves are diuretic and diaphoretic and are said to be useful "locally and internally in syphilitic, cancerous, and other foul ulcers". Dosages are given as one to two grains of the extract a day, or 30 to 40 grains of the leaves in infusion a day.

Other species include *Clematis Flammula*, sweet-scented virgin's bower, cultivated in gardens, *C. Vitalba* traveller's joy, and *C. virginiana* common virgin's bower.

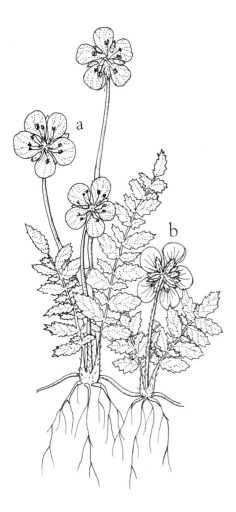

Silverweed
(Potentilla anserina)
(a) flower front (b) flower back

Coltsfoot

Coughwort, Ass's Foot, Bullsfoot, Horsehoof
Tussilago farfara
Compositae

Coltsfoot is a curious herb which seems to grow in two distinct stages. Very early in the growing season, the plant develops flat, orange flower heads. Only after the flowers have withered do the broad, hoof-shaped, sea-green leaves develop. This habit of growth earned coltsfoot its old name of *Filius ante patrem*, the son before the father.

In England and on the Continent, coltsfoot is a fairly common weed and its soil preferences are not too particular. But it does like full sun. It can be easily propagated from root cuttings or seed. Its spreading habits make it an excellent ground cover and account for its wide distribution.

Because of its two-stage growth, coltsfoot is easily harvested for its blossoms and its leaves, both of which have medicinal uses. It is usually listed as a demulcent, expectorant, and tonic, but its prime value was as a cough remedy. Indeed, its generic name *Tussilago* signifies "cough dispeller". The old herbalists, as far back as Pliny and Dioscorides, regarded coltsfoot as the best herb for lung and thoracic complaints. A decoction made of one ounce (28 g) of the leaves

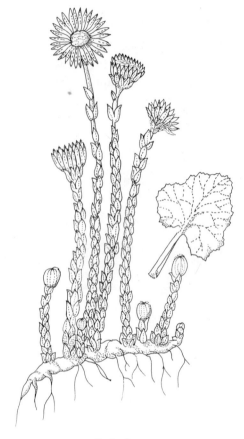

Coltsfoot
(Tussilago farfara)
Leaves appear after flowers

in a quart (1.1 l) of water boiled down to a pint (568 ml), sweetened with honey, and taken frequently in teacup doses is recommended for colds and asthma. But the old herbalists usually smoked coltsfoot to capture its curative values. Coltsfoot leaves are the primary ingredient in British herb tobacco, which also contains buckbean, eyebright, betony, rosemary, thyme, lavender, and camomile flowers. The tobacco is reputedly beneficial to sufferers of asthma, catarrh, and other lung troubles.

Comfrey

Knitbone, Knitback, Healing Herb, Ass Ear, Boneset
Symphytum officinale
Boraginaceae

Few herbs have had as many extravagant claims made for them as has comfrey. Known for centuries for its powerful abilities as a healer, comfrey was often granted purely miraculous ones as well. Culpeper claimed that comfrey root "is said to be so powerful to consolidate and knit together, that if they be boiled with dissevered pieces of flesh in a pot, it will join them together."

Aside from claims such as these, this showy member of the borage family has, indeed, been used for centuries by herbalists for a wide variety of ailments. Many of its uses are not as radical as the one suggested by Culpeper, but run the gamut from poultices made from the leaves and used to reduce swellings, to teas and infusions of the root used to treat diarrhoea.

The mature comfrey plant grows wild, but can be cultivated easily. It grows to about three feet (90 cm) high, erect and rough and hairy all over. The stem is stout and angular, the root branched, fleshy, and spindle-shaped. Roots are often a foot (30 cm) in length, an inch (2.5 cm) or less in diameter, and internally are white, fleshy, and juicy.

The lower leaves are very large (sometimes up to ten inches (25 cm) long, ovate in shape, and hairy—they resemble, in fact, a donkey's ears. The hairs cause itching if brushed. The size of the leaves decreases as they get higher up the plant.

Flower racemes are found at the top of the plant, bearing creamy-yellow or purplish-blue flowers on a stem that curves like a scorpion's tail. Each flower is followed by four seeds in a little cup-like fruit.

Comfrey blooms throughout the greater part of the summer. The first flowers appear in late April or early May and continue until the first frosts. Comfrey, however, is hardy and may not be harmed by the first light frosts. It often continues to produce foliage after other plants have been killed by frost.

Comfrey is beginning to gain some popularity among small farmers. But it is a difficult and expensive plant to grow in large quantities and is better suited to small-scale cultivation. Many find it a popular plant, not only for themselves, but for their animals as well.

It can be grown from plants, crown cuttings containing eyes or buds, and root cuttings. While the first two methods will produce a respectable crop the first year after planting, root cuttings are by far the cheapest method. Although older herbals mention growing comfrey from seed, few people have had success with this method.

Once established, comfrey is a hardy perennial. The roots will withstand temperatures down to −40°F (−40°C). In fact, it is a difficult crop to eradicate. Like horseradish, the roots will produce new plants from any sliver left in the ground.

Cuttings are planted three to six inches (8 to 16 cm) deep in a horizontal position. The soil should be well tilled and manured. Comfrey likes a sweet soil, with a pH value of between 6 and 7. Lime should be applied liberally. Other soil requirements can be met by dressing with ground phosphate rock for phosphates and greensand for potash.

The cuttings should be spaced three feet, or just under a metre, apart. Grasses and weeds should be kept down by cultivation or mulch. Once your cuttings are established, they can be divided for more plants. The best time to divide is in the spring when the leaves begin to appear above ground.

You can expect a moderate harvest from your cuttings the first year. Cuttings will come into full production in the third year. Some wild claims have been made for yields of comfrey plantings, and it seems to be difficult to determine just how much comfrey you can expect to harvest from a patch of a given size. You should, however, be able to harvest every ten to 30 days throughout the growing season, depending upon weather conditions.

Harvest comfrey just before it blooms. Nutritional and medicinal value seem to decrease once the plant flowers. Cut the plant with a sickle or knife when the leaves are 12 to 18 inches (30 to 46 cm) high, leaving a two-inch (5 cm) stem stub. It is important not to cut lower than this and damage the newly forming growth on the crown.

Herbal doctors seemed to have preferred fresh comfrey, giving little value to dried leaves. Nevertheless, the leaves can be dried. Cut the leaves at the end of the day when their food value is highest. Comfrey leaves are tender, so avoid bruising. They should be dried quickly in thin layers in the sun. Allow about two days for the drying to take place, then store in boxes between layers of grass hay. Be careful not to shatter or compress the leaves when packing them. Comfrey root can also be dried for winter use. Clean it carefully (avoid bruising or scraping) and dry slowly in the sun, turning often.

Modern science has established that comfrey is high in calcium, potassium, phosphorus, and other trace minerals. The leaves are rich in vitamins A and C. The virtues of comfrey as a vulnerary—the mediaeval term for a plant used to heal battle wounds—are due to the amount of allantoin it contains. Medical research has found that

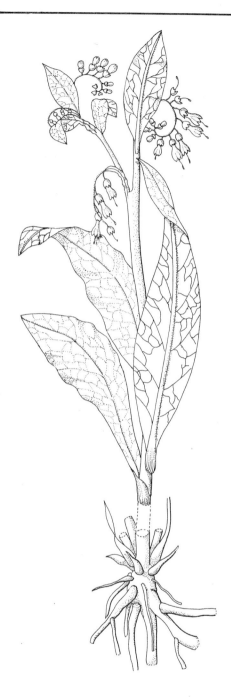

*Comfrey
(Symphytum officinale)*

allantoin is useful in treating wounds, burns, and ulcers. It is obtained from fresh extracts of the roots.

A decoction of comfrey root, made by putting one quart (1.4 l) of milk or water in the top of a double boiler, adding one ounce (28 g) of ground root, and cooking for 30 minutes, is said to be good for dysentery or diarrhoea when taken internally. It is also recommended for stomach or intestinal ulcers. As a remedy for bleeding haemorrhoids or other internal bleeding, half an ounce (14 g) of witch hazel leaves were added to the decoction before boiling. Lemon could be added to the decoction for a more pleasing taste. A strong tea made from the roots was used for whooping cough and lung troubles.

Comfrey leaves are also applied externally to swellings, bruises, or broken bones. As Culpeper believed, they hasten the healing of fractures, hence the names "knitbone" and "boneset". In fact, the name "comfrey" is thought to be a corruption of the Latin *confervere*, to heal. The generic name, *Symphytum*, is derived from the Greek *symphyto*, to unite. We now know that one of comfrey's chief effects is to act on the swelling through the allantoin present in the plant.

Culpeper said: "The roots of comfrey taken fresh, beaten small and spread upon leather and laid upon any place troubled with the gout presently gives ease: and applied in the same manner it eases pained joints and tends to heal running ulcers, gangrenes, mortifications, for which it hath by often experience been found helpful." At times, the entire plant was beaten into a pulp, heated, and applied as a poultice. In this form, it was said to ease the pain of an inflamed, tender, or suppurating part of the body.

In some parts of Ireland, comfrey is consumed as a cure for defective circulation and to strengthen the blood. The first leaves can be used in a green salad, or boiled and eaten like spinach. When older and larger, the leaves become coarse and unpleasant.

The leaves can also be dried, ground, and added to bread or muffins. This is a good way of using another unique component of the plant, vitamin B_{12}. So far, it is the only land plant discovered that contains this vitamin. It is also a good source of lysine, an amino acid lacking in the diets of those who use no animal products whatsoever.

Comfrey root, along with dandelion and chicory roots, can be made into a coffee substitute without the harmful effects of coffee. For this, roast equal quantities until they are dark brown. Grind and brew as you would coffee.

Comfrey has also been used, with moderate success, as a cattle food. It was first introduced into Britain for this purpose in 1811 when it met with only slight success. Although it grew well enough in wet places, it could not be adapted to dry climates. Another problem arises in determining yields. There are hundreds of varieties and strains of comfrey, some yielding a lot of forage and some little. Farmers found that cattle did not particularly take to comfrey, although this may have been due, in part, to the fact that they were not used to it.

Comfrey will not cause diarrhoea or bloating in young animals. It is also believed that comfrey will prevent foot and mouth disease if fed regularly to animals.

We feel at this point, however, we must include a caution regarding the internal use of comfrey by man or animals.

Recent research done by Dr. Culvenor in Australia indicated that certain alkaloids found in comfrey may be carcinogenic and cause liver damage, when the herb is taken internally in large quantities over long periods. Dr. Culvenor says "Thus, at the present time comfrey may be harmful or non-harmful to human beings. The experience of long-term users suggests that it is not. I believe that our warning is warranted until adequate investigations have been made. We are now setting about long-term studies which may provide the answer."

This warning does not apply to comfrey ointment or poultices applied externally which are still considered beneficial.

Coriander

Coriandrum sativum
Umbelliferae

One of the most ancient of herbs still in use today, coriander is known to have been cultivated in Egyptian gardens thousands of years before the birth of Christ. Its seeds were among the funeral offerings found in Egyptian tombs. Coriander then spread to Western civilizations, the great Greek physician Hippocrates having used it in the Fifth Century B.C.

By the time the herb had reached the Chinese continent, it had acquired a reputation for bestowing immortality and the Chinese herbalists developed several coriander compounds to that end.

Coriander also found itself a cherished place in the Bible. There are several Old Testament references to it as a herb whose fruit is similar to the mysterious food, Manna, that God showered upon the Israelites during their desert trek from bondage. In Exodus 16:31, it is recorded:

And the house of Israel called the name thereof Manna; and it was like coriander seed, white; and the taste of it was like wafers made with honey.

Coriander, though, is not so divine in all its aspects. The mature green plant, just before it goes to seed, emits a strong odour that some gardeners find highly offensive. Indeed, its generic name is derived from the Greek word *koris*, bug. Pliny described it as "a very stinkinge herb". Fortunately, as the plant dries the strong odour gives way to a pleasing aroma described as a combination of sage and lemon peel.

In the Arabian fantasy tales *The Thousand and One Nights*, coriander is mentioned as an aphrodisiac, a use

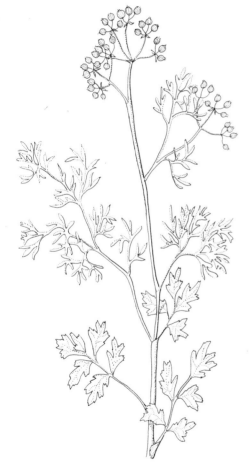

Coriander
(Coriandrum sativum)

substantiated by more recent findings that coriander seeds can be narcotic if consumed in excessive quantities. When coriander is combined with fennel it is supposed to conjure the devil. In a conjurer's mortar that may be a likely pairing, but in the garden, the two cannot stand being near each other as coriander hinders the seed formation of fennel.

Coriander was known widely in the British Isles at least as early as the Fifteenth Century and most likely long before that.

The plant is an annual with slender, erect stems bearing finely divided leaves. It reaches a height of up to three feet (90 cm). Coriander needs only moderately fertilized soil, but it cannot stand constant moisture. Because of its marked liking for well-drained soils and relatively dry climates, most of the commercially produced coriander is grown in arid areas of the world. Morocco, for example, is a major producer.

Delicate umbels of flowers, lavender to pale mauve, form late in June. Seeds germinate in darkness. They should be planted outside in late April or early May in drills half an inch (13 mm) deep and nine inches (23 cm) apart. Coriander prefers light, warm, and dry soil.

Coriander does not transplant well. It should, therefore, be sown directly in its bed. If you find it necessary to try a risky indoor start, plant in March and transplant in May. As much as coriander dislikes being near fennel, it welcomes anise as a neighbour and will benefit the formation of anise seeds.

Some gardeners make a common planting of coriander and caraway in the same row. Caraway is a biennial whose first-year growth is small and close to the ground and poses no threat to the young coriander shoots. In the second year, caraway is given the row to itself.

In any event, strict weed control is important while the early coriander fights to establish itself. By mid-August, however, it should be able to dominate its competitors and even mulching should be unnecessary.

Coriander attracts a great variety of pollinating insects to the garden. The swirl of activity around it may alone be well worth all the trouble of growing coriander.

Act swiftly to harvest the coriander when the fruits turn light brown. The small fruits, which envelope the seed, are one-eighth of an inch (3 mm) in diameter, globular, and will part into halves when they are dried and rubbed between the palms. It is this part of the plant that is most used in medicines and cookery. If the fruit balls aren't picked at the right time, the fast-dropping coriander will reseed itself.

Coriander is said by herbalists to have stimulant, aromatic, and carminative properties, although in modern times its chief medicinal use has been to disguise the disagreeable taste of active purgatives.

Its commercial uses now include the flavouring of foods and liqueurs and some confectioneries, including the fortification of inferior-grade cocoa. The crushed fruits and seeds are sometimes used in rich cakes, custards, and jellies. Along with the sugar-coated seeds of anise, caraway, and celery, coated coriander seeds are used in multi-coloured cake decorations, better known by children as "hundreds and thousands". In Peru and Egypt, it is common to put coriander leaves into soups and broths.

This herb imparts a wonderful spiciness to sausages and red meats. In pickles and beetroot salads, it makes an unusual and tasty addition.

Costmary

**Mace, Balsam Herb, Alecost,
Bible Leaf**
Chrysanthemum balsamita
(syn. *Tanacetum balsamita,
Pyrethrum balsamita*)
Compositae

Although not always the easiest herb to find, costmary is well worth the extra effort required to track it down. Its practical uses are enhanced by a charming appearance and sweet fragrance, and its history is filled with fascinating tales from all over the world.

The name of this sweet-smelling herb combines the Latin word *costus*, oriental plant, with "Mary", the mother of Jesus. Although in mediaeval France we find that costmary was called "Herbe Sainte-Marie", other historical references identify it with Mary Magdalene as often as with the Virgin Mary. This aromatic herb has always had a special place in Christianity. In Colonial times, the costmary leaf served as a book-mark in the Bibles and prayer-books of many devout church-goers. When the long sermon grew boring and drowsiness set in, the sleepy listener treated himself or herself to the minty flavour of the costmary leaves in an effort to stay awake. Thus arose the name "Bible leaf".

Originally found in the Orient, costmary was introduced into England in the Sixteenth Century, where it soon became extremely popular. In 1578, Lyte commented that it was "very common in all gardens", and Gerard, in 1598, confirmed the popularity of this herb when he said "it groweth everywhere in gardens". Not nearly as familiar today, it is nonetheless an important and precious part of many modern gardens.

Though closely related to tansy, costmary carries a soft, balsamic fragrance which is more aromatic. Culpeper calls costmary the "balsam herb". Its shiny, pear-shaped light green leaves are from six to eight inches (16 to 20 cm) long with finely-toothed margins. The two to three foot (60 to 90 cm) stems are stiff with short, sturdy, and slightly downy branches. Although attractive all year long, costmary is particularly charming in the spring, when it bears clusters of small, pale yellow, button-like flowers.

Another herb similar to costmary is maudlin. Parkinson tells us that, although maudlin is smaller that costmary, its fragrance is sweeter. Treasured for what Gerard calls "their sweet floures and leaves", maudlin and costmary were often used to make "sweete washing water".

There are so many useful ways to make costmary a worthwhile addition to your garden. Parkinson writes of its uses as a spicy flavouring in ale, from which comes the name "alecost" or "alecoast". In salads and soups, fresh costmary leaves lend a sweet aroma and taste, and the lingering fragrance of dried costmary makes it a fine herb for pot-pourri. Dainty bundles of lavender and costmary were commonly made by women "to lye upon the toppes of beds, presses, etc., for sweet scent and savour". It can also be used to sweeten the air of wardrobes and drawers. It makes a delicious tea and enhances the flavour of German sausage. In the garden, costmary keeps the weeds out, acts as a green background for spring flowers, and forms a beautiful, slow-growing edging.

Medicinally, costmary is known for its astringent and antiseptic properties. Until 1788, it was listed in the British pharmacopoeia as an aperient, particularly useful in the treatment of dysentery. Culpeper reported that costmary:

. . . provoketh urine abundantly, and moisteneth the hardness of the mother; it gently purgeth choler and phlegm . . . cleanseth that which is foul, and hindereth putrefaction and corruption; . . . and it is a wonderful help to all sorts of dry agues. It is astringent to the stomach and strengtheneth the liver and all the other inward parts: and taken in whey, worketh more effectually. Taken fasting in the morning, it is very profitable for pains in the head, that are continual; . . . It is very profitable for those that are fallen into a continual evil disposition of the body, called cachexia, but especially in the beginning of the disease. It is an especial friend and help in evil, weak, and cold livers. The seed is familiarly given to children for the worms, and so is the infusion of flowers in a white wine given them to the quantity of two ounces at a time; it maketh an excellent salve to clense and heal old ulcers, being boiled with oil of olive, and adder's tongue with it; and after it is strained put a little wax, rosin, and turpentine to bring it to a convenient body.

Gerard, writing even before Culpeper, stated that "the Conserve made with leaves of Costmaria and sugar doth warm and dry the braine and openeth the stoppings of the same; stoppeth all catarrhes, rheumes and distillations, taken in the quantitie of a bean."

Among its other uses, costmary was suggested as part of a very old remedy for "Aqua Composita", a kind of consumption. It is also mentioned in recipes for "oynment", to heal "bruises, dry itches, streins of veins and sinews, scorchings of gunpowder, the shingles, blisters, scabs and vermine".

Costmary is a perennial plant propagated only by the division of roots since there is no seed. Existing plants can be divided each spring. It spreads and grows easily, and requires minimal fertilization. Soil type is not important, and it will grow in sandy or heavy clay soils. It likes good drainage and will not thrive in areas where standing water is common. Mulching is unnecessary and not really feasible since costmary spreads above the ground in the same way that peppermint does. Unlike peppermint, however, costmary retains much more of the bush form, containing itself in more limited space.

Harvesting should be done before the leaves turn yellow and only in small amounts. Many leaves grow close to the ground, very few on stems. Harvesting, therefore, has to be done almost leaf by leaf. These take only a short time to dry at a temperature of about 100°F (38°C). Once they are dried, there are no problems in storing the plant, or the leaves, for a very long time.

Cowslip
(Primula veris)

Cowslip

**Herb Peter, Paigle, Peggle,
Fairy Cups, Arthritica**
Primula veris
Primulaceae

Cowslip is of the primrose family, many of which possess active medicinal properties. In addition to the cowslip and the primrose, the family also includes the tiny scarlet pimpernel *(Anagallis arvensis)*. The latter heralds the summer, while the cowslip and the primrose herald the spring.

Early in the spring the cowslip starts growing its leaves which are similar to those of the primrose but shorter and more round. All the leaves lie flat on the ground in that familiar "rosette". The flowers rise from the centre.

379

Shakespeare immortalised the cowslip:

Where the bee sucks there suck I:
In a cowslip's bell I lie;

He also wrote in *A Midsummer Night's Dream*:

The cowslips tall her pensioners be
In their gold coats spots you see;
Those be rubies, fairy favours,
In their freckles live their savours.

Cowslip is a sedative and an antispasmodic. In bygone days it was used extensively for home-made remedies. Among its attributes are its values in "strengthening the nerves and the brain, relieving restlessness and insommnia". It was said also to be good, along with betony, for alleviating pains in the head.

Cowslip wine, made from the flowers, used to be in great demand for homely remedies, being an excellent sedative. A traditional recipe is: take one pound (453 g) of freshly gathered blossoms and infuse them in one and a half pints (852 ml) of boiling water, simmered down with loaf sugar to a fine yellow syrup. This, taken with a little water, is reported to be admirable for giddiness from nervous debility, or from previous nervous excitement. This syrup was also administered aginst palsy.

Cumin

Cuminum Cyminum
Umbelliferae

While cumin is native to the eastern Mediterranean, especially the upper reaches of the Nile, it can be grown in England, but is rarely cultivated here. It was known early in history to the Persians, Egyptians, and Hebrews, and its use followed civilization around the Mediterranean and into France and England, though it has never become so popular in the northern countries as it has always been in the Near East. At one time, when pepper was rare and expensive, the Romans substituted cumin for it. In the time of Christ, the value of the cumin had increased until it had become negotiable in payment of taxes.

Cumin needs four warm months to mature its seed, and if it is to be grown successfully in a more temperate climate, plants should be started early indoors. Seedlings should be planted outside in sandy loam in warm spring weather. Plants are low and sprawling, because their weak stems will not support the weight of the large heads of flowers and seed. When they are planted outside, the seeds are sown at the rate of 16 to 20 to the foot (30 cm). Subsequently, the plants should not be thinned, since a thick growth helps to support the heavy heads and to keep them off the ground. Cumin plants have finely divided foliage and lavender-white flowers.

The seeds ripen late in the autumn. When the heads begin to turn brown, they should be cut and dried indoors. When thoroughly dried, the seeds may be separated from the heads by rubbing them between the hands. The small seeds may be separated from the chaff and stems by being strained through a sieve. They can be used to flavour cheese, bread, sausages, meats, vegetables, fish, and game. They are sometimes to be found among the ingredients of curry powder.

Dandelion

Priest's Crown, Swine's Snout
Taraxacum officinale
Compositae

Dandelion is a weed—at least to the harried farmer, the lawn fanatic, and to most other people. But the dandelion has a long and interesting history as a medicinal plant and as a foodstuff. That yellow-flowered, toothy-leaved plant prolific for most of the year on lawns, vacant lots, and open fields is not always what it appears.

Among country folk the delight of dandelion salad is common, as is dandelion wine. For a salad, the leaves should be picked before they reach

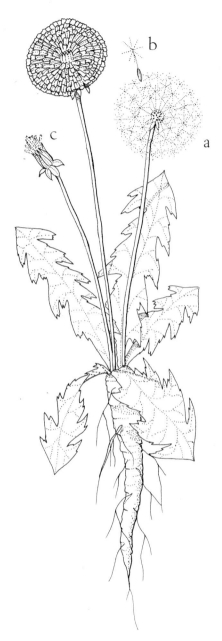

Dandelion
(Taraxacum officinale)
(a) seed head (b) seed (c) bud

maturity, otherwise they will be too bitter. They should be blanched before use. An alternative is to boil or steam the leaves and serve them as you would spinach.

Dandelion wine has been prepared for generations by country folk. It is made by pouring a gallon (4.5 l) of boiling water on a quantity of the flowers—enough to fill a gallon (4.5 l) jar. Then, stirring well, cover with a heavy cloth for three days, after which stir again at intervals; strain and boil the liquid for 30 minutes adding three and a half pounds (1.6 kg) of loaf sugar, a little sliced ginger, and the rinds of an orange and a lemon.

When cold, place a little yeast on a piece of toast and drop into the liquid. This causes fermentation. Now cover with the cloth and allow to stand for a couple of days until it has ceased fermenting, or "working" as the country folk say.

Now it is safe to pour into a cask and be "bunged down". And mind that it has stopped working; otherwise, if the liquid continues to ferment once the cask has been stoppered, it will explode! (This usually happens at dead of night, causing you to shoot out of bed thinking that the end of the world has arrived). After about two months, the wine can be taken from the cask and bottled. The result has been described by Maude Grieve as being "suggestive of sherry slightly flat, and has the deserved reputation of being an excellent tonic, extremely good for the blood".

Dandelion roots are the most valu-able part of the plant for medicinal uses. In some areas of Europe, dandelions were purposefully cultivated for the roots, which were collected and dried during the second year of growth. The most recent herbals suggest that the dandelion is merely a simple, bitter, and mild laxative. But it has been credited as a diuretic, laxative, hepatic, antiscorbutic, sialagogue, tonic, aperient, alterative, and stomachic.

A tea, said to be efficacious in bilious affections and much approved of in the treatment of 'dropsy' is made by infusing an ounce (28 g) of dried dandelion root in three-quarters of a pint (426 ml) of boiling water for ten minutes. Decant, sweeten with honey, and, during the course of the day, drink several glassfuls.

In Chinese medicine, dandelion is regarded as a blood cleanser, tonic, and digestive aid. It is ground and applied as a poultice for snake bites.

The ancients viewed the wide distribution of dandelions in nature as a sign, in keeping with the *Doctrine of Signatures*, that it was a cure-all. The bilious yellow flower was a sign that the plant was good for liver complaints. Even the name of the plant is apparently drawn from its appearance, though there is some disagreement as to which part of the appearance. The name dandelion is a corruption of the French *Dent de Lion*, lion's tooth. Some suggest the jagged, toothy leaves prompted the name. Others attribute the name to the resemblance of the flower to the golden teeth of the heraldic lion. Still others see some leonine characteristic in the roots.

Dill

Anethum graveolens
Umbelliferae

Dill is a hardy, annual plant that resembles fennel in so many ways that the herbalist Culpeper said the likeness "deceiveth many".

Like fennel, dill has a spindly tap-root, although dill roots are not usable. It also develops a round, shiny green main stem, but while fennel commonly shows many stems from a single root, there is seldom more than one on a dill plant.

Dill is prolific and, if a few are left to seed themselves, the gardener will have an entire season's supply without replanting.

Dill displays feathery branches along the main stem, which ends in a cluster of umbels with yellow flowers appearing at the tip of each umbel, several weeks after planting. Seeds are attached to the umbel tips in pairs.

The plant likes moderately rich, loose soil, and full sun. Because young plants are difficult to transplant, start dill outdoors either by rows a quarter-inch (6 mm) deep, by broadcast

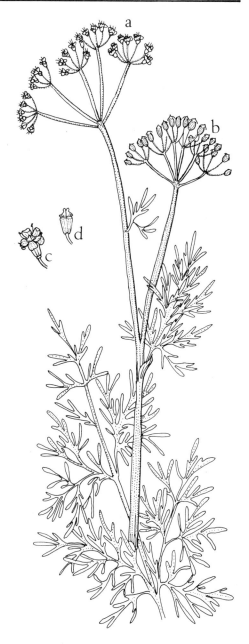

Dill
(Anethum graveolens)
(a) flower head (b) seed head
(c) flower enlargement
(d) seed enlargement

sowing, or by drills ten inches (25 cm) apart. Cover the new seeds with a light soil blanket. Germination takes place in ten to 14 days at about 60° F (16°C).

Both leaves and seeds are used. If plants are to be harvested before going to seed, plan successive replantings from April through to mid-July. For pickling—dill's major culinary use— seeding should be done in early May.

Leaves are harvested about eight weeks after seeding, with the outer leaves cut first, always close to the stem. Dry them in the shade within a day or two by placing them on a fine screen or paper. If necessary, use a low oven to complete the drying, because dill leaves will lose their colour and flavour if the drying time is prolonged. Finally, seal them in a tight jar. As an alternative to drying, you may freeze them while they are fresh.

Plants left to mature will grow up to three feet (90 cm) high, develop the flower-tipped umbels, and eventually go to seed. For pickling, harvest the flowering umbels and a few leaves. For oil and fragrance, of course, the seeds are used. Wait until they are a light brown, then cut the umbels, dry them in the sun for a few days, and shake the seeds loose. Cutting should be done in the early morning when the seeds are less likely to be accidentally shaken loose and lost. Seeds yield their oils to infusions of hot water or spirits, but it is necessary to bruise them first.

In the vegetable garden, small quantities of dill may be sown and allowed to mature and bloom for the benefit of honey-bees. It is a good herb to grow with cabbage and, when lightly sown, with carrots, cucumbers, lettuce, and onions. Dill should never be allowed to mature when sown with carrots because it has a severe depressing effect on them.

The medicinal uses of dill closely resemble those of fennel. A decoction of dill in white wine is "a gallant expeller of wind and provoker of terms", says Culpeper. Dill water is used as "gripe water" for babies. It is good, too, for easing swelling and pains, and is said to increase milk in nursing mothers and even to cure ulcers.

In the Middle Ages, dill was held to be a powerful charm against witchcraft. The Sixteenth Century poet Michael Drayton wrote of a woman:

> *Therewith her Vervain and her Dill*
> *That hindereth witches of their will.*

A 1640 recipe for pickling cucumbers with dill is as follows.

Gather the tops of the ripest dill and cover the bottom of the vessel, and lay a layer of cucumbers and another of dill till you have filled the vessel within a handful of the top. Then take as much water as you think will fill the vessel and mix it with salt and a quarter-pound of allom to a gallon of water and poure it on them and press them down with a stone on them and keep them covered close. For that use, I think the water will be best boyl'd and cold, which will keep longer sweet, or if you like not this pickle, doe it with water, salt and white wine vinegar, or (if you please) pour the water and the salt on them scalding hot which will make them ready to use the sooner.

Dill vinegar is easier to make. It simply necessitates soaking a few dill leaves in vinegar for a couple of days.

In France, dill is used to flavour cakes and pastries. Its chopped leaves add a distinct flavour to soups and salads. Creamed chicken and plain cottage or cream cheese take on a tangy snap with the addition of a few chopped leaves. Try it also with steaks and chops.

Docks

Yellow Dock, Curled Dock,
Round-leaved Dock, Patience Dock,
Red Dock, Water Dock,
Great Water Dock.
Rumex sp.
Polygonaceae

Dock is a name applied to a group of broad-leaved wayside plants. Docks and sorrels share the same generic name, *Rumex*, so they obviously have a lot in common. Both sorrels and docks have pot-herb uses, but the docks generally are less palatable. The docks also have much in common with ordinary garden rhubarb, and can be used as substitutes for it.

Yellow or curled dock, *(R. crispus)*,

Curly Dock
(Rumex crispus)
(a) flower

385

is probably the dominant variety. The plant grows up to three feet (90 cm) in height, and its broad leaves, six to ten inches (16 to 25 cm) long, have crisped edges. Hence, the specific name. The deep root makes the plant hard to eradicate, but it is the root that is used. Collected late in the summer and into autumn, the roots are split, dried, and stored for use as a gentle tonic, astringent, laxative, and alterative. In various compounds, it is useful in treating skin eruptions and itching. A simple ointment for such use is made by boiling the root in vinegar, then mixing the softened pulp with lard or petroleum jelly.

The round-leaved dock, *(R. obtusifolius)*, the common variety, is used today mostly in wool dyeing. The root yields a yellow dye. But the leaves have also been used as dressings for blisters, burns, and scalds. Round-leaved dock generally grows taller than yellow dock and has larger leaves, with rounded ends.

Other docks include: patience dock *(R. alpinus)*, a tall plant growing to six feet (1.8 m) high, with large, long, pointed leaves; red or water dock *(R. aquaticus)*, with an appearance and properties not unlike yellow dock; and great water dock *(R. hydrolapathum)*, the largest of the docks, which can grow to over six feet (1.8 m) and has lancet-shaped, dull green leaves up to three feet (90 cm) long. This latter dock has an affinity for riverbanks.

Elder

**Common Elder, Black Elder,
Pipe Tree**
Sambucus nigra
Caprifoliaceae

This familiar sight in the English countryside is a large rather coarse, deciduous shrub that grows rapidly and can reach a height of up to 12 feet (3.7 m) in a few seasons. Maude Grieve relates that it has been said that the English summer has not arrived until the elder is fully in flower and that it ends when the berries are ripe.

The elder leaves are large and dark green. It is most handsome in bloom during June and July, with creamy-white, umbel-like flower clusters up to ten inches (25 cm) across with a sweet, heavy scent. Later, it hangs heavy with purplish-black berries.

Elders are very effective in groups. They are hardy, and while not particular about the location, they do especially well in rich, moist soil with some shade. Elder can be propagated by cuttings of bare shoots in autumn, or it can be started from seed. It should be pruned in late autumn or early spring before growth begins.

All parts of the elder are useful—flowers, berries, leaves, bark, and root. The berries are prized for making wine, tarts, and jellies. A delightful tea is made from the dried blossoms, and it soothes cold sufferers by promoting sleep. Elder has been used for many medicinal purposes: in skin lotions, facials, and as an antiseptic wash for skin complaints.

Elder was widely used by the American Indians, who applied the bark as an antidotal poultice to painfull swellings and inflammations. They used an elder bark tea to ease parturition and a tea made from the dried flowers as a febrifuge. The flowers were considered as mildly stimulant, carminative, and diaphoretic.

The American Indians called elder the "tree of music" and made flutes from branches cut in spring and dried with the leaves. Large shoots were used for arrow shafts. So, elder not only can claim to have its roots in the calm of the English rural scene, but also in the Wild West.

The bruised leaves rubbed on the skin will keep flies away. Elders are said to protect garden plants from insect pests. An elder planted near the orchard will lure birds away from other fruit with its berries. A decoction of the leaves will keep caterpillars from eating plants on which it is sprayed; it is also used as a spray for mildew. Elder aids in fermentation of compost and creates humus in the soil around it which can be valuable to surrounding plants.

Elecampane

Scabwort, Elf Dock, Wild Sunflower, Horseheal, Velvet Dock
Inula Helenium
Compositae

Elecampane is a striking herb, tall, erect, and beautiful. It is a sturdy, almost unbranching plant, generally rising up to five feet (1.5 m) but ranging as high as ten feet (3 m). Its huge, tapering leaves, broad at the base, pointed at the apex, are offset by small, daisy-like flowers of orange discs bordered with a shaggy fringe.

It is one of this country's largest herbaceous plants, being widely distributed throughout England. However, it is confined to damp pastures and shady ground.

Provided with a moist, shady spot, it will grow well in any garden soil, although the better the soil, the better the plant. The seed germinates in about 15 days and may be sown in the spring or when ripe in a cold frame. Elecampane may also be propagated by root division in spring or by offsets of one bud and eye taken from the parent plant in the autumn.

Horseheal and scabwort, two of the country names of elecampane, are derived from early medical uses. A decoction of this herb is said to heal scabs on sheep, hence the name "scabwort". Likewise, it is reputedly effective in cutaneous diseases of horses; hence the name "horseheal".

The part used is the thickened root, which is generally gathered in the autumn of its second year. The dried, crushed root is an ingredient in many compound medicines. It is rarely used alone. Its action is that of a diuretic, tonic, diaphoretic, an expectorant, antiseptic, astringent, and an alterative, and it is gently stimulative.

Elm, Slippery

Sweet Elm, Indian Elm, Red Elm
Ulmus rubra (syn. *Ulmus fulva*)
Ulmaceae

A deciduous native of central and northern portions of North America, the slippery elm is a slim, wide-branching, flat-topped tree.

The dark brown bark is deeply furrowed, rough, and scaly. The under-bark is a ruddy brown; the innermost layer is buff-white and aromatic and is the portion used medicinally. The rough leaves are a deep yellowish, olive-green, lighter beneath. It blooms in March and April; the winged, round fruit or seed ripens in spring in two to four years. It is propagated by seeds sown as soon as ripe, or by layering and greenwood cuttings.

The inner bark is very mucilaginous and has been used and known as one of the more important healing plants. The powdered bark is used as a nutritious gruel or food and is recommended for its soothing and healing action for inflammations of the stomach and bowels; for bronchitis; and as a poultice for ulcers, wounds, burns, boils, and inflamed surfaces. It has been made into lozenges for coughs and sore throats.

Relief of inflammations of the digestive tract may be obtained by taking a decoction of slippery elm bark: Steep two or more ounces (56 g) of the bark in a quart (1.4 l) of boiling water for an hour or more. After straining, the decoction may be taken freely in tablespoonful doses. The same decoction is said to be useful as an enema. A lighter decoction, one ounce (28 g) of the cut bark to a quart (1.4 l) of water, has been recommended as a vaginal douche.

Eucalyptus

Blue Gum Tree
Eucalyptus Globulus
Myrtaceae

Although this plant is a native of warmer climates, Australia, South Africa, India, and southern Europe, for example, it is grown in this country, primarily in green-houses. But certain varieties can be grown out of doors in the south of England. Some varieties produce lovely blossoms in abundance which are a valuable source of honey nectar.

Eucalyptus is a heavy feeder and should not be planted too closely to other plants which might suffer from depletion of nutrients.

Insects are repelled by its aromatic oil, which is also used medicinally. One teaspoonful of the oil in half a pint (284 ml) of warm water, rubbed into the skin, is a powerful insect repellent for both humans and animals. Dried, finely powdered leaves are used as an insecticide.

The leaves and the oil distilled from them are used medicinally. The plant is said to have antiseptic qualities, which accounts for its use in treating ulcers and open wounds. The dried and powdered leaves can be inhaled in cases of bronchial inflammations and similar ailments, while the oil and infusions of the leaves can be used also in cases of fevers, muscle spasms, croup, and spasmodic throat troubles. But care must be exercised to avoid large doses of eucalyptus, as it may produce indigestion, nausea, vomiting, diarrhoea, muscular weakness, and related effects.

Eyebright

Euphrasia
Euphrasia officinalis
Scrophulariaceae

Eyebright is a tough but elegant little plant. It is a fairly common British

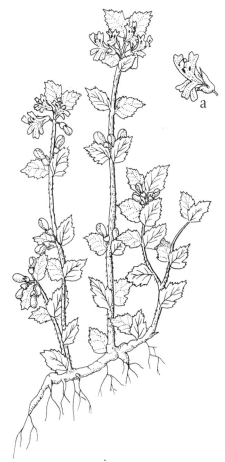

Eyebright
(Euphrasia officinalis)
(a) flower

weed and an annual, growing up to eight inches (20 cm) in height, with deeply cut leaves and numerous small, white or purplish flowers variegated with yellow.

Eyebright is a little difficult to grow, since it requires a symbiotic relationship with grass to survive. The eyebright roots send out tiny suckers, which attach themselves to the roots of grasses, drawing a measure of nourishment from the grass.

The medicinal use of the plant, as the name suggests, was for eye ailments. An infusion is made by putting an ounce (28 g) of the herb in three-quarters of a pint (426 ml) of boiling water. When cooled, the infusion should be used to bathe the eyes. Eyebright has also been used to alleviate hay fever.

Fennel

Fenkel, Sweet Fennel, Wild Fennel
Foeniculum vulgare
Umbelliferae

Portly herbalists might find it wise to develop an interest in fennel, for, in the words of the old master herbalist Culpeper, all parts of the fennel plant "are much used in drink or broth to make people lean that are too fat". It

is not the sort of plant that gardeners will want to integrate in *their* gardens, however, for it is the prime exception to the rule that herbs have a positive effect on surrounding plants.

Fennel is a biennial with a tendency to become a perennial where soil and climate are favourable. Its main tap-root is usually finger-thick, white and fleshy, with smaller horizontal side roots attached. An equally thick main stem of a highly polished green appearance extends vertically, to be capped by a small cluster of umbels the first year. In the second year, more main stems develop from the root and develop a multitude of umbels with tiny yellow, five-bladed flowers. Seeds of light to dark brown form in pairs at each bloom. Large feathery leaves of dark green adorn the main stem, which can reach up to five feet (1.5 m).

Fennel must be started from seed, which can be sown outside as soon as the soil can be worked. It prefers moderately fertile soil with adequate calcium and much sun. Avoid constant moisture.

Sow lightly in a bed or in drills six inches (15 cm) apart. Keep moist until two thin seed leaves are plainly visible. Germination takes place within two weeks. Thin to six inches (15 cm).

Fennel must be located with due regard to its neighbours. It has a decidedly harmful effect on beans, caraway, tomatoes, and kohlrabi. On the other hand, it is harmed by certain plants: coriander will prevent the formation of seeds if planted too

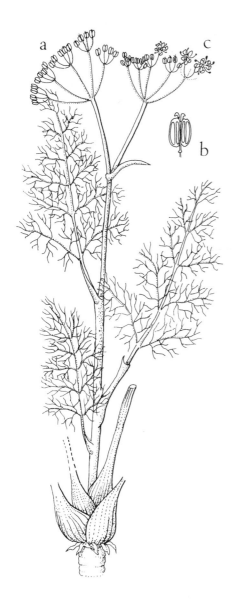

Fennel
(Foeniculum vulgare)
(a) seed heads (b) seed enlargement
(c) flower

close, and wormwood planted too close—within four feet (1.2 m)—cuts germination and stunts the growth of fennel plants.

At the end of the first year, dig up the tap-roots along with about three inches (8 cm) of stem. Treat them like carrots and potatoes: put them in sand in a humid, cool cellar or outside in a cold frame or trench. In the spring, shorten the roots a bit and plant them 36 inches (about a metre) apart. Harvest seeds as they turn from green to light brown. The morning is the best time to avoid unnecessary seed losses.

Fennel flowers will attract pollinating insects, but the powdered plant is used as an insect repellent around kennels and stables.

The ancient Greeks and Anglo-Saxons cheated on their fast days by nibbling a little fennel, which reduced the appetite.

With carminative and purgative qualities, fennel "expels wind, provokes urine, and eases the pains of the stone and helps it to break", Culpeper advised.

Fennel also can be a mother's friend. Leaves and seeds boiled in barley water are said to increase the yield of mother's milk and make it more wholesome. It is also the basis for gripe water given to babies to relieve wind.

One of the herb's chief medicinal qualities in olden times was its supposed ability to improve eyesight. The early Nineteenth Century poet, Longfellow, wrote of it:

Above the lower plants it towers,
The Fennel with its yellow flowers;
And in an earlier age than ours
Was gifted with the wondrous powers
Lost vision to restore.

The seeds are the part of the plant usually used for oil extraction. They yield their oil when distilled in water. Infusions work with hot water but even better with alcohol.

The leaves are used as both a garnish and a flavouring for salads, stews, and vegetables. Boiled with salmon and mackerel, fennel lessens the oily indigestibility of the fish.

The fennel stalk, stripped of its skin and dressed in vinegar and pepper, makes a tasty, celery-like salad that is popular in the plant's native Mediterranean area. The Italians call the dish *cartucci* and claim it calms and aids sleep.

Feverfew

Featherfew, Bachelor's Buttons, Bride's Buttons, Maydes Weed
Chrysanthemum Parthenium (syn. *Pyrethrum parthenium, Matricaria parthenoides*)
Compositae

Feverfew is a hardy biennial-to-perennial with what can only be described as a daring list of curative claims. A member of the daisy family, feverfew grows freely in fields and on untended ground. Reaching as high as three feet (90 cm), it bears golden-green leaves and white daisy-like flowers, which have inspired people to nickname the herb "bride's buttons" or "bachelor's buttons". In June, these inch-wide (2.5 cm) flowers completely cover the plant. The yellow centre of the flower is distinguished from the conical camomiles by its flatness. Gerard described the leaves of what he called "featherfew", a variation of the name, as being "tender, diversely torne and jagged, and nickt on the edges . . ." Unlike some of the sweeter herbs, feverfew emits a strong odour and possesses a bitter taste. The burning taste of the root explains why this herb is classified in some sources as a *pyrethrum*, derived from the Greek *pyr*, fire.

In the past, this versatile herb has offered numerous and varied benefits to humanity. It was once considered effective in cleansing the atmosphere and warding off disease. To combat insects, a tincture made from feverfew mixed with half a pint (184 ml) of cold water will keep away the gnats, mosquitos, and other pests. But if the insect bites, it's helpful to know that feverfew has the power to "relieve the pain and swelling caused by bites of insects and vermin". Particularly worth noting is the fact that bees find the odour and taste of feverfew highly repulsive.

In Finland, feverfew was administered as a tonic for consumption and its stimulant nature made it a good emmenagogue. Culpeper advised that:

The powder of the herb taken in wine, with some oxymel, purges both choler and phlegm, and is available for those that are short-winded, and are troubled with melancholy and heaviness, or sadness of spirits. It is very effectual for all pains in the head coming of a cold cause, the herb being bruised and applied to the crown of the head: as also for the vertigo, that is, a running or swimming of the head.

For opium addicts suffering from "overdose", feverfew would provide relief, Parkinson claimed. Victims of coughing, wheezing, and difficult breathing found that feverfew with honey eased the discomfort. The herb was fried with wine and oil and applied externally to eliminate colic. An infusion of feverfew flowers was believed to reduce the sensitivity to pain which highly nervous people experience.

According to Culpeper, feverfew is commanded by Venus, and thus addresses many of its healing powers to the ailments of women. He observed that feverfew is considered to be "a general strengthener of their wombs, and to remedy such infirmities as a careless midwife has there caused . . ." When boiled and drunk in white wine, feverfew "cleanses the womb, expels the afterbirth, and does a woman all the good she can desire of a herb". Among its many old, familiar names, "maydes weed" refers to the use of feverfew as a laxative for young

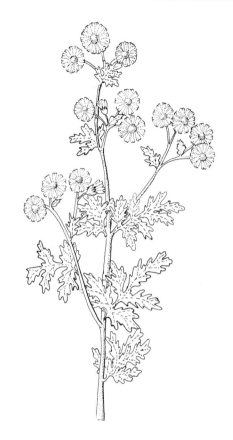

Feverfew
(Chrysanthemum Parthenium)

women suffering from suppression and inclined towards hysteria.

A hardy plant, feverfew needs very little attention. It may be grown and handled like camomile for the many medicinal uses or for the dainty blossoms it bears. The best time for planting is in April, although this is also feasible during the autumn. Although feverfew is not difficult to grow in almost any soil, a well-drained, loamy soil, well nourished with manure promises the best results.

393

To protect the fragile young plants from the hoe, it is recommended that weeding be done by hand in the early stages of growth.

Feverfew is propagated in three ways; by seed, by root division, and by cuttings. February and March are the most favourable months for sowing the seeds. It is recommended that they be thinned out to two to three inches (5 to 8 cm) between each plant, so that in June they will be hardy and ready to be transferred to permanent quarters on some rainy day in early June. Each plant should be spaced a foot (30 cm) or more apart, leaving two feet (60 cm) between the rows. Soon the plants grown from seed will be firmly established in the soil.

Propagation by division of the roots is done when these are most active, often in March. They should be sectioned into three to five large parts with a sharp spade or knife.

A third way to begin new feverfew plants is by taking cuttings from the young shoots which spring from the bases of mature plants. The heel of the old plant should be attached to these new shoots, since it will facilitate rooting. When the cuttings are ready for insertion, any time from October to May, shorten the foliage to three inches (8 cm) and plant firmly in a bed of light, sandy soil in a shady spot. Cover the top of the bed with sand and drench with water. Beware of snails and slugs which can be combatted by sprinkling the plants with soot, ashes, or lime. To protect the feverfew cuttings from black fly, sprinkle them with pepper.

Harvesting of the plants should be carried out at the peak of their maturity. The technique may require some practice, however, if undertaken according to Gerard's instructions. Feverfew, he said, is most effective against the fever or ague if it is gathered with the left hand while the name of the victim is spoken aloud and with "nary a glance behind".

Foxglove

Witches' Gloves, Dead Men's Bells, Bloody Fingers, Fairy Thimbles
Digitalis purpurea
Scrophulariaceae

Foxglove is the source of a most famous plant-derived medicine, digitalis. It is, without question, a true medicinal plant. But if misused, it can have dangerous effects.

Foxglove has thimble-like flowers two inches (5 cm) long, in a one-sided spray. The flowers develop on an unbranching three foot (90 cm) stalk, surrounded by the medically valuable leaves. It is one of the prettiest of England's wild flowers and can also be found throughout Europe. It grows freely in this country in woods, lanes, and on railway embankments, flourishing in siliceous and loamy soils. Little

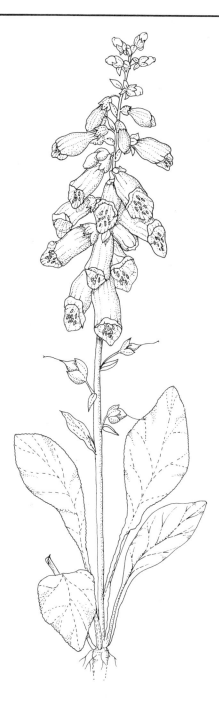

Foxglove
(Digitalis purpurea)

soil is needed. Foxgloves will grow in stone crevices and on rocky hillsides.

The leaves are picked in the second year just as the plant begins to flower. The drug derived from the leaves is used primarily as a blood circulation stimulant and for heart diseases. (It should be noted that digitalis can have deleterious effects and should be used only under proper supervision.) Curiously enough, the ancient herbalists tended to use foxglove for external uses. It was not until 1775 that an English doctor, having heard of internal uses from a folk healer, investigated its benefits on a scientific basis.

Foxglove is grown from seed, though the germination is somewhat uncertain. Seeds must be sown annually to maintain an annual bloom. The soil should be rich and moist. The plants should be fertilized annually with compost and mulched in the autumn to prevent frost damage in the winter.

Garlic

Poor Man's Treacle
Allium sativum
Amaryllidaceae

Garlic is a ruffian with a heart of gold. It has a wealth of talents serving men and women in the kitchen, the medicine chest, and the vegetable garden.

It has an undistinguished appearance and its smell is extremely stong.

Garlic has a long history. Its origin is unknown, though it is believed to have spread into the Middle East and Europe from somewhere south-east of Siberia. The Chinese have known and used garlic for centuries, as have the Jews and Arabs. Garlic was mentioned in the *Calendar of the Hsai*, a Chinese book dating back two thousand years before Christ. It is known to have been used by the Babylonians around 3000 B.C. and is a part of the ancient Hebrew Talmudic law, which stipulates it be used in certain dishes and on certain occasions.

Garlic is a small, vigorous relative of the onion. Like all the onions, it is a spare, functional plant, having a bulb sending up a few, thin shoots. Garlic's strap-like leaves grow to a foot or two (30 or 60 cm) in length, and surround a slender flower stalk which develops a globular cluster of tiny white blossoms. There is so little fanciness to it that some herbalists leave it out of their gardens. But the heart of garlic is underground. It is there that the pungent tasting and smelling bulb develops. It is a segmented globe, each segment called a clove. There are generally eight to 12 cloves to a bulb. With very rare exceptions, these cloves of garlic are all that are used although one herbalist suggests harvesting the garlic tops for use in salads.

Garlic is easily cultivated, although it does require a fairly long growing season. As early in the spring as possible, the bulb is split into its component cloves, and each is planted separately, about two inches (5 cm) deep and about six inches (15 cm) from its neighbours. Garlic will grow in almost any soil, although it prefers a moist, sandy one. A dressing of well-rotted manure or compost is helpful. Sun is important; a cold, damp growing season can seriously hinder garlic's development. Weeds, too, can crowd out garlic, so don't let them get the upper hand.

Garlic set out in March should be ready for harvest in August to September. Gather the bulbs after the leaves wither. They can be spurred to ripeness by bending the stalks to the ground in late summer. Once harvested, the plants may be braided together by their leaves or popped into an old nylon stocking or net bag, and hung to dry. If you are going to try the greens in a salad, gather and use them fresh.

Moderation is the byword in the culinary use of garlic. Begin, as most cookbooks suggest, by rubbing a clove of garlic around the salad bowl or the saucepan. As the taste for garlic develops, increase the amount. Eventually, you could be using whole cloves. A garlic clove finely chopped will add zest to a soup. A joint of lamb, mutton, or pork is improved in tenderness and flavour by the addition of garlic. Skin a few cloves and insert them into incisions made in the meat. Cook and serve. A simple method of experimenting with garlic seasoning on any dish is to use garlic salt, a powder made from dried garlic cloves and available in most supermarkets. A strong concoction is garlic butter, made by blending together a quarter of a pound (113 g) of butter and four macerated garlic cloves.

The problem with garlic always is its smell. If you like garlic, you might also get to like parsley, which is said to freshen your breath. Simply chew a sprig or two at the end of a garlic-rich meal. Milk, too, is said to be an antidote to the smell of garlic, although many a cow has tainted its milk simply by munching a bit of wild garlic.

Garlic's smell is inextricably tied to its essential oil which is a mixture of substances which are mainly allyl sulphides; the basic active principal is called allicin. The potency of the oil is such that it is claimed that the garlic odour will taint the breath of one who rubs the cloves on the soles of his feet. Garlic cloves were also bound to the feet of smallpox victims. Putting garlic cloves in the shoes of whooping-cough sufferers was another clove-to-foot remedy.

Organic gardeners have long believed that garlic has a positive effect in the garden as a deterrent to insect pests. Some gardeners scattered a little garlic amongst their vegetables most susceptible to insect damage, while others used the garlic cloves as an ingredient in home-made insect sprays. And within the last few years, scientific research has in fact verified that garlic is effective as an insecticide and insect repellent.

A British report on the research of David Greenstock of the Henry Doubleday Research Association, Braintree, Essex is most reassuring. Greenstock has been experimenting on a scientific basis with garlic and has developed a number of varieties of garlic-based insecticides said to be effective against a variety of insects. For example, it has been found to defect such insects as the malaria mosquito and the cockshafer larvae without being harmful to livestock or humans. Generally, the smell is credited for garlic's power as a garden guardian. And that's not far from wrong. Greenstock attributes the herb's power to the allyl sulphides, the source of the smell.

A simple do-it-yourself recipe from Greenstock is; "Take three ounces (85 g) of chopped garlic bulbs and let them soak in about two teaspoonfuls of liquid paraffin for 24 hours. Then slowly add a pint (568 ml) of water in which three-quarters of an ounce (21 g) of oil-based soap (Palmolive is a good one) has been dissolved, and stir well. Strain the liquid through fine gauze, and store it in a china or glass container (it reacts with metals). Try it against your worst pests, starting with a dilution of one part to 20 parts of water, then going down to one to 100."

Historically, however, garlic's primary positive qualities have been related to health. It has a long list of medicinal uses. There was a time in this century, for example, when herbalists were drawing parallels between the

Bulgarians' use of garlic and their longevity. Pills made from garlic are marketed as a dietary supplement.

Medicinally, garlic is a diaphoretic, diuretic, an expectorant, and a stimulant. For centuries garlic has been a common European remedy for colds, coughs, and sore throats. A syrup of garlic is made by pouring a quart (1.1 l) of boiling water over a pound (454 g) of sliced garlic cloves, allowing the mixture to brew about 12 hours, then stirring in sufficient honey to produce a syrup. Vinegar may be added to improve the syrup. The garlic smell may be masked by bruising a bit of sweet fennel seed or caraway seed and boiling it for a short time in vinegar, then adding the decoction to the syrup.

A syrup recommended for children troubled by a cough, but not inflammation, is made by melting an ounce and a half (42 g) of sugar in a fluid ounce (28 ml) of raw garlic juice (the juice squeezed from the garlic bulb).

These folk remedies are not without medical approval. A number of experiments have been conducted and the results reported are interesting. In the March, 1950 issue of *Medical Monthly*, a German magazine, Dr. J. Klosa reported that garlic oil kills dangerous organisms without attacking other organisms vital to the body. Klosa experimented with a solution of garlic oil and water, sometimes adding fresh extract of onion juice, which enhanced the solution's effectiveness. Studies by Dr. F. G. Piotrowsky of the

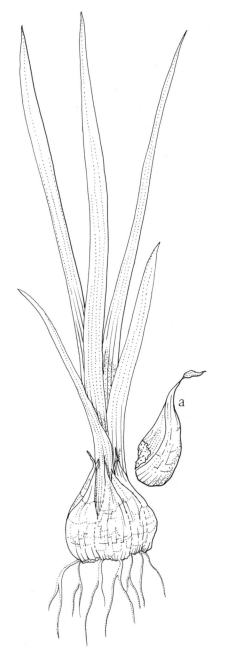

Garlic
(Allium sativum)
(a) clove

University of Geneva revealed that blood pressure was effectively lowered in 40 per cent of his hypertensive patients after being treated with garlic. In the July 1, 1948, issue of *Praxis*, Dr. Piotrowsky reported that garlic opens up blood vessels, thus reducing pressure. He also noted that dizziness, angina pains over the chest, and headaches often disappear with garlic therapy. More recently, Polish scientists reported from Warsaw in 1969 that bacteria which resist other antibiotics, including staphylococci, succumb to a pulverized garlic preparation. Scientists in the Soviet Union reported in 1972 the production of an actual pharmaceutical antibiotic, allicin, which they say destroys only harmful germs, leaving natural bacteria untouched.

The reports from the Communist-bloc countries confirm what has been effectively demonstrated through centuries of application. The use of garlic as an antiseptic has, of course, passed into history as medical science has progressed, but for years it was used in hospitals and by herbalists. During World War I, there was a boom in "garlic commerce", and the herb is credited with saving thousands of lives. Pads of sphagnum moss were sterilized and saturated with water-diluted garlic juice. When applied to open wounds, the garlic helped control suppuration.

Among the other ailments, garlic is said to remedy rheumatism, whooping cough, and intestinal worms. Garlic cloves were bruised and mixed with lard and the resulting ointment rubbed on the chest and back to cure whooping cough. Garlic syrup was said to be effective against rheumatism, as was simply rubbing the ailing joint with garlic. For intestinal worms, raw garlic juice, or milk which had been boiled with garlic, was suggested. For baldness, a lotion was made by macerating several bulbs in a quart (1.1 l) of wine or alcohol.

The ancient Egyptians held garlic in great esteem, invoking its name as one might that of a deity, in the taking of oaths and in some areas, refusing to eat it because it was too sacred. It was, as mentioned earlier, an important part of the diet of the Egyptians' slaves, who reportedly refused to work when it was withheld. The Greeks too, had a certain religious awe for garlic. They placed garlic on piles of stones at crossroads as a supper for Hecate, the triple goddess (Phoebe in heaven, Diana on earth, and Hecate in hell). But they also refused entrance to the Temple of Cybele to anyone who had garlic on his breath.

"When Satan stepped out from the Garden of Eden after the fall of man, Garlick sprang up from the spot where he placed his left foot, and Onion from that where his right foot touched." Such is the legend some herbalists attributed to the Mohammedans.

Garlic has appeared in writings of all ages, from the epics of Homer to the plays of William Shakespeare. Theophrastus and Pliny the Elder recorded much of what we know of garlic's uses in the ancient Egyptian and Greek civilizations. Aristophanes, the Greek playwright, wrote that garlic juice would restore lost virility, and told of famous athletes who made garlic a part of their training diet. Hippocrates, the medical pioneer, classified garlic as a sudorific, diuretic and laxative. Aristotle wrote: "It is a cure for hydrophobia and a tonic, is hot, laxative, but bad for the eyes."

The Renaissance herbalist John Evelyn had much to say about garlic:

Garlick, Allium; dry towards Excess; and tho by both Spaniards and Italians and the more Southern People familiarly eaten with almost everything, and esteemed of such singular Vertue to help concoction, and thought a Charm against all Infection and Poyson (by which it has obtain'd the Name of the Country-man's Theriacle) we yet think it more proper for our Northern Rustics, especially living in Uliginous and moist places, or such as use the Sea; Whilst we absolutely forbid it entrance into our Salleting, by reason of its intolerable Rankness, and which made it so detested of old that the eating of it was (as we read) part of the Punishment for such as had committed the horrid'st Crimes.

Culpeper noted that "Mars owns this herb". He listed a variety of applications for garlic, adding that "for all those diseases the onions are as effectual. But the garlic," he continued, "has some more peculiar virtues besides the former, *viz.* it has a special quality to discuss inconveniences, coming by corrupt agues or mineral vapours, or by drinking corrupt and stinking waters; as also by taking wolf-bane, hen-bane, hemlock,

or other poisonous and dangerous herbs. Authors quote many other diseases this is good for; but conceal its vices. Its heat is very vehement; and all vehement hot things send up but ill-savoured vapours to the brain. In choleric men it will add fuel to the fire; in men oppressed by melancholy, it will attenuate the humour, and send up strong fancies, and as many strange visions to the head; therefore, let it be taken inwardly with great moderation; outwardly, you may make more bold with it."

One legendary commendation of garlic concerns the Great Plague which swept England in the mid Seventeenth Century. A household was immunized from the Plague, it is said, because garlic was stored in the building. Another story is told of French clerics, who used garlic, ministering freely to the needs of the Plague victims without contacting the disease, while English clerics, who didn't use garlic, died.

The most famous story of garlic and the Plague tells of "Four Thieve's Vinegar", which is a vinegar infused with garlic. According to one version of this legend, four thieves confessed to plundering the bodies of victims during the Plague which swept Marseilles in 1721. They protected themselves by imbibing vast quantities of the vinegar. In another version, the thieves are condemned men released from prison to help dispose of the thousands of bodies. Ultimately, they gain pardons by revealing how they carried out their assignment without contracting the Plague themselves. Of course, the garlic vinegar was their secret.

The legends and stories, of course, do go on and on. Bull fighters carry garlic to prevent the bulls from charging. Jockeys in Hungary used to carry garlic to prevent another horse and rider from getting in front of them. In India, garlic is worn for protection against evil spirits and spells. But perhaps the most familiar is the one that has dragged garlic down; the one voiced by so many, including William Shakespeare: "And, most dear actors, eat no onions nor garlic, for we are to utter sweet breath."

Gentian

Yellow Gentian, Gentian Root, Bitter Root
Gentiana lutea
Gentianaceae

Gentian does not grow in the British Isles. Nonetheless, it is of interest since it is imported into the country. The larger proportion of our imports used to come from Germany, but a certain amount also comes from Switzerland, France, and Spain.

Gentian is a native of the mountainous regions of Europe. It has long been a recognized medicinal herb, chiefly as a tonic. It was first listed in old Arabic

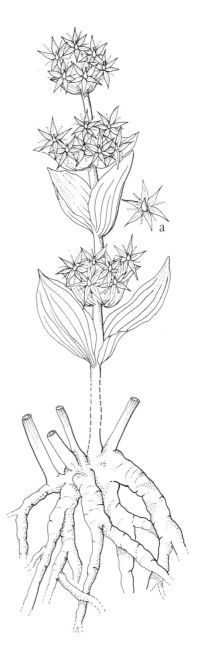

Gentian
(Gentiana lutea)
(a) flower

401

and Greek herbals and has been included in herbals and pharmacopoeias to this day. It is said to have been named after Gentius, a King of Illyria, who first discovered its tonic qualities.

Many varieties of this perennial are cultivated for rock gardens and woodland settings abroad. *Gentiana lutea* is the recognized medicinal species. The stem is three to four feet (1 to 1.25 m) tall, leaves oblong, bright, pale green with large yellow flowers that have a faint aromatic fragrance. Gentians need frost to germinate and require a cool situation, with good drainage and ample amounts of humus and compost. The very small seeds are slow to germinate and should be as fresh as possible.

The dried root and rhizome are used medicinally. They were regarded as a splendid tonic to invigorate digestion and purify the blood. A gentian root tonic was made by filling a pint bottle (568 ml) half full of the dried root, filling it with a half-water, half-alcohol mixture, and allowing it to stand for 14 days. A teaspoonful was taken before meals. The plant was also said to be helpful in fevers and general debility.

Geranium, Scented

Pelargonium sp.
Geraniaceae

The most striking thing about the scented geraniums or pelargoniums is their incredible variety. They may be the most delightfully varied aggregation of plants in the herb world.

Curiously enough, the scented geraniums aren't true geraniums, though they are related through botanical family membership. The scented geraniums all share an elongated seed case resembling a stork's bill, a resemblance which led to the generic name *Pelargonium*. They share, too, qualities of scent, colour, and form unsurpassed in the botanical world. All are half-hardy, leafy semishrubs.

Practically all herbal writers speak of the remarkable scents of these herbs for the strength and variety of pelargonium fragrances are the dominant herbal virtue of the plants.

Of course, the pelargoniums have a colourful history as houseplants, but they were houseplants chiefly because of their fragrance. Herbalists given to such things wax nostalgic about grandmothers and Victorian mansions and brushing the gargantuan rose geraniums, thereby releasing their strong fragrance of roses. The Victorian Era was the heyday of the pelargoniums, but there are pockets of revived interest today.

The pelargoniums were first introduced into Europe in the Seventeenth and Eighteenth Centuries by sailors who stopped off while rounding the Cape of Good Hope. The plant then, as now, was popular simply as a pretty, fragrant houseplant.

The French did find commercial value in several of them, when it was discovered that they could be substituted for attar of roses in perfume making. Since that discovery, the perfume-makers have grown large amounts of scented geraniums in North Africa and southern France. About one pound (453 g) of leaves will produce a gram (.04 ounces) of oil. Three ounces (85 g) of oil dissolved in alcohol serves as an essence that is one of the principal ingredients in scented soaps, perfumes, and pot-pourris. The leaves themselves are used in home-made pot-pourris.

The ingenious cook can find a variety of culinary uses for the various scented geraniums. Perhaps the most familiar is the use of rose geraniums in apple jelly. One places two or three rose geranium leaves in the bottom of a jar and pours in hot apple jelly; it is as easy as that. Rose geranium sugar is made, similarly, by layering the herb leaves with the sugar. Rose geranium tea is fragrant and refreshing. The challenge for the true pelargonium lover is to experiment with the many varieties. The rose geranium is cited here merely because it is the most popular of the pelargoniums.

Little is made of the medicinal values of the pelargoniums. One herbal reports that most pelargoniums have astringent properties and says they have been found valuable in dysentery and for ulceration of the stomach and upper part of the intestines. A folk remedy for an aching head was to bathe the head in geranium vinegar.

The pelargoniums are all started from cuttings. The growing presents no particular problems. The small plants should be set outside during the summer, where they will develop rapidly and produce many leaves. Since they are quite tender, they must be brought inside during cold, winter months. Frost will kill them.

Cuttings should be taken in the early autumn, using a sharp knife to cut just below the node where the leaf grows from the stem. Four to five inch (10 to 13 cm) cuttings should be taken from the larger varieties and three inch (8 cm) cuttings from the smaller ones. These are then inserted into clean sand, deep enough to hold them erect and spaced so as to permit free air circulation. Keep the cuttings well watered and shaded for several days, gradually introducing them to sunlight. After two or three weeks, the cuttings should be sufficiently well established to survive transplanting to individual pots, preferably two to three inches (5 to 8 cm) in size. The more vigorously growing varieties will have to be retransplanted into larger, four inch (10 cm) pots, as their roots fill the smaller pot.

Lemon Scented Geranium
(Pelargonium graveolens)

When transplanting pelargoniums outside, they should be placed in a spot with fertile soil, high in humus. They must be well watered to develop properly.

Scented geraniums, of course, can be kept in containers, and moved back and forth from indoors to outdoors as the weather changes. By so doing, some very impressive-sized plants can be developed. Grown indoors, the plants need all the sunlight they can get and regular watering, and they thrive best in a temperature of about 70° F (22°C). They should be planted in boxes or pots at least five inches (13 cm) deep; preferably twice that.

Use a good potting mixture to assure adequate drainage, and fertilize the plants occasionally with a manure or fish emulsion tea.

Insects present no problem. Scented geraniums are very resistant to insect attack. Moreover, the companion planter may find white-flowered scented geraniums valuable in the vegetable garden.

The leaves of the pelargoniums can be used fresh, especially if grown indoors. The main harvest of those grown seasonally outdoors should be before the slightest frost, as the plants are highly sensitive and die off at the first touch of frost. Leaves harvested in this way should be dried in the shade. Dried properly they will store well.

The real problem with growing pelargoniums is selecting particular varieties to grow. Without doubt, the basic scented geranium is the one commonly called the rose geranium, *P. graveolens*. This is a large plant with deeply cut grey-green leaves, lavender flowers, and a rose-like fragrance. It will grow to three feet (90 cm) in height unless pruned regularly. Within this species there are a stunning number of varieties.

There are many other species of pelargoniums, each with its distinctive leaf shape, colour, and flower. *P. fragrans* or the nutmeg geranium, has small, smooth, grey-green leaves, spreading branches, sprays of small white flowers, and a pungent nutmeg-like fragrance. *P. torento* or the ginger geranium, has roundish leaves with sharply toothed margins, darkly marked lavender flowers, and a ginger-like aroma. *P. nervosum* or the lime-scented geranium is quite similar to the ginger geranium, but has small, darker foliage.

There are a variety of lemon-scented geraniums, two of the most common being *P. limoneum*, lemon geranium, and *P. mellissinum*, lemon balm geranium. The former has fan-shaped, toothed leaves, and is strongly lemon scented. The latter has light green leaves which resembles those of a maple tree, and small lavender flowers. It smells like lemon balm, and is one of the fastest growing pelargoniums.

Two other interesting pelargoniums are the peppermint geranium and the attar of roses geranium. The peppermint type, *P. tomentosum*, has large, flat, downy-covered leaves. It is strongly aromatic in the tradition of its namesake. *P. capitatum*, the attar of roses type, has divided foliage and pinkish flowers.

The listings above, of course, ignore the dozens of varieties existing within each species designation, as well as the scores of other species.

Germander

Sage-leaved Germander, Wood Sage, Hind Heal, Wall Germander, Water Germander
Teucrium sp.
Labiatae

There are several varieties of germander, all fine bordering plants for the small garden. *Teucrium lucidum* is a hardy perennial with small, stiff, glossy dark green leaves which lends itself to clipping as a low hedge. It grows up to one and a half feet (45 cm) tall. *T. Chamaedrys*, commonly known as "wall germander", is a low, creeping variety which makes good ground cover. It is hardier than *T. lucidum*, and its leaves will turn reddish in autumn and in dry weather. *T. Scorodonia*, known as "sage-leaved germander", is a hedge-like plant that draws its common name from its grey-green, sage-like leaves. A fourth variety, *T. Scordium*, is a creeping plant with an affinity for marshy, damp places; hence its common name, "water germander".

Germander can be started from seed, but the germination takes as long as 30 days. Perhaps a better method is to start plants from cuttings early in the growing season. The plants may be divided in the autumn. The soil should be rich, light, and moist. A sunny spot is preferred but not essential. In England, the plant flowers from July to September.

Apart from its place in the landscaped garden, germander has a history of medicinal uses. A decoction of the herb has been taken as a remedy for gout. It is often listed as a diuretic, and each variety has different uses.

Ginger

Zingiber officinale
Zingiberaceae

This is another plant that is not natural to this country, but which everyone knows of, if not uses. It is imported dried, largely from the West Indies, primarily Jamaica.

The root or rhizome is the part used medicinally, but the flowers of the ginger plant have a pleasant aromatic smell and the bruised stalks a characteristic fragrance. The root should not be used until the plant is one year old.

The root has stimulant and carminative properties and is useful in dyspepsia, flatulent colic and especially valuable in alcoholic gastritis or for diarrhoea which is not accompanied by inflammation. It is excellent to add to bitter infusions.

Maude Grieve says: "Ginger Tea is a hot infusion very useful for stoppage of the menses due to cold, externally it is a rubefacient."

Ginger is also used in many culinary dishes especially curries and oriental specialities. Green ginger (the young green roots) steeped in syrup makes a delicious preserve.

Ginger, Wild

Hazelwort, Wild Nard
Asarum Europaeum
Aristolochiaceae

Wild Ginger is a low, spreading plant with heart-shaped leaves which covers the ground in hilly woods. It flowers between May and August.

The parts used are the dried roots and leaves. The root smells like pepper and has a spicy flavour. When dried it

Wild Ginger (Asarum Europaeum)
(a) flower (b) rhizome

can be made into an ash-coloured powder. The dried leaves give a green powder which has the same properties as the root.

It has been used medicinally as an emetic, cathartic and errhine, "for which latter purpose it has been principally used in affections of the brain, eyes, throat, toothache and paralysis of the mouth," writes Maude Grieve. In France drunkards used it as an emetic. It is also useful for head colds as it promotes sneezing.

The powdered roots or leaves are usually mixed with hot water or alcohol, and have proved useful in chronic chest complaints and painful spasms of the bowels and stomach.

Ginseng

Five Fingers, Tartar Root
Panax quinquefolius
Araliaceae

A native of Manchuria, China, and other parts of Asia, ginseng was first introduced into England in 1740 by the botanist Collinson. It is difficult to cultivate here successfully, but for those who wish to try, a rich compost is necessary and it should be grown in greenhouses.

Ginseng is perhaps the most fascinating wild herb. It is a plant cloaked in mystery and superstition. It evokes

407

visions of mountain men, inscrutable Orientals, clipper ships, fortunes made and lost overnight. It is almost irrevocably tied to the past, and yet it may be a herb of the future.

Ginseng is a plant whose root is valued by the Chinese above all others as a cure-all. Their centuries-old esteem provoked incredible market demands, astronomical prices, over-harvesting, largely ill-fated cultivation schemes, and a lingering curiosity. Today, the root remains as important in Chinese folk medicine as ever, as expensive as ever, as untamed as ever, and as mysterious as ever.

It is easy enough to be suspicious of ginseng. Although the Chinese have used extracts of ginseng root for a thousand years or more as a general tonic, curative, strength-builder, and aphrodisiac, there has until recently been no evidence of a scientific character that ginseng really does the things the Chinese say it does. The greatest value is placed upon the root which is primate-shaped. This has a trunk and extremities approximating arms and legs. It smacks of the *Doctrine of Signatures*, and indeed, it is believed by some that the shape of the ideal root suggested it as a panacea for man. The shape, incidentally, prompted the Asiatic species of *Panax* to be named *schinseng*, Chinese for man-shape, from which the Anglicised gingseng is obviously derived.

Outside China, ginseng historically has been denigrated by the established medical authorities, although it has been widely used in folk medicine. "It would be difficult to find any plant with a reputation so disproportionate to its actual virtues." This was, and still is, the typical judgement of respectable, responsible authorities. In Russia scientists are researching many ideas and substances that are thought to be part of the "lunatic fringe" by scientists in the West. They have been working to find the true medicinal value of plants, and trying to promote a plant of their own, *Acanthopanax senticosus*, which they claim has characteristics very much like ginseng. Brekhman, author of a book on that plant, recently made these rather interesting comments about it:

By its pharmacological properties, *Acanthopanax* is in many features similar to ginseng. It is a stimulant, increasing the general tone of the organism, normalizing the arterial pressure and reducing an elevated blood sugar level. Owing to its capacity to strengthen the protective forces of the organism and to increase resistance against various adverse effects, *Acanthopanax* may be regarded as representative of those rare substances which possess an adaptogenic action, and contribute to the realization of its adaptive, "protective" reaction of the organism.

In other words, they say that *Acanthopanax* helps people resist the bad effects of stress more effectively. This research may eventually substantiate the long-held belief that ginseng is indeed "the queen of medicinal herbs".

The ginseng story must begin with the ancient Chinese medical texts. Among the properties attributed to ginseng are: alterative, tonic, stimulant, carminative, and demulcent. In Chinese medicine, ginseng is "a tonic to the five viscera, quieting animal spirits, establishing the soul, allaying fear, expelling evil effluvia, brightening the eye, opening up the heart, benefiting the understanding, and if taken for some time it will invigorate the body and prolong life". Moreover, it is regarded as an aphrodisiac wholly capable of prolonging sexual potency far into advanced years.

Perhaps as much for the latter as for any of the former properties, ginseng became an extremely desirable commodity. One emperor declared himself the sole ginseng dealer, buying all that was harvested, keeping the best for himself, and selling the remainder to make a fat profit. But demand eventually outstripped supply with the result that there was widespread over-harvesting.

P. quinquefolius is a small plant ranging between ten and 23 inches (25 and 60 cm) in height when mature. It likes shady ravines, gentle north slopes, and other spots with light, well-drained soil, rich in leaf-mould from hardwood forests. Ginseng grows very slowly, the seed taking as long as 18 months to germinate, the shoot taking another three to six years to mature. It begins with two leaves, each with five lobes. The flowering stem terminates in a greenish-white umbel of bisexual flowers. During its development, the plant's root expands very slowly indeed, each year adding a growth ring. The larger the root, of course, the more valuable it is.

Although it is not a plant that can be grown readily in this country, ginseng has become increasingly popular, and a selection of ginseng products can be purchased in health food shops in various forms. Ginseng tea, for example, snaps you to attention in a subtle way, clearing the sinuses with a faint liquorice-like aroma, and leaving you with the relaxed feeling of satisfaction that only a truly great hot beverage can produce. As you sip your ginseng tea, you can ponder the mystery surrounding the curious root, its history, and its aura.

Goldenrod

Goldruthe, Woundwort, Aaron's Rod, Solidago
Solidago virgaurea
Compositae

There are many varieties of Goldenrod but *Solidago virgaurea* is the only one native to Great Britain. It grows from 18 to 36 inches (46 to 91 cm) high with alternate leaves and terminal panicles of golden flowers.

This herb was known as a vulnerary and its generic name *Solidago* is derived from the word *solidare* meaning 'to make whole'.

The leaves are the part used medicinally. Infused, one teaspoonful to a cup of boiling water, they are reported to have aromatic, stimulant, diuretic and carminative properties. They have been used as an astringent and in bladder disorders. A warm infusion was used to relieve dysmenorrhoea and amenorrhoea, and was also found helpful to allay sickness and nausea arising from a weak digestion. It used to be used in the treatment of diptheria.

Goldenrod is a traditional cottage garden plant and makes a lovely showy display in the flower border. When bruised it emits a smell like wild carrot. The leaves and flowers yield a yellow dye.

Goldenrod
(Solidago virgaurea)
(a) flower

Goosefoot, White

Lamb's Quarters, Wild Spinach,
Fat Hen, Frost Blite
Chenopodium album
Chenopodiaceae

This herb, also well known as lamb's quarters, is one of the gardener's most persistent adversaries. But the gardener would do well to let the weed grow and harvest it along with other foodstuffs, for it is a palatable and nutritious plant. Moreover, the weed—so long as it doesn't get out of hand—is a companionable plant for the garden, thanks to its long tap-root.

Chenopodium album is a relative of garden spinach and a blood brother of Good King Henry (*C. Bonus-Henricus*), a more domesticated pot-herb. The plant is erect, growing up to three feet (90 cm) high, with wedge-shaped leaves and densely flowered spikes. The colour is slightly silvery, hence the specific name *album* and the common name "white goosefoot".

The plant grows wherever there is rich soil, and it particularly likes

edible. The greens, which may be eaten raw in salads or cooked as a vegetable, are rich in vitamins C and A (richer, in fact, than spinach) and in calcium. The seeds are collected and ground into a meal after drying, the meal being used to make bread. They can also be eaten raw.

White Goosefoot
(Chenopodium album)

Guelder Rose

**Water Elder, Snowball Tree,
Rose Elder, May Rose**
Viburnum Opulus
Caprifoliaceae

This deciduous shrub which can grow up to 15 feet (4.5 m) high usually has several stems from the same root. The leaves have three lobes and are broadly wedge-shaped. Showy clusters of snow-white flowers, up to five inches (13 cm) across, bloom in June, with the outer blossoms larger and sterile. These large blossoms contain inner complete blossoms, and it is these that provide the nectar for fertilizing insects. The large, heavy clusters of juicy scarlet berries remain after the leaves have fallen, until spring. The fruit is very acid; it is edible and can be substituted for cranberries.

The bark can be used medicinally as a nervine and antispasmodic. It is also reported to be very effective for cramps, spasms, and convulsions.

manure piles and compost heaps. Since most regard it as a nuisance, it is easily gathered where it grows. One presumably would neither want nor need to cultivate it.

Both the foliage and the seeds are

411

Guelder roses are hardy and not very particular as to soil, but prefer a situation that is not too dry. They may be grown from seed that has been stratified, green-wood cuttings under glass, hardwood cuttings, and layering.

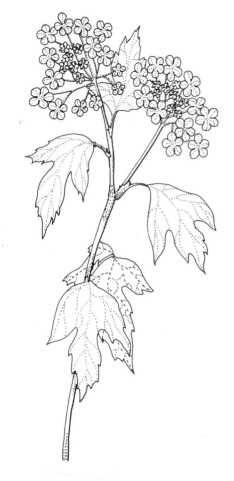

Guelder Rose
(Viburnum Opulus)

Hawthorn

Haw, May, May Blossom, Quick, Whitethorn
Crataegus oxyacantha
Rosaceae

A very showy, deciduous bush or small tree, growing to 15 feet (4.6 m), hawthorn has white flowers in May followed by bright red berries in September. Branches are spiky, and even when leafless, picturesque in effect. They are excellent in a shrubbery border, their lines carrying the vision from lower shrubs upwards to trees in the background. They are frequently grown as hedges.

Hawthorns grow readily in almost any soil. They are propagated by division of young roots or by cuttings made in September and set in a cold frame. They can be started from seed, but germination may not take place until the second or third year.

Hawthorn is widely used as a hedge. It has escaped cultivation and is seen in waste places and around untilled fields. It is also found in many other countries.

Apart from its ornamental uses, hawthorn has been valued as a heart tonic, and this value has been increasingly studied in recent years. Promising results have been reported in connection with a variety of heart ailments, including angina pectoris and abnormal heart action. It is also said to be effective in stemming

Hawthorn
(Crataegus oxyacantha)
(a) flower (b) berry

a pint (568 ml) of ethyl alcohol and an ounce (28 g) of the hawthorn berry powder. The tincture is given in doses ranging from one to 15 drops. Although non-toxic, hawthorn can produce dizziness if taken in large doses.

Hawthorn has also been used in treating arthritis and rheumatism, and for emotional stress and nervous conditions.

Hellebore, False

Adonis, Red Camomile,
Pheasant's Eye, Sweet Vernal, Ox-eye
Adonis autumnalis
Adonis vernalis
Ranunculaceae

Growing six to 12 inches (15 to 30 cm) high with delicate, finely cut leaves, false hellebore, *(Adonis vernalis)* has large yellow flowers of about ten to 20 petals in early Spring. It may be grown from seed sown in spring or early autumn, or by root divisions in spring. It prefers light, sandy soil.

False hellebore's primary medicinal use is for heart troubles. It has an action similar to digitalis, although it is said to be far more powerful, and has been used in cases where digitalis has failed. The plant is listed in some herbals as a poison. Consequently,

arteriosclerosis, commonly known as hardening of the arteries. The berries are the part used and are dried and reduced to a powder. Doses range from three to 15 grains three to four times daily. But the powder may also be made into a tincture by combining

413

herbalists recommend that it be used only under medical supervision.

An insecticide is made from the roots and sold in the form of a dry powder. It is potent only when fresh, and although rather expensive, is used on ripening fruit and vegetables. It is a slow stomach poison for insects and especially useful against crop-eating insects such as beetles, caterpillars, grubs, and grasshoppers. Usually mixed with flower or hydrated lime and used as a dust, it can also be mixed with water for a spray, about one ounce (28 g) to two gallons (9 l) of water.

A near relative of false hellebore, *Adonis autumnalis*, is also sometimes called false hellebore, as well as pheasant's eye and red camomile. It is a native of Europe, growing about a foot (30 cm) high and having finely cut leaves and small scarlet flowers.

Hepatica

Liverleaf, Noble Liverwort, Trefoil
Hepatica acutiloba
Ranunculaceae

Hepatica is a small herb of the buttercup family whose three-lobed, leathery, evergreen leaves are shed for new ones after flowering. Blossoms, often fragrant, appear very early in spring. They may be white, pinkish-lavender, or purple. These natives of open, rich woodlands can be easily transferred to the wild garden. They require neutral soil, rich in humus, and can be propagated by division of roots, or seeds. *Hepatica acutiloba* has three pointed lobes, and *H. triloba* has rounded leaves which are maroon in winter.

Hepatica is a mild mucilaginous astringent, made into an infusion or tea for coughs and colds.

Holly

Holm, Holy Tree, Christ's Thorn
Ilex Aquifolium
Aquifoliaceae

Hollies are well-known for their glossy, evergreen leaves and red berries, used extensively for Christmas decoration. There are several varieties, but the English holly, although not so hardy as some, will survive some pretty severe winters. However, it is more beautiful than some of the others since it bears larger, more dense clusters of berries. Holly is used in border shrubberies, as hedging, or as a small decorative tree in the garden.

Hollies are slow-growing and do best in rich, rather moist soil. Plants can be readily purchased from nurseries. They should be moved in spring before new growth starts, or in late summer. When transplanted, a daily

Holly (Ilex Aquifolium)

spraying with the garden hose for several weeks will prove beneficial.

Propagation is by cuttings of ripened wood, placed in a cold frame and kept well moistened. They may also be started from seed, which requires stratification and will germinate the second year.

The leaves and berries are used for medicinal purposes. The leaves are astringent and are utilized for fevers and rheumatism. The berries help to alleviate dropsy.

Holly, Sea

Sea Hulver, Eryngo
Eryngium maritimum
Umbelliferae

Sea holly is plentiful on sandy seashores in Britain, especially on the East Coast and in some parts of Cornwall. It does not seem to grow much at all in Scotland.

A beautiful, very hardy perennial,

415

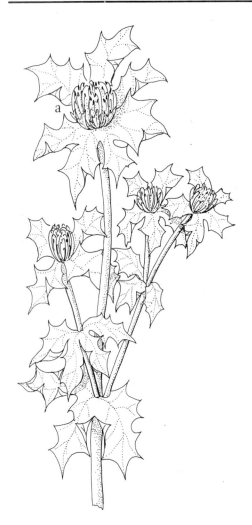

Sea Holly
(Eryngium maritimum)
(a) flower

sea holly grows one foot (38 cm) tall, and has broad, prickly, greyish-blue leaves and pale blue flowers surrounded by spiny bracts. The flowers are frequently dried for winter bouquets.

It should be planted in light, rich soil, in an open sunny location. It is an excellent plant for the rock garden. It can be propagated by seed sown as soon as ripe or by root division.

The root and leaves are used for uterine irritation and bladder diseases, glandular deficiencies, as a nervine, and tonic. The roots are nutritious and can be candied. They are rich in minerals, especially iron, magnesium, silica, and iodine.

Hops

Humulus Lupulus
Cannabinaceae

Hops are natives of Europe and western Asia, and are best known as the principal ingredient in beer. They were not always used in beer, but have long been used medicinally as a tonic, diuretic, and sedative.

Hopped ale was first brewed in Europe late in the Middle Ages, and was introduced into England in the Fifteenth Century. Hops have been cultivated as a commercial crop ever since, their culture being spread wherever conditions are suitable. The female flower, which resembles a globe artichoke, is the part used by brewers. It yields essential oils and resins which give the hop its aroma and beer its taste. The male flowers are borne on separate plants and have a different appearance to the female flowers.

In cultivation, hops are usually trained up a framework of poles and wires, making a good summer screen.

The vines are usually propagated by cuttings of young shoots from the crown, but they can also be started from seed.

Hops
(Humulus Lupulus)

A perennial vine, the hop produces new shoots each spring which grow rapidly, extending as much as 30 feet (9 m) before drying down to near-ground level at the end of the season.

Horehound, White

Hoarhound
Marrubium vulgare
Labiatae

The perennial horehound, native to England but adaptable to almost any climate, has been respected since ancient times for its wide variety of uses, from flavouring to curing colds to counteracting poisons.

Although it is found in the greatest quantities in England, particularly the southern counties, it grows throughout Europe. The herb thrives in poor, dry ground where other plants can't survive, although it is only half-hardy in severely cold climates. It flourishes in the wild.

The plant is bushy and produces annual branching stems up to two feet (60 cm) in height. Whitish flowers are borne on the wrinkled leaves, which are covered with white, felted hairs, giving the plant a woolly appearance.

417

The plants have a musky smell which is diminished by drying and eventually disappears. It flowers from June to September.

Called a herb of Mercury by Culpeper, the horehound was used widely as a medicine by the Egyptians, Greeks, and Romans. The Greeks often used it as an anti-spasmodic drug and as an antidote for the bite of a mad dog, hence its common name, "horehound".

There are various theories for the origin of the Latin name. Some scholars believe it was named after Maria Urbs, an ancient town in Italy, but most attribute its name to the Hebrew, *Marrob*, a bitter juice. The herb is one of the five plants which the Jews took for the feast of the passover.

Used by the ancients as an antidote for many poisons as well as a cure for respiratory diseases, the herb gained fame for a long list of uses through the centuries, including a cure for snakebites, an ointment for wounds and itches, an insect repellent and a worm killer. With honey, the leaves were said to cleanse ulcers, and the juice was considered excellent for clearing the eyesight, either by dropping it directly into the eyes or sniffing it up through the nostrils.

The most popular use was for clearing the lungs. According to Gerard, "Syrup made of the greene fresh leaves and sugar is a most singular remedie against the coughing and wheezing of the lungs . . ."

Culpeper claimed horehound:

Helpeth to expectorate tough phlegm from the chest, being taken with the roots of the Irris or Orris . . . and purges away yellow jaundice; and with the oil of roses, dropped into the ears, eases the pain of them.

It opens obstructions of both the liver and spleen and used outwardly cleanses, abates the swollen part and pains that come by pricking thornes; with vinegar, it cleanses and heals tetters.

Culpeper and other authorities also recommend the herb for women to increase the menstrual flow, and in childbirth, to help expel the afterbirth. It acts as a laxative when taken in large doses.

To make a good syrup for coughs and colds, mix half an ounce (14 g) each of horehound, rue, hyssop, liquorice root, and marshmallow root with a quart (1.1 l) of water; boil it down to a pint and a half (752 ml) of liquid, strain, and give in half-cup doses. A horehound tea for colds can be made by pouring boiling water on the fresh or dried leaves, one ounce (28 g) of the herb to three-quarters of a pint (426 ml) of water. For a more pleasant-tasting syrup, boil one part dried horehound with eight parts of water for ten minutes. Strain the mixture after five minutes. Combine one part of the horehound mixture with two parts of honey and stir until smooth.

Horehound drops can be made by combining the above mixture (without honey) with 16 ounces (454 g) of raw sugar. Place the sugar in a small, deep saucepan and stir in one-eighth of a teaspoon of cream of tartar, then add the horehound mixture. Stir until the

418

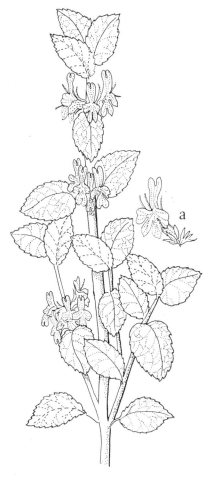

White Horehound
(Marrubium vulgare)
(a) flower

propagation is by seed grown indoors. Old plants should be divided and planted 20 inches (51 cm) apart.

Horehound needs a warm, sunny location to grow properly, but the soil can be dry and of low fertility. Weeding in the early stages of growth is, of course, of major importance, but mulching will have little effect on the plant. If mulch is used, it should consist of materials which are able to hold or raise the soil temperature.

Horehound is harvested by cutting all growth three inches (7.5 cm) above the ground. To preserve the herb, it should be chopped and dried within a short time and sealed tightly in a jar.

Horseradish

Mountain Radish, Red Cole
Cochlearia Armoracia,
Armoracia lapathifolia
(syn. *Amoracia rusticana*)
Cruciferae

sugar has dissolved, then cook over a low heat until a drop of the mixture in cold water becomes a hard ball. Pour on a buttered dish and cut into cough-drop sizes when it is half-hardened. Keep in a cool place until used.

The herb gardener generally doesn't need much horehound because of its great potency. The best method of

Horseradish has been famed for its medicinal qualities from ancient times. The Greeks knew it as *Raphanos agrios*, wild radish, and used it as a stimulant, laxative, plaster, diuretic, and antiseptic. It was also used as a cure for scurvy. Modern science has again proved the wisdom of the ancients by discovering that horseradish is a source of vitamin C.

419

Horseradish, however, is much more familiar as a condiment; the chief ingredient of a tangy sauce for beef and other meats or fish. This use of the root is a comparatively recent one. In 1597, Gerard spoke with wonder of the German practice of eating horseradish sauce with fish and meat. In 1657, Coles wrote that the root, "sliced thin and mixed with vinegar is eaten as a sauce with meat, as among the Germans". However, he made it clear that the practice was not one a gourmet would adopt. Horseradish root was also eaten by the French. The old French name for it was *Moutarde des Allemands*, indicating that they had learned of its use from their German neighbours.

Horseradish is a perennial. The plant develops large, green to yellow-green, elongated leaves that attain a length of up to two feet (60 cm). It has been cultivated since the earliest times and may have originated in Hungary.

The plant does not develop any seed, and propagation is by root cuttings only. Cuttings should be made from straight roots and should be six to seven inches (15 to 18 cm) long and should include a bud, although any piece of root will develop buds and shoots. For this reason, horseradish should be planted in a corner of the garden that will be kept strictly for it. If you decide to eradicate your horseradish bed, make sure that every piece of root is removed from the ground. Any left in the soil will develop into a new plant.

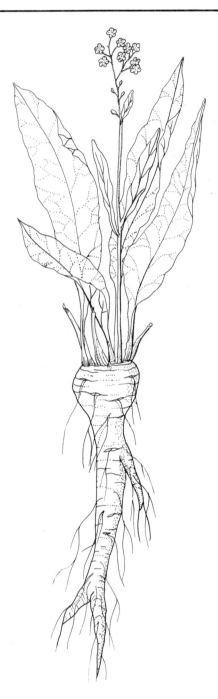

Horseradish
(Cochlearia Armoracia)

Horseradish prefers wet, clay soil and must be planted early for a good autumn crop. The ground should be deeply tilled in January and well fertilized with rotted manure or compost. Planting is done in February. Plant your root cuttings 12 to 15 inches (30 to 38 cm) deep or more, and 12 to 18 inches (30 to 46 cm) apart each way. The horseradish bed should be weeded regularly. Early mulching will help.

Expect to harvest your crop in the autumn. Wash the roots and store them in damp sand in a root cellar. They should last through the winter and can be grated fresh as needed. The roots can also be left in the ground and dug when needed. In this case, mulch as you would for beets or turnips.

In the spring, you will find that you can also harvest and eat the first leaves that appear from the crown. Use them in salads, chopped fine and mixed with other salad greens. They can also be boiled and mixed with other greens; their taste is too strong to serve alone.

When you harvest your first horseradish root, you will find that it has no odour. Horseradish root contains two chemical components responsible for the characteristic smell and taste; sinigrin, a crystalline glucoside, and myrosin, an enzyme. Sinigrin is decomposed in the presence of water by myrosin, and a volatile oil, allyl isothiocyanate, is formed. This oil is chiefly responsible for the taste and smell. Since myrosin and sinigrin exist in separate cells of the roots, they do not normally come into contact with each other until the root is bruised or cut.

On exposure to the air, the root loses its colour and volatile strength. It should never be boiled, but always used raw and freshly grated.

Horseradish was a great value to the ancient herbalists as a plaster. Culpeper said, "If bruised and laid to a part grieved with the sciatica, gout, joint-ache, or hard swellings of the spleen and liver, it doth wonderfully help them all." Grated horseradish applied to chilblains and secured with a light bandage is said to help cure them.

Horseradish when infused in wine will stimulate the nervous system and promote perspiration. It serves much the same purpose when used as a condiment with meat or eaten as a relish with vegetables. For a condiment, use four parts grated horseradish root to one part vinegar. Other herbs can be mixed with the horseradish; dill or mustard, for example, will go well with meats.

An infusion of horseradish in milk makes an excellent cosmetic for the skin and helps restore freshness and colour to the cheeks. The juice, mixed with white vinegar and applied externally, is supposed to remove freckles.

Horseradish juice and vinegar, well diluted with water and sweetened with glycerine, was used to relieve whooping cough in children. A syrup for hoarseness was made by infusing one dram (3.5 g) of freshly grated horseradish root with four fluid ounces (114 ml) of water in a closed vessel for two hours, then adding double its weight in sugar. The dose was a teaspoonful or two repeated occasionally.

Horseradish was also employed as a remedy for worms in children. Coles said: "Of all things given to children for worms, horseradish is not the least, for it soon killeth and expelleth them."

Hydrangea

Common Hydrangea, Seven Barks, Wild Hydrangea
Hydrangea arborescens
Saxifragaceae

A deciduous shrub of the saxifrage family, hydrangea grows in sheltered places in the south of England as it can stand only a few degrees of frost. It grows from four to ten feet (1.25 to 3 m) high and has almost heart-shaped leaves three to six inches (7.5 to 15 cm) long. Rounded clusters of long-lasting white flowers appear in June and July (there are accepted ways of colouring these blooms usually blue or pink). The common name "seven barks" refers to the peculiar characteristic of its stem bark, which peels off in seven thin layers of different colours.

Hydrangeas thrive best in rich, moist soil, but will grow under varying conditions. Shoots should be cut back severely and weak growth thinned for good flower-heads. They are propagated by cuttings of half-mature shoots, rooted under glass and also by hardwood cuttings. Good plants can be grown from cuttings in one year. They can also be layered and divided.

Hydrangeas are mildly diuretic and cathartic and were once considered a valuable remedy for removal of stone and gravel in the bladder.

Hyssop

Hyssopus officinalis
Labiatae

Hyssop is historically known as a holy herb, used for cleaning sacred places. The herb also has many medicinal uses and makes an excellent tea. It is a perennial shrub native to Europe and temperate Asia. But it also grows in other countries where it has been introduced.

It was used by the Egyptians to cleanse lepers, and the herb is often mentioned in the Bible as a purifier. Hyssop is a name adopted from the Greek *azob*, a holy herb.

In Psalm 51:7, David says in a prayer, "purge me with hyssop and I shall be clean", and in John 19:29, hyssop is mentioned at the crucifixion: "There was a vessel full of vinegar: and they filled a sponge with vinegar and put it upon hyssop and put it in

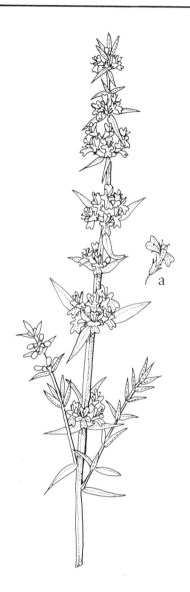

Hyssop
(Hyssopus officinalis)
(a) flower

been resolved. Throughout the history of the church, hyssop has been revered for its cleansing powers. When Westminster Abbey was consecrated, hyssop was sprinkled on the altar.

Culpeper reported, "The herb is Jupiter's, and the sign Cancer. It strengthens all parts of the body under Cancer and Jupiter." His listing of the medicinal virtues of hyssop covered all of those typically attributed to the herb.

Hyssop boiled with honey and rue, and drank, helps those that are troubled with coughs, shortness of breath, wheezing, and rheumatic distillations upon the lungs; taken with oxymel, it purges gross humours by stool; with honey kills worms in the belly; and with fresh new figs bruised, helps to loosen the belly, and more forcibly if fleur-de-lys and cresses be added thereto. It amends and cherishes the native colour of the body spoiled by the yellow jaundice, and taken with figs and nitre, helps the dropsy and spleen; being boiled with wine, it is good to wash inflammations, and takes away the black and blue marks that come by strokes, bruises, or falls, if applied with warm water. It is an excellent medicine for the quinsy, or swelling in the throat, to wash and gargle it, when boiled with figs; it helps to cure toothache, if boiled in vinegar, and the mouth rinsed with it. The hot vapours of the decoction taken by a funnel in at the ears, eases the inflammations and singing noise of them. Being bruised with salt, honey, and cumin seed put to it, helps those stung by serpents. The head anointed with the oil kills lice and takes away the itching of the head. It is good for falling sickness, expectorates tough phlegm, and is effectual in all cold griefs, or diseases of the chest and lungs, when taken as a syrup. The green herb bruised with sugar, quickly heals any cut or green wounds, if properly applied. The pains

His mouth . . ." Some scholars, however, believed the hyssop mentioned in the Bible is not the herb known today, and the controversy has never

and discolourings of bruises, blows, and falls may be quickly removed by a cataplasm of the green leaves sewed in a linen cloth, and put on the place.

An essential oil derived from the green portions of the plant is used in making perfumes, especially Eau de Cologne.

Hyssop was used by monks in the preparation of some liqueurs. The recipe book of John Nott, a cook to the Duke of Bolton, written in 1723, recommends hyssop water for a good complexion. He calls for six spoonfuls of hyssop juice in ale every morning.

Externally, the herb is recommended for curing rheumatism and for bruises and contusions. It is also supposed to heal cuts promptly.

Hyssop tea is made by pouring a pint (568 ml) of boiling water over an ounce (28 g) of the green tops and is considered to taste excellent. It is considered useful in chest diseases and coughs, colds, hoarseness, fevers, and sore throats. It is thought to be especially good for loosening phlegm.

Hyssop adds a bitter minty taste to salads and is also used in soups, stews, fruit cocktails, and pies.

The companion planter will find some value in hyssop. Planted near grapevines, it increases their yield. It should not be grown too close to radishes, but planted near cabbage, it lures away the cabbage butterfly. Hyssop tea is said to be useful against bacterial diseases of plants.

If nothing else, the herb adds beauty to any garden. This fragrant attractive plant is extremely hardy and can grow up to three feet (91 cm) high. The leaves are thin and long, and have a shiny green colour and strong scent when brushed. The flowers form in the leaf axles and, according to variety, are blue, pink, or white. The blue variety is most commonly used as a medicinal herb. The seeds, having a long, oval shape, are dark brown to black and germinate in darkness within ten days at a temperature of 70° F (21°C).

Hyssop is best started indoors from seed because it is a slow grower. If direct seeding outdoors is desired, it should be done as soon as weather permits. Older plants can be divided early in the spring and reset at a minimum distance of 12 inches (30 cm).

The main requirements for growing are a dry and sunny location and a soil with good calcium reserves. Many gardeners choose the herb as a herbaceous border because it responds well to pruning and makes a beautiful showing when in flower. The blue variety, which is more vigorous and hardy than the other two, is considered by most gardeners to be the most beautiful.

For a hedge, the distance between plants should be kept at 12 inches (30 cm), while a space of two feet (60 cm) is best for general planting. If the seeds are sown outside, hoeing, weeding, and thinning will be necessary during the first three weeks, followed by mulching once the plants have reached a height of six inches (15 cm).

In most cases, it will be more convenient for the beginner to buy a few plants of hyssop, unless he intends growing a long hedge. These will produce enough material for tea to last the whole year.

Hyssop can be used fresh and green from the garden. Otherwise, the harvesting takes place when the first flowers are about to open. This step should not be delayed since hyssop tends to become woody within a short time. The oils and flavours of all herbs, of course, are in the leaves and green stems and not in the woody parts.

In order to encourage fresh growth, cutting should be done close to the ground. If the harvest is too woody, the leaves should be stripped off the branches. The use of a liquid fish emulsion fertilizer is advisable after each harvest.

The stripped leaves are dried whole, while the soft growth can be chopped with the stem and dried in warm shade or low oven heat. Drying is generally completed within two days.

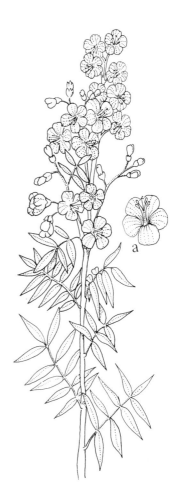

Jacob's Ladder
(Polemonium caeruleum)
(a) flower

Jacob's Ladder

Greek Valerian, Charity
Polemonium caeruleum
Polemoniaceae

A perennial growing two to three feet (60 to 90 cm) high with feather-shaped leaves, Jacob's ladder has bright blue flowers with yellow stamens. It grows easily from seed or root division, in rich, loamy soil with good drainage.

Culpeper says: "It is useful in malignant fevers, and pestilential distempers; it helps in nervous complaints, headaches, trembling, palpitations of the heart, vapours etc. It is

425

good in hysteric cases, and epilepsies have been cured by the use of this herb."

It is perhaps interesting to note that its common name "Greek valerian", is a misnomer since the plant is not a valerian at all, but belongs to the natural order Polemoniaceae—the family of phlox. But cats are not so erudite, since they are almost as fond of Jacob's ladder as valerian proper.

False Jacob's Ladder *(Polemonium reptans)*, or abscess root as it is sometimes called, has creeping roots, grows six to 12 inches (15 to 30 cm) high and has white or light blue flowers that droop in loose clusters. The root is used for fevers, inflammations, pleurisy, coughs, colds, and bronchial and lung complaints. The plant has diaphoretic and astringent properties as well as being a good expectorant.

Juniper

Genevrier, Ginepro, Enebro
Juniperus communis
Cupressaceae

Small or medium-size evergreen trees or shrubs, many types of junipers are used in landscaping. Junipers are hardy, attractive, and varied in form. The needle-like leaves are mostly grey-green or blue-green. The green berries which take two or three years to ripen to a blue-black colour are harvested in autumn. Leaves and shoots can be collected any time of the year.

A strong aromatic scent emanates from all parts of the shrub. The berries taste slightly bitter-sweet and are fragrant and spicy. Junipers are hardy even in the coldest areas. They prefer dry, sandy, or gravelly soil with full exposure to wind and sun. They will tolerate average garden conditions, but resent shade and wet ground.

Among the varied forms, there are dense, columnar trees; medium-size, rounded shrubs; irregular bush forms; and creeping prostrate types. Irish and Swedish junipers are tall, narrow, and quick-growing; the Greek and Chinese varieties are very compact and slow-growing; Pfitzers are irregular, massive types, while the California juniper may reach a height of 40 feet (12 m).

This is a most important group of ornamental shrubs used for landscaping. Propagation by seed is extremely slow; they will not germinate until the second or third year. Most varieties can be started from cuttings. Tips four to six inches (10 to 15 cm) long are cut in August; the needles are stripped an inch (2.5 cm) or so from the butt, which is then placed in a cold frame bed of sand four or five inches (10 to 13 cm) deep. Water thoroughly, cover with glass, and keep shaded. They will be rooted by the following summer. Most varieties can be found in nurseries.

In the past, juniper was regarded as

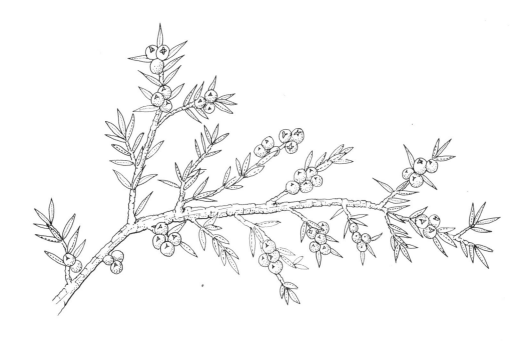

Juniper (Juniperus communis)

a magic shrub to use against devils, evil spirits, and wild animals. It is mentioned in the Bible as a symbol of protection. Its aromatic scent made it a popular strewing herb, and shoots were burned to disinfect the air in a room. Juniper berries are used for making gin. They are also an excellent seasoning for game, marinades, poultry, and sauerkraut, and will take away the strong taste of venison, wild duck, and other wild animals. Before roasting, parboil the meat in a beef stock to which lemon, bay leaves, and about four to six juniper berries have been added.

Juniper is considered one of the most useful medicinal plants. It stimulates appetite and digestion and helps to eliminate mucus in coughs. It has a diuretic effect on the functions of the kidney and bladder. A strong tea of the berries is considered an excellent wash for the bites of poisonous insects, snakes, dogs, and bees.

A useful infusion of the berries may be prepared by soaking several tablespoonfuls of berries in water, then adding them to a pint (568 ml) of boiling water, leaving them to infuse for half an hour or more. It is recommended that the infusion be taken in four doses during the course of the day.

Lavender

English Lavender
Lavandula vera syn. *L. officinalis*
Spike Lavender
Lavandula Spica syn. *L. latifolia*
French Lavender
Lavandula Stoechas
Labiatae

Lavender today, is so familiar that its name is instantly associated, not only with the delicate, sweet fragrance of its oil but with the specific mauve-like hue of its tiny petals. Known since ancient times, it was popular among the pre-Christian Greeks and Romans as a perfume for baths and soaps. The generic name *Lavandula*, probably came from the Latin *lavare*, to wash.

Lavender has not always been popular. In the Dark Ages it was obscured by other herbs which commanded more significance due to their religious and medicinal connotations. However, it came into its own in the late Renaissance period as a herb of celebrated fragrance.

Today, it supports one of the largest herbal industries in the world, the perfume industry, with centres of cultivation for commercial use being in England and France.

There are three basic species of lavender, and each has several varieties. English lavender *(Lavandula vera)* is also known as true lavender because its oil is of the highest, most fragrant quality. It is highly valued for commercial production, although Spike lavender *(L. Spica)* produces a greater volume of oil.

Maude Grieve wrote that the flowers of spike lavender yield three times as much oil as those of English lavender but it is of a second-rate quality, less fragrant than that of the true (English) lavender, its odour resembling a mixture of the oils of lavender and rosemary.

She added that oil of the third main species, French lavender *(L. Stoechas)*, has an odour that is more akin to rosemary than to ordinary lavender.

To decide which variety to grow in your garden, decide whether the main object will be the flowers or the leaves. If it's the flower you want most, the English lavender is your plant. For leaves, the spike lavender will produce a broader leaf and more oil.

All the lavenders are shrubby perennials. English and French lavenders prefer sandy, coarse, even rocky soils that are warm and moderately fertilized. Spike lavender tends to prefer alluvial soil. Originally natives of the warm Mediterranean areas they all like a sunny location. English lavender is the hardiest, but severe frosts will kill it.

Leaves of all the species are light green-grey, resembling those of rosemary. English lavender carries the narrowest leaves, and sometimes is referred to as the narrow-leafed plant. French and spike lavender have broader leaves.

Flowers form in June and July in

Lavender
(Lavandula spica)

spikes at the top of the plant. French lavender flowers tend to be a darker hue than those of the other species.

Seeds, which form later in the season, are a shiny, dark, greyish-brown and generally rather difficult to germinate. They take up to four weeks to sprout, and they have a very low percentage of survival. Lavender started from seed should be planted inside in February because of its long germination period.

Alternatively, lavender can be started by taking August cuttings, which will form productive young plants by the next spring.

The lavender spot in the garden should be neutral to alkaline in acidity. Add lime if the pH level is more than four. Mulching is not necessary, in fact not even desirable, since it lowers the soil temperature to the discomfort of the plant. Fertilizing is of minor importance, and if the soil has to be enriched, use only well-rotted compost or manure, never fresh.

The harvesting of the leaves is not critical, but the flowers must be taken just before they open. They lose their aromatic properties quickly after opening. Both flowers and leaves are dried in shade at 90° to 100°F (32° to 38°C). They dry well and pose no storage problem.

Lavender's medicinal properties in the old days were said to be aromatic and carminative, with especial emphasis on the plant's soothing effect on nerve disorders. "It profiteth them much that have the palsy if they be washed with the distilled water from lavender's flowers," advised Gerard in 1597. A hundred years after that, a popular herbalist said a lavender tincture, "if prudently given, cures hysterick fits though vehement and of long standing".

Lavender water has been used for centuries as a home remedy for hoarseness and sore throats, and oil of lavender is a traditional balm for sore joints and toothaches. Up until the First World War, oil of lavender was used as an antiseptic for wounds as well as a vermifuge.

Lavender has only minimal uses in the kitchen, although Queen Elizabeth I was known to have been fond of lavender conserve.

One of lavender's finest uses is in sachets and pillows to perfume linen. Said to repel moths, flies, and mosquitoes, a folk formula for making an insect repellent for the living room is to absorb a few drops of lavender oil in a cottonwool ball, then suspend it from the ceiling.

The dried flowers, sewn into a linen pillow, can be tucked among dainty linens to impart to them a lovely scent. For lavender water, add a drop of musk and a fluid ounce (28 ml) of lavender oil to 12 fluid ounces (336 ml) of light white wine. Shake well, leave to settle for a few days, then shake again and pour into airtight bottles. Or add two ounces (56 ml) of refined essence of lavender to 12 fluid ounces (336 ml) of good brandy for a powerful concentrate of lavender water.

A refreshing toilet preparation is made by mixing six parts of rosewater, one part spirits of lavender, and two parts of vinegar. Or, steep fresh lavender tops in vinegar for a week, shaking the mixture each day. At the end of the week, filter the vinegar and store it in airtight bottles.

Lavender Cotton

Santolina
Santolina Chameacyparissus
Compositae

Lavender cotton, not really a true lavender, has the density, texture, and colour necessary for successful use in knot gardens and other formally laid-out herb gardens. Its spreading branches, which range as tall as two feet (60 cm), have very fine blue-grey leaves, said by some to resemble coral. It has small, yellow flowers, but these are usually trimmed off. *Santolina virens*, or green santolina, is a similar plant in a contrasting colour.

Plants can be grown from seed, although perhaps a better method is to take root cuttings. Santolinas like the sun and a light, dry soil. They are not terribly hardy, and protection from snow is necessary for survival.

Although santolinas are primarily used in the garden, the leaves are reputed to have value as a moth repellent, and a perfume oil has been extracted from them, although their natural fragrance isn't particularly pleasant.

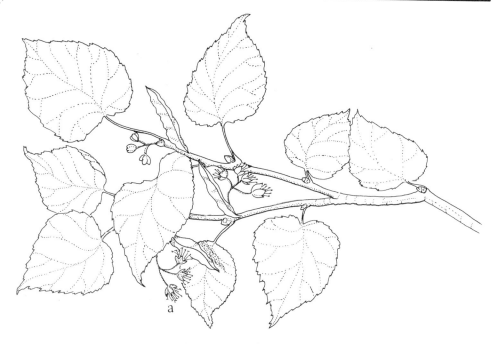

Lime (Tilia Europoea)
(a) flower

Lime Tree

Limeflowers, Basswood,
Linden Flowers, Common Lime
Tilia sp.
Tiliaceae

Lime, or linden is a popular tree, commonly used along avenues and entrance driveways for the uniformity it produces. The lime tree can attain a height of 130 feet (40 m) or more, with dense, attractive foliage. The leaves are perfectly heart-shaped, two and a half to four inches (6 to 10 cm) long, and coarsely double-toothed Produced with them is an abundance of fragrant white to yellowish flowers, attractive to bees. The fruits or seeds are about the size and shape of a pea. The trees are generally pyramidal in form, the dark brownish-grey bark is scored with elongated perpendicular fissures.

Limes are all hardy and thrive in rich soil. They require moisture, but not too much. The leaves will drop in warm weather if they are too dry. Seeds require two years to germinate. Lindens can be propagated by layers or cuttings.

The fibre of the wood was once used for making strong ropes. Lime flowers and leaves are an old household remedy for nervousness, colds,

431

headaches, and indigestion. A hot infusion was used to check diarrhoea, and to promote sleep. Linden flower wine acts as a tonic to stimulate appetite and aid digestion. The foliage can be dried like hay for winter feed for animals.

Lobelia

Indian Tobacco, Pukeweed, Eyebright
Lobelia inflata
Campanulaceae/Lobeliaceae

Lobelia is said to be the discovery of Samuel Thomson, who tried it first on a friend while mowing a field. "He first fully satisfied himself that it had emetic properties," one record of the event says, "by coaxing his partner, who was mowing with him in the field, to chew the green plant, which he did, and became deadly sick and relaxed, and upon drinking some water he vomited and rapidly recovered from its effects, and felt better afterwards than he did before."

The record tells two tales, one of Indian tobacco's first use by a white man in America, and the other of the hazards of blind herbal experimentation. There is no clear-cut agreement among herbalists and doctors as to the propriety of using Indian tobacco; some contend the herb is potentially poisonous, others dispute that claim. But it is a fact that Thomson himself was sued over the death of a patient for whom he had prescribed Indian tobacco. He was found not guilty, incidentally.

The herb was named after the French botanist Matthias de Lobel of Lille. It is an erect annual or biennial herb growing to between one and two feet (30 and 60 cm) high, with numerous oval-shaped leaves. Several species are grown in this country, such as *Lobelia Dortmanna* and *L. Urens.* Their flowers come in a variety of scarlets, purples, and blues. These bloom between July and October, giving way to seed-bearing fruits.

L. inflata was used medicinally by American Indians, and is the only variety to be recognized as an official drug plant. Blue lobelia *(L. syphilitica)* was once regarded as an emetic, purgative, and anti-syphilitic, hence the specific name. *L. Cardinalis,* commonly known as the "cardinal flower", or "Red lobelia" was believed to have the same properties as *L. inflata,* though to a lesser degree.

The plant is currently the subject of intensive research in America. Scientists there are experimenting with large-scale cultivation of the plant. They are conducting research into the source of the alkaloid lobeline, and a number of other derived drug substances. Lobeline, like nicotine, acts as a stimulant in small dosages, but as a nerve depressant and poison in large doses.

Lovage

Old English Lovage, Cornish Lovage
Levisticum officinale
Umbelliferae

An ancient cure for a variety of diseases, lovage is enjoying a surge of popularity for use in salads, soups, pies, confectioncries, and just for itself.

Native to the Balkans and the Mediterranean area, lovage was introduced to much of Europe and to Great Britain by the Romans. Both the Greeks and the Romans used the herb as a medicine, and in the Middle Ages it was used as a panacea for most illnesses. In Central Europe, women wore lovage around their necks when meeting lovers, and the herb was often put in love potions as an assurance of everlasting devotion.

Lovage has been used for disorders of the stomach and feverish attacks in case of colic and for flatulence in children. It was also used for gravel, jaundice, and urinary problems.

Culpeper recommended the herb, saying:

. . . a liquid, extracted by boiling the herb in water . . . being dropped into the eyes taketh away their redness and dimness . . . It is highly recommended to drink the decoction of the herb for agues . . . The distilled water is good for quinsy if the mouth and throat be gargled and washed therewith . . . The decoction drunk three or four times a day is effectual in pleurisy

. . . The leaves bruised and fried with a little hog's lard and laid hot to any blotch or boil will quickly break it.

The herb was also added to baths, probably as a deodorant.

Today, the herb is used primarily for salads and other dishes. In some countries lovage leaves are used to make sweets, while oil from the plant is occasionally mixed with tobacco to add flavour.

This tall, hardy perennial reaches six feet (1.8 m) high in ideal conditions, with roots that average one inch (2.5 cm) thick and grow irregularly in different directions. Its diameter can measure as wide as four to five feet (1.2 to 1.5 m). The dark green leaves resemble those of celery, but, of course, have an entirely different aroma.

The stalks and leaf stems are hollow tubes with the flower stalks growing above the leaf mass, developing true umbels at the tips with light yellow flowers. When ripe, the seeds are dark brown and grow in pairs like those of dill. The best germination begins in darkness, within two weeks.

Lovage is extremely easy to grow. The seeds can be sown in the spring, or preferably in late summer. Transplant the seedlings to their permanent location later in the autumn or very early in the spring.

Only a few plants are needed because growth is more abundant than most other plants. As the plants get older, they should be divided every fourth year to keep them vigorous,

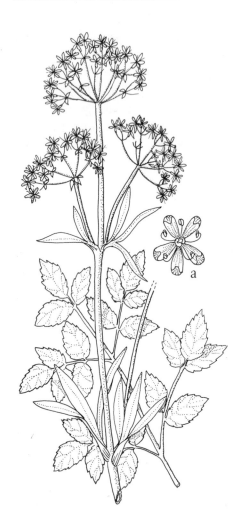

Lovage
(Levisticum officinale)
(a) flower

one. The only areas to avoid are spots which are too sunny or too dry. The fertility of the soil needs to be high, and heavy fertilization with manure compost and lime is advisable in order to achieve optimum results.

Even high soil moisture is beneficial, but not to the extent of standing water or poor drainage. Heavy mulching with hay or straw is well received by the plant, partly because of the increase of soil life and earthworms in particular, which digest the mulch and keep the soil supplied with calcium. Top-dressing with compost during the season, or drenching the soil around the lovage with a fish emulsion solution aids vigorous growth. If the leaves should ever turn prematurely yellow, it is a sign of a lack of nutrients or water, or both.

Fresh leaves should be picked all year round in small amounts for soups, gravies, or salads. Obviously the older leaves should be used first to avoid yellowing, cutting each one off close to the ground. A family will rarely be able to consume the leaves as fast as they grow, leaving the only alternative to cut the plant off about two inches (5 cm) above the ground before the leaves turn yellow and become useless.

Since one leaf with stem is often more than two feet (60 cm) long, it is advisable to cut small leaflets off the ribs before attempting to dry them. The stem parts hold so much water it would take days to dry the whole; but the leaf parts alone will dry within two days, in warm shade. Lovage

preferably very early in the spring when the first shoots push through the soil. The plant can live 20 years or more when cared for in this fashion.

Almost every location in the garden is suitable for lovage. One plant could be placed in a corner, even a shaded

should be dried until it is crisp enough to crush in your hand. It should be stored in a closed container away from light. It tends to yellow with age, even when dried, and becomes useless after one year.

Madder

Dyer's Madder, Krapp, Robbia
Rubia tinctorum
Rubiaceae

Madder is known almost exclusively as a plant used for dyeing. The long fleshy roots, when dried and milled, yield a variety of colours—red, pink, brown, orange, black, lilac, and purple—depending upon the mordant used. Madder has been grown commercially for its value as a dye.

Medicinally, madder has been used in experiments to determine the characteristics of bone growth. When eaten by cows, for example, it dyes their bones. In addition to this, it also dyes urine and milk. Madder is also used as a textile dye. Medicinally, it has been reputed to be effective in dropsy and jaundice.

The plant develops a long, spindly stalk, up to eight feet (2.5 m), with whorls of narrow, lance-like leaves. But, because of the weakness of the stalks, the plants generally lie along the ground. In its second year, the

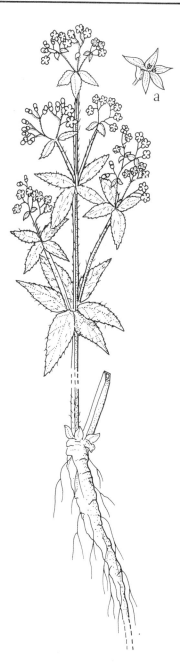

Madder
(Rubia tinctorum)
(a) flower

435

plant develops tiny, yellow, star-like clusters of flowers on spikes at the top of the stalks.

Madder is most easily propagated from root divisions, since it is a spreading plant, sending up new plants wherever its root surfaces. It can be started from seed and likes a light, sandy soil and lots of sun.

Marigold, Common

Pot Marigold, Mary Gowles,
Golds, Calendula
Calendula officinalis
Compositae

The common marigold is a familiar but welcome sight in gardens for many months of the year. Originally from southern Europe it is a hardy annual plant of the Compositae family with light greenish-yellow leaves and flowers in different shades of yellow and orange. The history of this herb is filled with poetry and symbolism, most of which has been in reaction to, and in appreciation of, an unusual behaviour characteristic which has fascinated poets and prose writers alike. At dawn, the moist blossoms open and rise with the sun, creating the poetic image of the awakening of a "weeping" flower. Its more familiar

golden-orange colour brightens the day until sunset when the "early-to-bed" marigold closes for the evening.

Of all the allusions made to the marigold in literature, the most beautiful may be John Keats's poem *"I stood tiptoe upon a little hill"* (London 1817):

> Open fresh your round of starry folds,
> Ye ardent marigolds!
> Dry up the moisture from your golden
>   lids,
> For great Apollo bids
> That in these days your praises should
>   be sung
> On many harps which he has lately
>   strung;
> And when again your dewiness he kisses
> Tell him I have you in my world of
>   blisses!
> So haply when I rove in some far vale
> His mighty voice may come upon gale.

It was the Romans who recorded that the marigold was usually in bloom on the first day, or *calends*, of every month. From this observation, the Latin generic name *Calendula* and the common Italian name *fiore d'ogni* were given to the herb. Because of the flower's sensitivity to the sun, it was also appropriate in some writings and reports to call the plant *solsequia* or *solis sponsa*. Nevertheless, the Anglo-Saxons perceived the lovely golden plant from another perspective and labelled it *mersomeargealla*, or marsh marigold, the obvious precursor of its familiar name today. In mediaeval England, a popular religious legend described the Virgin as being accustomed to wearing golden blossoms, which the monks of the period decided should be named in her honour; from that association of the golden herb with the Virgin Mary, old poets began calling the herb "Mary Gowles" and "Mary Golde".

The Latin specific name *officinalis* was the standard term applied to herbs with official medicinal qualities. According to Fuller, the medicinal powers of the marigold were familiar to all: "We all know the many and sovereign virtues in your leaves, the Herbe Generalle in all pottage." (Antheologie, 1655). In *Maison Rustique,* or the *Countrie Farme* (1699), Stevens listed some of the body pains and problems which marigold was considered effective in healing—headaches, jaundice, red eyes, toothache, and ague.

The Seventeenth Century herbalist, Culpeper, had some other suggested uses for the marigold:

They strengthen the heart exceedingly, and are very expulsive, and a little less effectual in the smallpox and measles than saffron. The juice of Marigold leaves mixed with vinegar and any hot swelling bathed with it, instantly gives ease, and assuages it. The flowers, either green or dried, are much used in possets, broths, and drink, as a comforter of the heart and spirits, and to expel any malignant or pestilential quality which might annoy them.

To provide aid to an ailing heart or any kind of fever, Culpeper recommended placing a "plaister" made from a mixture of powdered, dried flowers and lard, turpentine, and rosin on the breast of the ailing. From Stevens, we get another formula, this time using marigold flowers for a cure of Plague or pestilence; he writes, "a conserve made of the flowers and sugar, taken in the morning fasting, cureth the trembling of the harte, and is also given in the time of Plague or pestilence." Generally, only the deep-orange marigold was expected to fulfil any healing obligations.

These early herbalists had, in accordance with certain religious and astrological principles, a very specific and mystifying set of instructions for picking the beautiful marigold flower. To preserve the virtue of the herb, which Culpeper said was commanded by Leo, one famous herbalist recorded that it must be gathered only when the moon is in the sign of the Virgin; picking it during the rise of Jupiter will result in its loss of all virtue. The person assigned to the gathering of the plant must be free of deadly sin and must remember to say three *Pater Nosters* and three *Aves*. Once gathered and worn by someone, the marigold plant can give that person the power to perceive and recognize anyone who has robbed him or her. Moreover, it will strengthen the eyes of anyone who so much as looks at it.

In modern times, the marigold has been used primarily as a local remedy with a stimulant and diaphoretic effect. Chinese herbals list the common marigold as a remedy for persistent bleeding piles. It can provide local relief and prevent suppuration when taken internally or applied externally and has been known to be helpful in the treatment of chronic ulcers and varicose veins. During the American Civil War and the First World War, the marigold flowers were used as a haemostatic. Even today, calendula ointment serves as a dressing for small wounds.

For relief from the pain of a wasp or bee sting, one might try rubbing a marigold flower on the affected part. Sprains and cuts can be much less painful if a lotion made from the marigold flower is applied to them. When a fever attacks, an infusion of freshly gathered blossoms will encourage perspiration and expel any collected mucus or suppuration. The stinging effect of the plant has also been proven to be effective in removing warts.

The culinary uses of the marigold herb are primarily in salads and, dried, in broths and soups. The taste of the leaves is at first pasty and sweet and then quite salty. The strong-tasting juice which can be extracted from the leaves has been effective as a remedy for constipation. Although Gerard once said, "No broth is well made without dried marigold blossom in cooking," he wrote in his essay on 'Christ's Hospital' (1823) about "boiled beef on Thursday, with detestable marigold petals floating in the pail to poison the broth."

The seeds of the marigold plant are unusual in shape and formation. Light yellow in colour with at least half a dozen shapes ranging from a winged seed to a curled seed, the calendula seed holds its germination for only a year. Thus, fresh seeds are needed for each planting.

Marigold
(Calendula officinalis)

Sometime in April or May—when the sun is shining—the seeds can be planted. The soil temperature should be at least 60° F (16° C) for the seeds to germinate well. Although the plants need to be kept free of weeds and thinned out to nine or ten inches (22 to 26 cm) apart, there is not much more cultivation necessary in the care of marigolds. The different varieties offered by seedsmen usually represent various forms of double or single-flower plants with colour ranging from yellow to deep orange, the latter-coloured marigold being excellent for herb teas. If the soil is fairly rich, the flowers will begin to appear anytime from June to August. If you are interested in retaining a healthy flowering until early October, the phosphate content of your soil will be important. Although marigolds may survive the first frost, a harder frost of $25°F$ ($-4°C$) will damage it.

As far as harvesting is concerned, most people are interested in the marigold flower, which on sunny days can be pinched off the stem. Each petal of the harvested flower head is pulled out by hand, leaving the green centre of the flower. Because the only part of this plant generally used in food and medicine is the flower petal, it is considered to be a very expensive herb. In order to produce a cheaper quality medicinal or cooking herb, some growers harvest the flower head and dry the whole head. After shredding and grinding it, they offer the petals mixed with the green flower centre which is, of course, an impure product. The petals should be dried in the shade on paper rather than on screens, since once they are dried they have a tendency to hold tight to the screen, making it difficult to remove them. They should also be kept from touching one another, since this can lead to dis-colouration.

Because the marigold petals are so hydroscopic, they should be stored in a moisture-proof container to preserve colour and flavour ordinarily lost in humid conditions.

Marjoram, Sweet

Knotted Marjoram
Origanum majorana (syn. *Majorana Hortensis*)
Labiatae

Of nearly thirty varieties of marjoram, perhaps the most popular as seasonings are wild marjoram *(Origanum vulgare)*, pot marjoram *(O. Onites)*, and sweet marjoram *(O. marjorana)*.

Historically, wild marjoram, *(O. vulgare)* has been used more for medicinal applications than for kitchen purposes, when compared with the rest of the marjoram family.

Several varieties share many characteristics of the herb commonly called oregano. In a few cases, the common properties are so close that confusion reigns over whether the plant is a marjoram or an oregano.

Some herbalists, for example, say *O. heracleoticum* is oregano while Maude Grieve lists it as winter marjoram. And *O. vulgare*, according to Maude Grieve is wild marjoram; other herbalists have accepted it as oregano. Still others

439

have dubbed *O. vulgare* "British marjoram" because it flourishes in these islands.

There seems to be no disagreement, however, that the plant designated *O. marjorana* by Linneaus and *Marjorana hortensis* by Moench is sweet marjoram and nothing else.

Sweet marjoram is a tender perennial in its native Portugal and similar Mediterranean climates, but in temperate climates it is almost impossible to keep the plant alive through even the mildest winter. So consider it an annual that must be started anew from seed each year.

The dense, shallow root system of sweet marjoram can utilize no more than the top few inches of soil, and so a fairly rich humus is desirable. The plant's square stems grow upright to about 12 inches (30 cm). Stems are surrounded by a profusion of branches bearing oval, slightly fuzzy leaves with short stems. White or pink flowers appear in mid-summer but are almost entirely covered by small leaves that form a little ball at the end of each stem. Seeds are light brown. They look like small nuts and reach a mature size of just over 1/32 inch (1 mm). Under diffused light, they take eight days to germinate.

Because the seeds are so small, it is almost impossible to tend them properly outside. Sweet marjoram should be started indoors in March in trays. Pat them lightly into well-sifted soil, which should be kept moist. Weeds are fierce competitors with young marjoram; keep them

Sweet Marjoram
(Origanum majorana)
(a) flower

under strict control if they're evident during marjoram's slow early growth. Transplant when the soil has warmed.

Outside, the plants should be spaced six to eight inches (15 to 20 cm) apart, although they can be placed in three-plant clumps if the shoots are still small. Five such clumps should provide enough sweet marjoram, both fresh and dried, for a year's use.

Well-rotted compost (never fresh manure) should be supplied to impart a pleasant flavour to sweet marjoram. Regular hoeing is essential to control weeds; in fact, this plant can be "hoed to maturity" and will respond to hoeing in the same way that other plants respond to heavy fertilization. For that reason, mulching should be delayed until two weeks before the first harvest.

The first harvest comes at the time the green ball-like tips appear at the ends of the stems, although for early use some young shoots may be pinched off. When flowers appear, the whole plant should be cut back to an inch (2.5 cm) above the ground to stimulate a second growth.

That second growth, lush and more full than the first, is really the main crop. Cut the plants again when flower heads form the second time.

For drying, place the cut plant on a fine screen or paper and put it in a warm, dry, shaded area. When dry, rub the plant through a fine screen. The leaves will powder and sift through the screen while the woody stems will remain behind. Sweet marjoram, unlike some other herbs, retains its full flavour when it is dried.

Traditionally, sweet marjoram has been a symbol of youth, beauty, and happiness. Legend has it that the plant is a transfiguration of a handsome youth once in the service of King Cinyrus of Cyprus. One day he dropped a vessel of sweet perfume. In terror of displeasing the king, he swooned into unconsciousness and soon was transfigured into the sweet marjoram plant to grace the palace forever after.

William Shakespeare, who knew his herbs well, immortalized the attributes of the plant in *All's Well that Ends Well*. In Act IV, scene V, there is this repartee:

> Lafeu: 'Twas a good lady, 'twas a good lady:
> we may pick a thousand salads, ere we light on such another herb.
> Clown: Indeed, sir, she was the sweet marjoram of the salad, or, rather, the herb of grace.

The "herb of grace", though, was a typically scampish double-entendre that actually compared the lady in question to rue, a herb whose disagreeable qualities are in stark contrast to the sweetness of marjoram.

An even earlier literary tribute to marjoram was paid by Virgil who, in his *Aeneid*, wrote of being "where the sweet marjoram, breathing its fragrance, surrounds him with flowers and soft shade."

The French, too, cherished the sweetness of the herb. It was the custom to tuck a few sprigs of it away in hope chests and linen drawers.

Oil of sweet marjoram was once used as a polish for furniture and as the main ingredient in sweet washing water. Also, people used to steep leaves of sweet marjoram, sometimes mixed with those of mint to obtain a different kind of tea as a change from their more traditional brew.

In the kitchen, try using marjoram with green vegetables, turkey, pork, lamb, or eggs. Pot-pourri, too, is enlivened by this tangy herb, whose fresh tops are sometimes added to home-brewed beer for an unusual flavour. Sprinkle a few cut-up leaves of fresh marjoram on lightly buttered whole-wheat bread and grill it slightly for a tasty herb toast. Mix one part of sweet marjoram to three of brown sugar to make a tasty dressing for roast leg of lamb, and stick a few whole cloves into the meat as well for a delicious dish.

O. vulgare, or wild marjoram, is preferred to sweet marjoram for medicinal uses. They include the relief of nervous headaches (an infusion of the fresh leaves) and a toothache remedy (a few drops of the oil on a piece of cottonwool). Used as an emmenagogue and mild tonic, wild marjoram is stimulant, carminative, and diaphoretic.

The herbalist Gerard said marjoram is a good measure:

. . . against cold diseases of the brain and head . . . The leaves dried and mingled with honey put away black and blue marks after stripes and bruises, being applied thereto . . . There is an excellent oyle to be drawn forth from these herbes, good against the shrinking of sinus, cramps, convulsions, and all aches proceeding of a cold cause.

For headache or nervousness, mix equal parts of marjoram, sage, catnip, and peppermint. Steep one teaspoonful in a cup of hot water for five minutes. Sip a cup slowly every hour until relieved. Omit the sage for a good stomach soother.

Mezereon
(Daphne mezereum)
(a) flower (b) fruit

Mezereon

Daphne, Dwarf Bay, Mezereum
Flowering Spurge, Spurge Laurel
Daphne sp.
Thymelaeaceae

Daphne is valued chiefly for its fragrant flowers. It does best in well-drained sandy loam, well supplied with leaf mould. Propagation is by seeds, cuttings, and layers.

Daphne Mezereum is a pretty little deciduous shrub, growing to about three feet (90 cm) with fragrant pink or lilac-purple flowers in winter and early spring, before the leaves appear. In summer it has scarlet fruits. *D. Mezereum* var. *alba* has white flowers and yellow fruit.

D. Laureola (spurge laurel) is an evergreen shrub, with a sweet-scented fragrance, growing to six feet (1.8 m) high with large shiny green leaves and yellowish-green flowers in very early spring. It grows best in partial shade and moist soil.

Daphne has been used as a stimulant and vesicant, and also as an ointment for ulcers. The bark was found useful for treating venomous bites. It has also been found effective as a purgative.

The bark of the root and stem and the berries and roots are the parts used medicinally.

Mint

Mentha sp.
Labiatae

To many people, especially children, the word *mint* is more likely to mean a certain type of sweet or chewing gum, rather than coolly scented green plants. But there were green plants before there were any other mints, and those green plants have a long and colourful history, as well as a place as the most economically significant herb today.

The mint family, Labiatae, is large, having about 160 genera, which include the thymes, sages, marjorams, basil, hyssop, horehound, rosemary, lavender, and lemon balm. But the true mints are the many members of the genus *Mentha*, and it is those herbs which are of concern here. The best known of the mints are spearmint and peppermint, the two most common flavours of chewing gum. Mints are legion. They are known under such names as garden mint, mackerel mint, green mint, wild mint, corn mint, water mint, curled mint, and horsemint. There are dozens of other species, varieties, and odd hybrids.

As members of the same genus, the mints share a common background and some common characteristics. The most significant of the latter are their square stems and opposite leaves (meaning simply that each leaf has

443

one opposite it on the stem). Most are rampantly spreading perennials which inhabit moist, rich soils throughout the world. Originally natives of the Near East, the mints spread across the globe, thanks in part to their growth characteristic, but also to the great esteem in which they were held by all who came in contact with them. There is no better evidence of this than the number of literary references to the mints in the Bible, Chaucer's writings, the herbals of all ages, and in Greek mythology.

The generic name *Mentha* was first connected with the mint plant by the Greek philosopher-scientist Theophrastus more than three hundred years before Christ. He based the connection on Greek mythology. Mintho, the story went, was a beautiful nymph who was loved by Pluto, god of the underworld. Persephone, who had been abducted by Pluto to reign with him over his domain, became jealous and changed Mintho into a fragrant and lowly plant which to this day waits at the shady edges of Pluto's dark world. The plant, of course, is the mint.

In another myth, fragrant mint leaves were used to clean and deodorize a table set by an old couple for strangers travelling through their country. The strangers turned out to be the gods Zeus and Hermes, disguised. They richly rewarded Philemon and Baucis, the old couple, for their hospitality.

The mints can be used in preparing fragrant baths, pot-pourris and sachets. A room can be scented simply by hanging a bunch of mint in a doorway. This is a common practice in India and other hot countries, for the fragrance gives the impression of coolness. These uses derive from the use of mint as a strewing herb. Spread across the floors of churches and temples, the herbs, bruised by the feet of worshippers and penitents, cleared the air of unpleasant odours. This practice spread from public places to private houses throughout Europe.

Mint was also used in cooking and food preparation, as much for its cooling effect as for its carminative, stomachic properties. In the Middle East, mint-laced salads are popular to this day. The mint has been used as a condiment, garnish, and to make beverages.

It is impossible to pinpoint a single most common use of mint. There is mint tea, mint jelly, or mint sauce, all everyday commodities. There are as many ways to make mint sauce, it seems, as there are cooks to make it. A very simple approach is to combine a quantity of well-chopped mint leaves with just enough boiling water to thoroughly moisten them. After the mass has cooled, stir in an equal amount of orange marmalade. Mint tea is made as are most herbal teas, by infusing about an ounce (28 g) of the dried herb in three-quarters of a pint (426 ml) of water (when using the fresh leaves, more than an ounce (28 g) may be required to brew a satisfying tea).

But there are some relatively uncommon ways to use mint. Mix chopped mint leaves with cream cheese and spread it on whole-grain bread. Mix a quantity of chopped leaves in a salad, toss it well, and dress it with oil and vinegar. Fresh green peas can be perked up by adding a little chopped mint. The ingenious cook can find a variety of dishes that benefit from mint.

The medicinal virtues of the mint have been reported throughout history. The ancient Chinese herbals listed it. Pliny the Elder commented, "The smell of mint stirs up the mind and appetite to a greedy desire of food." The Elizabethan herbalists had much to say about it; Culpeper alone listed forty distinct ailments for which mint was a good remedy.

Gerard commented, "The smelle rejoiceth the heart of man, for which cause they used to strew it in chambers of places of recreation, pleasure, and repose where feasts and banquets are made . . . It is applied with salt to bitings of mad dogs. They lay it on the stinging of wasps with good success." And echoing Pliny he said, "The smell of minte does stir up the minde and the taste to a greedy desire of meate."

Parkinson wrote, "Mintes are sometimes used in baths with balm and other herbs as a help to comfort and strengthen the nerves and sinews. It is much used either outwardly applied or inwardly drunk to strengthen and comfort weak stomackes."

As a wild plant, mint provides enjoyment for foragers everywhere. It often cross-pollinates, producing variations, most of them small, from plant to plant. For the grower, this means a cutting or root division must be used to ensure getting the desired plant variety. For the botanist, it means a continuing challenge.

The oil and its constituents distilled from mint are used in medicines, culinary preparations, cigarettes, cosmetics, toiletries, and, of course, sweets and chewing gum.

Peppermint *(Mentha X piperita)*, is the most useful of the mints. It can be used in many of the culinary applications already described, and it has a history of medicinal use. It has been listed for more than 140 years as an official drug plant. Used in a variety of compound medicines, it often serves to make disagreeable preparations palatable. Of itself, it has strong antispasmodic action. Most herbals list it as a stimulant, stomachic, and carminative. It has been used in cases of flatulence, colic, cramps and other muscle spasms, dyspepsia, cholera, diarrhoea, and a variety of other ailments.

A recommended home remedy for colds and flu is prepared by infusing equal quantities of peppermint and elder flowers (boneset or yarrow may also be added). The tea may be taken freely.

A drink of a peppermint-milk infusion is said to help abdominal pains, while insomniacs can find relief in an infusion of two parts peppermint and one part each of rue and wood betony.

In the garden, peppermint can be a worthy companion. Planted or strewn between cabbage plants, it protects

Peppermint
(Mentha X piperita)
(a) flower

them from the white cabbage butter-fly. It must be watched carefully, however, to keep its spreading tendency in check. Most herb gardeners keep peppermint, and the other mints as well, in a separate bed to prevent them

from crowding out other herbs.

Peppermint has a shallow root system which seems to channel all its energies into the formation of runners which form below and, more abundantly, above ground. The pointed, oval leaves are attached to square stems of a purplish-green colour which extends to the undersides of the leaves. The small flowers are violet and form at the far ends of the shoots only. The seeds are tiny, round, and dark brown. Germination takes place in diffused light within ten days. The viability of the seed declines rapidly after the second year.

The only sensible way to establish a good peppermint bed is to purchase a plant or two. Peppermint has been selected for oil content and flavour and is reproduced vegetatively to retain the desired strains. Though peppermint seed germinates well, it must be remembered that plants from seed do not come true to parent plants and constitute a wide variety of different strains. On the other hand, the enthusiast might see a challenge to develop his own special variety.

The chosen strain, or the purchased variety, is reproduced from cuttings or "stolons", another name for the runners of the mint. Either way is simple and quite often more successful than desired—meaning that a mint bed can easily get out of hand. Peppermint requires a good fertile soil with a high moisture-holding capacity, free of weeds, especially grasses or clovers. The spacing of individual plants should be at least two feet (60 cm) because the runners will fill in this distance within one year. As soon as the runners begin to spread, hoeing has to be entirely replaced by hand weeding. Mulching can be done only in a thin layer in order not to interfere with the development of the shoots which grow out of the nodes of the runners or stolons. The main purpose of the mulch material in this case is to keep the plants clean. Up to three cuttings are possible each year. After the final harvest in the autumn, all exposed roots and runners are best covered with a one to two inch (2.5 to 5 cm) layer of compost or well-rotted manure. This will protect the plants from frost damage and at the same time fertilize them for the following year.

The time for harvesting is judged by the flowering tendency and the yellowing of the lower leaves. As soon as either or both stages have been reached, the entire plant, including the shoots of runners, is cut one inch (2.5 cm) above the ground. Stems with leaves should not be left after the harvest, because they could become hosts for disease. A layer of compost in the autumn also covers all crop residues and aids in their decomposition. The second or third harvest will be smaller and may be done as soon as plants are large enough to handle.

The best quality of peppermint is achieved by stripping the leaves off their stems, and drying them whole in warm shade.

Spearmint *(M. spicata)*, while somewhat less potent than peppermint, is the mint most people think of as "mint". It is the one most commonly used in juleps, sauces, and jellies, and is useful chiefly for these purposes. It does have some effect as a carminative, stimulant, and antispasmodic, but to a lesser degree than peppermint. It is sometimes used as a child's remedy in the same preparations in which peppermint would be used to remedy an adult's complaint.

Spearmint grows in erect, unbranched plants rising as high as three feet (90 cm). It has smooth, bright green leaves with unevenly toothed margins. The flowers, which appear in July or August, vary from almost white to a deep purple and are clustered on a single flower spike. It is a hardy perennial plant, found growing in abundance along roadsides. But it is often grown in gardens because it is easy to cultivate. It is increased by root division and, planted at distances of one foot (30 cm) apart, it quickly forms a mass, which may be cut for many years without removal. This herb is grown to a considerable extent in greenhouses, in much the same way as lettuce. Its treatment there is very simple, being merely to lift up the roots in a solid mass, placing them on three or four inches (7.5 to 10 cm) of earth under glass and to water freely as soon as it begins to grow.

It is most easily differentiated from peppermint by its taste and by the lack of down on the leaves. It is cultivated in much the same way as peppermint.

Apple mint, *(Mentha X rotundifolia)*,

447

is often found on rubbish tips, compost heaps, and waste places. It is a small, unassuming plant, not difficult to please as to sun or shade and soil fertility. It has soft, grey-green woolly leaves, somewhat round, as its specific name suggests, and grey-white blossoms, shading to pink or pale purple.

Pennyroyal, *M. Pulegium*, is treated separately.

Bergamot or orange mint, *(Mentha X piperita* var. *citrata)*, is notable for its distinctive, citrus-like fragrance. Its rounded, broad leaves are dark green with a hint of purple. The undersides of the leaves often have a reddish hue, and in spring the entire plant is distinctly reddish-purple. Easily cultivated, it adds an interesting fragrance to the herb garden, and, harvested, to tea and pot-pourri.

Egyptian mint *(Mentha X niliaca)*, has leaves that are so velvety they have earned the name "fairy blankets" among children. This is a tall mint, growing to three or four feet (90 cm to 1.2 m) in height, and it is thought to be a hybrid between apple mint and either spearmint or long-leaved mint, *M. longifolia*.

Water mint *(M. aquatica)*, bears its flowers in little rounded balls at the tips of the stems and in the axils of the uppermost leaves. The hairy leaves are egg-shaped and have stalks. One well-known variety has crisped or crinkled leaves and is sometimes called *M. aquatica* var. *crispa*. There are also forms of other mints that have crisped leaves.

Corsican mint *(M. Requieni)*, is a delightful little creeping plant with minute, rounded leaves, forming an almost moss-like mat. When lightly brushed it emits a very strong, pleasing odour of mint. Corsican mint is used to flavour liqueurs, and is delightful as a ground cover for small spots.

It thrives in moist shade, but will also grow in the sun. Since it does not survive cold winters unless well covered by snow, it is better to keep indoors in pots through the winter. Propagation is by division.

Mugwort

Felon Herb, St. John's Plant
Artemisia vulgaris
Compositae

Mugwort, famed for the protection against fatigue, sunstroke, wild beasts, and evil spirits it offered travellers, got its name because it was once used in place of hops to flavour beers. The dried flowers were boiled with malt liquor and the liquid was added to beer. It was used for this purpose fairly widely among country people until quite recently and, no doubt, by a few today.

It has been suggested that the name of the herb has been derived from *moughte* (maggot), because from Greek times the plant has been regarded as useful in driving away moths.

Wherever its name came from, mugwort has been surrounded by legends and superstitions for centuries. A crown made from sprays of the plant was worn on St. John's Eve to protect the wearer against evil possession. In Germany and Holland, it is known as "St. John's plant", and it is believed that if mugwort is gathered on St. John's Eve, it will give protection against diseases and misfortunes. It is said that John the Baptist wore a girdle of mugwort in the wilderness, and that the powers of the plant protected him against harm there.

In China, mugwort is hung up during the time of the Dragon Festival (fifth day of the fifth moon) to ward off evil spirits. It is also used as a *moxa*, a herbal preparation placed on the skin and ignited to cauterize ulcers, ease pain, and restore sensation to numbed limbs.

Mugwort is a tall plant, normally reaching three feet (90 cm) in height, and may grow to seven feet (2.1 m) under favourable conditions. Its stems are angular and of purplish hue. The leaves are smooth and dark green on top, covered with a cottony down underneath, and are light greyish-green.

The flowers are in small, oval heads. They are pale yellow or reddish and are arranged in long, terminal panicles. The seeds that form after pollination are light grey, in the form of very small sticks of about one millimetre by a quarter of a millimetre in size.

Mugwort
(Artemisia vulgaris)
(a) flower

Mugwort is closely related to common wormwood, but can be readily distinguished by its pointed leaves and by the fact that the leaves

449

are lightly coloured only on the under-surfaces. It also lacks the oil of the wormwood.

Mugwort is easily grown from seed. Germination of the seed takes place quickly at fairly low temperatures, from about 55° to 60° F (13° to 16° C). However, since the seeds are so small, the best way to start mugwort is indoors for transplanting outside. It can also be reproduced by dividing old plants, or by buying a new plant from a nursery. Both of these methods yield faster results.

The plants may reach a height of six to seven feet (1.8 to 2.1 m) under the right conditions, so it is best to plant them near the perimeter of the garden where they will not have to compete with other plants for space or sunlight. Once established, mugwort will spread rapidly unless it is cut back. Plant it in moist and well-fertilized soil. It should be well composted, and cultivated or mulched until established.

Harvesting depends on the part to be used. If you are brewing tea from mugwort, harvest it before it flowers. The dried leaves are used for tea, and were used quite extensively a long time ago at a time when the price of ordinary tea was exorbitant. The flowering buds are used as a seasoning for goose. Together with the leaves they should be dried in the shade. They retain their colour and dry well.

Mugwort root, collected in the autumn, is also used medicinally. Roots should be free from rootlets and washed with cold water. Drying is begun in the open air: spread the roots thinly and don't let them touch each other. When they have begun to shrink take them indoors and finish drying in a drying room or shed or in the oven under a low heat. Drying should take two weeks or more. The root is not dried until it is brittle, snapping when bent.

Astrologers regarded mugwort as a plant under the influence of Venus, and recommended it for treating ailments of women. One of its chief uses was to stimulate the menstrual flow, often when combined with penny-royal and southernwood. It was also used to stimulate perspiration.

Mugwort was administered as an infusion, prepared in a covered vessel using one ounce (28 g) of the herb to three-quarters of a pint (426 ml) of boiling water. Adminster in half tea-spoonfuls while still warm. The infusion may also be taken cold as a tonic in similar doses three times a day.

Mugwort was also recommended for palsy or epilepsy. Gerard wrote: "Mugwort cureth the shaking of the joynts inclining to the Palsie." A dram of the powdered leaves given four times a day was reported to have cured a patient who had been affected by hysterical fits for many years.

Culpeper, recommending that the tops of the plant be used freshly gathered, reported:

A very slight infusion is excellent for all disorders of the stomach, prevents sickness after meals and creates an appetite, but if made too strong, it disgusts the taste. The tops with the flowers on them, dried and powdered, are good against agues, and have the same virtues with wormseed in killing worms. The juice of the large leaves which grow from the root before the stalk appears is the best against the dropsy and jaundice, in water, ale, wine, or the juice only. The infusion drank morning and evening for some time helps hysterics, obstruction of the spleen and weakness of the stomach. Its oil, taken on sugar and drank after, kills worms, resists poison, and is good for the liver and jaundice. The root has a slow bitterness which affects not the head and eyes like the leaves, hence the root should be accounted among the best stomachics. The oil of the seed cures quotidians and quartans. Boiled in lard and laid to swellings of the tonsils and quinsy is serviceable. It is admirable against surfeits.

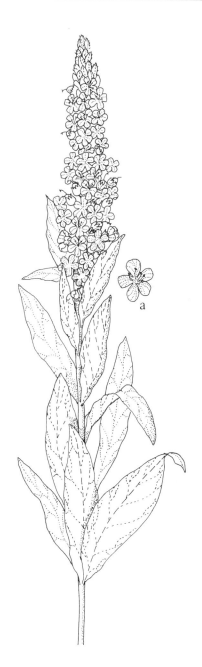

Mullein, Great

**Golden Rod, Aaron's Rod,
Candlewick Plant, White Mullein**
Verbascum Thapsus
Scrophulariaceae

Mullein is found throughout the British Isles, with the exception of the far north of Scotland. Medicinally, it has served for centuries as a demulcent and emollient, being used, paradoxically, for both diarrhoea and constipation, and was especially valued as a remedy in bronchial and lung ailments.

*Great Mullein
(Verbascum Thapsus)
(a) flower*

451

The plant is a striking one, with a tall, flower-studded spike arising from a thick stake of leaves. Mullein is a biennial, and the flower stalk does not develop until the second year. In the first year, the large, woolly leaves develop and they persist through the winter. The flower stalk, with its yellow blossoms, rises from four to eight feet (1.2 to 2.4 m) in the second year. Both leaves and blossoms are used.

The dried leaves have been smoked to ease throat congestions. Dried and powdered, the leaves are used in soothing infusions. A popular remedy called for boiling an ounce (28 g) of dry powdered leaves in three-quarters of a pint (426 ml) of milk for ten minutes, straining the infusion carefully (to remove the hairs which give the leaves their woolly character), stirring in a teaspoonful of honey and serving warm, a wineglassful at a time. The infusion is useful primarily as a remedy for coughs, but it has also been recommended for diarrhoea and constipation. The flowers usually are steeped in olive oil for several weeks, and the resulting ointment used on bruises, frostbite, haemorrhoids, and even in aching ears.

Mullein is easily established in the garden. The seeds germinate in about ten days, and the resulting plants will ultimately self-sow freely. It grows well in poor soil.

Mustard, Black

Brassica nigra syn. *Sinapis nigra*

Mustard, White

Brassica hirta syn. *Brassica alba*
Cruciferae

Both kinds of mustard, black and white, have been used as condiments for many centuries. Use of the seed is thought to date back to the time of the Greeks, who also used the plant's green leaves as a pot-herb and salad.

Black mustard (*Brassica nigra* or *Sinapis nigra*) is a hardy annual which grows to a height of four feet (1.2 m), even in poor soil. But when grown for its seed, it must be kept fairly moist and well nourished.

White mustard (*Brassica hirta* or *B. alba*) is more often grown in the garden for its seed. It is a plant that grows to a height of eighteen inches (46 cm). Its leaves are useful for salad. It may become a pest, however, because it self-sows freely, so it is inadvisable to plant it in the regular vegetable garden or flower border.

When grown for the seed—which is used in pickling and as a peppery condiment—the pods must be picked before they are completely ripe, or they will shatter and the fine seed will be lost. Pods are spread on muslin to dry, and are crushed to remove seeds and hulls. The seed must be further

Black Mustard
(Brassica nigra)
(a) flower (b) seed pod

Mustard seeds are also used medicinally. They are said to have stimulant, diuretic, and aperient properties. The seeds of the black mustard are more pungent than those of the white.

Old herbals say that mustard seeds excite the stomach, stimulate nervous energy, and act as a laxative. They act very mildly yet effectively as an aperient and are supposed to be useful for indigestion.

Mustard is often used externally and is generally beneficial when applied over the seat of inward inflammation of the chest, stomach, or throat. A mustard poultice is made by mixing good, fresh-ground mustard seed with water (it can be moderated by adding flour to the mixture). It should be spread thickly on a piece of linen or calico and covered with a thin piece of muslin, and then applied to the affected area for 15 to 20 minutes to redden the skin without producing a blister. If it burns when taken off sprinkle the part with flour.

Mustard lotions and ointments have sometimes been used for local friction, chilblains, and other swellings. In cases of poisoning, torpor, or paralysis, a mustard footbath was used to rouse the system. Country people still use mustard footbaths to relieve discomfort of colds and chills and to revive tired feet.

Mustard has a strong irritant action internally and externally and must be used with great care or it may cause serious inflammation.

crushed and milled to remove the fine hulls before they are used. Commercially, mustard seed is ground to a flour to provide dry mustard. This process, however, is normally beyond the scope for home gardeners.

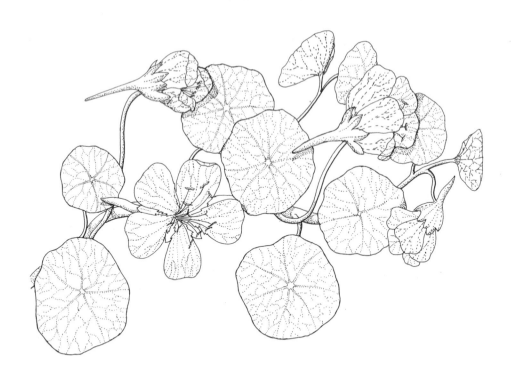

Nasturtium (Tropaeolum majus)

Nasturtium

Indian Cress
Tropaeolum majus
Tropaeolacae

Nasturtium is one of the most familiar companion plants used by the organic vegetable gardener. The low, creeping plant with its saucer-like leaves and bright-coloured flowers attracts some pests and repels others. Both the leaves and flowers are edible and are, in fact, a tasty and attractive ingredient for fresh salads.

The genus *Tropaeolum* includes more than 50 annual or perennial plants, mostly climbing. Common nasturtium *(T. majus)* is a tender annual, and one of the most popular because of its showy flowers in many shades of red, orange, and yellow. Large varieties climb as high as ten to twelve feet (3 to 3.7 m). Dwarf varieties grow in low, compact, rounded bushes slightly less than one foot (30 cm) high and about a foot (30 cm) in diameter. These forms are excellent for bedding.

Common nasturtium is a native of South America, and is sometimes known as Indian cress—a reference to the Peruvian Indians who made good use of it. It made its way from the land of the Incas to Europe by way of conquering Spaniards and pirating Englishmen, first appearing in English gardens at the very end of the Sixteenth Century.

The common name "nasturtium" should not prompt one to confuse *T. majus* with the botanical genus *Nasturtium*. The most familiar variety of the latter family is *N. officinalis*, watercress. The only real connection between watercress and nasturtium is the taste. Nasturtium is sometimes regarded as a substitute for watercress. The name *Tropaeolum* is derived from the Latin *tropaeum*, for trophy, and was an allusion to the shield-like leaves and helmet-like flowers.

Nasturtium is most useful in cooking and in the garden. The entire plant has a spicy, yet delicately pungent flavour. Both the flowers and young leaves are fine for salads and sandwiches, used in the same manner as lettuce. The seeds also make a good snack, and the Chinese have relished pickled nasturtium seeds for centuries. Simply gather seed clusters when about half-grown, leaving some of the stem still attached. Clean them and put them in a jar, covering them with freshly boiled cider vinegar. Seal the jar tightly and store in a cool place.

Another technique for pickling the seeds involves gathering them as soon as the blossoms are gone from the plants. Soak them for three days in cold salt water, changing the brine each day. Prepare a pickle of nutmeg, peppercorns, horseradish, and vinegar,

warming but not boiling the mixture. Drain the seeds, place them in a jar, add the warm pickle, and seal.

The primary use of nasturtium remains in the garden. It is a popular ornamental flower, and an even more popular companion plant. It is particularly useful in keeping vegetables and fruits susceptible to aphids free of the pest. Nasturtium does this by attracting the aphids to itself. An infusion of the plant can be made by covering it with water in a pan, bringing it just to the boil, and immediately taking it off the heat; dilute four to one with water and use as a spray.

Nasturtiums do best in a sunny, well-drained location. When planted in a shady spot or in wet ground, they tend to produce a large growth of foliage with relatively few flowers. Since it is a climbing plant, enough space should be allowed so it can hang down a bank or slope, or even be allowed to trail over a compost heap.

The seeds should be sown outside as soon as the danger of frost has passed. Cultivate the soil well. Cover the seed with about an inch (2.5 cm) of soil and firm well. Thin plants to about a foot (30 cm) apart. If the soil is poor and hard, dig it over deeply, adding several inches of finished compost to the surface. Harvesting can take place at any time, the leaves and flowers being used fresh.

Nettle, Stinging

Greater Nettle, Common Nettle
Urtica dioica
Urticaceae

Nettle is like a beast with a heart of gold. It makes good eating, and it has a variety of healing virtues, but its embodiment turns away many. For the stinging nettle has come by its name for good reason, as anyone who has been stung by it knows.

Stinging nettle is a familiar plant inhabiting roadsides, vacant lots, and waste places. It's a perennial with persistent, spreading roots. It has heart-shaped, finely toothed leaves, and its one to two foot (30 to 60 cm) stems are covered with downy hair and venomous spines. Each spine is a hollow needle filled with poison which is released whenever the plant is brushed against. The sting produces a red rash. Dock, incidentally, is an antidote. Its leaf, if bruised and the juice rubbed on the nettle sting, will alleviate the pain. It is said that wherever nettle grows, dock grows, also.

Fortunately, the virulent qualities of nettle are destroyed by cooking or drying the plant. Simply boiling or steaming the foliage can produce a satisfying vegetable, but nettle is more tasty when made a part of some fancier dish. Old herbals contend that nettles are useful in weight-reducing diets.

A variety of cosmetic properties were attributed to it. Nettle water was

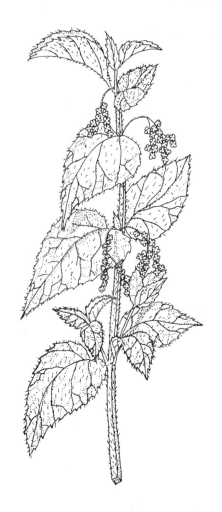

Stinging Nettle
(Urtica dioica)

reputed to be an excellent wash to clear the complexion and give brightness to the eyes. Boiling the entire plant in a mixture of vinegar and water, then adding Eau de Cologne, was supposed to produce a good hair lotion. Combing the hair with expressed nettle juice was supposed to stimulate hair growth.

The plant was reported to have many medicinal properties. It was said to be anti-asthmatic and was used in bronchial and asthmatic ailments, as well as consumption. The seeds were recommended as antidotes to venomous bites and stings and such poisonous plants as henbane, hemlock, and nightshade. A novel use of the plant was as a counter-irritant in rheumatism cases. The afflicted person was "whipped" on the rheumatic joint with whole plants. The idea was that the pain of nettle stings would make the sufferer forget the pain of the rheumatism!

Onion, Common

Allium Cepa

Onion, Tree

Top Onion, Welsh Onion
Allium Cepa var. *proliferum*
Liliacaea

Most people are familiar with the onion, a plant which is unremarkable as a plant, but quite remarkable as a food and seasoning. But few are familiar with the onion family's curiosity — the tree onion.

The most curious thing about the tree onion is that it develops bulbs at the top of its slender green shoots, as opposed to the typical onion, which develops its bulb at the bottom. The bulbs are set in the ground and send up shoots typical of the onions. But instead of a seed head, the tree onion develops a bulb, which sends up its own shoot, in turn developing a bulb, and so on. Of course, the weight of the several stages of bulbs eventually bends the plant to the ground, where the stalk-end bulbs can take root and establish themselves as new plants.

Onions are plants worthy of the herbalist's attention, and the tree onion in particular could be the variety best suited for one interested in the plant as a herb. The tree onion can, in fact, be used in the same way as the common onion. Moreover, it is an interesting garden plant as well, making an arresting back border for a culinary garden.

Like their relative, garlic *(Allium sativum)*, onions were a favoured food of the Egyptian slaves. According to the Greek historian Herodotus, something like nine tons of gold were given in payment for the onions consumed by the slaves building the great pyramids. The Egyptians themselves held onions in high regard, for Pliny reports that they "make their oaths" by garlic and onions. They regarded the brittle brown skin which envelops the onion bulb as a symbol of the universe.

Later, Europeans had superstitions about onions, too. One practice was the suspending of onion slices in each room to purge "evil spirits" from a house. The slices were collected and burned daily. A London herbalist, Dr. Fernie, recorded a story attributing the immunization of a household to the Plague, to a sack of onions. A similar story recorded by another herbalist attributes the immunization to garlic. The conflicting stories serve to demonstrate the inherent similarities of the two herbs. Culpeper noted under his entry for garlic that for most ailments, onions served as well as garlic.

The ancient herbalists recommended onions. Parkinson, for example, said onions had many uses: "so many I cannot recount them, everyone pleasing themselves, according to their order, manner, or delight". Gerard listed a variety of applications. He said:

They do bite, attenuate, or make thinne, breake winde, provoke urine . . . they open passages that are stopped . . . the juice sniffed up into the nose, purgeth the head . . . stamped with salt, rue and honey, and so applied, they are good against the biting of a mad dog . . . The juice annointed upon a pild or bald head in the sunne, bringing the hair again very speedily . . . Onions sliced and dipped in the juice of Sorrell will take away a fit of the Ague.

Evelyn reported: "Boiled they give a kindly relish, raise appetites, corroborate the Stomach, cut Phlegm, and profit the Asthmatical."

Culpeper, noting that the onion is "so common and well known that it needs no description", listed most of the applications that the other herbalists listed and added a few of his own:

The onions increase sperm, especially the seed: they kill worms in children, if they drink the water fasting wherein they have been steeped all night. Being roasted under the embers, and eaten with honey, or sugar and oil, they much conduce to help an inveterate cough, and expectorate tough phlegm . . . The juice is good for either scalds or burns. Used with vinegar it takes away all blemishes, spots, and marks in the skin; and dropped into the ears, eases the pains and noise in them. Applied also with figs beaten together, helps to ripen and break imposthumes, and other sores . . . Onions are good for cold watery humours, but injurious to persons of bilious habit, affecting the head, eyes, and stomach. When plentifully eaten, they procure sleep, help digestion, cure acid belchings, remove obstructions of the viscera, increase the urinary secretions, and promote insensible perspiration . . . Onion bruised, with the addition of a little salt, and laid on fresh burns, draws out the fire, and prevents them blistering. The use is fittest for cold weather, and for aged, phlegmatic people, whose lungs are stuffed, and breathing short.

Quite a number of medicinal applications of the onions are still listed in herbals. A simple onion tea acts as a diuretic. The antiseptic properties of the onions may be put to use by macerating the bulb and applying it to sores, boils, and the like as a poultice. There is a surprising variety of folk cures which are onion-based.

Warts are said to be eliminated by the daily application of salted onion. The same application is reputed to take the heat out of scalding burns. Calluses can be removed through a curious onion treatment: fresh onions are cut in half, then steeped for at least three hours in strong wine vinegar. The onion halves are then securely bound to the calluses and left overnight. In the morning, the surface layer of the callus will be sufficiently softened to permit it to be scraped or picked away. Repeat the process until it is wholly removed. A reputed cure for athlete's foot is onion juice. Merely rub the juice between the toes two or three times daily until the condition disappears.

For sprains, mix a finely chopped onion with sugar, spread on a cloth, and wrap around the sprained joint. A variation on this remedy is to mix a tablespoon of olive oil with a finely chopped onion and apply the mixture as a thick poultice. A third variation calls for a poultice made from chopped onion and salt.

Onions are also believed to be useful in cases of asthma, bronchitis, and other respiratory ailments. The odour of the onion alone is prescribed for some such ailments, although it is more often suggested that a raw onion be made a part of the diet until the ailment is gone. A croup remedy is made by thinly slicing an onion, and sprinkling sugar on each slice. The syrup that this concoction yields should be taken by teaspoonful doses every 15 minutes until the croup is gone.

Other onion cures can be cited for ear-aches, gall stones, protruding piles, headaches, and skin blemishes. Most seem centred around the vegetable garden onion, rather than the curious tree onion, but the qualities are very similar.

In the kitchen, the tree onion is serviceable in all the dishes in which one would use onions. They are particularly good for pickling. Moreover, the stalks of the tree onion may be diced and used as a substitute for chives.

Since the tree onion has no seed, it has to be started from the little onion bulbs, which can be planted at any time of the year. The little onions are very hardy, and if the plant is not cared for, these onion bulbs bend down to the ground over winter and, in spring, sprout anew. The growing of the plant is easy, simply because it is so rugged and frost-hardy.

The tree onion grows in almost any type of soil, but needs some fertilization if a good formation of little onion bulbs is to be expected. The best fertilizer is a compost not too rich in nitrogen, such as a leaf compost. Manures should be avoided.

Bulbs and stalks may be harvested throughout the growing season. The bulbs will generally make their appearance in early July and can be used fresh immediately or allowed to dry on the plant before harvesting. When dried to a dark brown, the bulbs store very well—better, in fact, than the common garden variety. The stems should, of course, be used fresh.

As mentioned, tree onions present an arresting appearance in the herb garden, but they can also be of value in a vegetable garden. They like to grow with beetroots, and camomile and, in good soil, they are helped by summer savory and lettuce. Do not plant onions with peas or beans, however, for they will inhibit their growth.

Oregano

Wild Marjoram
Origanum sp.
Labiatae

There is no agreement among herbalists as to which species of the genus *Origanum* is referred to by the common name "oregano". Two groups of authorities differ over calling oregano either *O. heracleoticum* or *O. vulgare,* while a third group cites the two species without attaching the common name "oregano" to either, calling *O. heracleoticum,* "winter marjoram" and *O. vulgare,* "wild marjoram".

A curious element of the mystery is that the plants, although of the same genus, are in fact quite different.

O. heracleoticum is a perennial native to Greece and the Island of Cyprus. It isn't fully acclimatized to harsh winters, so where this is the case it should be treated as a tender perennial. A dense system of fine roots produces a low-growing, almost creeping plant with very hairy leaves. The flower stalks grow erect, about 12 inches (30 cm) tall, and develop

small clusters of white flowers at their ends. The seeds are light brown and particularly tiny.

O. vulgare is also a perennial, and a native of the Mediterranean. It is, however, quite hardy. The plant is erect, rising to two feet (60 cm) in height. It has dull, grey-green, oval leaves, far less hairy than those of *O. heracleoticum.* The flowers can be pink, white, purple, or lilac.

The flavour is the heart of oregano's usefulness. Indeed, it is most famous as a seasoning herb. This fame is due primarily to its use in pizzas, spaghetti sauces, and other tomato dishes. Add the leaves sparingly, fresh or dried, to any of these dishes. Oregano is also a good garnish for beef or lamb stews, gravies, soups, salads, or tomato juice. *O. heracleoticum* is limited to such uses, but the capacities of *O. vulgare* are more extensive.

O. vulgare has an ancient medicinal reputation, the Greeks having used it both internally and externally as an antidote to narcotic poisoning, convulsions, and dropsy. The Elizabethan herbalists noted these properties, and added many of their own. Culpeper, for example, wrote:

It strengthens the stomach and head much; there is scarcely a better herb growing for relieving a sour stomach, loss of appetite, cough, consumption of the lungs; it cleanses of the body of choler, . . . and helps the bites of venomous beasts. It provokes urine and the terms in women, helps the dropsy, scurvy, scabs, itch, and yellow jaundice. The juice dropped into the ears, helps deafness, pain, and noise in them.

Oregano
(Origanum vulgare)
(a) flower

More recent herbalists have listed it as mildly tonic, diaphoretic, carminative, stimulant, and useful as an emmenagogue. They have noted that its warming qualities have made it useful as a liniment and rubefacient.

A frequently mentioned toothache remedy is oregano oil. Moisten a piece of cottonwool with a few drops of the oil and place it on the aching tooth. A warm infusion of oregano is said to spur the fever and eruption of measles and to be helpful in cases of nervous headache. The ancient Greeks made warm poultices of the leaves to apply to painful swellings, and even Twentieth Century herbalists have recommended such use.

Because of the strong balsamic odour of the whole plant, it has had some use in pot-pourris, sachets, and aromatic waters, although it takes a secondary role to sweet marjoram in such applications. The flower tops of the plant are said to yield a dye, although one of limited durability. It dyes wool purple and linen a reddish-brown.

If all this mystery has aroused your curiosity, perhaps you would like to try cultivating some oregano. The plant can be grown from seed or cuttings. The real trick seems to be getting the seed or a cutting from a true oregano plant.

The demand of oregano on soil fertility is modest, though good drainage and tilth are essential. Planting outside with a distance of twelve inches (30 cm) between plants should be delayed until danger of frost has passed. Hoeing and weed control are important; mulching with hay helps to keep the plants clean. Water requirements are minimal and generally supplied by average rainfall. As soon as the white flowers appear, oregano is ready for harvest, unless of course, continued picking for fresh use during its growth never allowed it to flower. Even then, oregano should be trimmed about six weeks after planting, cutting off all shoots to within one inch (2.5 cm) of the growing centre. This practice stimulates dense, bushy growth.

Oregano can be dried inside or outside in the sun after harvesting without losing much of its properties. It dries very quickly. Rubbing the dried material through a fine screen will prepare the oregano for culinary use.

Parsley

Carum petroselinum
Umbelliferae

One of the best-known herbs, parsley is also one of the most effective and versatile. Pliny considered the bright green biennial among the most important of his time for its medicinal values. Today, parsley is mostly used as a decorative herb, but it has high nutritional and medicinal values which are often overlooked.

Parsley is believed to be indigenous to Sardinia, Turkey, Algeria, and Lebanon, where it still grows wild. The Romans are credited for bringing the herb to England, from where it was carried and cultivated throughout the world.

Curiously enough, this widely known and much-used herb has had a long history of identity troubles. Gerard preferred the name *Apium hortense* for the plant he identified as garden parsley. The more commonly used name for that plant was *Petroselinum*, a name believed to have been ascribed to the plant by Dioscorides, the Greek herbalist and physician. The name was meant to distinguish parsley from celery. Both were *selinons*; celery was called *heleioselinon*, or marsh *selinon*, and parsley was called *petroselinum*, or rock *selinon*.

Linnaeus named the plant *Apium Petroselinum*. Later, botanists reclassified and renamed it *Petroselinum lativum* and *Carum Petroselinum*.

P. crispum is a widely cultivated, curly-leaved variety of parsley. It is a very old variety, having been mentioned in the writings of Pliny. It has very similar properties to *C. Petroselinum* but is less hardy.

The Greeks believed the god Hercules chose parsley for his garlands, and consequently it was woven into crowns for victors in their athletic games. Greek warriors used to feed it to their horses before races with the belief that it would help them run faster. At Greek banquets, chaplets of parsley were worn to absorb the fumes of the wines and to help the men from becoming inebriated. It was also used to subdue the odour of garlic, onions, and other strong-smelling foods.

Theocretus wrote:

> At Sparta's palace twenty beauteous
>   maids
> The pride of Greece, fresh garlands
>   crowned their heads
> With hyacinths and twining parsley
>   drest
> Graced joyful Menelaus' marriage feast.

On the other hand, the Greeks were also believed to have associated parsley with oblivion and death. According to Greek legend, parsley sprang up where the blood of the Greek hero Archemorus spilled when he was eaten by serpents. Because of this legend, the expression "in need of parsley", meant one was seriously—almost hopelessly—ill. The Greeks also used the herb to make wreaths for their graves. As the parsley became transplanted onto the ground around the graves, it made a beautiful carpet of green.

Parsley is slow to germinate, which gave rise to the superstition that, before it grew, it had to go to Satan and back seven times. Some believed that only a witch could grow it but that a fine harvest was assured if it was planted on Good Friday or by a pregnant woman. Transplanting parsley was never done, because it was said to displease the herb and bring bad luck to the household of the offender.

The medicinal uses of parsley are almost endless. Parkinson said, "the rootes boiled into broth help open obstruction of the liver, veines and other parts . . . The rootes likewise boiled with leg of mutton . . . will have their operation to cause urine."

Gerard agreed that parsley was just the thing to "take away stoppings and provoke urine;" either in a broth or by eating the seeds. He added that parsley seeds "waste away winde, are good for suche as have dropsie, draw down the menses, bring away the afterbirth; they be commended also against the cough, if they be boiled or mixed with medicines for such a purpose . . . They are also good to be put into clysters against the stone or torments of the guts."

That was not all, of course. It was claimed that the bruised leaves were used successfully to cure bites and stings of insects, and that the seeds would exterminate vermin in the hair. It was also said to be poisonous to birds. But certainly not to rabbits, who love parsley more than any vegetable. Another novel use for parsley: if thrown into a fishpond it would "heal the sick fishes therein".

Culpeper recommended parsley for most of the above uses, and added several of his own. Being under the dominion of Mercury, it was very comforting to the stomach and was good against the falling sickness. If the leaves were laid on the eyes, it helped to ease swelling and pain, and dropped into the ears with a little wine, it would ease earaches. "If used with bread or meal, or fried with butter," he said, "and applied to women's breasts that are hard through

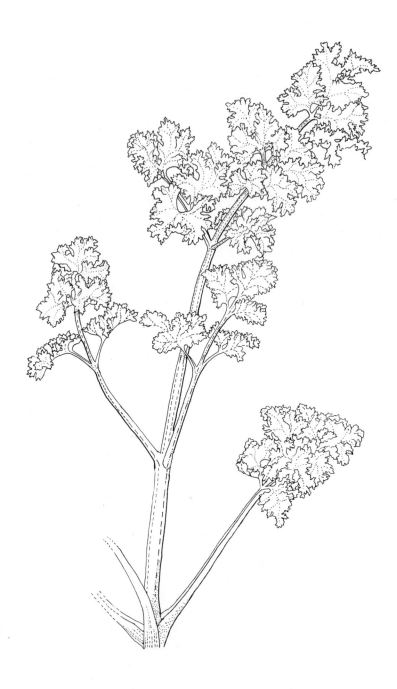

Parsley (Carum Petroselinum)

the curdling of their milk, it abates the hardness and takes away the black and blue marks coming of falls or bruises."

Some of these uses may be questionable, but parsley's value as a diuretic is still highly regarded today. In Greek, the word *parsley* means "stone-breaker".

The herb is a rich source of calcium, thiamin, riboflavin, and niacin. It abounds in vitamin A, and has more vitamin C than oranges. Because of its richness in vitamins, some consider it excellent to ease the pain of arthritis. A useful infusion is made by pouring boiling water over firmly packed parsley in a ratio of four parts water to one part parsley, both leaves and stems. Allow to infuse for 15 minutes, then strain through a coarse cloth and bottle immediately. Cool quickly and keep under refrigeration. Parsley is also useful for eliminating bad breath.

In the first year, this biennial herb develops a multitude of green leaves on long stems until the winter halts its growth. White roots of various thicknesses, depending on variety, penetrate the soil to a depth of a foot (30 cm). Flower stalks, reaching a height of over three feet (90 cm), develop the second year, with greenish-yellow flowers on clusters of umbels. The seeds are greyish-brown and germinate within three weeks.

Since the herb gardener is generally interested only in the leaves, the herb is usually planted each year and treated as an annual. The superstition about the hazards of transplanting parsley are based on the fact that parsley doesn't transplant well. Thus, the gardener should plant the herb outside in rows bordering the garden. Early and shallow seeding will aid germination.

Parsley grows best in fertile soil, full of humus, with good moisture-holding capacity. Well-rotted compost is excellent fertilizing material, worked into the soil with a hoe or by roto-tilling. The gardener should avoid manure, however, because it attracts flies and could result in an infestation of maggots.

Naturally, weed control in all cultivation is important, but this is especially true with parsley because it develops so slowly at first. It is a good idea to hoe around the herb once a week until a hay or straw mulch takes control over the weeds.

Because parsley is preferably used fresh, it is usually picked almost daily in the summer months. The larger, outer leaves should be cut or broken first, always close to the core of the plant, leaving no part of the stem attached. Parsley can also be harvested by cutting the whole plant about an inch (2.5 cm) above the ground. But be sure not to damage the growing point.

The harvested plant should be dried quickly in the shade. It may be necessary to finish the drying process in the oven. Once dried, parsley should be crushed and stored in a tightly sealed container. Keep it away from moist places.

465

Pennyroyal

Pulegium, Pudding Grass,
Run-by-the-Ground
Mentha Pulegium
Labiatae

Pennyroyal is an official member of the mint family, being of the genus *Mentha*. It is a low-growing creeping plant; only the lavender-blossomed flower stalk rises above the ground. The leaves are tiny.

Nonetheless, pennyroyal was noticed very early on because it seemed to have the power to drive away fleas. Pliny remarked on it, and Linnaeus selected a specific name indicative of this power in naming the plant, *pulex* being the Latin for flea. Both its old botanical name, *Pulegium regium*, and its old common name, *Pulioll-royall*, are references to the insect-repelling properties of the herb, and the fact that even Royalty had problems with body lice.

Pennyroyal is not a native of England; originally, it came from the Near East, from whence it spread across the cooler parts of Europe and north to Finland. Both the Greeks and the Romans used and valued the little herb, and Pliny listed a considerable number of disorders that it was said to remedy.

Culpeper noted that pennyroyal:

Drank with wine, it is good for venomous bites, and applied to the nostrils with vinegar revives those who faint and swoon. Dried and burnt, it strengthens the gums, helps the gout, if applied of itself to the place until it is red, and applied in a plaster, it takes away spots or marks on the face; applied with salt, it profits those that are splenetic, or liver-grown . . . The green herb bruised and put into vinegar, cleanses foul ulcers and takes away the marks of bruises and blows about the eyes, and burns in the face, and the leprosy, if drank and applied outwardly . . . One spoonful of the juice sweetened with sugar-candy is a cure for hooping-cough.

Culpeper's contemporaries generally echoed his sentiments towards pennyroyal.

More recent herbals have listed pennyroyal's properties as carminative, diaphoretic, stimulant, and emmenagogic. It is also said to be antispasmodic and stomachic.

Pennyroyal may be propagated from seed, which germinates in the dark at a temperature of 65° to 70° F (18° to 21° C), but it is slow to develop and takes a long time to establish itself. As a perennial, it is best to use cuttings or root divisions. It roots very easily, provided it is kept sufficiently moist at all times. As pennyroyal creeps along the ground, it forms roots wherever the stem touches the soil, which makes it easy to subdivide an older plant.

Growing pennyroyal is similar to growing any other mint. It likes a rich soil, and will do well in the shade. It likes a good water supply and especially a high humus content in the soil. If the humus conditions are poor, pennyroyal will develop a light

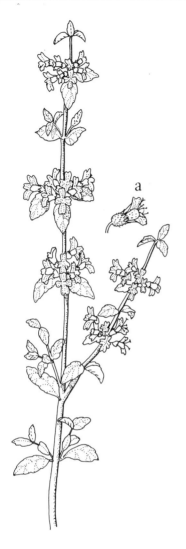

Pennyroyal
(Mentha Pulegium)
(a) flower

is so small. It is very often difficult to harvest the shoots without collecting up some soil, stones, or foreign leaves and growths. For the home gardener it is easier, of course, simply because only one or two shoots are needed to flavour a meal and one can take more trouble. The plant should be used fresh as long as it is available, but it can also be dried in the shade, preferably before chopping. The dried herb should be stored in tightly sealed, non-metallic containers.

Sewn into sachets and fragrant bags, pennyroyal will repel moths and lend your clothing a minty aroma.

Maude Grieve tells us that there are frequent references to pennyroyal in Anglo-Saxon and Welsh works on medicine.

The boke of Secrets of Albertus Magnus of the Vertues of Herbes, Stones and Certaine Beasts states that by putting drowning bees in the warm ashes of pennyroyal "they shall recover their lyfe after a little tyme as by ye space of one houre," and be revived.

She also says that "an infusion of the leaves, known as Pennyroyal Tea, is an old fashioned remedy for colds and menstrual derangements".

Pennyroyal used to be used in making stuffings especially for hog's pudding, hence its common name "Pudding Grass". A famous stuffing was made of pennyroyal, honey and pepper.

green or yellowish appearance and look starved. Thus, the application of good manure or compost is most important.

Harvesting pennyroyal is difficult because it grows so low and the leaf

467

Lesser Periwinkle (Vinca minor)

Periwinkles

**Running Myrtle, Cockles,
Pennywinkle, Blue Buttons,
Sorcerer's Violet**
Vinca major and *Vinca minor*
Apocynaceae

A useful plant for ground cover, periwinkles are very hardy, thrive in shade, and are one of the best plants to grow beneath trees and other areas where a carpeting effect is desired. They have shining evergreen leaves and blue flowers in spring.

Greater Periwinkle *(Vinca major)* is larger, taller, and faster-growing than the Lesser Periwinkle *(Vinca minor)* and can be used to cover shaded banks quickly. It is propagated by root divisions and cuttings.

Medicinally, it was used as an astringent and nervine, or made into an ointment to heal piles and inflammatory conditions of the skin. A tincture was used for haemorrhages. Culpeper says that this herb is good for nervous disorders and female complaints. If chewed it is supposed to stop bleeding in the mouth and nose.

468

Pipsissewa

Ground Holly, False Wintergreen,
Pipsisway
Chimaphila umbellata
Pyrolaceae

This small evergreen of the heath family has shiny, leathery, dark green leaves in irregular whorls. The fragrant flowers, from white to rose-pink or light purple, rise above the leaves in a cluster of four to seven blossoms. The fruit is an erect five-celled capsule.

Found mostly in the more temperate northern areas of the world, it prefers an acid soil, rich in leaf-mould. It has a creeping yellow rhizome with several erect or semi-procumbent stems. It is propagated by soft wood cuttings, taken when the leaves are half-grown.

It is used in long-standing rheumatic and kidney ailments. The medicinal properties are listed as astringent, alterative, diuretic, and tonic.

The fresh leaves when bruised and applied to the skin act as a rubefacient. It is said to diminish lithic acid in the urine and it is very useful for skin diseases.

The variety, Spotted Wintergreen *(Chimaphila maculata)* has variegated foliage and very fragrant white flowers. It is said to act medicinally as a diuretic with an antiseptic influence on the urine and has been used for cystitis. The leaves and sometimes the stems are used although all parts have active properties.

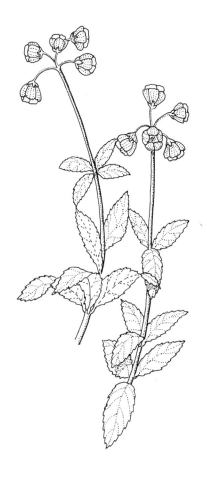

Pipsissewa
(Chimaphila umbellata)

469

Plantain

**Ripple Grass, Great Plantain,
Snakeweed, Waybread,
Englishman's Foot**
Plantago major
Plantaginaceae

Plantain is considered by many today to be a weed, but its great reputation in the herbal lore earned it notice in some of the world's great literature. Both Chaucer and Shakespeare mention the plant in their writings. It is known all over the Western world, having spread widely from its European origins.

There are many varieties of plantain, as there are more than 200 genera in the family Plantaginaceae. The most familiar, *Plantago major*, or common plantain, is characterized by its ribbed, ovate leaf and its spiky stalk with purplish-green blossoms. It has a short rhizome with many long, straight, yellow roots. The roots, leaves, and seeds can all be used.

Plaintain has been used externally to treat stings and bites and as a poultice, and internally as a tea for kidney ailments.

Culpeper noted, "Briefly, the plantains are singular good wound-herbs to heal fresh or old wounds or sores, either inward or outward." Shakespeare had characters in at least two plays recommend plaintain leaf for a "broken skin".

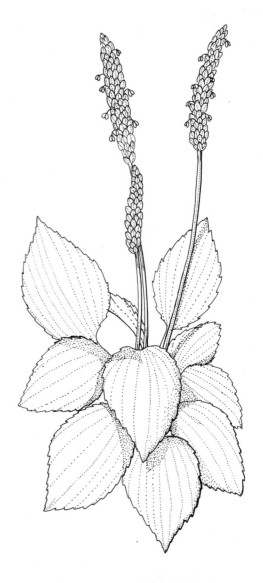

*Common Plantain
(Plantago major)*

470

Poplar

White Poplar, Quaking Aspen
Populus sp.
Salicaceae

The poplars are fast-growing, soft-wooded, deciduous trees of the willow family. They have alternate leaves, followed by catkins, Poplars grow readily in any soil, and because of their rapid growth, are often planted for wind-breaks. They are easily propagated by seed or hardwood cuttings.

White poplar is a small tree with slender, alternating branches. The broad leaves are heart-shaped, whitish with white veins, and hang on such slender stalks that they flutter restlessly. The trunk and limbs are silvery white. It should be planted against dark-leaved trees or evergreens so one may benefit from the full beauty of its form and colouring. The autumn foliage is a clear yellow.

The buds, leaves, and bark are used for their soothing, balsamic qualities, and can be made into a useful wash for burns, cuts, and scratches. The bark is regarded as a universal tonic and takes the place of Peruvian bark or quinine. It may be given freely for cases of debility, indigestion, fever, kidney, and liver ailments.

Balm of Gilead *(Populus balsamifera)* is a strong growing tree with a balsamic fragrance. The buds are boiled in olive oil or other good oil to make an excellent salve. The buds

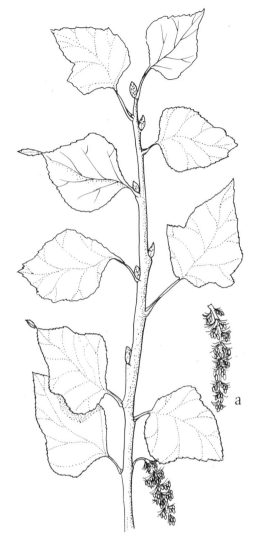

Lombardy Poplar
(Populus nigra)
(a) catkin

and bark are a stimulating tonic. The buds are used for colds, coughs, stomach and kidney ailments and as a gargle. To dissolve the resin, the buds are soaked in alcohol before being used for a tea.

471

Poppy, Opium

White Poppy, Mawseed
Papaver somniferum
Papaveraceae

Opium poppies are native to Greece and the Orient. They were grown by the Greeks, Romans, and early Chinese primarily for their seed, which was used in cooking and as a source of oil. A variety of poppy with very flavourful seeds has been developed by the Dutch from a combination of the Opium Poppy *(Papaver somniferum)* and the corn poppy *(P. Rhoeas)*. This poppy is widely grown in India, Turkey, and Persia, both for seed and for opium. The seed does not retain any of the narcotic properties, which are present only in the green seed pod.

The opium poppy is an annual which grows about one foot (30 cm) high. Its four-petalled white flowers are tinged with blue and grow to four inches (10 cm) in diameter. It requires a long growing season, and cannot be matured in the north unless plants are started indoors. This is a precarious undertaking, because the roots are very sensitive and resent transplanting. Seed may be sown in pots then the whole root ball should be transferred to the garden when the weather becomes warm. Six inches to a foot (15 to 30 cm) should be allowed for each plant, depending on variety. Soil should be rich and moist. Poppies bloom very indifferently in the shade,

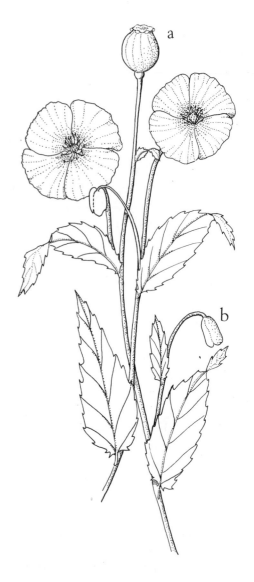

Opium Poppy
(Papaver somniferum)
(a) seed pod (b) bud

so a sunny location is important.

Pods should be allowed to dry on the plant, but must be caught before

472

they turn their salt-cellar like openings to the ground to spill their seeds. Drying can be finished on muslin indoors. When the pods are crisp, the seeds may be removed by rubbing the pods between the palms. The tiny seeds can be separated from the chaff by putting them in a coarse strainer and shaking.

Poppy seed is used principally for baked products of all kinds. It is also one of the main ingredients of commercial birdseed mixtures. Oil from the crushed seed is used as a substitute for olive oil.

Purslane

Green Purslane, Pigweed
Portulaca oleracea
Portulacaceae

Purslane is familiar to most gardeners, for it is a very common garden intruder. But those who would root it out for the compost heap would do well to save it for the salad bowl, for purslane can be cultivated as a pot-herb. It is a fleshy annual whose many branches and tiny green and reddish leaves, reddish stems, and minute yellow flowers spread rapidly along the ground. Both stems and foliage are succulent.

A native of India and Africa, purslane was introduced into Europe

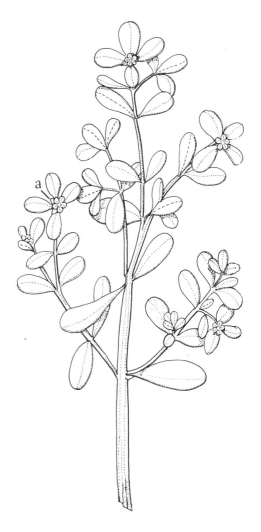

Purslane
(Portulaca oleracea)
(a) flower

as a salad plant during the Fifteenth Century. The old herbals list many medicinal applications for purslane. Culpeper, Gerard, Parkinson, and others agreed it was a good coolant, serving in "ailments of heat", fevers, inflammations, and the like. The expressed juice of the plant, taken with honey, was believed to relieve dry coughs, shortness of breath, and immoderate thirst. For fevers and inflammations of the eyes, it was bruised and applied externally. Nowadays the most common use of this succulent and nutritious herb is in salads.

Pyrethrum

Dalmation Pellitory, Insect Plant
Chrysanthemum cinerariaefolium
Compositae

Pyrethrum is the source of a safe insecticide of the same name which is widely used by organic gardeners. The flowers are dried and powdered. The powder is best used alone, but it is sometimes used as a base for more toxic and dangerous pesticides.

The plants themselves are not only pretty but useful, since the quality which makes the powdered flowers useful to the gardener makes the plants valuable in the garden. The flowers are white or pink daisy-like blossoms topping stems reaching as high as two feet (60 cm).

Pyrethrum is hard to grow from seed. It should be started in a sterile planting medium. Once established, the seedlings should be transplanted

to a limey soil in a sunny spot. Regular cultivation is important to eliminate competition from weeds. Avoid excessive watering. In the spring, the plants may be increased by root division.

The word *pyrethrum* is derived from the Greek *pyr*, meaning fire. The reference is apparently to either the colour of the flowers or to a use of the plant as a febrifuge. Curiously enough, although a genus *Pyrethrum* exists, the plants commonly known as pyrethrums are members of the *Chrysanthemum* genus.

Rose

Rosa sp.
Rosaceae

Roses have been known throughout the northern hemisphere as far back as literature records. Early poets of Greece, China, and Persia all sang praises of the rose. Dried roses have been found in Egyptian tombs. An indication of its antiquity is the fact that the name for a rose is almost the same in every European language.

To most people, the rose is best known as an aromatic and ornamental shrub, but it is used medicinally and also for culinary purposes.

There are probably more varieties of roses than there are of any other plant considered a herb. Linnaeus, in 1762, described 14 rose species, a number which he soon increased to 21. After Linnaeus had pointed the way, other botanists followed with more and more complete classifications. John Lindley in 1820 described 76 species and sub-species. In recent years over 296 species have been classified.

Species described by botanists are pure strains. They do not include crosses, hybrids, doubles, bud mutations, and "sports". The latter varieties, although not recognized by academic botanists as separate species, account for 95 per cent of the roses listed in current catalogues. It has been estimated that through the latter half of the Nineteenth and the first half of the Twentieth Century, at least 16 thousand varieties of roses were developed. Each year sees a new crop of hybrids presented to the gardener.

The herbalist is probably interested in very few of these 16 thousand varieties. One of these is the Damask rose *(Rosa damascena)*, a principal ancestor of many of the hybrids we have today. It is said to have first appeared in France at about the time of the Crusades. This rose was the source of the very best attar of roses. The whole bush is graceful, growing about three feet (90 cm) in height. The flowers come in many colours ranging from pale pink to deep red and pure white. A second important rose is the Provins rose *(R. gallica)*. It has deep red blossoms appearing one to three on a branch. It grows up to three feet (90 cm) tall and has stocky branches.

These two kinds of roses bloom only once a year. But they are historic roses, fragrant, beautiful and well worth having in the garden.

Another interesting rose is the Japanese rose or rugosa *(R. rugosa)*, a hardy shrub rose which bears many attractive fruits, or hips, in the autumn. The hips are a rich source of vitamin C. The rugosa grows six to 15 feet (1.8 to 4.6 m) tall, will endure heat, cold, dryness, sandy or clay soil, and even salt sea air. Its flowers are single, double, or semi-double, in white, pink, and red. The rugosa is a native of China, Korea, and Japan. Because it is a distinct species, it can reproduce itself from seed.

The petals of the rose are the aromatic heart of the plant. These have been traditionally harvested and processed for their oil for centuries, the French and Bulgarians producing the most sought-after attars of roses. A technique for extracting attar of roses on a small scale is outlined in Chapter Four, which also covers the use of rose petals in pot-pourris, sachets, and other aromatic items.

While the rose is undoubtedly best known for its fragrance, it is also valuable as a culinary herb. Most of us have heard of rose hip tea, but the fruit or "hips" of the rose can be used in a variety of ways by the imaginative cook. After the petals drop in the autumn the hips appear as pods of various sizes and colours. The quantity of vitamin C concentrated in rose hips is said by experts to be as much as 60 times that found in oranges. In addition to this goodness, hips have a pleasant flavour, being fruity and sweet. In the early autumn the large bushes are covered with the orange and red fruits. Some people enjoy eating them fresh, but usually they are collected, trimmed, and cooked lightly before being used in a variety of recipes.

Because vitamin C is elusive and difficult to retain through a drying process, rose hips are not easily prepared in powder form. It is best to make an extract or pureé of them. This can then be stored with a minimum loss of food value, and used throughout the year by the tablespoonful or in fruit juices, salads, soups, and sauces.

If you wish to prepare your own rose hip syrup, follow these four simple rules:

1. Trim both ends of the rose hip with a pair of scissors before cooking.

2. Use stainless steel knives, wooden spoons, earthenware or china bowls, and glass or enamel saucepans.

3. Cook quickly with the lid on, to avoid excessive loss of vitamin C.

4. When the hips are cooked, strain out the seeds or break them down by rubbing the cooked pulp through a sieve.

To prepare an extract of the rose hip one must first chill the hips to inactivate the enzymes which might otherwise cause the loss of vitamin C. Remove blossom ends, stems, and

leaves, then quickly wash the hips. Boil up one and a half times as much water as you have rose hips, then add the rose hips and simmer 15 minutes. Let it stand in a pottery utensil for 24 hours, after which strain off the extract. Boil, add two tablespoons of lemon juice for each pint, and finally pour into jars and seal.

A rose hip pureé may be made as follows: Take two pounds (just under one kilo) of rose hips and 32 fluid ounces (909 ml) of water. Stew the hips in a saucepan with the lid on until tender. This will take about 20 minutes. Then press the mixture through a sieve. The result will be a brownish-tinted pureé of about the same consistency and thickness as jam.

In Sweden, rose hip soup is a popular, healthy dish. It is easy to make. The hips are crushed and boiled for ten minutes, then strained and again brought to the boil and thickened with four level teaspoonfuls of potato flour (you can use soy-bean or whole wheat flour) which has been prepared with 16 fluid ounces (454 ml) of cold water. This soup can be served hot or cold.

The rose is also used medicinally. The red rose *(R. gallica)* has been listed as an official drug plant. The petals are used to mask unpleasant odours in medicinal preparations. The hips of the dog rose *(R. canina)*, with the pulp separated from the seeds, can be made into a conserve which can be used as an astringent, and is also reported to be good for diarrhoea, dysentery, and coughs. A tea made

Dog Rose (Rosa canina)

from the powdered dried buds is supposed to check profuse menstruation.

A volatile oil is made by distilling the leaves of the cabbage rose *(R. centifolia)*. Mixed with water it makes a soothing eye-water, and is much used in beauty lotions. The petals make a laxative syrup. The flowers of the damascus rose *(R. damascena)* were also used for laxative purposes. The flowers of the red or French rose *(R. gallica)* can be made into a conserve or infusion useful as a gargle and for fevers. Culpeper says, "the distilled water, made of the full blown flower is cooling, and of good use for sore inflamed eyes."

The rose is primarily a beautiful ornamental shrub. Many gardeners devote their space solely to roses.

Roses require sun, free circulation of air, and porous, well-drained, acid soil with an alkalinity value of between pH 5 and 6.

The best plants to buy are two-year-old, field-grown, budded stock. Roses may be planted in the autumn or spring. Most nurseries dig their roses in the autumn, store them through the winter, and plant in the spring. If they are purchased in the autumn and held over for spring planting, they should be heeled in at the bottom of an 18 inch (46 cm) trench, covered with loose soil, and mulched after the ground is frozen.

A trench should be dug in the soil to a depth of 24 inches (60 cm) for best results. Experiments have proved that roses planted in more shallow soil will give equal results with those in deeper beds during the first year, but after the second year the roses in 24 inch (60 cm) beds will be superior.

In preparing a rose bed, the top spade's depth of soil is removed and put aside. The lower spade's depth should then be removed and discarded. Replace it with the top loam, plus amounts of rotted manure and humus equal in volume to about one-quarter and one-half that of the loam. This mixture should be allowed to settle for two weeks before planting.

A hole slightly larger in diameter than the spread roots of the plant should be dug just deep enough to bury the bud graft when planting. Soil should be heaped cone-shaped in the centre of the hole, and the plant seated on it. Damaged roots should be pruned back. Long straggly roots should also be cut back and the tips of most others removed. Once the rose is in place, the hole should be half-filled with soil and a pail of water poured into it, to wash soil among the small rootlets. When the water has seeped away, the hole should be filled flush and the soil tamped. Finally, prune to six to eight inches (15 to 20 cm) above the ground.

Roses are seldom grown from seed because seed-grown plants will revert to species. It is possible to propagate species from seed, but this requires too much work for most gardeners.

Several methods of handling rose seeds, which are contained in the hip, are suggested. One is the "ripening" method. Hips are mashed to a pulp and permitted to ferment at a low temperature of about 40°F (4°C) for about 60 to 120 days. Then they are washed and layered in humus in a seed box or flower pot, and placed outdoors on the north side of a building to stay cool.

A second method is to remove the seed from the hip and, without fermenting, place it in leaf-mould or peat-moss in a tray or pot outside. Weathering during the cold months helps the seed to germinate. A third, and simpler method, is to plant the seed directly in the garden in the autumn. If this method is adopted, seed should be sown about an inch (2.5 cm) deep, and six inches (15 cm) apart. After germination, plants may be moved to stand a foot (30 cm) apart and permitted to grow for two years before being moved to the shrubbery border.

A practical method for propagating roses true to the parent is by cuttings or slips. Cuttings, taken from the most healthy plants, are made at a point where the cane breaks with a snap. If it bends, the wood is too tough. If it crushes, it is too green.

Cuttings may be set directly into an existing rose bed or in a corner of the garden where they will receive the morning sun only. Cover them with glass jars, pushing the jars securely into the soil, then water well. It is not necessary to water them too often, because the moisture which condenses inside the glass jar will keep them sufficiently wet.

If the cutting forms roots, new

shoots will appear within three or four weeks. Jars are not removed until the cuttings have roots enough to supply plenty of moisture to the leaves, possibly not until the following spring. Cuttings may be made at any time from June until the first frosts. If they are made during July or August, it is well to shade them from a strong afternoon sun.

Roses need plenty of water when the season is dry, but it should be supplied at weekly intervals in quantities large enough to reach the deepest roots rather than in small daily doses. Mulch may be spread around the plants to conserve moisture if the weather becomes hot and dry. Compost made up of such waste as wheat hulls, straw, decayed or shredded leaves, or lawn clippings may be used. If peat moss is used, it should be moistened before it is applied. It is advisable to mix a nitrogen fertilizer with the mulch.

A formula developed especially for spring and summer rose feeding contains the following: two parts fish-meal, two parts dried blood, one part wood ashes (if soil is very acid), one part phosphate rock, and one part greensand. The first two ingredients supply nitrogen; wood ashes supply potash; and phosphate rock and greensand provide phosphorus. Application of this fertilizer may be repeated each month until the beginning of August.

Bedding roses are pruned in the spring when new shoots are about a quarter of an inch (6 mm) long. Dead wood, all wood with brown, dried, or shrivelled bark, should be trimmed off first. The plant should then be inspected for injury, and any branches injured by the winter winds or frost should be trimmed back. Next, rough, gnarled branches with weak twigs, and thin, weak, shoots should be removed. Then, if many good blooms are required, the remainder of the branches must be shortened by a third of their length. If fewer blooms are required, shorten by two-thirds.

Rosemary

Polar Plant, Compass-weed
Rosmarinus officinalis
Libiatae

Rosemary is steeped in religious traditions. It is a symbol of fidelity and remembrance in two of the holiest of Christian ceremonies, the wedding and the funeral. Its more temporal uses as a medicinal and culinary herb are dazzling in number and variety. And it is an attractive addition to any garden.

The most common variety, *Rosmarinus officinalis*, is a perennial evergreen shrub that grows to a height of two to four feet (60 cm to 1.2 m). A native of the Mediterranean, rosemary sometimes reaches six feet (1.8 m) in warm climates and good soil, such as can be found in that part of the world. Legend has it that the

479

rosemary bush grows to six feet in 33 years—the stature and life of Christ—and then, in obeisance to Him, ceases its vertical growth so as never to stand higher than He did.

Rosemary can be propagated by seeds, cuttings, or layering. Seeds are usually avoided because of the low percentage of germination. Generally, only one to five of every ten seeds planted will germinate. And it may take up to three years to produce a reasonable bush from seed. For gardeners who have no choice but to seed, planting should be done indoors in light, rich, and well-drained soil as early as January. Save at least one plant for cuttings in subsequent years.

Cuttings are made by taking a six-inch (15 cm) end tip of new growth and burying its lower four inches (10 cm) in sand or vermiculite, along a shady border of the garden. August is the best time. If the cuttings are planted outside, cover each one with an inverted glass. They will be ready to transplant in two to three months. To layer new shoots, just weight one or two of the lower branches of a mature bush beneath the soil.

Rosemary will develop into a highly ornamental shrub with a woody stem and boughs of evergreen needles which are dark green on top and lighter on the undersides. Blue flowers, light to dark, form at the tips of branches in the spring. The flowers are white on the more obscure variety *Rosmarinus officinalis* var. *alba*. Otherwise, there is little difference.

Legend attributes the delicate blue of the *R. officinalis* flowers to the Virgin Mary. As this one goes, Mary draped her azure cloak over a white-bloomed rosemary bush during the flight from Egypt, whereupon the noble plant embraced the hue of the Virgin's garment.

The name "rosemary" sometimes is said to be a similar Virginal tribute. More likely, the name is a derivative of the Latin *ros*, dew, and *marinus*, of the sea. The plant's native habitat was among the misty hills bordering the Mediterranean Sea.

Rosemary flourishes with occasional watering, although it needs well-drained, slightly alkaline soil. It cannot stand being dehydrated, a danger that exists particularly indoors.

Although rosemary can be left outside all year round, it cannot stand heavy frosts. The best approach is to plant along the south face of a wall where plastic or glass winter green-houses can be constructed around the plant. Plants can also be brought inside for the winter, but care must be taken to supply enough room and enough moisture for the roots. Spray the branches every few days as well. Neither the blue nor the white *R. officinalis* varieties can stand temperatures below about 27°F (−2.8°C). The danger point for *R. officinalis* 'Prostratus', a creeping blue-flowered variety, is a few degrees higher.

R. officinalis 'Prostratus', in addition to making a bright and fragrant covering for banks, is a lovely indoor plant when planted in a hanging pot and allowed to cascade over the sides.

Rosemary
(Rosmarinus officinalis)
(a) flower

All varieties prefer sunny or semi-shady locations.

It is uncertain how rosemary was dispersed from its Mediterranean homeland. One theory is that Roman conquerors brought it to northern Europe and England. Another says the Crusaders brought it home after adopting it from their Saracen foes, who used it as a balm for their wounds.

European herbalists quickly bestowed on rosemary a reputation for the ability to strengthen the memory. That attribute, no doubt, gave rise to the use of rosemary as a symbol for constancy. Rosemary sprigs, dipped in scented water, were woven into bridal bouquets or exchanged by the newly-weds as a token of their troth. Richly gilded and bound in multi-coloured ribbons, the sprigs were presented to the wedding guests as reminders of virtuous fidelity.

At funerals, rosemary sprigs were tossed into the grave as a pledge that the life and good deeds of the departed would not soon be forgotten. The Seventeenth Century poet Robert Herrick wrote:

> *Grow for two ends, it matters not at all,*
> *Be't for my bridal or my burial.*

Shakespeare's Ophelia, mourning Hamlet's madness in Act IV, Scene VI of *Hamlet*, laments:

> *There's rosemary, that's for*
> * remembrance:*
> *pray you, love, remember;*
> *and there is pansies, that's for*
> * thoughts.*

Mediaeval herbalists bedecked rosemary with wonderous abilities to cure nervous afflictions, and even to

481

restore youth. William Langham in the Sixteenth Century prescribed: "Seethe much Rosemary and bathe therein to make thee lusty, lively, joyfull, likeing and youngly." *Bankes Herbal* adds: "Make thee a box of the wood and smell it and it shall preserve thy youth."

Rosemary was also used extensively in manufacturing a favourite Renaissance instrument, the lute.

As a curative tonic, elixirs of rosemary extract were said to be of value, in the words of Parkinson, "inwardly for the head and heart; and outwardly for the sinews and joints."

Rosemary tea is made by infusing three-quarters of a pint (426 ml) of water with one ounce (28 g) of young rosemary tips or a heaped teaspoonful of dried leaves. Taken with the juice of half a lemon and a touch of honey, the tea is said to alleviate headaches and help the restless sleep at night.

Rosemary wine can be made, according to an ancient recipe, by soaking a handful of six-inch (15 cm) tips in 3¼ pints (1.8 l) of white wine for a few days.

From a 1759 recipe book comes a formula for spirit of rosemary:

Gather a Pound and a half of the fresh Tops of Rosemary, cut them into a Gallon of clean and fine Melasses Spirit (probably dark rum), and let them stand all Night; next Day distill off five Pints with a gentle Heat. This is of the Nature of Hungary-water, but not being so strong as that is usually made, it is better for taking inwardly. A Spoonful is a Dose, and it is good against all nervous Complaints.

Hungary water itself, according to legend, was invented by a gnarled hermit to cure his queen, Elizabeth of Hungary, of paralysis of the joints. The water, actually a powerful distillate of rosemary oil in alcohol, is said to cure stiffness of the joints when rubbed on externally.

What is thought to be an elaboration on the original Hungary water formula is offered in a 1732 herbal. Take a handful of 12 inch (30 cm) tips and chop them into one inch (2.5 cm) slivers. Add them to 6½ pints (3.7 l) of brandy. Add almost as much myrtle as rosemary, and let the concoction stand three days. Then distill it to an oily reduction.

Culpeper says a "coarser way" of making Hungary water is to add a few drops of oil of rosemary to spirits, possibly vodka. Pure oil is available commercially, but Culpeper suggests filling a narrow-mouthed bottle with flowers, covering the mouth with a fine cloth, and inverting the bottle into a waterglass. When set in the sun, the solar heat will drive the oil from the flowers, and it will collect in the lower glass "to be preserved as precious for divers uses, both inward and outward. . ."

A pleasant sachet and insect-deterrent can be made from equal parts of rosemary, lavender, and grated lemon peel. For a pleasant mouthwash, infuse one-third of a teaspoonful each of rosemary, anise, and mint in 8 fluid ounces (227 ml) of water.

One ounce (28 g) each of rosemary and sage infused for 24 hours in three-quarters of a pint (426 ml) of water makes a pleasant hair tonic that can be used to combat dandruff. After infusion, strain the liquid and add a teaspoonful of powdered borax.

A delightful fragrance can be made by mixing a handful each of crushed rosemary and juniper berries in a pan of water. Heat well and stir; then keep the mixture on a radiator in winter or in sunlight during summer. The aromatic emissions were used for centuries in French hospitals and courts to ward off disease. This is called the *incensier* method. Culpeper recommended burning rosemary, "to expel the contagion of the pestilence".

Rosemary also has a major place in the modern kitchen as a tangy herb to flavour beef, veal, pork, lamb, poultry, soups, stuffings, sauces, and salad dressings. It can be purchased in the form of dried and chopped leaves. If it is available fresh, cuttings from the new growth can be laid directly on roasts and poultry to add garnish as well as flavour.

Rue

Herb-of-Grace, Garden Rue
Ruta graveolens
Rutaceae

Rue, the herb of grace, has been used as a herbal medicine for thousands of years. It was prescribed for at least 84 different ailments in Pliny's day. Its generic name, *Ruta*, is derived from a Greek word meaning "to set free", indicating the ancient belief in its potency to relieve maladies and illnesses.

Rue was famous as an antidote to poisons of all kinds. Gerard wrote: "if a man be annointed with the juice of rue, the poison of wolf's bane, muchrooms, or todestooles, the biting of serpents, stinging of scorpions, spiders, bees, hornets and wasps will not hurt him."

Rue is said by some to have been the main ingredient in the poison antidote for Mithridates, the King of Pontus, who experimented with poisons and their antidotes. When he tried to commit suicide, he found that he was unable to die from the poison (some sources attribute this immunity to herbs of the genus *Eupatoria*). He finally persuaded a slave to stab him to death. Rue is used in China today to counter poisons and is recommended as an antidote to malarial poisoning.

Rue is a hardy evergreen perennial, native to southern Europe. The lower stem is woody, and the leaves are alternate and bluish-green in colour,

483

and bi-pinnate or tri-pinnate. The foliage is very aromatic, emitting a powerful odour. The taste is bitter. The flowers are greenish-yellow in terminal panicles, blossoming from June until September. The seeds that form after pollination are greyish.

Rue is easily propagated from seeds which should be started indoors in February for planting outside in May. When the seedlings are about two inches (5 cm) high, they may be planted outdoors, allowing 18 inches (46 cm) between each plant. Rue should be planted in a sunny place for best results, although the plants will do fairly well almost anywhere.

Rue can also be propagated by cuttings or rooted slips made in early spring. Cuttings should be planted in the shade until well rooted, when they can be transplanted into a permanent, sunny location.

The herb can be harvested several times a year. Harvest the leaves (the part of the plant used in herbal remedies) before the flower forms. After the first cutting, top-dress the plant with good compost or organic fertilizer to stimulate a second growth.

The herb is usually used fresh, but it can be dried in the shade. It should be stored in an air-tight container to avoid loss of quality.

Rue's nickname, "herb of grace", lends it holy connotations. Brushes made from rue were, at one time, used to sprinkle the holy water at the ceremony preceding High Mass. It was also called the "herb of repentance", presumably because of this same use.

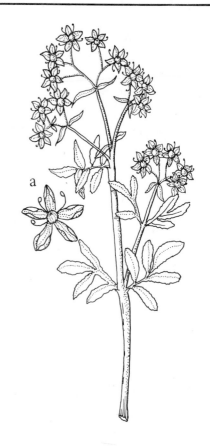

Rue
(Ruta graveolens)
(a) flower

Ophelia, in *Hamlet*, refers to this use of the herb when she says, "There's rue for you and here's some for me; we may call it herb of grace o'Sundays."

Presumably, the herb's use in the church led many during the Middle Ages to believe that it was a powerful defence against witches. Rue was commonly used to ward off spells. It is said that rue was the herb given by Mercury to Ulysses to free him from the charms of the witch Circe.

Rue has been regarded from the earliest times as being successful in warding off contagious diseases, and for preventing the attacks of fleas and other noxious insects. It was an important part of the bunch of aromatic herbs carried into court by judges as a safeguard against the fevers, diseases, and pests that prisoners brought with them from the jails. It was often strewn in the court, and sprigs were placed on the dock benches to disinfect them. Gerard gives an interesting recipe for a disinfecting paste: "The leaves of rue eaten with the kernels of Walnuts or figs stamped together and made into a masse or paste, is good against all eville aires, the pestilence, or plague."

Rue water was sprinkled about the house to kill fleas. It was also placed or grown near stables or around manure piles to repel flies.

Culpeper recommends it as a cure for sciatica and pains in the joints. For these purposes, the affected area was commonly "annointed" with rue. Culpeper also recommends:

. . . the juice thereof warmed in a pomegranate shell or rind, and dropped into the ears, helps the pain of them. The juice of it and fennel, with a little honey, and the gall of a cock put thereunto, helps the dimness of the eyesight.

Leyel said that rue "bestows second sight, and it certainly preserves ordinary sight, by strengthening the ocular muscles." Pliny tells us that Greek painters used rue to achieve a second sight and to relieve their eyes after working long hours in dim light. It was used for similar purposes during the Middle Ages.

Both the fresh and dried plants are used in compounding herbal remedies, although the latter is less powerful. One common use is as a tonic with sedative qualities against colic, and as a stimulant for the circulation. It is also taken as infusion of one teaspoonful of the dried herb to a cup of boiling water, to prevent ageing.

The medicinal virtues of rue are due to a volatile oil found in glands distributed over the entire plant. Oil of rue is made from the fresh herb, and may be administered in doses of from one to five drops. The oil may, however, cause allergic reactions in some people in the form of a long-lasting rash similar to poison ivy rash. In this case, it is best to avoid any future contact with this herb.

Rue is little used as a condiment because of its strong taste. However, the Italians sometimes add a few chopped leaves of the herb to salads. Rue leaves are also eaten to refresh the mouth and to relieve giddiness, hysterical spasm, or nervous headaches.

If you have some doubt as to where to obtain rue, remember that the Greeks believed that rue stolen from a neighbour's garden did better than a plant acquired honestly. But if you are caught red-handed, don't blame the publishers of this book!

485

Safflower

Dyers Saffron, Fake Saffron,
Flores Carthami, Bastard Saffron
Carthamus tinctorius
Compositae

Safflower is an important annual with dark green and shiny leaves which have prickly orange hairs on the margins. It resembles the thistle in foliage and form. The flowers are made up of clusters of green bracts, topped by tufts of deep yellow florets, turning orange as they mature. They are very ornamental when grown in clumps. Seeds ripen in August and look like curious white teeth with stained ends.

The seeds are the source of safflower oil. Dried blossoms are used as a substitute for saffron for colouring chicken gravy, soups, and pickles; the orange colouring is water-soluble.

From the dried flowers a resinous red dye was made and used for dying silk, or mixed with talcum powder for rouge.

The plant was found in the Egyptian tombs. It grows in poor, dry soil, in full sun. Sow seeds in April where they are to grow as they do not transplant well.

The flowers infused in boiling water are used medicinally as a laxative and diaphoretic.

Saffron

Crocus
Crocus sativus
Iridaceae

Saffron is the herb that brings late-season colour to the garden. As the weather turns cold and the trees begin shedding their leaves, the lovely lilac flowers of the saffron appear. Without the flowers, however, the plant itself is undistinguished, having narrow, grass-like leaves.

The flower, in addition to providing the plant with distinction in the garden, holds the useful element, the stigma. Each flower has three scarlet-orange stigmas which are collected and dried, then used to dye a variety of foodstuffs and textiles. Medicinally, it is a carminative, diaphoretic, and emmenagogue.

It is best to purchase saffron plants, since the new plants do not blossom for three years. Moreover, saffron must be hand-pollinated to get seed, so the best method of propagation is bulb division. The bulbs can be divided annually or only once in three years. But whichever method is used, the plants should not remain in the same spot more than three years. The corms are planted in late July to early August. Place them six inches (15 cm) deep and six inches (15 cm) from neighbouring plants. The soil should be light and rich, the location sheltered.

If you expect to collect the stigmas,

be sure to plant thousands of saffron, because 60 thousand stigmas weigh only a pound (just under half a kilo). Obviously, the dried material is very expensive, and, as might be expected, the stigmas are often adulterated (or stretched) with arnica or calendula petals or safflower florets.

Sage

Garden Sage, Sawge
Salvia officinalis
Labiatae

Sage enjoyed widespread popularity as a virtual panacea for all ailments of the body when herbal medicine was practised universally. Fortunately, the decline of herbal medicine did not leave this pleasant herb in present-day obscurity, for as the medicinal use of sage waned, its role in cookery increased. Nevertheless, sage still has a place in herbal medicine. Although there are few who still believe that sage can cure tuberculosis and treat snake bites effectively, it is said to be of value in reducing nervous headaches and sore throats.

The plant's very name is an off-shoot of its once-held power to pro-long life. An ancient Latin proverb says: *"Cur moriatur homo cui Salvia crescit in horto?"* (Why should a man die

when sage flourishes in his garden?)."

The generic name *Salvia* means "health" or "salvation". The specific name *officinalis* indicates that sage was among herbs of medicinal value listed in the official pharmacopoeia.

A native of the Mediterranean, sage was spread throughout Europe by the Romans. Centuries later, when East-West trade developed, European sage became such a highly prized export item that it was worth three or four times its weight in China tea.

The Seventeenth Century herbalist Gerard said of sage, "It is singularly good for the head and brain, it quickeneth the senses and memory, strengtheneth the sinews, restoreth health to those that have the palsy, and taketh away shakey trembling of the members."

Sir John Hill, another herbalist, wrote that sage:

will retard that rapid progress of decay that treads upon our heels so fast in the latter years of life, will preserve the faculties and memory, more valuable to the rational mind than life itself without them; and will relieve under that faintness, strengthen under that weakness and prevent absolutely that sad depression of spirits, which age often feels and always fears, which will long prevent the hands from trembling and the eyes from dimness and make the lamp of life, so long as nature lets it burn, burn brightly.

In the Ninth Century, a European herbalist proclaimed, "Amongst my herbs, Sage holds the place of honour; of good scent it is, and full of virtue for many ills."

It was, and still is, a popular plant.

There are more than a dozen varieties of sage with varying colourations, leaf shapes, and life cycles. *S. officinalis*, being the most popular, is the one discussed here.

Even the *S. officinalis* will vary in colouring and leaf markings from plant to plant. If you should happen to cultivate a plant whose markings please you, propagate others from that plant by cutting or pegging. Plants started from seed often will not be consistent in markings.

The typical *S. officinalis* is a foot (30 cm) or more high with a squarish stem and rounded oblong leaves supported by short stems. Purplish flowers appear in August in whorls at the upper end of the plant. The leaves and stems are coated with stubbly silver-grey hair that has earned the plant the Arabic common name of "camel's tongue".

Sage is a hardy perennial that will withstand most British winters, but it should not be allowed to outlive three or four years, because of the tendency of its stems to become woody and tough. Each spring, the woody growth should be trimmed away. Sage is easy to start from seed because the seeds are large and can be spaced and observed well in their early growth. Start the seeds indoors in March or outside in April. Plant the seeds a foot (30 cm) apart.

Decisive factors are a sunny, wind-protected area with neutral soil, a good calcium supply, and plenty of moisture, especially in the early stages. Compost can be applied, but fresh

Sage
(Salvia officinalis)
(a) flower

manure should be avoided because it produces an undesirable flavour in the herb. Because sage likes a well-aerated soil, early spring hoeing and cultivation are important.

The last autumn harvesting should be no later than September, and only leaves and stems high up on the plant should be taken. A light September harvest is all that will be possible the first year. In subsequent years, at least two cuttings will be available.

Dry the leaves in the shade until they're crisp. For tea, just break them up by hand. For seasoning, rub them through a fine sieve. The flavour keeps well after drying.

Experts on companion planting suggest growing sage near rosemary. They say the two herbs stimulate one another. Sage will also protect cabbage from its insect enemies and make it more digestible. Young cucumber and grass shoots, however, are inimical to sage and their growth could be stunted by a nearby sage bush.

The old herbalist Culpeper said sage is "of excellent use to help the memory, warming and quickening the senses". He said it's also "profitable for all pains in the head coming of cold rheumatic humours, as also for all pains in the joints, whether inwardly or outwardly."

Maude Grieve, the Twentieth Century herbalist, said an infusion of sage can be prepared "simply by pouring three-quarters of a pint (426 ml) of boiling water onto one ounce (28 g) of the dried herb, the dose being from a wineglassful to half a teacupful, as often as required, but the old-fashioned way of making it is more elaborate and the result is a pleasant drink, cooling in fevers, and also a cleanser and purifier of the blood. Half an ounce (14 g) of fresh sage leaves, one ounce (28 g) of sugar, the juice of one lemon or one and a quarter ounces (35 g) of grated rind, are infused in a quart (1.1 l) of boiling water and strained off after half an hour." She added a Jamaican variation in which lime juice is substituted for the lemon juice. She said this sage tea "is highly serviceable as a stimulant in debility of the stomach and nervous system and weakness of digestion generally." One use for a super strength distillate of sage tea is as a tinting agent to darken greying hair. Sage, rubbed daily on the teeth, however, is said to keep them sparkling white.

A tonic wine can be made by blending a quantity of fresh sage leaves with a good red wine such as claret or burgundy. Run the blender on high speed for a couple of minutes, until the sage leaves have been pulverized and suspended throughout the wine. Then return the sage wine concentrate to its original bottle.

Use finely crushed sage leaves to flavour cheese, or sprinkle them over buttered bread. Use sage to flavour sausages, fowl and pork; one of its properties is that it aids the digestibility of heavy, greasy meats.

Use it sparingly at first because it has a heavy, almost dominating flavour. To tone sage down, some cooks say that parsley added in large measure will take the edge off its pungency.

For a unique after-dinner delicacy, brush egg white diluted with a little water over fresh sage leaves. Sprinkle powdered sugar lightly over the leaves. In addition to making an interesting light dessert, the sage leaves will soothe the dyspeptic.

An early Nineteenth Century recipe for sage and onion sauce recommends:

Chop very fine an ounce (28 g) of onion and a half-ounce (14 g) of green sage leaves, put them in a stamper with four teaspoonsful of water, simmer gently for ten minutes, then put in a teaspoonful of pepper and salt and one ounce (28 g) of fine breadcrumbs. Mix well together then pour to it a 4 fluid ounces (112 ml) of broth, gravy, or melted butter, stir well together and simmer a few minutes longer. This is a relishing sauce for roast pork, goose, or duck, or with green peas, or Maigre Days.

Sage is no stranger in today's cookbooks either. You will find it mentioned often in any book that believes a herb rack is to be used for more than decorating a blank wall in the kitchen.

St. John's Wort

St. John's Blood, Mary's Sweat
Hypericum perforatum
Hypericaceae

St. John's wort is a perennial which grows to a height of one to three feet (30 to 90 cm). It has bright yellow flowers and unusual black-spotted leaves. The specific name *perforatum* is a reference to the leaf spots, which

appear to be holes, but which are actually subsurface oil glands.

The source of the most common name is open to speculation. Some tie it to a relation between the flowers and St. John the Baptist's birthday, which was the summer solstice; others relate it to the blood red oil that the

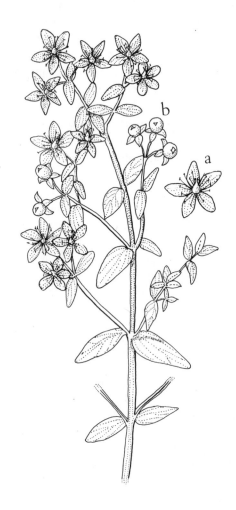

St. John's Wort
(Hypericum perforatum)
(a) flower (b) seed pod

leaf glands contain. It is sometimes called St. John's blood and is also known as Mary's sweat. The somewhat mystical religious ties of the plant are clear, however, and the plant was considered valuable in exorcising evil spirits. The generic name *Hypericum* is from the Greek, meaning "over an apparition".

It has been used as an astringent, nervine, and aromatic. Some valued it as a vulnerary. Others used it for coughs, lung ailments, and particularly in urinary troubles. An infusion of one ounce (28 g) of the herb to three-quarters of a pint (426 ml) of boiling water was prescribed in wineglass doses.

Salsify

Salsafy, Purple Goat's Beard,
Vegetable Oyster
Tragopogon porrifolius
Compositae

Salsify, sometimes spelt salsafy, is a pot-herb, grown for its root, which is harvested, stored, and cooked much as one would carrots or beetroots.

The plant was not originally a British species, but it can be found here in moist meadows, where it has escaped from garden cultivation.

The plant is fairly easily grown,

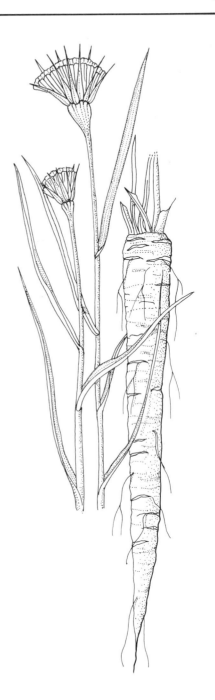

Salsify
(Tragopogon porrifolius)

provided the seeds are well watered from the time of sowing until the seedlings are well established. The seeds should be sown early. For the roots to form properly, the soil must be open and friable.

Savory, Summer

Satureia hortensis

Savory, Winter

Satureia montana
Labiatae

Sarsaparilla

Smilax Aspera
Liliaceae

This herb is a native of Central and South America and the West Indies, which was brought to Europe during the Sixteenth Century by the Spaniards. It is grown in Italy and Spain and other warm countries throughout Europe and Asia.

Sarsaparilla is a perennial climber with roots up to a yard (1 m) in length. It has dark green, glossy leaves which are heart-shaped and clusters of star-shaped greenish-white flowers. Depending on the variety the berries are either black or red.

The root is the part of the plant used medicinally which is reputed to have tonic, demulcent, alterative, stimulant, and sometimes diuretic and diaphoretic properties. Nowadays it is used in the making of soft drinks.

Summer savory is by far the most popular of more than a dozen different species of the aromatic *Satureia* genus. Several species have been introduced into Britain, but only two, the annual summer or garden savory and the perennial winter savory, are grown here.

A hardy annual that tends to grow symmetrical branches, summer savory can be grown outdoors, where it reaches 18 inches (46 cm) high, or indoors where it will be somewhat smaller. Now used almost exclusively in the kitchen, it nonetheless was once held to have medicinal properties.

Culpeper said:

Both summer and winter savory are good for heating, drying, and carminative actions, expelling wind from the stomach and bowels, and are good in asthma and other affections of the breast . . .

Keep it dry and make conserves and syrups of it for your use, for which purpose the summer kind is best. This kind is both hotter and drier than the winter kind.

Both savories were applied to the stings of bees and wasps to ease the pain. Culpeper went as far as recommending this herb as a remedy for deafness.

Summer savory makes a delightful tea. Make it in the usual manner by infusing one ounce (28 g) of the herb in three-quarters of a pint (426 ml) of boiling water. Add one and a half tablespoonfuls to 4 ounces (113 g) of creamery butter for a tasty spread. Egg dishes profit by the addition of summer savory, and so do nearly all kinds of meat, fowl, and green salads.

The ancient Romans used summer savory to flavour vinegar. Virgil, renowned as a beekeeper as well as a poet, made sure his hives had easy access to the herb, for it enhanced the honey.

Roots of the summer savory bush are well-divided and spread laterally through the upper layer of soil. They produce a plant that is equally well-branched above ground, with leaves that are dark green in the shape of wide needles, half an inch (13 mm) long. It flowers in July, producing light pink to violet flowers in the leaf axles, in little bunches of up to five flowers. The nut-shaped seeds are dark brown to black; they germinate in two or three weeks when exposed to light at outside temperatures. Their viability decreases rapidly after the first year.

Savory is a fast grower and is best sown directly in rows outside, nine inches to a foot (23 to 30 cm) apart, or broadcast and later thinned. Shallow seeding, not deeper than one-eighth of an inch (3 mm) is important for proper germination. If the top soil dries out quickly, water the seed lightly

Summer Savory
(Satureia hortensis)

to keep it moist. Water after sunset to avoid crusting of the top soil.

Since it grows quickly and will shade the soil in a short time it acts as its own mulch. Special care should be taken, though, to keep the soil free from weeds in its early growth. Weeding can become very difficult if

493

they are allowed to develop and tangle themselves around its early growth. Mounding slightly around the base will help to keep the plants upright.

Dwarfing or slow growth will most likely be due to lack of water. Savory's moisture requirements are very high, so be sure to keep it moist during dry weather. Indoor pots of summer savory should be hand-sprayed with an atomizer at least twice a week. Moderate feeding is sufficient, for it prefers a soil that is light and only modestly nutritious. Avoid fresh manure.

Experts on companion planting have noted that summer savory aids onions in their growth, so it makes a pleasant as well as a useful border around them. It also makes a beneficial neighbour to green beans, both in the garden and in the cooking pot.

Harvest when the plants are six inches (15 cm) high, and continue all summer. The object is to prevent summer savory from flowering, after which the leaves will curl and turn yellow and brown. Early harvesting should take just the tops off the plants. The main harvest, when the plant insists on flowering, should be carried out as soon as the flowers open. The whole plant should be taken and dried.

Because summer savory is a "hot" herb, drying takes little time. Spread the whole plant on a fine screen or paper, and allow it to dry in warm shade. In a climate with low humidity, summer savory could even be dried outside in the sun provided the drying would be complete within two days. However, this is unlikely in Britain

and artificial means will be necessary; nonetheless, the leaves dry well. They can also be frozen.

A word about winter savory. This hardy, dwarf bush perennial prefers a poor, coarse soil. It does not need as much water as its summertime counterpart. As a matter of fact, too much moisture will decrease its hardiness. This variety develops pale lavender flowers a month earlier than summer savory. It is propagated either from seed sown the same way as summer savory, or by dividing its root cluster in April. The vitality of this perennial will decline after a few years, so the wisest course is to grow a new crop by seed or division every other year. Take clippings as you need them, but be sparing in cold weather.

Sedge, Sweet

Calamus, Sweet Flag, Sweet Root, Sweet Myrtle
Acorus calamus
Araceae

This is a reed-like aquatic plant thriving in ditches, on the banks of lakes and streams, and on marshy ground. The sword-shaped leaves are sheathed about the stalk at their base. They arise erect, falling at the tips, and are about three feet long (1 m). A flower stalk projects at a slight

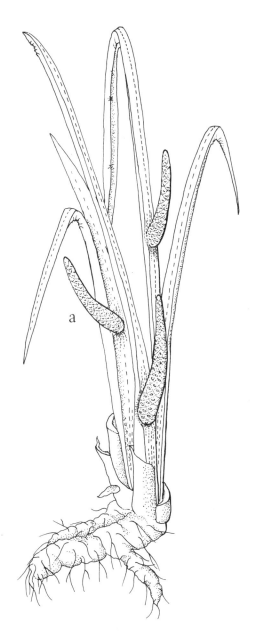

Sweet Sedge
(Acorus calamus)
(a) flower

angle from the axils of the outer leaves. The entire plant has a spicy, lemon fragrance.

While marshes, low meadows, and the waterside are the favourite habitat of sweet sedge, it is easily grown in any spot, as long as moisture is abundant. The clumps of plants or the rhizome, or rootstock, are divided in early spring or autumn, and the divisions are set about a foot (30 cm) apart and well covered.

The aroma of the plant is the basis for its long history in herb lore. The foliage was widely used as a strewing herb, as the aroma released when bruised under foot could mask odours. The lower stem and rhizome can be dried, cut into pieces, and used to scent drawers, and chests.

The rhizome is collected in the early spring or late autumn of its second or third year, dried, and powdered. The scent is sweetly aromatic, but the taste is somewhat bitter and quite pungent. The rhizome powder is infused one ounce (28 g) to three-quarters of a pint (426 ml) of water, then taken in wineglass doses for fevers and dyspepsia. The dried root or rhizome may be chewed to ease digestion and to clear the voice.

In cooking, the root is sometimes used as a substitute for ginger, cinnamon, or nutmeg because of its spicy nature. Commercially, the rhizome has found its way into hair preparations, tooth-pastes, and beverages, including beer, bitters, tonics, liqueurs, and cordials.

Senna

Purging Cassia, Pudding Pipe-Tree
Cassia sp.
Leguminosae

The cassias are common in tropical countries. However, they were recorded as having been grown in England in

Senna
(Cassia Acutifolia)
(a) flower (b) seed pod
(c) open pod showing seeds

the mid-Seventeenth Century by keeping them in hot beds throughout the summer, but, although they frequently flowered, their seeds did not mature. They are well known for their medicinal, purgative action.

Cassia fistula, purging cassia, is a small tree from India with evenly pinnate leaves. It has long racemes of showy yellow flowers and pods up to two feet long (60 cm). These are the cassia pods used commercially and are mildly cathartic. The leaves and flowers are also purgative, and the bark is used as an astringent.

A useful infusion of senna can be made with two ounces (56 g) of the leaves to three-quarters of a pint (426 ml) of boiling water. The leaves should be soaked for at least an hour, then strained off. Wineglass doses should be given every few hours until the purging action is experienced.

Sesame

Benne, Gingilly, Teel
Sesamum indicum
Pedaliaceae

Although not a native of this country, sesame is well known here. It is native to Africa and the warmer parts of Asia. Earliest records show that sesame seed was a staple food and oil source in China, Japan, and India, and was also used in ancient Greece. The Egyptians and Persians of Biblical times ground it into a kind of flour, from which they made bread. The Romans crushed the seed and used it like butter. Today it is still used as a spread and the oil is used in the manufacture of some margarines.

Sesame is a strong, slender annual growing to 18 inches (46 cm) high. It has slim dark green leaves and one inch-long (2.5 cm) flowers, which lie along the square stem. The flowers resemble foxgloves. It is a plant which loves warmth and will not grow naturally in the British Isles.

If used in large enough quantities, sesame seeds are a very good source of vitamins C and E, calcium, and unsaturated fatty acids. The seeds need to be baked or roasted to bring out their nut-like flavour. In the Orient, they are often mixed with honey and dried fruits to make a sweetmeat.

Skirret

Sium sisarum
Umbelliferae

Skirret is an old-world pot-herb. It is a native of China, naturalized in Europe. Under favourable conditions, the plant grows up to four feet (1.2 m) in height. It is topped with umbels of white flowers. The part of the plant used is the root, which resembles clusters of little parsnips.

The plants are most easily increased by dividing the root each spring. They can be grown from seed, but germination is not always successful.

The root is cooked as a vegetable. It is supposed to be a valuable addition to the diet in cases of chest ailments, and a useful diuretic.

It has been cultivated in this country since the Sixteenth Century. When boiled and served with butter, the roots form a dish, declared by Worlidge, in 1682, to be "the sweetest, whitest, and most pleasant of roots."

Sorrel

Green Sauce, Sally Sour, Sour Sauce
Rumex sp.
Polygonaceae

Sorrel is a prolific herb found growing in damp ditches and meadows all over the countryside.

Of the most commonly cultivated of the sorrels, the broad-leafed French sorrel *(Rumex scutatus)* dominates the narrower-leaved garden sorrel *(R. acetosa)* because of the former's tastier leaves.

The sorrels are closely related to the docks, but they are more palatable. Both are of the genus *Rumex*, a Latin

497

allusion to the spear-shaped leaves of the genus.

Of a different genus altogether is a plant whose common name is wood sorrel. Probably lumped in with the sorrels because it tastes quite similar, wood sorrel *(Oxalis Acetosella)* bears absolutely no botanical kinship to the sorrels.

What wood sorrel and the real sorrels share is the same high content of the chemical salt, binoxalate of potash, which imparts a highly acid taste to them. Common garden rhubarb similarly has a high concentrate of that salt, and as a result, an acid taste.

French sorrel likes a dry, friable soil in a sunny location. Garden sorrel, though, prefers plenty of moisture. They both like rich soil.

Both species may be grown from root divisions made in the spring or the autumn, but the sorrels are hardy, frost-resistant plants and can be started easily from seed. Seed should be planted outside in March or April, or earlier indoors in rich, moist soil. When the shoots reach one or two inches (2.5 or 5 cm) thin them to six inches (15 cm). Mulch as soon as possible, especially if you are growing garden sorrel. That will hold moisture and prevent the top-soil from crusting, a condition that the sorrels abhor.

Stalks of small, bell-shaped flowers, usually yellow-green with purple veins, will form early in the spring and bloom by May. Seeds form rapidly and, if not harvested immediately, will start a new crop the same summer.

Goldfinches and greenfinches will help keep the sorrel seed under control; it is a favourite food for them. But you will probably have to do your part too. Removing the seed pods helps to rejuvenate the plant, so that it will keep producing green leaves for your kitchen well into the autumn.

Sorrel leaves can be harvested any time the plant is growing. Use fresh leaves if you can; drying them does not preserve their distinctive citrus-like flavour.

The following is a novel suggestion for preserving sorrel leaves. It is based on an Eighteenth Century French recipe. Extract the water from sorrel leaves by lacing them with plenty of salt and frying them very slowly with a generous amount of butter. After the water has evaporated, turn off the stove and allow the sorrel butter to become tepid. Ladle it into jars and allow the mixture to cool thoroughly. Seal each jar with a layer of pure melted butter, cover it with an air-tight cap, and refrigerate.

Another traditional sorrel recipe is for the sweet-and-sour sauce that gave garden sorrel one of its common names, "green sauce." This old English recipe involves beating sorrel leaves to a mash and adding sugar and vinegar. It was used as a sauce with cold meat, fish, and fowl. Gerard, in his 1597 treatise on useful plants, said such a "Greene Sauce is good for them who have sicke and feeble stomaches . . . and of all sauces, Sorrel is the best, not only in virtues, but also in pleasantness of his taste." The

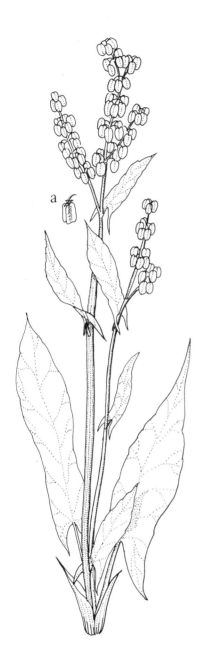

Garden Sorrel
(Rumex acetosa)
(a) flower

favoured species in England at that time, though, was probably French sorrel, which had succeeded garden sorrel about the time of Henry VIII, whose reign ended in 1547.

Peasant cooks tied sorrel leaves around tough cuts of meat in the belief that the leaves' acidity would tenderize the meat.

Boiled sorrel leaves are a succulent substitute for spinach. Remove the stalks, and place the leaves in a saucepan. A cast iron saucepan, or one with a cast-iron core, is best for cooking vegetables because the heat is distributed evenly. Cover the leaves with a minimum of water and simmer slowly for half an hour, turning the sorrel frequently. Strain the leaves, but save the juice. Chop the leaves finely and return them to the juice. Add pepper, salt, and butter to taste. Stir for another ten minutes over a low heat and serve.

The renowned French provincial *Potage aux herbes* is a heavenly blend of herbs and vegetables, the perfect illustration that a vegetarian's diet need not be a drab one.

One recipe is as follows:

Chop four ounces (113 g) sorrel leaves together with one heaped tablespoon of fresh chervil, and the heart of a small lettuce. Melt one tablespoon of lard in a saucepan, add the herbs, and simmer for 30 minutes. Add a small teaspoonful of honey and two and a half pints (1.4 l) of stock (this can be made with two stock cubes). Cover saucepan and boil for 30 minutes. Mix two egg yolks with a little warm stock and add them to the soup. Serve sprinkled with tiny knobs of butter and fried croutons.

As an ingredient in green salads, sorrel lends "so grateful a quickness to the salad that it should never be left out". That was the advice of John Evelyn, in 1720. He added that a sorrel salad "renders not plants and herbs only, but men themselves, pleasant and agreeable."

Irish peasants commonly used sorrel leaves as a side dressing to fish and milk, and it was believed throughout Europe, probably with some accuracy, to be a tonic against scurvy.

Some historians believe that the ternate leaves of sorrel, rather than those of clover, were the instruments St. Patrick used to illustrate the Trinity, and that sorrel was the original shamrock.

Medicinally, sorrel is said to have diuretic, antiscorbutic, and coolant properties and is taken to reduce fevers and to quench thirst. Herbalists caution against sorrel for persons with gout and rheumatism for its acid composition is believed to aggravate those conditions.

Culpeper wrote in the Sixteenth Century:

. . . all the Sorrels are under the dominion of Venus. It is useful to cool inflammation and heat of the blood in agues, pestilential or choleric, or sickness and fainting, arising from the heart; to quench thirst and procure an appetite in fainting or decaying stomachs; for it resists the putrefaction of the blood, kills worms, and is a cordial to the heart, which the seed does more effectually, because it is more drying and binding, and thereby stays the fluxes of women's courses, or flux of the stomach.

An outmoded use for extract of sorrel leaves is as a stain remover on linen cloth. Related to that was an ancient Chinese belief that sorrel juice could remove freckles. The *Rumex* genus is well known to the Chinese, for in two thousand years of weed-like wanderings it has spread throughout the world.

Southernwood

Old Man, Lad's Love
Artemisia Abrotanum
Compositae

Southernwood is a relative of wormwood, tarragon, mugwort, and all the other artemisias, but its relationship to wormwood is particularly close in that it is regarded in Europe as the southern variety, hence the name. Like wormwood, it is an ornamental shrub that grows up to seven feet (2.1 m) high, and has been used widely in landscaping. Its foliage is finely divided and grey-green in colour. It has a lemon odour, although varieties having camphorous and tangerine-like odours exist. It rarely flowers in Britain.

Southernwood cuttings are easily rooted, and this is the way to establish the plants. Its soil requirements are not remarkable and it is a hardy plant.

It is said to prevent drowsiness. In the days of long, tedious church services, the worshippers used to steel themselves with southernwood and lemon balm.

Branches placed in chests and wardrobes are said to guard clothing against moths. Southernwood is also used in sweet baths, and aromatic waters. Medicinally, it is astringent, anthelmintic, and deobstruent. The branches dye wool a deep yellow.

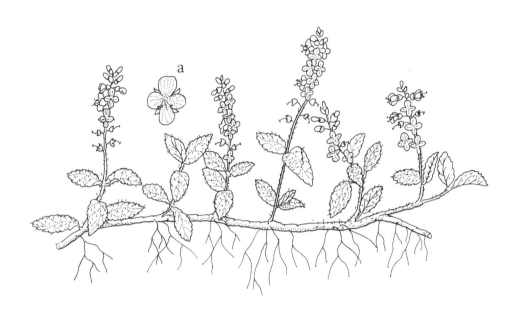

Common Speedwell
(Veronica officinalis)
(a) flower

Speedwell

Common Speedwell
Veronica officinalis
Scrophulariaceae

This small perennial creeps over the ground, and roots form at the joints of the woody stems and send up branches three to ten inches (8 to 25 cm) high. Leaves are opposite, soft and hairy, and greyish-green. The flowers arranged in spires bloom from May to July in shades of blue. It is a hardy, free-flowering plant and thrives in light shade or open sunny locations. It can be easily grown from seed or by division, and is useful in rock gardens or for ground cover.

Speedwell is found in the British Isles on heath and moorlands, dry hedge banks and in woodlands.

A tonic, alterative, and diuretic, it is

501

used as a remedy for coughs, catarrh, and skin diseases.

two to three times daily in wineglass doses. The bark may also be steeped in ethyl alcohol to make a tincture, given in doses of five to ten drops, usually mixed with water or honey.

Spindle Tree

Pigweed, Dogwood, Burning Bush, Wahoo, Fusoria
Euonymus europaeus
Celastraceae

Burning bush, as it is also known, is a smooth-leaved shrub found in bushes and woods. Bearing small greenish-white flowers in loose clusters, it flowers during May and June, followed by an abundance of scarlet-crimson fruit. The fruit is emetic and is harmful if eaten; it has been known to be fatal when eaten by sheep.

In the Nineteenth Century the bark was used in various patent medicines and became extremely popular as a laxative, diuretic, and tonic. It was listed as an official drug plant, and in 1912 a report was published indicating that the plant produced a digitalis-like effect on the heart.

For medicinal use, the bark should be gathered in the autumn. The fruits, though attractive, are considered poisonous and should not be used. A decoction is made by boiling one ounce (28 g) of the bark slowly in three-quarters of a pint (426 ml) of water. When cooled, it should be taken

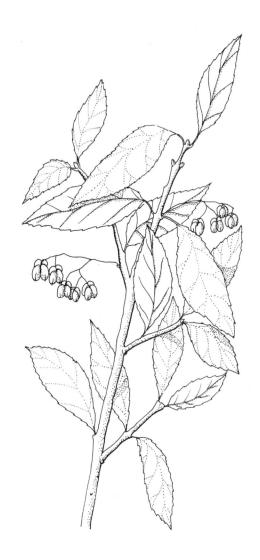

Spindle Tree
(Euonymus Europaeus)

502

Sumac

Smooth Sumach
Rhus sp.
Anacardiaceae

The sumac is a decorative ornamental shrub, with compound leaves that turn brilliant scarlet in the autumn. The small flowers in panacles are followed by bunches of red berries. It grows well in poor, dry soil and can be found on dry hillsides. It can be propagated by root cuttings or seed, which is sown in the autumn, or stored at freezing temperatures for germination in the spring.

The root, bark and berries of the scarlet sumac are used medicinally for diarrhoea, leucorrhoea, and febrile diseases. The astringent berries were also used for a gargle. A native of North America, but also widely distributed throughout Europe, the roots were used by the American Indians for a yellow dye, the crushed leaves as a poultice for skin diseases, and a decoction of the leaves as an antidote for venereal disease.

The fragrant sumac or sweet sumach *(Rhus aromatica)* is a smaller shrub with aromatic, three-part leaves. The yellowish flowers develop before the leaves, and the fruit is red and hairy. The root bark was used in the treatment of diabetes, for discharges of kidney and bladder, and for incontinence in both children and aged persons.

It grows about 4 feet (1.21 m) high, and was first introduced in England as an ornamental shrub in 1759. Its bark is used in tanning.

R. Vernix, the poison sumac, is the only moisture-loving species and should be avoided.

Sunflower

Marigold of Peru, Corona Solis
Helianthus annuus
Compositae

The sunflower is perhaps one of the most commercially important herbs in the world today, yet very few people think of it as a herb. This familiar giant, looking much like a colossal golden daisy, is very much a herb, although its history is not so widely chronicled as other herbs.

The sunflower is an American native. The Indians used the seeds as a source of meal, and the Spanish conquerors of South and Central American civilizations found the plant was much revered. The Incas of Peru, particularly, made the sunflower a part of their religious practice: the priestesses in the Inca temples of the Sun were crowned with sunflowers and also carried them in their hands. Reproductions of sunflowers sculpted in pure gold were placed in many of their temples.

The Spaniards and other visitors to the New World were quick to carry seeds back to the Old World, and the sunflower soon spread across Europe. The Europeans apparently didn't put the plant to immediate use. Gerard noted, for example, that the virtues were not known. He stated:

There hath not anything been set downe either of the ancient or later writers concerning the vertues of these plants, notwithstanding we have found by triall, that the buds before they be floured, boiled and eaten with butter, vinegar and pepper, after the manner of Artichokes, are exceedingly pleasant meat, surpassing the Artichoke in provoking bodily lust. The same buds with the stalks near to the top (the hairiness being taken away) broiled upon a gridiron, and afterward eaten with oile, vinegar, and pepper, have a like property.

Parkinson, too, reported that the sunflower had no use, "in Physicke with us but that sometimes the heads of the Sunne Flower are dressed, and eaten as Hartichokes are, and are accounted of some to be a good meate, but they are too strong for my taste."

Both Parkinson and Gerard acknowledge the ancestry of the plant, referring to it as the floure (or flower) of the Sunne, the golden floure (or flower) of Peru, or the marigold of Peru. Culpeper didn't acknowledge the plant at all.

The fact that these herbalists knew of no use "in Physicke" shouldn't prompt us to discount the sunflower as a medicinal herb. Maude Grieve's *Modern Herbal* reports, "The seeds have diuretic and expectorant properties and have been employed with success in the treatment of bronchial, laryngeal, and pulmonary affections, coughs and colds, also in whooping cough." It was also considered useful against dysentery, malaria, and inflammations of the bladder and kidneys. The root was used for snake bites, and crushed, it was applied as a wet dressing to draw blisters. The leaves are astringent and have also seen use in herbal tobaccos.

A recommended preparation is made by boiling two ounces (56 g) of the seed in a quart (1.1 l) of water, continuing until only twelve ounces (341 ml) of fluid are left. Then strain the liquid and add six ounces (170 ml) of gin and six ounces (170 g) of sugar. The preparation is given in doses of one to two teaspoonfuls, three or four times daily.

An infusion said to be useful in cases of whooping cough may be made from seeds that have been browned in the oven. The oil might also be used, given in doses of ten to fifteen drops, two or three times daily.

Perhaps one of the more curious home remedies has long been practised in the Caucasus, using sunflower leaves. It is employed in cases of malarial fever. A large cloth is spread over a bed, and the sunflower leaves are spread over the cloth, then moistened with warm milk. The fever victim is then wrapped up in it. This is said to stimulate perspiration, and the process is repeated daily until the fever breaks.

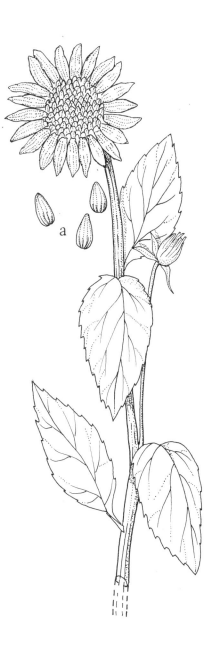

Sunflower
(Helianthus annuus)
(a) seeds

The sunflower is a remarkably versatile commercial plant. The entire plant can be used as fodder for livestock. The flowers yield a yellow dye. The pith of the stalks can be used to make paper and is used as a mounting medium for microscope slides. Having a specific gravity lower than cork, the pith was for years used in the making of life preservers and life belts. But the part of the plant of major economic significance today is the seed.

Sunflower seed is one of the richest among herb seeds for its nutritional value. They are 25 per cent protein, putting them on the same protein level as meat. They contain liberal amounts of vitamins, especially A, B complex, and the sparsely found E. All these are to be found in unsaturated oils. The mineral content includes much more calcium than cottonseed, soyabean, or linseed. The potassium content is comparable to that of raisins, nuts, and wheat germ. The seeds have the highest rating for magnesium, and have more iron than any other food (with the exception of egg yolk and liver). Sunflower seed meal is highly digestible and is over 50 per cent protein. The top-quality oil is rich in lecithin and unsaturated fatty acids. It contains 30 per cent protein as well as its share of vitamins and minerals.

Already an important crop in Canada, South America, and Russia, sunflower seed is rapidly becoming a major world-wide commodity. Primarily, its market is as a protein-rich feed for cattle, pigs, poultry,

505

birds, and humans. Apart from sunflower's nutritive value, more people are becoming aware of the appealing taste of its crunchy seeds. The oil is useful industrially in the manufacture of soap, candles, burning oils and certain varnishes, and paints.

The seeds can be used much as you would use nuts. Ground into a meal, they can be used in baking or as a supplement in a variety of dishes. Combine some meal with several eggs to make a breakfast omelette—a departure from any other you've tasted. Just mix 4 ounces (112 g) of sunflower seed meal, four lightly beaten eggs, and half a teaspoonful of caraway seeds; pour the blended ingredients into a hot, oiled frying pan and brown on both sides.

Sunflower seeds are becoming increasingly popular. In Russia and China they are well known. Here in Europe the seeds are available already hulled. But in countries peopled with dedicated sunflower seed eaters, the seeds are hulled by fingers and teeth. Here is how it's done. You first insert the seed between the teeth, the seed standing on edge, still holding on with your fingers until you give it the first crack with the teeth. Then the tendency of the seed, when the pressure of the teeth is removed, is to lie down flat. You quickly insert the lower teeth into the opening you have made in the seed, removing your fingers. The lower teeth exert sufficient pressure to remove the kernel from the shell with the gradual aid of your upper teeth. You will find that

your tongue comes to your rescue and helps to push the shells to one side. It is all done in a twinkling. The Russians poke them into one corner of the mouth, with a stream of hulls flowing from the other corner, and they do it rapidly. They accomplish the act without the aid of the hands, using the tongue and teeth working in conjunction with one another.

From the point of view of the gardener, growing sunflowers is an enjoyable occupation. If you plant the mammoth Russian variety, you will be amazed at the magnitude of the plant, often reaching over 12 feet (3.6 m) in height. When the plants are young, each morning their heads will turn to face the sun. There are many varieties, including some that do not produce seed. These are used chiefly as ornamental plants.

Sunflowers which produce seed come in dwarf, semi-dwarf, and tall varieties; the best kind for the average gardener is the giant sunflower *(Helianthus giganteus)*. This is a strong-growing perennial that climbs to 12 feet (3.6 m) or more and carries a huge head packed with really big seeds; the type suited for harvesting and eating.

Most popular and widely grown of the giant varieties is the mammoth Russian, which matures in about 80 days. Besides being the largest and tallest of all sunflowers, it bears big, striped seeds that are thin-shelled, meaty, and rich in both flavour and food value. The plant's towering, husky stalks make excellent screens or field backgrounds. When grown close together, their broad leaves will keep the sun from reaching weeds and can be extremely effective as weed smotherers.

Sunflowers grow very well with mild, organic fertilizers and have few insect pests, so there is seldom need to spray them. For giant-size heads, space the plants at least three or four feet (90 cm or 1.2 m) apart, but for production of seed, space them more closely. Giant heads are not as easy to harvest or dry as smaller heads, so crowd the plants a little. But don't over-crowd them. Over-crowding of any sunflower, especially the taller-growing varieties, causes the plants to fall in heavy winds. Usually sunflowers are planted in rows of 36 or 42 inches (91 or 107 cm), with a seed planted every five or six inches (13 or 15 cm). While they are hardy to light spring frosts, it is a good idea to allow a growing period close to 120 days before the first autumn frosts. As the heads grow heavy, the stalks may need support of some kind.

When you approach the problem of harvesting the seed, you will do well to note the time when the birds begin to pick out the seed around the rim of the head. Naturally, the outer seeds mature earlier than those nearer the centre of the head. As soon as about two-thirds of the seeds are well filled, the head may be gathered. If you wait for the centre seeds to fill out you may lose the outer ones. The easiest way to harvest the crop is to cut off the heads with a foot or two of the stalks attached and hang them up in an airy, dry place to cure before attempting to separate the seeds from the husks.

Much later, after the rush of harvesting your other garden crops is over, you may remember your collection of sunflower seedheads hung to dry in the attic. By that time, the rough stalks will have become brittle. The fat seeds separate easily as you run your thumb lightly over the surface of the head and will rattle like peas as they fall into the pan placed below.

Tansy

Bachelor's Buttons, Bitter Buttons, Stinking Willie
Tanacetum vulgare syn.
Chrysanthemum vulgare
Compositae

If tansy has an essential character, it is that of preservation and immortality. Its very name is a derivative of the Greek name *Athanasia* meaning "immortal". Used as an embalming agent from ancient times, it was also used to preserve meat.

Tansy also developed into a symbolic and pragmatic ingredient in the holiest of Christian springtime rites; those of Eastertide. Tansy, by the Seventeenth Century, had been embraced by the church as one of the Bitter Herbs of Passover. Tansy cakes became an Easter-day tradition symbolizing the Passover herbs.

A more practical attribute was its proclaimed ability to rejuvenate the human body after a long winter of existence on salted meat and fish. Tansy cakes were also said to purify the humours of the body after the sparsities of Lent.

Here is an old recipe for tansy cakes believed to date back to the Seventeenth or Eighteenth Century:

Beat seven eggs, yolks and whites separately; add a pint (568 ml) of cream; near the same of spinach juice; and a little tansy juice gained by pounding in a stone mortar; a quarter of a pound (113 g) of Naples biscuit; sugar to taste; a glass of white wine; and some nutmeg. Set all in a saucepan, just to thicken, over the fire; then put into a dish lined with paste, to turn out, and bake it.

Tansy itself is a hardy perennial that is difficult to grow from seed but, once established, inclined to take over nearly everything in sight. It might be worth the trouble in the long run to plant tansy in a sunken bottomless container such as half of a clean 44 gallon (200 l) drum. This should prevent the aggressive root structure from spreading into neighbouring plants.

The plant consists of a stem, two to three feet (60 to 90 cm) high, with fern-like leaves four inches (10 cm) wide and six inches (15 cm) long. Late in summer, heads of flat, round, yellow flowers develop and last several weeks. The leaves are the part of the plant

Tansy
(Tanacetum vulgare)
(a) flower

used for seasoning and medicinal purposes.

Tansy likes modestly fertilized soil with adequate nitrogen. It's best started from purchased plants which can be propagated by dividing the roots or taking slips. Plant young shoots at least a foot (30 cm) apart.

Harvest the leaves at the peak of growth, but avoid yellowing leaves. For tansy tea, however, take the young green shoots and strip the leaves off the stem. Drying will take about two days in 90° F (32° C) shaded heat or a warm oven.

It is interesting to note that the common name "Stinking Willie" was given to tansy by the Highland Scots, who considered it a weed. They named it contemptuously after William of Orange.

Tansy was strewn on the floors of English manor houses to repel insects which were attracted to the leavings of feasts and revelry. Adding tansy to the debris apparently was preferred to sweeping it out of the house. In addition, oil of tansy rubbed on the body is said to repel insects.

Medicinally, tansy was said to increase fertility when applied externally and to cause abortions when consumed. It has all the properties of aromatic bitters and was taken in tonics and teas to soothe the nerves, aid digestion, and calm a number of female discomforts such as hysteria, kidney weakness, amenorrhoea, and fevers. It was used externally for skin eruptions and sprains.

Among the better-known culinary uses of tansy is in the preparation of the liqueur Chartreuse. Once used as a substitute for pepper, tansy has a place in salad dressings and omelettes. Use it sparingly because it is a powerful seasoning agent.

Tarragon

Little Dragon, Mugwort
Artemisia Dracunculus
Compositae

Tarragon, affectionately known as "little dragon", is one of the herbs that has been passed down to us from antiquity. Like rosemary, sage and thyme, tarragon traces its historic roots back over two thousand years.

Its use was recorded by the Greeks about 500 B.C. Tarragon was among the so-called "simples", or one-remedy herbs, used by Hippocrates. European gardeners knew tarragon in the Middle Ages, but it wasn't until the end of those dark times that it crossed over the English Channel, and it entered England during the Tudor reign, probably as a preferred gift for the Royal herb garden from a Continental monarch. For many years, tarragon was relatively unknown outside the Royal garden.

Tarragon's common name probably is a corruption of the French *esdragon*, derived from the plant's Latin specific name *Dracunculus*, a little dragon. It seems likely that the plant earned this common name because its brown coiled roots resemble a cluster of small, gnarled serpents.

In ancient times, tarragon was considered valuable in drawing the venom from the bites of snakes and insects and in treating the bite of a mad dog.

In the Middle Ages, it was thought to increase physical stamina, and sprigs of it were tucked into pilgrims' shoes before they set out on their long fatiguing journeys. Herbalists of the day maintained that tarragon, taken inwardly, was "good for the heart, lungs, and liver". More specific prescriptions for its medical uses are hard to find.

In the kitchen, however, it has a wide range of uses that begins with the traditional tarragon vinegar. This best known of tarragon elixirs can be made simply by filling a wide-mouthed bottle with fresh sprigs, then soaking them in fine quality cider, or white wine vinegar. A delicately flavoured vinegar is important so as not to stifle tarragon's relatively light flavour.

In combination with other herbs, however, tarragon can be overpowering. It should be used with discretion.

Considered to be one of the more refined herbs, as opposed to robust herbs, tarragon makes a delicious additive to all kinds of white sauces, fish, cheese, eggs, and green vegetables such as spinach and peas. Cauliflower, too, benefits from a sprinkling of tarragon. As an ingredient of tartar sauce, the herb is indispensable, and it's almost *de rigeur* in *sauce Béarnaise* as well.

Try this for a heavenly light lunch: to your favourite recipe for creamy white sauce, add parsley and tarragon. Serve it over poached eggs nestled in shells of the lightest pastry. Serve with a chilled, light dry white wine.

When it comes time to acquire your first tarragon bush, beware! There are two distinct varieties. The most desirable is commonly called German or French tarragon. Unless you have access to an established bush from which you can take a slip or some roots you will have to buy the bush from a commercial herb grower. The European variety rarely produces fertile flowers which go to seed.

The other variety is the less desirable Eastern variety, commonly called Russian tarragon. It does not seem to have a separate specific name, but it differs greatly from the Western variety. Russian tarragon produces seeds copiously and seems more vigorous a plant than the aromatic European variety, but it is unfortunately lacking in the oils that make European tarragon such a delight to taste and smell.

Cuttings can be taken early in spring, after the main plant has begun to show new growth. Place the new slip under an inverted drinking glass to keep it warm. Keep the plants about 20 inches (50 cm) apart, because tarragon sends out a lateral root structure rather than a vertical one.

Tarragon likes moderate sun in a fertile, well-drained location. Heavy mulching is advisable to improve the soil's capacity to hold moisture, although too wet a soil is not advisable. Fertilize established plants with a fish emulsion after taking cuttings.

Root division can be done in March or April by dividing the root cluster of a single mature plant into two or

Tarragon
(Artemisia Dracunculus)

three clumps. In any event, mature plants should be divided every four years to rejuvenate them.

It would be a wise idea to set up a rotation system for dividing some plants each year if you plan to make tarragon a mainstay of your herb garden. Be very careful if you hoe your tarragon, for its lateral, shallow root structure makes the roots vulnerable.

With good care, tarragon will grow up to three feet (90 cm) high. Upright green stalks will carry elongated leaves, green or dark green. Small yellow and black flowers form in August.

Harvest tarragon early in July or when the lower leaves start to turn yellow. This yellowing is a sign either of insufficient fertilization or of ageing. In either case, the yellowed leaves will not turn green again, so gather them before discolouration sets in. Leave two or three inches (5 or 8 cm) of stem.

The first cuttings, however, may be taken as early as June. Older plants are more likely to give a heavy first cutting and second, or even third, crops.

Tarragon leaves brown easily, so dry them carefully. Strip them from the stem and dry in a warm, shaded, and well-ventilated area. The temperature should not exceed 90° F (32° C). When leaves are dry, seal them in tight, dry containers. They will re-absorb moisture at the first chance.

Tarragon winters well if its beds are covered with straw or hay to protect the roots slightly. Consider, though, that taking one or two plants inside for the winter will enhance your home with the sweet aroma of fresh-mown hay all winter long.

Towards the end of the autumn, transplant a tarragon root cluster into a pot no less than ten inches (25 cm) in diameter. Leave plenty of room for the roots to spread out. If the potting soil is not sandy, add some light gravel for airiness.

Don't over-water tarragon indoors. It should be allowed to dry out for a day or two before re-watering. Twice-monthly waterings will make it thrive.

Thyme

Common Thyme, Garden Thyme
Thymus vulgaris
Labiatae

When the time has come to plant even the most meagre of herb gardens, the time has come to plant thyme. Another of the herbs whose beginnings go back two millennia or more, thyme has a wide usefulness both medicinally and in cookery.

Traditionally, this herb has been graced with many positive associations, not the least of which has been humour. During the Renaissance, when wits were keen and words well chosen, it was said that thyme could hardly enter a conversation between two persons of quick mind without a welter of puns developing. The first allusion to the herb soon became jokingly known as "punning thyme".

Thyme has always been associated with honey, without doubt because it attracts bees in great profusion. It is common practice to plant thyme in Mediterranean orchards to attract pollinating insects to the fruit trees.

Virgil praised honey made from thyme. It is a delicious Greek speciality, and those who have tasted it say the delicate flavour of thyme is unmistakable.

In the plant's native Mediterranean region, lambs are sometimes put out to graze in fields of wild thyme, which many believe enhances the flavour of the meat.

Thyme was believed to be among the three or four herbs which Mary and the Child used for bedding in Bethlehem of Judea, and so it has become a herb to be included in Christmas creches. It also has been a favoured plant in the gardens of churches and monasteries.

The bee, honey, thyme, image lasted through the centuries and bloomed in the European age of chivalry, when thyme flourished as a symbol of strength, activity, and bravery. Many a lady embroidered a pennant for her knight showing a bee hovering over a sprig of thyme.

French republicans embraced thyme as a symbol of their own courage, and a sprig delivered to the door of a loyal republican was a silent summons to a clandestine meeting.

In early Greece, thyme signified graceful elegance. One of the highest compliments a suitor could pay his lady was to tell her she was sweet as thyme. In many cases, she was indeed sweet as thyme because oil of thyme was used in those days as a lady's perfume. It is still used in scented soaps and bath oils today.

Thyme's generic name *Thymus* is thought by many lexicographers to be a derivation of the Greek *thumus* (courage). Others believe it evolved from an ancient Greek expression meaning "to fumigate". Thyme was considered to have strong antiseptic properties, and it was used as an incense to purify the air. A similar belief was that a hillside of thyme not only sweetened the air near it, but cleansed it of bad vapours as well.

Maude Grieve wrote at length about thymol, a commercially valuable component of oil of thyme as well as several other plants.

Thymol, she reported, was used extensively as a battlefield antiseptic in World War I. It also had other uses; as a deodorant, local anaesthetic, meat preservative, paint for infectious irritations of the skin, mouthwash, and several other germicidal agents.

Thyme, especially when made into a tea, is said by herbalists to be aromatic, stimulant, diuretic, carminative, diaphoretic, emmenagogic, antispasmodic, as well as an antiseptic.

If you can't locate thyme honey, which is the delicious base for several herbal remedies, you can make a substitute using a good domestic honey and thyme tea. To prepare the tea, make the usual herbal infusion of one ounce (28 g) of the dried leaves

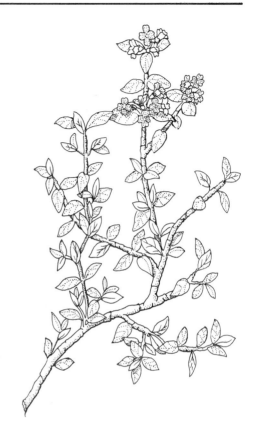

Thyme
(Thymus vulgaris)

to three-quarters of a pint (426 ml) of boiled water. Allow the infusion to cool to room temperature, then strain it and add 13 tablespoons of pure honey. Stir until mixed uniformly. This thyme syrup must be refrigerated. Taken in tablespoonful doses several times a day, it is good for sore throats, coughing spells, and colds.

In the kitchen, dried thyme leaves are as nearly universal a seasoning as any herb could be. One recent expert on herbal cookery advocated using thyme "as freely as salt"; in other words, in practically everything. It adds flavour to red meat, poultry, fish, and most vegetables.

Botanically, there are many closely related species in the *Thymus* genus. Most of them bear a close resemblance to *T. vulgaris*, a species that itself has at least three varieties; English thyme, German winter thyme, and French summer thyme. They differ mainly in the width of their leaves, being respectively variegated, broad, and narrow.

The different varieties of thyme are also grouped generally into upright and trailing types with *T. vulgaris* being the most common of the uprights, and wild thyme *(T. Serpyllum)* being foremost among the creeping thymes.

Common thyme, *(T. vulgaris)*, is usually started from seed, although cuttings or root divisions can be used. Seeds should be planted in indoor trays because a temperature of around 70°F (21°C), is needed for germination. The seeds are exceptionally small. It takes some 170 thousand to make an ounce (28 g). They should be evenly distributed over the seed box, and covered only lightly or not at all. They should germinate in about two weeks.

After the young plants have taken root, they can be moved outdoors. They should be planted nine inches (23 cm) apart in full sun, in a sandy, dry soil that is moderately fertilized. Thyme's nutrient requirements are

not great, but it is important to avoid heavy, wet soils.

A dense system of fine roots will develop along with a surface structure of woody stems and branches to which are attached small oval-shaped leaves. The plant will reach eight to ten inches (20 to 25 cm) in height. Leaves will be grey-green, and pink or violet flowers will appear in the leaf axils of the tip ends from May to August.

Weed control is important because weeds can be a debilitating competitor for nutrients with the small, slow-developing young thyme. Once the shoots are established, mulching will hold soil warmth and discourage weeds.

Open cultivation and hoeing should always be avoided around low herbs because the actions of hoeing and rain on the bare earth will make the lower branches of the plant dirty.

Harvest just before flowers begin to open by cutting the entire plant one and a half or two inches (3.7 or 5 cm) from the ground. A second growth will develop that should not be cut at all. Harvesting the second growth will reduce its winter hardiness, especially if the ground is bare and temperatures fluctuate widely. If you must have more thyme late in the summer, prune just the upper third of the plant, and then be sure to give it extra attention in the cold months.

After harvesting, lay the entire plant on a fine screen or a sheet of newspaper and dry it in warm shade. When dried, the leaves will separate from the woody stems with light winnowing or simple rubbing. Throw the stems onto the compost heap; the leaves alone are usable. Drying is easy, and thyme stores well at low humidity.

If you move your thyme to another corner of the garden, be sure to fertilize the plants' old area heavily before planting another herb there, as it tends to rob the soil of nutrients.

Tobacco

Tabacca
Nicotiana tabacum
Solanaceae

Tobacco can and should be considered a herb. While growing tobacco is an industry in many sub-tropical climates, it is hardly that in this country. In any event there are laws governing the growing of tobacco here. But during the last war there were concessions to allow home production during national shortage.

There is no solid evidence that the plant was seriously used by the American Indians who cultivated it. But the arrivals from the Old World quickly plunged into efforts to turn the plant to economic gain, efforts most notably marked by the introduction of tobacco to England by Sir Walter Raleigh. Then, as now, the noxious weed was denounced. It was

Tobacco
(Nicotiana tabacum)
(a) flower (b) buds

reported at the time that King James I offered a "counterblaste to Tobacco", labelling smoking as "a custome lothsome to the eye, hatefull to the Nose, harmefull to the braine, dangerous to

515

the Lungs, and in the blacke stinking fume thereof, nearest resembling the horrible Stigian smoke of the pit that is bottomlesse."

In time, however, a great many applications developed in folk medicine, and tobacco found its way into the official pharmacopoeias. Gerard listed 25 virtues of tobacco, six of which required the smoking of it. It was said to be a sedative, a diuretic, an expectorant, a discutient, a sialagogue, and an emetic. The smoke was blown into the ear to relieve earaches. Suppositories of tobacco leaves were used for "strangulated hernia". The leaves were applied as a poultice to bee stings, swellings, and sores.

An annual growing six feet (1.8 m) tall, tobacco is a handsome garden plant. Its broad leaves may be a foot (30 cm) or more in length, and the stem is covered with sticky hairs. The two-inch (5 cm) flowers are white, rose, or purple-rose, borne in racemes.

The seeds are sown in a very rich and friable soil under glass in late winter. The minimum temperature of the hotbed must be 70° F (21° C). Some varieties require shading. Probably no other crop needs a rich organic soil more than tobacco; fine tilth is of the greatest importance to good growth and health. The plants are set out 12 inches (30 cm) apart in rows three feet (90 cm) apart and cultivated until they cover the soil. The tops are picked off just before flowering to prevent the plants from going to seed. Drying is a process that must be carried out very carefully in a special curing house.

516

Tree of Heaven

Chinese Sumac, Vernis de Japon, Ailanto

Ailanthus altissima

Simaroubaceae

The tree of heaven is a native of China and India, but it is cultivated throughout Europe. It was first introduced into England in 1751 and is now frequently planted in English gardens.

The tree of heaven is useful where rapid growth is desired, as it will grow ten feet (3 m) or more in one season, and may reach a height of 60 feet (18 m). A tall hedge can be quickly grown by setting trees close together, then pruning at the desired height each spring.

A hardy, deciduous tree, it has a tropical appearance with large pinnate, compound leaves resembling sumac. It can be of particular importance in city gardens because of its resistance to smoke, dust, and disease.

The crushed leaves and flowers have a strong odour, offensive to most insects. It can be propagated by root cuttings, but grows easily and rapidly from seeds, and frequently self-seeds.

The bark and root bark are used as a cardiac depressant, for dysentery, diarrhoea, leucorrhoea, and to eliminate tape worm.

An infusion of the bark can be administered in orange-flower water sweetened with honey to reduce the bitterness and resultant sickness.

Valerian

Garden Heliotrope, All-Heal,
Spikenard
Valeriana officinalis
Valerianaceae

Valerian, a perennial member of the Valerianaceae family, is probably the most tranquillizing herb you can grow in your garden.

Indigenous to Britain, it also grows throughout the world. Valerian has dark green, serrated leaves grouped in pairs. The plant, which grows three to five feet (90 cm to 1.5 m) tall, develops a flower stalk early in the year with fragrant, light lavender flowers. Its seed is flat and heart-shaped, and coloured either light or dark grey.

Most people find valerian's scent disagreeable, but some like it. In ancient times, an Asian version of valerian apparently had a very pleasant scent. It is believed that valerian is the spikenard referred to in the Bible as a perfume brought from the East.

During the Middle Ages, valerian roots were laid among clothes as a perfume. The herb can intoxicate cats like catnip, but also attracts rats. Legend has it that the Pied Piper of Hamlin carried valerian roots in his pockets when he led the rats into the river.

Valerian's greatest use is as a medicine. Its historic uses are varied.

Culpeper said the root was under the influence of Mercury, and thus "hath a warming faculty". He highly recommended the herb for bruises, coughs, and the plague. Others have claimed that valerian is useful in treating hypochondria, hysteria, epilepsy, migraine headaches, some forms of fever, and most diseases of the nervous system.

Gerard said "valerian is excellent for those burdened, and for such as be troubled with croup and other like convulsions, and also for those that are bruised with falls." He added that "no broth or pottage or physicall meats be worth anything if [valerian] be not there."

Valerian's chief use is as a sedative. It has remarkable calming effects and is one of the most frequent remedies for nervousness and hysteria. If taken too often or in excessive doses, however, it can cause headaches, spasmodic movements, or hallucinations.

An excellent compound for nervousness, therefore, is an infusion of half an ounce (14 g) each of valerian, skullcap, and mistletoe in one and a half pints (752 ml) of boiling water, covered and left standing for at least two hours. A tablespoonful can be taken two to four times daily.

Another infusion of an ounce (28 g) each of powdered valerian, powdered ginger, powdered lobelia, and two ounces (56 g) of powdered pleurisy root is also considered good as a tranquillizer.

In the garden, valerian makes a handsome and useful border. The

517

Valerian
(Valeriana officinalis)
(a) flower

companion planter will find it helps most vegetables, as it is said to attract earthworms. A recommended garden practice is to make an infusion of valerian, and spray plants and soil

with it once a month throughout the summer. The result should be strengthened plants and an abundance of earthworms.

As valerian seeds don't germinate very easily, the best method of propagation is by division. If an older plant is not available in the garden, the plant will have to be purchased.

Valerian has a peculiar habit of growing out of a "crown", a short, conical root stock. The crown may develop several years before the sleeve and flower stalks. The crown can be transplanted and used to start individual plants. This should be done in March or April, as soon as the crown appears.

The plants very easily over-crowd themselves, so occasional dividing is necessary to ensure good growth. At least every three years, all the plants should be divided and replanted in rows at least one foot (30 cm) apart. The plants should also be spaced one foot (30 cm) apart.

The root is the most important part of the plant for medicinal purposes, and should be harvested in the autumn before the first frost. When harvested, it should be washed thoroughly to remove all stones and debris and dried.

Drying roots is different from drying leaves. They should be dried at a high temperature, such as 120°F (49°C) until brittle. If after this they are rubber-like, they should be dried even further. Once dried, the roots should be carefully stored to keep them free from moisture.

Verbena, Lemon

Lemon-scented Verbena,
Herb Louise, Verveine citronelle
Lippia citriodora syn.
Aloysia triphylla, Aloysia citriodora
Vervenaceae

Lemon verbena, native of the Amerricas, was first introduced into England in 1784 where it thrives best in the south and can grow to a height of 15 feet (4.6 cm). However, it is in South and Central America where it still thrives best, especially in Peru and Chile.

Europe was introduced to lemon verbena by the Spanish conquistadors who found space among their cargoes of gold booty for a few emigrant plants.

It is probably because of its New World origins that lemon verbena is lacking in the lore and traditional apothecary uses that surround most other herbs. Moreover, it has limited use in the kitchen.

Its primary role, however, is as a domestic houseplant grown purely for its pleasing scent of fresh lemons. But for that pleasure, there is a price to pay in care and work, for the lemon verbena is a tender plant that needs constant attention.

Lemon verbena is a tender perennial shrub that must be protected from frost. Starting the plant is a problem because its seed formation is infrequent and spotty. Greenhouses that handle exotic plants commonly maintain lemon verbena bushes from which they should be able to cut you a piece in March. If you have a bush, you can take cuttings in August provided you maintain the mature bush in a rich, well shaded area and keep it moist. The mature plant tends to wilt when cuttings are made, and the cuttings themselves are hard to establish.

Once rooted, though, the bush grows easily and will develop to maturity in one season, eventually reaching a height of some 15 feet (4.6 m) in the south of England.

Be sure to bring lemon verbena inside before the first frost. Indoors, the plant should be fed well-rotted compost or manure every two weeks. Its leaves should be misted or washed weekly with tepid water.

Lemon verbena is a deciduous plant, so don't be concerned when you bring the shrub indoors and it promptly moults its leaves. They will come back, although the indoor leaves are more apt to be a yellow-green colour than the grey-green of outdoor foliage. Flowers generally form in little white clusters at the end of the branches. Seeds, however, are rare.

Harvesting the leaves can be done almost anytime, although waiting until late summer will give you maximum enjoyment of the aromatic properties of the plant. Strip the leaves off a branch, or cut the whole shoot and chop it and the leaves. Dry in the shade.

Generally, the leaves may be

substituted for lemon or mint in recipes for poultry, fish, and stuffings. It also makes a pleasant tea.

Lemon verbena is believed to possess properties of a stomachic and antispasmodic, although it has never gained widespread use in herbal medicine.

Vervain

Herb of Grace, Herbe Sacrée
Herba veneris
Verbena officinalis
Verbenaceae

Vervain is a common roadside plant, but one with a magical, mystical past. It is a perennial bearing numerous small, pale lilac flowers. Leaves are opposite and have toothed lobes.

Vervain has been used as a tonic, diaphoretic, and expectorant, but no strong claims have ever been made as to its efficacy. In China, it is used to induce menstruation, to relieve rheumatism, and as an astringent and vermifuge.

Historically, the plant has been associated with sorcerers, witches, and magic. In ancient times, it was bruised and worn about the neck as a charm against headaches and venomous bites. An old legend claims that vervain was used to staunch the wounds of Christ on Calvary.

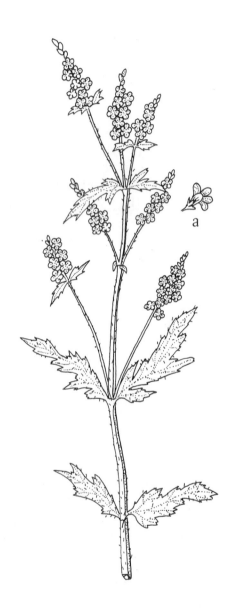

Vervain
(Verbena officinalis)
(a) flower

Violet, Sweet

Viola odorata
Violaceae

There are over two hundred varieties of violets. The flowers are usually deep purple, but there are other colours, lilac and white, for example. They are commonly cultivated in Britain.

They should be planted in rich, loamy soil in a sheltered position. Partial shade and moisture are required. Add a generous amount of compost to the soil. Plants multiply by runners, and also from seed. There are many cultivated varieties. *Viola tricolor*, known as wild pansy or hearts-ease, is an all-summer blooming variety with small purple and gold flowers, which grows very easily because it self-sows readily.

In addition to their ornamental value in the garden, violets have several uses in cooking. The blossoms can be candied and added to cakes as decorations. The flowers may also be floated in party punches.

The leaves and flowers are said to have antiseptic and expectorant properties. In China, violet blossoms were burned under abscesses in the belief that the smoke would aid in healing the wound. The Chinese also used the blossoms in decoctions and poultices. Violet flowers were said to have demulcent and mildly laxative properties.

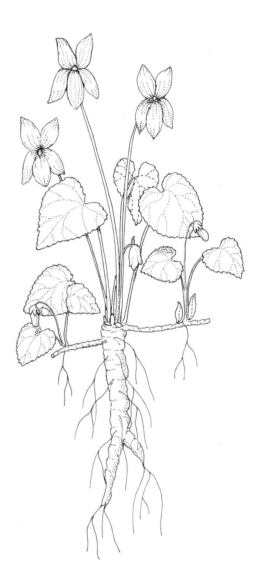

Sweet Violet
(Viola odorata)

521

Willow

**Pussy Willow, Weeping Willow,
Crack Willow**
Salix sp.
Salicaceae

The shrubs and trees of this group are related to the poplars. They come in various forms, some upright, others weeping, and there are also prostrate varieties. Willows are hardy and deciduous, and bear flowers in catkins, covered with silky hairs.

The willows are highly valued as ornamental shrubs. The graceful form, lovely foliage, and on some varieties, decorative silvery catkins make them an important feature of garden design. They also provide a quick growth and can be used as a protective shelter for young, slower-growing plants.

They thrive in a moist location and the extensive root system makes them valuable for planting on river and stream banks to prevent erosion. A weeping willow, drooping near a pool, makes an artistic setting. Willows prefer moist locations, but will grow in most situations. They grow easily from cuttings and may also be grown from seed, which should be planted as soon as they are ripe.

Willows are cultivated for basket-making. The dry bark is bitter, astringent, and detergent. It was used for diarrhoea, to staunch bleeding, and for dandruff. It is used for fevers, rheumatic ailments, and headaches.

Crack Willow
(Salix fragilis)
(a) catkin

The bark and berries are the parts used medicinally and contain salicin, the prime ingredient in aspirin.

Wintergreen

**Spiceberry, Teaberry, Checkerberry,
Creeping Wintergreen**
Gaultheria procumbens
Ericaceae

Wintergreen is an evergreen shrub of the heath family and is often found in woods and clearings. It is a low-growing plant with creeping stems. The broad leaves are elliptical, leathery, glossy green above, and paler below. The nodding white flowers are followed by edible crimson berries.

Wintergreen prefers non-limy soil and is often found near rhododendrons. It grows to a height of between 5 and 6 inches (13 and 15 cm). It needs a well-drained, preferably sandy soil with acidity between pH 4.5 and 5.5, and shade. It can be propagated by seeds, cuttings, and layers. Divisions may be set out in the autumn or spring.

It is very difficult to establish plants taken from the woods. Nursery-grown stock is more satisfactory, having been accustomed to artificial conditions. Cultivated wintergreen should be planted on a shady slope and mulched with two to four inches (5 to 10 cm) of pine needles.

The leaves are considered a valuable remedy in the treatment of rheumatism. They are aromatic, astringent, and stimulant, used both internally and externally. As a poultice, they can be applied to boils, felons, swellings, and inflammations. The tea is beneficial as a gargle.

Berries and leaves are both used for flavouring, but are not dried. The berries in brandy made a drink similar to bitters. Oil distilled from the leaves is used for flavouring and for perfume.

Witch Hazel

**Spotted Alder, Winterbloom,
Snapping Hazelnut**
Hamamelis virginiana
Hamamelidaceae

As a garden plant witch hazel reaches about 12 feet (9 m) in height. It provides, among other things, a stock for the slow-growing Japanese species, *Hamamelis mollis*, popular with British gardeners for its yellow and brown frilly flowers which bloom in February. The hard-shelled fruits, nut-like capsules or pods, shoot out their seeds like bullets from a gun; hence the common name "snapping hazelnut".

Witch hazels do well in moist, sandy loam and can take shade and moisture. They grow in damp woods in all parts of the country and several species are available in nurseries.

The branches are used as divining rods to detect subterranean water and metals, and perhaps this is why they came to be called "witch hazel".

The medicinal properties of witch hazel are astringent, tonic, and sedative. An old-time remedy still in popular use is a decoction of the bark and leaves used as a mouthwash, a vaginal douche to check internal and external haemorrhaging, and for treatment of piles. An ointment is also made for local application. The distilled extract of fresh leaves and twigs is used both externally and internally. For relief of varicose veins it is applied as a moist compress. For diarrhoea, it is administered as an enema and is used as a wash for tumours, inflammations, bed sores, and inflamed eyes.

An official drug plant, the waters distilled from the bark are sold by the hundreds of thousands of gallons annually. Nevertheless, there is still some disagreement over the efficacy of the herb.

Woad

Wad
Isatis tinctoria
Cruciferae

Woad is a biennial with a long history of use as a dye; hence the specific name *tinctoria*. During the first year the plant develops into a rosette of long, narrow, blue-green leaves. Stalks grow in the second year, rising as much as four feet (1.2 m), followed by bright yellow flowers in June.

Woad
(Isatis tinctoria)
(a) flower (b) seed

The plant can be grown from seed, and once established, it will self-sow freely. It requires fertile soil, good draïnage, and some sun.

Woad has been widely cultivated in Britain since earliest times, for the blue dye from the leaves. It is well known that the ancient Britons used it as a body dye to scare their enemies and Caesar found the natives stained with it when he visited Britain. Even in the Twentieth Century, some commercial use is still made of it in dyeing, as a fixative for true indigo and as a mordant for black dye, rather than for its colour.

The leaf and stem had some medicinal use in making plasters and ointments for ulcers, inflammations, and bleeding wounds, although it is too astringent for internal use.

Woodruff, Sweet

Wuderove, Muge-de-boys
Asperula odorata
Rubiaceae

Sweet woodruff is a beautiful, fragrant, little herb often found in the deepest recesses of the forests, where the sun penetrates only with difficulty. A native of Asia and Europe, it has been traditionally used as an ointment and a perfume.

In the Fourteenth Century, the plant was used in England and Scandinavia to make a water for cordials. It first appears in print in the Thirteenth Century as "wuderove", derived, some scholars believe, from the French "rovelle", a wheel, which refers to its spoke-shaped leaves.

In France, the plant was called "Muge-de-boys", musk of the woods. In Germany, as early as the Thirteenth Century, the herb was used to flavour May wine. The "Mai Bowle" is served today in Germany on May Day, and thereafter for the rest of the month.

Throughout the Middle Ages, woodruff was hung in churches and placed in boxes with lavender and roses on special days, such as St. Peter's and St. Barnabas' Day.

It was also used for stuffing mattresses and placed between the pages of books. Kept among sheets and towels, it will preserve them from insects and impart a pleasant scent. Gerard suggested it be used frequently indoors to "attemper the air, coole and make fresh the place".

Besides its use as a perfume, woodruff was credited as a valuable medicine to remove biliary obstructions of the liver and relieve upset stomachs. When the fresh leaves are applied to cuts and wounds, they bring relief. Gerard added that the herb was good for the heart and liver.

A good punch can be made from dried sweet woodruff. It can also be used as a flavouring for soda water or white wine.

It is a perennial herb about eight inches (20 cm) tall, with slightly shiny yellow-green leaves in whorls of six to eight around the stem. When crushed, the herb smells of sweet hay and slightly of vanilla. The plant thrives in moist soil.

Woodruff is extremely difficult to grow from seed. The most frustrating part of growing the plant from seed is

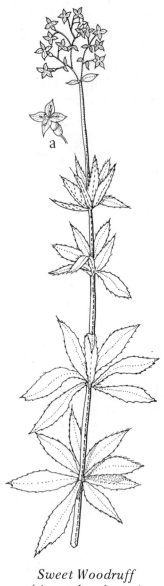

Sweet Woodruff
(Asperula odorata)
(a) flower

(just under half a square metre).

Its first and foremost requirement is shade, accompanied by slightly acid soil with a high humus content. The best medium for growth is leaf-mould compost; no other fertilization is needed. Occasional weeding might be necessary, while hoeing is out of the question as it might destroy parts of the spreading root system.

Woodruff may be harvested at any time during the growing season. It is different from most herbs in that the lovely fragrance develops only when it is dried. The fresh green plant itself is almost odourless. The shoots should be cut close to the ground in any quantity desired, or, as is most often the case, as much as the gardener feels he can spare without ruining the lovely green carpet they produce. The small amounts that are harvested should be chopped and dried instantly in warm shade.

Wormwood

Green Ginger
Artemisia Absinthium
Compositae

its long germination period, which can be up to two hundred days. The herb can be divided and replanted when it has covered an area of two square feet

Wormwood, like its relative mugwort, has been shrouded with superstitions for centuries. It took its generic name from Artemis, the Greek goddess, because she discovered the plant's virtues and gave them to mankind. However, another story suggests it was named after Artemisia, Queen of Caria, who gave her name to the plant after she had benefitted from its treatments.

Wherever its name came from, wormwood is one of the bitterest herbs known. Its common name comes from its ability to act as a de-wormer in children and animals. In fact, it was used in granaries to drive away weevils and insects, and as a strewing herb in spring to repel fleas. A strong decoction of wormwood was also employed as a wash for the floors of sickrooms to purify them from the illnesses of their inhabitants. The ancients also believed that wormwood was a counter-poison against toadstools, hemlock, and the bites of the sea dragon.

Wormwood is a perennial, and can be quite decorative in the garden. However, it does not make a good companion plant as it contains large amounts of a toxic substance called "absinthin", which rain washes off the leaves of the plant and into the ground, inhibiting the growth of nearby herbs or plants. This can be particularly bad in years of heavy rainfall.

The stem of the wormwood is branched and firm, almost woody at the base. Reaching a height of up to two and a half feet (76 cm), it is covered with fine silky hairs. The hairy leaves are three inches (nearly 8 cm) long by one inch (2.5 cm) wide and thrice-pinnate with linear, blunt segments. They are greyish-green and have a distinct odour.

Flowers are small and globular, and are arranged in erect, leafy panicles. They bloom from July until October with a greenish-yellow tint.

Wormwood is very easy to grow. Soil fertility requirements are minimal, but the plants should be weeded regularly. It can be propagated from cuttings, seeds or by root division in autumn. Seeds can be started indoors in winter and transplanted outside in the spring or sown directly outdoors in the autumn. Germination is quick. Allow two feet (60 cm) between plants.

The whole plant is used. Gather it in July and August and dry in a warm room in bunches. Use only the upper green portion for drying; discard the woody stem and the roots. If after a few days the leaves are dry but the stalk is still damp, hang the bunches near a stove to finish drying. When dry, rub through a sieve to remove the coarser stems, and pack immediately in jars. Seal at once to prevent re-absorption of moisture.

Wormwood has been used as a tonic and diuretic, to promote digestion, and to restore appetite. An infusion of one ounce (28 g) of the herb to three-quarters of a pint (426 ml) of water was taken by the wineglassful four times a day. Grieve's herbal says, "A light infusion of the tops of the plants, used fresh, is excellent for all disorders of the stomach, creating an appetite, promoting digestion, and preventing sickness after meals, but producing a contrary effect if used too strong."

Wormwood
(Artemisia Absinthium)
(a) flower

The latter is a caution that should be well observed by the experimenter with herbal remedies. In fact, wormwood in concentrated form is a volatile poison. It produces trembling, dullness of thought, and convulsions, classic signs of narcotic poisoning. In small doses, it is probably safe, but home experimenters would be well advised to use wormwood only as a strewing herb, or natural pest control.

Wormwood is too bitter to have many culinary properties, but it was used to flavour beer before the common use of hops. Vermouth is also made with wormwood, since it contains absinthe. It has been used since ancient times to make wine more intoxicating.

The classic use of wormwood was as a vermifuge. The dried, powdered flowers were usually used, although diluted absinthe liqueur was also given.

In the garden, wormwood will repel beetles and moths, and protect nearby cabbage plants against the cabbage-worm butterfly. A weak tea bath will discourage slugs if sprayed onto the ground in the autumn and spring. The same spray can be used in storerooms to keep weevils away from grains. It also repels aphids. However, don't use the spray too often, as it may retard plant growth.

There are two other species of wormwood commonly used in herbal remedies; Roman wormwood and sea wormwood. Roman wormwood is much more delicate than common wormwood, and has many dark, small flowers. Vermouth is made from this species because its flavour is less bitter. Sea wormwood grows in salty soils, and is smaller than the common wormwood. Both the sea and Roman wormwoods were used in remedies, but they were considered weaker than the common wormwood.

Dr. John Hill, writing in 1772,

recommended wormwood in many forms. He wrote:

The leaves have been commonly used, but the flowery tops are the right part. These, made into a light infusion, strengthen digestion, correct acidities, and supply the place of gall, where, as in many constitutions, that is deficient. One ounce of the Flowers and Buds should be put into an earthen vessel, and a pint and a half of boiling water poured on them, and thus to stand all night. In the morning the clear liquor with two spoonfuls of wine should be taken at three draughts, an hour and a half distance from one another. Whoever will do this regularly for a week, will have no sickness after meals, will feel none of that fulness so frequent from indigestion, and wind will be no more troublesome; if afterwards, he will take but a fourth part of this each day, the benefit will be lasting.

Yam, Wild

Colic Root, Rheumatism Root
Dioscorea villosa
Dioscoreaceae

Althouth this is a native to warmer climates, yams are imported, and available in specialist shops in most major cities.

The wild yam is a twining perennial. It has a long, branched, and crooked root which has been used medicinally as an expectorant, a diaphoretic, and, in large doses, an emetic. It was officially listed for a time as a diaphoretic and expectorant.

The colloquial names applied to the use of the root for colic and muscular rheumatism. American Indians have used the root to relieve the pains of childbirth, and it is reputed to be particularly helpful in relieving morning sickness so often associated with pregnancy.

There are nearly 150 varieties of *Dioscorea*, many of them developing edible tubers like potatoes. An interesting ornamental variety is *D. Batatas*, sometimes known as the Chinese yam, the red velvet yam, or the cinnamon vine.

A herbaceous, tall-climbing plant with slender twining stems, it is useful and decorative where a heavy screen is not desired. It is grown for its large edible tubers, up to three feet (90 cm) long and its attractive foliage. The leaves are shiny, ribbed, and veined, and small clusters of cinnamon-scented flowers blossom out of the axils of the leaves. Little tubercles form in the leaf axils, and from these, new plants can be started. Easy to grow, they can also be started from seeds, tubers, and cuttings.

529

Yarrow

Soldier's Woundwort, Bloodwort, Devil's Nettle
Achillea Millefolium
Compositae

If you were a Twelfth Century knight at arms, you would probably have carried a pouch of fresh yarrow leaves with you as nature's own first-aid kit, but being a Twentieth Century gardener, you will undoubtedly turn to yarrow as a wonderfully decorative border around your garden instead.

Despite the plant's principal use for its bright, long-blooming flowers, there are still several practical reasons for cultivating yarrow. In companion planting it repels beetles, ants, and flies. In addition, its diaphoretic, styptic, tonic, and astringent properties continue to justify its place in the herbal medicine chest.

Yarrow gets its generic name *Achillea* from the legend that comrades of the Greek hero Achilles used yarrow to heal their wounds during the Trojan War. The specific name *Millefolium* derives from yarrow's feathery leaves, so well divided that the plant appears to be thousand-leaved.

Yarrow is a hardy perennial that grows wild and will exist, although perhaps not thrive, in almost any grade of soil. It is considered, with some justification, to be a weed by many gardeners.

The flowers lend themselves to drying for bouquets. You can choose from among the white, red, orange, and yellow-blooming varieties, although the white and red seem to be the ones usually cultivated for medicinal and culinary purposes. Orange and yellow ones are more often grown for their floral attributes.

A word of caution when using the white medicinal variety; it must be removed annually because it excretes a toxin to the soil that eventually will defeat even its own growth. If you need to have it you might grow it for a season; just long enough to get to know and recognize the plant.

Yarrow can be grown either from seed or by dividing the root clumps of established plants. The seed will germinate in light. Sow it on top of fine soil and keep it moist until it germinates. Start it indoors in March so it will be ready for harvesting in June or July. Although fertilization is of minor importance because of yarrow's hardiness, annual applications of bone-meal will promote its growth. Furthermore, yarrow will produce a more pleasing aroma in light, sandy soils than in heavy, clay ones.

For medicinal and culinary uses, cut the whole plant at the peak of flowering. Chop the stem and leaves and dry them rapidly at 90° to 100°F (32° to 38°C). Because of its fine division, yarrow will darken quickly if not dried rapidly and thoroughly.

Yarrow used as a companion plant will drive away many common garden

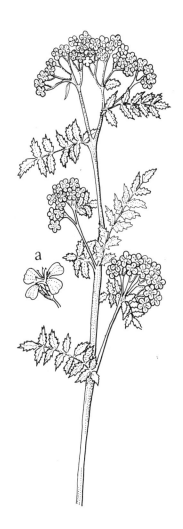

Yarrow
(Achillea Millefolium)
(a) flower

of their future loves". This is accomplished by sowing an ounce (28 g) of the herb into a small square of flannel and putting it under the pillow. Before retiring, the visionary recites this plea:

> *Thou pretty herb of Venus' tree,*
> *Thy true name is Yarrow;*
> *Now who my bosom friend must be,*
> *Pray tell thou me tomorrow.*

During the night, the dreamer's true love is supposed to appear in a vision.

A more down-to-earth application of yarrow is for breaking colds and fevers. For this sip an infusion made by pouring three-quarters of a pint (426 ml) of boiling water over an ounce (28 g) of yarrow, then adding a teaspoonful of honey and three drops of tabasco sauce. The patient should be heavily covered. This remedy will open the pores and cause profuse sweating to purify the blood of toxins.

Minus the honey and tabasco, the straight infusion can be used as a shampoo that's said to prevent baldness. A parallel formula for breaking colds and fevers is to substitute elder flowers and peppermint for the honey and tabasco. As a general tonic, yarrow is said to have a salutary effect on the entire nervous system.

Yarrow has been used throughout the centuries as snuff, a toothache remedy, and as a substitute for hops in brewing homemade beer. In the kitchen, its usefulness is limited to an occasional stand-in for cinnamon or nutmeg.

insects, and increase the content of volatile oils in nearby herbs.

Among its reputed powers is the ability to bestow on "young squires and maidens a heart-throbbing vision

531

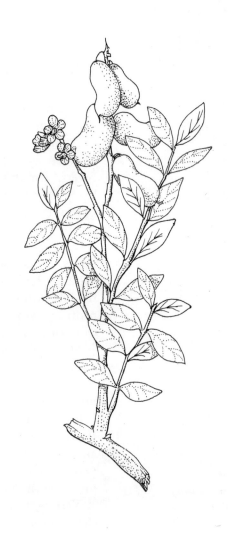

Glossary

Abortifacient: A drug which causes abortion.

Alterative: A medicine which gradually alters or changes a condition. A treatment that alters processes of nutrition.

Annual: A plant that completes a cycle of development from germination of the seed to flowering and death in a single growing season.

Anodyne: A medicine that relieves pain.

Anthelmintic: A medicine that expels or destroys intestinal worms. Such medicines are also called *vermifuges*.

Antidote: A medicine which counteracts the action of another, particularly a poison.

Antiperiodic: A medicine which prevents the periodic return of attacks of a disease, such as a recurring fever.

Antipyretic: A medicine which tends to reduce or prevent a fever. Such medicines are also referred to as *febrifuges*.

Antiseptic: A substance that will destroy infection-causing bacteria.

Antispasmodic: A medicine that relieves or prevents involuntary muscle spasms or cramps in ailments such as epilepsy, spastic paralysis, and painful menstruation.

Aperient: A mild and gentle-acting *laxative* medicine.

Aromatic: A fragrant substance with a spicy and pleasantly pungent smell.

Astringent: Medicinally it refers to a substance which causes the tissues to contract, thus checking the discharge of mucous, blood, and the like.

Axil: The upper angle between a leaf and the stem it springs from, or between a branch and trunk.

Balsamic: Healing or soothing.

Biennial: A plant that requires two seasons to complete the growth cycle from germination of seed to flowering and death.

Bitter tonic: A substance with an acrid, astringent, or disagreeable taste which stimulates the flow of saliva and gastric juice. Such tonics are taken to increase the appetite and to aid the digestive process.

Bract: A small leaf, often modified, which forms either on the flower stalk or as part of the flower head below the *calyx*. It bears a flower in its *axil*.

Calyx: Whorl of leaves forming outer case of a bud.

Carminative: A substance which checks the formation of gas and helps expel flatulence.

Catarrh: A discharge of fluid from the inflammation of a mucous membrane, especially the nose.

Cathartic: A medicine which causes the evacuation of the bowels. A *laxative* is a gentle cathartic, while a *purgative* is a much more forceful one and is used only in severe conditions.

Catkin: A downy or scaly spike of flowers produced by certain trees. They often hang down and can be commonly seen on willow and hazel trees.

Cholagogue: A medicine which promotes the discharge of bile from the system.

Composite: A plant of the Compositae or daisy family, with flowers made up of many small separate flowers, united in a single head, which looks like one flower.

Corm: A short, bulbous subterranean stem, found on plants such as garlic or anemonies.

Corroborant: A tonic or other substance which is invigorating, and strengthening.

Counter-irritant: An irritant used to relieve another irritation. It is usually an agent applied to the skin to produce a superficial inflammation which reduces or counteracts a deeper inflammation.

Crucifer: A plant of the Cruciferae family which has flowers of four petals arranged in a cross-like formation.

Decoction: A preparation made by simmering a substance in water. A decoction is often made of hard substances, such as roots, bark, or seeds, since it takes long exposure to heat to extract their active principles. The water is only simmered, however, for vigorous boiling may destroy the vital properties of the plant. Usually an ounce of the herb is combined with a pint of boiling water, covered, and simmered for half an hour or more. Some herbalists prefer to use more than a pint to compensate for the liquid lost during the simmering. The preparation is strained and cooled before administration. It should be used immediately for it loses viability rapidly.

Demulcent: Oily or *mucilaginous* substance which soothes the intestinal tract, providing a protective coating and allaying irritation.

Deobstruent: A medicine which clears obstructions from the natural ducts of the body.

Detergent: In medicine, a substance used for cleansing.

Diaphoretic: A substance taken internally to cause sweating. Such medicines are also called *sudorifics.*

Diuretic: A medicine which promotes the flow of urine.

Emetic: An agent which induces vomiting.

Emmenagogue: A medicine taken internally which restores or brings on menstruation.

Emollient: A substance which, when applied externally, softens and soothes the skin.

Expectorant: A substance that loosens and helps to expel phlegm from the throat, breast and lungs by coughing.

Extract: A medicine or other substance which contains the essence of a plant. Extracts are made in a variety of ways, depending upon the best method of drawing out the principle elements from the plant. *Decoctions, infusions,* and *tinctures* are all extracts.

Febrifuge: A medicine which helps reduce fever, sometimes called *antipyretic.*

Flatulence: Gas in the stomach or bowels.

Hemostatic: Any substance used to stem internal bleeding.

Hepatic: Any substance which affects the liver, whether helpfully or harmfully.

Herbarium: A collection of dried plants systematically arranged to permit easy study of them.

Hygroscopic: Having the ability to readily absorb and retain moisture from the air.

Infusion: An *extract* of a particular substance derived by soaking the substance in water. A tea is an infusion. With herbs, an infusion is usually made by combining an ounce of the dried and powdered herb with a pint of boiling water and allowing them to steep for five to ten minutes.

Laxative: A gentle *cathartic,* that helps to promote bowel movements.

Mucilaginous: Refers to a slimy substance, often a viscous or gummy fluid which soothes inflamed parts.

Nervine: A substance which calms or quiets nervousness, tension, or excitement.

Pectoral: Relieves ailments of the chest and lungs.

Perennial: A plant which continues a cycle of new growth and flowering for many seasons between germination of the seed and death. It will live for several years.

Physic: A medicinal substance or preparation.

Poultice: Material applied to the surface of the body as a remedy for some disorder. Usually, a poultice is made of fresh vegetable matter that has been crushed or soaked into a pliant mass, then placed between two pieces of cloth for application.

Purgative: A strong *cathartic*, given to relieve severe constipation.

Raceme: A flower cluster with the separate flowers attached by short equal-length stalks at equal distances along a central stem with the lowest flowers blooming first and the youngest blossom at the top.

Rheumatism: A disease characterized by inflammation, stiffness, and pain in the joints.

Rhizome: A thick prostrate root-like stem, usually horizontal, which sends out roots below and shoots above. It is differentiated from ordinary rootstock by the presence of nodes, buds, and occasionally scale-like leaves.

Rubefacient: A substance which, when rubbed into the skin, reddens it by attracting blood to the area. It acts as an external *stimulant* and *counter-irritant.*

Scrofula: Tuberculosis, especially of the lymphatic glands.

Sedative: A medicine which calms the nerves.

Serration: Notched like a saw. Many herbs have serrated leaves.

Sessile: Refers to leaves and flowers which have no stalk, but are attached directly by the base.

Sialagogue: A substance which stimulates the flow of saliva.

Soporific: A substance that tends to induce sleep.

Specific: A medicine that has a special effect on a particular disease.

Stimulant: A substance which increases or quickens the various functional actions of the body, such as speeding up digestion, raising body temperature, and so on. It does this quickly, unlike a *tonic*, which stimulates general health over a period of time. Unlike a narcotic, it does not necessarily produce a feeling of general well-being.

Stomachic: A medicine which aids the action of the stomach. It promotes digestion and stimulates the appetite.

Styptic: A substance that stops or checks bleeding. It is usually an *astringent* which shrinks the tissues, thus closing exposed blood vessels.

Sudorific: A substance which causes sweating. It is similar to a *diaphoretic.*

Tincture: A solution of organic material in alcohol. Some plants will not release their principles in water, so they are soaked in alcohol, or a mixture of alcohol and water. Usually an ounce of the herb is combined with a pint of alcohol, or alcohol and water, and allowed to steep, with daily agitation, for two weeks. The liquid is strained before use. This type of extract stores well.

Tonic: A substance which invigorates or strengthens the system. Often tonics act as *stimulants* and *alteratives*.

Tuber: An enlarged part of a root or underground stem. The potato is perhaps the most familiar tuber.

Umbel: A cluster of flowers formed by stalks of nearly equal length springing from a common centre. The individual flowers form a flat or convex or concave surface. This type of flower cluster is characteristic of the Umbelliferae family.

Vermifuge: A medicine that destroys intestinal worms and helps expel them. Also called *anthelmintic*.

Vulnerary: A substance used for healing wounds.

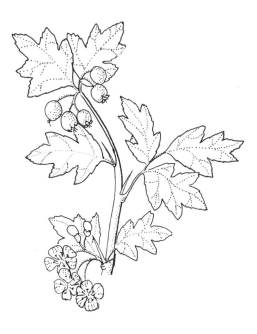

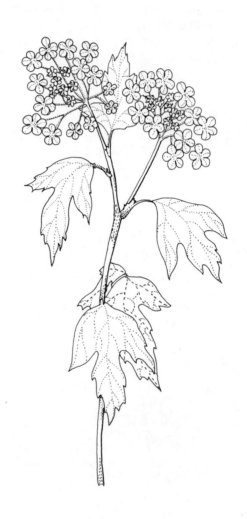

Bibliography

Adrosko, Rita J. *Natural Dyes and Home Dyeing.* New York: Dover, 1971. Distributed through Constable & Co. Ltd., London.

Aichele, Dietmar. *A field Guide in Colour to Wild Flowers.* London: Octopus Books, 1975. ´

Beau, Georges. *Chinese Medicine.* Translated by Lowell Blair. New York: Avon Books, 1972.

Beston, Henry. *Herbs and the Earth* (Dolphin Books Edition). New York: Doubleday, 1973.

Bonar, Ann & MacCarthy, Daphne. *How to Grow and Use Herbs.* London: Ward Lock Ltd., 1974.

Budge, Sir E.A. Wallis. *The Divine Origin of the Craft of the Herbalist.* London: Culpeper House, 1928.

Clarkson, Rosetta E. *Herbs and Savoury Seeds.* New York: Dover, 1972. Distributed through Constable & Co. Ltd., London.

Culpeper, Nicholas. *Culpeper's Complete Herbal.* London: W. Foulsham & Co. Ltd.

Damney, Janet & Pomeroy, Elizabeth. *All About Herbs.* London: The Hamlyn Publishing Group Ltd.

Davenport, Elsie G. *Your Yarn Dyeing.* Pacific Grove, Ca., USA: Craft & Hobby Book Service, 1970.

Defoe, Daniel. *A Journal of the Plague* (Limited Edition). London: The Falcon Press, 1950.

Dioscorides. *The Greek Herbal.* Oxford: Oxford University Press, 1934.

Emmart, (translator). *Badianus Manuscript (1552).* Baltimore, USA: John Hopkins Press, 1940.

Evelyn, John. *Acetaria, A Discourse of Sallets — 1699* Reprint. Brooklyn N.Y. USA: Brooklyn Botanic Garden, 1937.

Everard, Barbara & Morley, Brian D. *Wild Flowers of the World.* London: Ebury Press and Michael Joseph, 1970.

Fernald, M.D. *Gray's Manual of Botany* (8th Edition). Boston, USA: American Book Co., 1950.

Fernie, W.T. *Herbal Simples.* London: J. Wright, 1914.

Fitter, Richard & Alastair. *The Wild Flowers of Britain and Northern Europe.* London: William Collins, Sons & Co. Ltd., 1974.

Fox, Helen Morgenthau. *Gardening with Herbs.* New York: Dover, 1972. Distributed through Constable & Co. Ltd., London.

Fox, William. *Family Botanic Guide.* Sheffield, England: Fox & Sons 1916.

Gibbons, Euell. *Stalking the Healthful Herbs.* New York: David McKay Co., 1966.

Grieve, Maude. *A Modern Herbal.* London: Peregrine Books, 1978.

Hall, Dorothy. *The Book of Herbs.* London: Angus & Robertson Ltd., 1972.

Harriman, Sarah. *The Book of Ginseng.* New York: Pyramid Books 1973.

Harris, Ben Charles. *Eat the Weeds.* New Canaan, Connecticut, USA: Keats Publishing Inc., 1975. Distributed through Thorsons Publishers Ltd., Wellingborough, Northants.

Harrop, Renny (Editor). *Encyclopaedia of Herbs.* London: Marshall Cavendish Ltd., 1975.

Hart, Cyril & Raymond, Charles. *British Trees in Colour.* London: Michael Joseph Ltd., 1973.

Hatfield, Audrey Wynne, FRHS. *How to Enjoy your Weeds.* London: Frederick Muller Ltd.

Healey, B.J. *A Gardener's Guide to Plant Names.* New York: Charles Scribner's Sons, 1972.

Heffern, Richard. *The Herb Buyer's Guide.* New York: Pyramid Books, 1973.

Hersey, Jean. *Cooking with Herbs.* New York: Charles Scribner's Sons, 1972.

Hutchinson, John. *British Wild Flowers* (Vols. 1 & 2). London: Penguin Books Ltd., 1955.

Jain, K.K., M.D. *The Amazing Story of Health Care in New China.* Rodale Press, 1973.

Kadans, Joseph M. *Encyclopaedia of Medicinal Herbs.* New York: Arco, 1975. Distributed by Thorsons Publishers Ltd., Wellingborough, Northants.

Keen, Barbara & Armstrong, Jean. *Herb Gathering.* Brome & Schimmer, 1941.

Kierstead, Salie Pease. *Natural Dyes.* Boston, USA: Bruce Humphries, 1950.

Laurence, D.R. & Black, J.W. *The Medicine You Take.* London: Fontana, 1978.

Law, Donald. *Herb Growing for Health.* (2nd Revised Edition). East Sussex, England: John Gifford Ltd., 1975.

Law, Donald. *Herbs and Herbal Remedies.* London: W. & G. Foyle Ltd.

Levy, Juliette de Bairacli. *Complete Herbal Book for the Dog.* (4th Revised Edition). London: Faber & Faber Ltd., 1975.

Levy, Juliette de Bairacli. *Herbal Handbook for Farm and Stable.* London: Faber & Faber Ltd., 1963.

Levy, Juliette de Bairacli. *The Illustrated Herbal Handbook.* London: Faber & Faber Ltd., 1974.

Levy, Juliette de Bairacli. *Natural Rearing of Children.* London: Faber & Faber Ltd., 1970.

Leyel, Mrs. C.F. *Elixirs of Life.* London: Faber & Faber Ltd., 1958.

Leyel, Mrs. C.F. *Green Medicine.* London: Faber & Faber Ltd., 1952.

Loewenfeld, Claire & Back, Philippa. *The Complete Book of Herbs and Spices.* Newton Abbot, England: David & Charles Ltd., 1978.

Loewenfeld, Claire. *Herb Gardening.* London: Faber & Faber Ltd., 1971.

Looch, Dr. F.R. *Les Plantes Medicinales.* Bienne, France: Ernest Kuhn, 1906.

Lucas, Richard. *Common and Uncommon Herbs for Healthful Living.* London: Parker 1969.

Lucas, Richard. *Nature's Medicines.* London: Parker 1966.

Lusch, (Editor). *About Herbs.* Thomsons.

Mabey, Richard. *Plants with a Purpose.* London & Glasgow: William Collins, Sons & Co. Ltd.

Marks, Geoffrey. *The Medicinal Garden.* New York: Charles Scribner's Sons, 1971.

Martin, W. Keble. *The Concise British Flora in Colour.* London: Ebury Press and Michael Joseph Ltd., 1965.

Mawson. *Herb and Spice Cookery.* London: The Hamlyn Publishing Group Ltd.

Messegue, Maurice. *Of Men and Plants.* London: Weidenfeld & Nicolson 1972.

Mitton, F. & V. *Mitton's Practical Modern Herbal.* Slough, England: W. Foulsham & Co. Ltd.

Quelch, Mary Thorne. *Herbs for Daily Use.* London: Faber & Faber Ltd., 1946.

Raray, Jean. *A Guide to the Wild Flowers of Great Britain and Europe.* London: The Hamlyn Publishing Group Ltd., 1963.

Robinson, M., M.D. *The New Family Herbal and Botanic Physician.* Wakefield, England: W. Nicholson & Sons, 1886.

Rohde, Eleanour Sinclair. *A Garden of Herbs.* New York: Dover, 1969. Distributed through Constable & Co., London.

Rose, Jeanne. *Herbs and Things: Jeanne Rose's Herbal.* New York: Grosset and Dunlap, 1972.

Sanecki, Kay N. *Wild and Garden Herbs.* London: W.H. & L. Collingridge Ltd., 1956.

Shay, & Dirasek. *Herbs: A Concise Guide in Colour.* London: The Hamlyn Publishing Group Ltd.

Simmonite, W.J. *The Simmonite-Culpeper Remedies.* London: W. Foulsham & Co. 1957.

Simons, Adelma G. *Herbs to Grow Indoors.* New York: Hawthorn, 1969.

Smith, William. *Wonders in Weeds.* Health & Science Press.

Step, Edward. *Herbs of Healing.* London: Hutchinson, 1926.

Strange, Richard le. *A History of Herbal Plants.* London: Angus & Robertson, 1977.

Strassburger. *Strassburger's Textbook of Botany.* London: Macmillan Publishers Ltd., 1898.

Thomson, William A.R., M.D. (Editor). *Healing Plants — A Modern Herbal.* London: Macmillan Publishers Ltd., 1978.

Thomson, William, A.R., M.D. *Herbs that Heal.* London: A. & C. Black Ltd.

Thurstan, Violetta. *The Use of Vegetable Dyes.* Leicester, England: Dryad, 1964.

Vogel, Virgil J. *American Indian Medicine.* Norman, Okla. U.S.A.: University of Oklahoma Press, 1970. Distributed through Bailey Bros. & Swinfen, Ltd., Warner House, Folkestone, Kent.

Weiner, Michael A. *Earth Medicine — Earth Foods . . . Of The North American Indians.* London: Collier Macmillan Ltd., 1973.

Wickham, Cynthia. *The House Plant Book.* London: Marshall Cavendish Ltd., 1977.

Woodward, M. *Leaves from Gerard's Herball.* New York: Dover Publications, 1969. Distributed through Constable & Co. Ltd.,

542

London, 1978. Wellingborough, Northants: Thorsons Publishers Ltd., 1972.

Wren, R.C. *Potter's Encyclopaedia of Botanic Drugs and Preparations.* London: Pitman 1956.

Yates, Lucy H. *The Country Housewife's Book.* London: Country Life Ltd., 1934.

Herbal Suppliers
and Useful Addresses

AMERSHAM HEALTH FOODS, 156 Upper Station Road, Amersham, Bucks. Tel: Amersham (024 03) 6752.
Carries a range of the more common herbs and spices. Personal shoppers only.

ARJUNA WHOLEFOODS, 12 Mill Road, Cambridge.
Carries a range of the more common herbs and spices.

ASHFIELDS HERB NURSERY, Hinstock, Market Drayton, Salop. Mr. & Mrs. J. Hugo. Tel: Sambrook (095 279) 392.
Plants, seeds, books, charts, and catalogue.

ASSOCIATION OF BRITISH HERB GROWERS & PRODUCERS, THE, 17 Hasker Street, London SW3. Mr. T. Whittaker (Secretary). Tel: 01-584 2093.

AUGUSTA SEEDS, Crown Chambers, 22 South St. Mary's Gate, Grimsby, South Humberside.
Herb seeds.

BALDWINS, 173 Walworth Road, London SE17. Tel: 01-703 550. Mon.-Sat. 9.00-5.30, Thurs. 9.00-1.00.
Carries a range of the more common herbs and spices.

BINSTED HERBS, The Old Rectory, Binsted, Arundel, Sussex. Mr. D. Tristram. Tel: Yapton (0243) 551277.
Wholesale herb growers, culinary and ornamental. Sell mainly to garden centres.

BLACKDOWNS, Moreton-in-Marsh, Glos. Mr. T. Canning. Tel: Paxford (038 678) 354.
General arable farmer growing sage for drying. Fresh sage available for sale with due notice.

BRISTOL BOTANIC PRODUCTS, 43 Picton Street, Bristol 6. Mr. I. Hughes. Tel: Bristol (0272) 421118.
Herb and spice blender, wholesale herb and spice merchant.

BRITISH HERBAL MEDICINE ASSOCIATION LTD., THE, The Old Coach House, Southborough Road, Surbiton, Surrey KT6 6JN. General Secretary — K.E. Rusby. Tel: 01-399 6693/6.

CHASE COMPOST SEEDS LTD., Benhall, Saxmundham, Suffolk. Tel: Saxmundham (0728) 2149.
Suppliers of herb seeds (limited selection).

COLMAN FOODS, Carrow, Norwich, Norfolk. Mr. J. G. Hemingway. Tel: Norwich (0603) 60166.
Large scale growing, drying and cleaning of mint, parsley and tarragon. Crop experimentation on these and other herbs.

CULPEPER
Fresh herbs sold in pots at all shops except Bruton Street. All shops sell every culinary herb. Please enclose a s.a.e. when applying for Culpeper catalogues, which also contain full details concerning mail order supply, post, packaging etc. Addresses of shops are listed below:

21 Bruton Street, Berkeley Square, London W1X 7DA. Tel: 01-629 4559. Mon.-Fri. 9.30-5.30, Sat. 10.00-5.00.
Personal shoppers, catalogue, mail order.

9 Flask Walk, London NW3. Tel: 01-794 7263. Mon.-Sat. 9.00-5.30, Thurs. 10.00-1.00.
Personal shoppers only. Catalogue.

12D Meeting House Lane, Brighton, Sussex. Mon.-Fri. 9.30-5.30, Sat. 10.00-5.00.
Personal shoppers. Catalogue.

25 Lion Yard, Cambridge. CB2 3NA. Tel: Cambridge (0223) 67370. Mon.-Fri. 9.30-5.30, Sat. 10.00-5.00.
Personal shoppers. Catalogue.

Hadstock Road, Linton, Cambridge. CB1 6NJ. Tel: Cambridge (0223) 891196. Mon.-Fri. 9.30-5.00.
Personal shoppers, mail order, catalogue.

The Friary, Grosvenor Centre, Northampton NN1 2ER. Tel: Northampton (0604) 39288. Mon.-Fri. 9.30-5.30, Sat. 10.00-5.00. Personal shoppers. Catalogue.

14 Bridwell Alley, Norwich. NR2 1AQ. Tel: Norwich (0603) 618911. Mon.-Sat. 9.30-5.30, Thurs. 9.30-1.00. Personal shoppers only. Catalogue.

DAPHNE FFISKE HERB NURSERY, 2 Station New Road, Brundhall, Norwich. Tel: Norwich (0603) 712137. Plants, catalogue.

DOBIE SEEDS, Upper Dee Mills, Llangollen, Clwyd. Tel: Llangollen (0978) 860119. Suppliers of herb seeds (limited selection).

DOWN TO EARTH SEEDS, See Swardmaster Agricultural Seeds.

DORWEST HERB GROWERS, Shipton Gorge, Bridport, Dorset. Tel: Burton Bradstock (030 889) 272. Mail order only. Catalogue.

ENGLISH WOODLANDS LTD., 125 High Street, Uckfield, Sussex. Tel: Uckfield (0825) 4235. Trees and shrubs.

FORGE HERBS, THE, Tunstall, Woodbridge Road, Suffolk. Tel: Snape (072 888) 342.

GOUGH-THOMAS, DR. HUGH, 5 Springfield Road, St. Johns Wood, London NW8. Tel: 01-624 4294. Concerned with plant physiology of herbs.

HAELEN CENTRE, 39 Park Road, London N8. Tel: 01-340 4258. Mon.-Thurs. 11.00-6.00, Fri. 11.00-7.30, Sat. 9.00-5.30. Mail order, personal shoppers, no catalogue. Carries a range of the more common herbs and spices.

HARVEST BARN FARM, Aldsworth, Cheltenham, Glos. Mr. and Mrs. C. Cliff. Tel: Windrush (045 14) 210. Fresh cut herbs — specialities french tarragon and basil.

HECHES HERBS, St. Peter in the Wood, Guernsey, Channel Islands. Tel: Guernsey (0481) 63545.

547

HERB CENTRE, THE, Carlton Crafts, Middleton Tyas, Richmond, Yorks. Mrs. H. Bates.
Plants, fresh herbs in season, dried herbs and herb pillows. Visitors welcome and goods may be ordered by post.

HERB FARM, THE, Broad Oak Road, Canterbury, Kent.

HERB FARM, THE, Ivegill, Carlisle.
Plants.

HERB GARDEN, THE, Thunderbridge, Kirkburton, Huddersfield, Yorks. Mr. M.C. Brierly. Tel: Kirkburton (048 483) 2993.
Plants; largest collection in the north of England.

L'HERBIER DE PROVENCE, 134 Fulham Road, London SW10.
Tel: 01-352 0012.
Carries a range of the more common herbs and spices.

HERBS FROM THE HOO, 46 Church Street, Buckden, Huntingdon, Cambs. PE18 9SX. Mrs. E. Peplow. Tel: Huntingdon (0480) 810818.
Traditional herb garden and nursery with herb workshop. Day courses, lunches with guest speaker and visits to garden for groups. Some mail order. Plants.

HERB SOCIETY, THE, 34 Boscobel Place, London SW1.
Tel: 01-235 1530.

HEREFORD HERBS, Remenham House, Ocle Pychard, Herefordshire. Mr. G. Lloyd. Tel: Burley Gate (043 278) 379.
Producers of frozen culinary herbs — retail, catering and industrial. Suppliers of leading food companies. Retail and gourmet products marked under 'Herba' label. Plants.

HIMALAYAN HERBS, 124 Chiswick High Road, London W4.
Tel: 01-995 7239.
Carries a range of the more common herbs and spices.

HOAR CROSS HERB GARDEN, Hoar Cross, Burton-on-Trent, Staffs. The Hon. Armca Meynell. Tel: Hoar Cross (028 375) 306.
Plants.

HOBBITS, Downham, Billericay, Essex. Mr. R. Lunn.

HOLLINGTON NURSERIES. Woolton Hill, Newbury, Berks. Mr. & Mrs. S. Hopkinson. Tel: Newbury (0635) 253908.
Container plants to the wholesale and retail trade. Earthenware pots.

HONEYROSE PRODUCTS LTD., P.O. Box 4, Creeting Road, Stowmarket, Suffolk. Mr. Ollie. Tel: Stowmarket (044 92) 2137.
The world's leading herbal cigarettes and smoking mixtures. Tobacco free and nicotine free. Manufactured from selected aromatic herbs and fruit juice.

HULLBROOK HOUSE HERB FARM, Shamley Green, Guildford, Surrey. Mr. & Mrs. D. E. Freed. Tel: Bramley (048 647) 3666.
Herb vinegars, herb butters and plants.

HURST, GUNSON, COOPER TABER LTD., Witham, Essex. Mr. B. C. Palmer. Tel: Witham (0376) 516600.
Growers, exporters and importers of seed for agriculture and horticulture. 'Hurst Garden Pride' packets include a range of the most popular herb varieties. Obtainable through retail stockists.

ILEX FARM, British Bee Breeders Association, Clay Cross, Handley, Chesterfield, Derbyshire.
Herbs.

IDEN CROFT NURSERIES, Frittenden Road, Staplehurst, Kent. Mrs. R. Titterington. Tel: Staplehurst (0580) 891432.
Specialists in all the year round fresh cut culinary and aromatic herbs for chefs and catering establishments. Some plants available in spring and summer.

LATHBURY PARK HERB GARDENS, Newport Pagnell, Bucks.

LIGHTHORNE HERBS, Lighthorne Rough, Moreton Morrell, Warwickshire. Mrs. B. Joseph. Tel: Moreton Morrell (092 685) 426.
Wholesale suppliers of herb plants, dried herb packs, herb posters, and cottage garden plants.

MANOR HOUSE HERBS, Wadeford, Chard, Somerset.
Tel: Chard (046 06) 2213.
Catalogue.

MATTHEWS, MRS., The Manor House, The Chenies, Nr. Rickmansworth, Herts.

MIDSOMER HERBS, Byways, Silver Street, Midsomer Norton, Bath, Somerset. BA3 2EU. Tel: Midsomer Norton (0761) 412168.
No catalogue.

NORFOLK LAVENDER LTD., Caley Mill, Heacham, Kings Lynn, Norfolk. Mr. H. Head. Tel: Heacham (0485) 70384.
Largest growers and distillers of lavender in Great Britain. Developing a herb garden.

OAK COTTAGE HERB FARM, Nesscliffe, Shropshire. Mrs. R. Thompson. Tel: Nesscliffe (074 381) 262.
Plants, fragrant and old fashioned plants, pot-pourri. Herb gardens planned and restored. Lectures.

OLDFIELD NURSERIES, Norton St. Philip, Bath, Somerset. BA3 6NG.
Catalogue.

OLD RECTORY HERB FARM, Ightham, Nr. Sevenoaks, Kent. Mr. & Mrs. B. Leary. Tel: Borough Green (0732) 882608.
Walled herb garden, plants, dried lavender, pot-pourri, and large selection of plants and wild species.

ON THE EIGHTH DAY CO-OPERATIVE LTD., 111 Oxford Road, All Saints, Manchester. Tel: 061-273 4878.
Personal shoppers only. Wholefood restaurant. Carries a range of the more common herbs and spices.

ORCHARD HOUSE NURSERY, 105 Abbey Road, Leiston, Suffolk. Tel: Leiston (0728) 830350.

POYNTZFIELD NURSERY GARDEN, By Cannon Bridge, Black Isle, Rosshire. No telephone.
Herbs.

R. V. ROGER LTD., The Nurseries, Pickering, North Yorkshire. Tel: Pickering (0751) 72226.

SENNI HERB FARM, Senni, Sennybridge, Brecon, Powys. Mr. & Mrs. J. Morgan. Tel: (087 482) 717.

SESAME, 128 Regents Park Road, London NW1. Tel: 01-586 3779. Mon.-Sat. 9.30-7.00.
Personal shoppers only, no catalogue. Carries a range of the more common herbs and spices.

STOKE LACY HERB FARM, Bromyard, Herefordshire. Tel: Burley Gate (0432 78) 232.

SUFFOLK HERBS, Sawyers Farm, Little Cornard, Sudbury, Suffolk. Tel: (0787) 227247.
Organically grown herbs and seeds.

SWARDMASTER AGRICULTURAL SEEDS, Cade Horticultural Products, Streetfield Farm, Cade Street, Heathfield, East Sussex. Tel: Heathfield (043 52) 3964.
Seeds (agricultural).

THOMPSON HERBAL, 75 Corporation Street, Coventry, Warwickshire. Fresh loose herbs.

THOMPSON & MORGAN, Seedsmen, Crane Hall, London Road, Ipswich, Suffolk. Tel: Ipswich (0473) 214226.
Variety of seeds.

TIDEBROOK MANOR FARM, Wadhurst, Sussex. Mr. H. Zeylstra (Secretary to the National Institute of Medical Herbalists).
Growing and harvesting, drying of medicinal herbs and preparation of fluid extracts, tinctures and powdered herbs.

TIPPELL, MRS. J., 57 Ormesby Way, Kenton, Harrow, Middlesex. Tel: 01-204 3663.
Variety of usual and unusual herbs.

TRESARE HERB FARM, Taman Bay, Looe, Cornwall.
Please send s.a.e. with enquiries.

TUMBLERS BOTTOM HERB FARM, Kilmersdon, Radstock, Nr. Bath, Somerset. Mr. G. Cooper and Mr. G. Taylor. Tel: Radstock (0761) 34452.
Plants, agricultural shows, shops at Woburn and Beaulieu. Catalogue.

VALESWOOD HERB FARM, Little Ness, Shropshire. Mrs. B. Keen. Tel: Baschurch (0939) 260376.
Plants, dried herbs, pot-pourri, and lavender. Wholesale and retail. Lectures.

WEALD HERBARY, THE, Park Cottage, Frittenden, Cranbrook, Kent.
No telephone.

WELLS & WINTER, Mere House, Nr. Maidstone, Kent. Tel: Maidstone (0622) 812491.

WHOLEFOOD, 110-112 Baker Street, London W1. Tel: 01-935 3924. Plants, fresh herbs in season, and dried herbs.

WOODLANDS FARM NURSERIES, Broad Oak Road, Canterbury, Kent. Tel: Canterbury (0227) 52254.

Index of Latin Names

Page numbers in *italic* refer to photographs

Achillea var. sp., yarrow 73, 86, 190, 213, 244, 289.

Achillea Millefolium, yarrow 56, 61, *72,* 87, 267, 530—31 (with ill.); var. *rubra,* yarrow 10

Acanthopanax senticosus, name promoted by Russian scientists, having the characteristics of ginseng 408

Aconitum Napellus, aconite 74, 313—14 (with ill.)

Acorus calamus, sweet flag, sweet sedge 69, 73, 79, 134, 149, 160, 494—95 (with ill.)

Adonis autumnalis, red camomile 413—14

Adonis vernalis, false hellebore 413—14

Agrimonia Eupatoria, agrimony 153, 192, 314—15 (with ill.)

Agropyrun repens, couch ("quack") grass 84, 203, 238

Ailanthus altissima, tree of heaven 516

Ajuga chamaepitys, common bugle 342

Ajuga pyramidalis, erect bugle (Highland sp.) 342, 343

Ajuga reptans, creeping bugle 55, 342—43 (with ill.); var. *atropurpurea* (bronze) 342—43; var. *multi-colour* (red, brown, and yellow foliage) 343; var. *rubra* (dark purple foliage) 343; var. *variegata* (cream and blue flowers) 343

Alchemilla vulgaris, lady's mantle 86, 213, 221, 301

Allium Cepa, common onion 54, 183, 194, 244, 254, 259, 457—60; var. *proliferum,* Tree onion 457—60

Allium Moly, golden garlic 248

Allium sativum, garlic 19, 48, 61, 63, 90, 198, 213, 221, 238, 245, 248, 254, 257—58, 263, 293, 395—401 (with ill.) 457

Allium Schoenoprasum, chives 10, 93, 100, 120, 198 213, 217, 221, 235, 245, 259, 263, 293, 364—65 (with ill.); var. *sibricum,* giant chive 248

Alnus glutinosa, alder 49, 186, 191, 284, 315—16

Aloysia citriodora and *triphylla,* see *Lippia citriodora*

Althaea officinalis, marshmallow 16, 46, 54

Anagallis arvensis, pimpernel 54

Anethum graveolens, dill, 10, 68, *121,* 124, 158, 160, 198, 213, 231, 233, 235, 238, 254, *255,* 263, 322, 383—85 (with ill.). See also *Peucedanum graveolens*

Angelica Archangelica, angelica 10, 59, 66, 74, 76, *77,* 91, 124, 127, 134, 154, 198, 202, 316—20

Angelica sylvestris, wild angelica 320

Anthemis arvensio, corn camomile 354

Anthemis Cotula, wild camomile, stinking camomile, 354

Anthemis nobilis, common camomile, Roman camomile 52, 54, 78, 90, 124, 126, 151, 153, 156, 198, 221, 231, 245, 251, 256, 259, 281, 301, 349—54 (with ill.)

Anthemis tinctoria, ox-eye camomile, 193, 354

Anthoxanthum odorata, sweet vernal grass 75

Anthriscus Cerefolium, chervil 10, 14, 63, 213, 216, 235, 361—63 (with ill.). See also *Scandix Cerefolium* and *Myrrhis odorata*

Apium graveolens, wild celery 360 (with ill.)

Apium hortense, garden parsley 462

Arctium Lappa, burdock 54, 71, *83,* 343—45 (with ill.)

Arctostaphylos Uva-ursi, bearberry 49, 80, 82

Armoracia lapathifolia, syn. *Armoracia rusticana,* horseradish 66, 202, 213, *264,* 419—422. See also *Cochlearia Armoracia*

Armoracia rusticana, see *Armoracia lapathifolia*

Arnica montana, arnica 46, 278, 325

Artemisia var. sp., wormwood 73, *148,* 149, 244, 259, 278, 284, 289, 299. See also *Artemisia Absinthium*

Artemisia Abrotanum, southernwood 10, 12, 149, *150,* 213, 256, 259, 265, 284, 293, 500—01

Artemisia Absinthium, wormwood 12, 61, 79,

Index of Common Names

Page numbers in *Italic* refer to photographs

561

Common Lime *see* Lime Tree
Common Nettle 52, 56, 75, 79, 90, 190, 198,
    213, 256, 259, 456—57 (with ill.)
Common Onion *see* Onion
Common Speedwell 501—02 (with ill.)
Common Thyme *see* Thyme
Compass-weed 479—83 (with ill.)
Conifers 283, 284
Convolvulus 238
Coreopsis 175, 182, 186, 193
Coriander 22, 93, 124, 127, 198, 213, 233,
    246, 254, 375—76 (with ill.)
Corn Camomile 354
Corn Feverfew 354
Corn Poppy 472
Cornish Lovage 433—35 (with ill.)
Corona Solis 503—07 (with ill.)
Corsican Mint 299, 448
Costmary 251, 377—79
Cottonseed 505
Couch Grass 84, 203, 238
Coughwort 370—71 (with ill.)
Cow Chervil 366—68 (with ill.)
Cowslip 79, 251, 379—80 (with ill.)
Crack Willow 522 (with ill.)
Cranesbill 56, 69
Creeping Wintergreen 523
Crocus *see* Saffron
Crowfoot 250, 348 (with ill.)
Cucumber 89, 111, 244, 245
Cudbear 190
Cumin 94, 127, 233, 322, 380—81
Curled Dock 48, 385—86 (with ill.)

Daffodil 76
Dahlia 193
Daisies 90, 251, 257
Dalmation Pellitory 474
Damask Rose 167, 475, 477
Dandelion 70, 71, 74—75, 80, 82, 84, *85*,
    90, 94, 186, 190, 198, 240, 254, 256,
    301, 381—83 (with ill.)
Daphne 442—43 (with ill.)
Dead Men's Bells 394—95 (with ill.)
Dead Nettle 261
Devil's Nettle 530—31 (with ill.)
Dill 10, 68, 94, *121*, 124, 158, 160, 198,
    213, 231, 233, 235, 238, 254, *255*, 263,
    284, 285, 383—85 (with ill.)
Dock 52, 191, 193, 385—86 (with ill.)
Dog Fennel, *Anthemis Cotula* 354
Dog Rose 476—77 (with ill.)

Dogwood 60, 502 (with ill.)
Dwarf Basil 331
Dwarf Bay 442—43 (with ill.)
Dwarf Nasturtium 301
Dwarf Sage 289, 299
Dyer's Broom 193
Dyer's Madder 190, 435—36 (with ill.)
Dyer's Saffron 486

Egyptian Mint 448
Elder 44, 61, 75, 78, 386—87
Elf Dock 387—88
Elm *see* Slippery Elm
Enebro 426—27 (with ill.)
English Alder 315—16
English Lavender 428—30
English Oak 44, 48, 49, 50, 56, 69, 256
Englishman's Foot 470 (with ill.)
Erect Bugle 342
Eryngo 415
Eucalyptus 50, 54, 57, 149, 243, 388—89
Euphrasia 44, 389—90 (with ill.)
Eyebright, *Euphrasia officinalis* 44, 389—90
    (with ill.)
Eyebright, *Lobelia inflata* 432

Fairy Cups 379—80 (with ill.)
Fairy Thimbles 394—95 (with ill.)
Fake Saffron 486
False Dittany, *Dictamnus alba* 347 (with ill.)
False Hellebore 413—14
False Jacob's Ladder 426
False Wintergreen 469 (with ill.)
Fat Hen 410—11 (with ill.)
Featherfew 392—94 (with ill.)
Felon Herb 448—51 (with ill.)
Fenkel 390—92 (with ill.)
Fennel 44, 66, *67*, 68, 94, *95*, 124, 197,
    202, 213, 216, 233, 244, 245, 254, 263,
    376, 383, 384, 390—92 (with ill.)
Fenugreek 94
Fern *see* Sweet Fern
Feverfew 256, *257*, 278, 392—94 (with ill.)
Five-Fingers, *Panax quinquefolius* 407—09
Five-Fingers, *Potentilla* sp. 368—69
Five-Leaf Grass 368—69
Flags *see* Iris *and* Sweet Flag
Flax 52, 54, 71, 256
Flammula Jovis 369
Fleabane 56
Florentine Iris 133

General Index

Rosewood
Rose beads 166—67
Rose Elder (guelder rose) 411—12 (with ill.)
Rose Geranium, *see* Geranium
Rose lavender powder 154
Rose lilac (sachet) 147
Rose water 44, 156—57 (with ill.)
Rosemary 479—83 (with ill.), 509; aromatic 152, 154, 158, 160, 166, 482—83; companion planting 245, 256, 265; culinary 97, 108, *115,* 483; cultivation and propagation of 213, 217, 224, 480; decorative 90; Hungary water, recipes for, 482; in Christian legend 480; in landscaping 269, 284, 293, 301; in pot-pourris and sachets, 139, 482; insect spray 259; medicinal 68, 78, 482; moth repellent 147; symbol of fidelity 479; tea, recipe for 482; wine, recipe for 482
Rosemary potatoes 108
Rosewood, oil of 160
Rotenone 231
Round-leaved Dock 385, 386
Royal Society 28
Rubiaceae 10, 335, 435, 525
Rue, 441, 483—85 (with ill.); culinary 485; cultivation and propagation of 484; flea repellent 485; harvesting, drying, and storing of 484; medicinal *53,* 483, 485; oil of 485; used against witches 484
Rugosa Rose, *see* Japanese Rose
Run-by-the-Ground (pennyroyal) 466—67 (with ill.)
Running Myrtle (periwinkle) 468
Rutaceae 10, 347, 483

Sabarth, Erica 244
Sachets and pot-pourris 138—146; exotic pot-pourri 145; for linen 146; herb garden 145; lavender blend 145; lemon verbena 145; old English pot-pourri 147; rose lilac 147; spicy perfume for

sachets 146; wild flower 146; woody mixture 146
Safflower, 486; culinary 100, *101;* description of 486; habitat 486; in dyeing 188, 486; medicinal 486; oil, containing vitamin F 89; seeds, source of oil 486
Saffron 486—87; culinary 100; cultivation and propagation of 486—87; description of 486; medicinal 64, 486; stigmas, collecting the 486—487
Sage 10, 487—90 (with ill.), 509; aromatic 152, 158, 160, 166, 169; companion planting 245, 250, 251, 252, 255, 265, 489; culinary 98 (with ill.), 487, 489, 490; cultivation and propagation of 213, 217, 488; decorative 90; habitat 487; harvesting and drying of 489; in landscaping 289, 301; insect spray 259; medicinal 66, 487, 489
Sage-leaved Germander 405—406
St. Anthony's Turnip (bulbous buttercup) 348 (with ill.)
St. John's Blood (St. John's wort) 490—91 (with ill.)
St. John's Plant (mugwort) 448—51 (with ill.)
St. John's Wort 490—91 (with ill.); in dyeing 188; medicinal 50, 69, 87, 491; religious ties 490—91
St. Peter's Wort 55
Salad Burnet *see* Burnet, Salad
Salads and salad dressings, recipes for 112
Salicaceae 471, 522
Sally Sour (sorrel) 497—500 (with ill.)
Salsafy (salsify) 44, 68, *106,* 491—92 (with ill.)
Salsify 491—92 (with ill.); culinary *106;* cultivation and propagation of 491—92; habitat 491; medicinal 44, 68
Salvia Dorisiana 99
Sandalwood 154, 160; oil of 166; root 149, 160
Santolina (lavender cotton) 10, 430; cultivation and

propagation of 213, 224; in landscaping *280,* 284, 289, 293
Sarsaparilla 82, 492
Sassafras 38, 46, 78, 124; oil of 166; root 149, 160
Sauces, recipes for 104, 113
Savory 122, 213, 299, 492—494 *see* Summer Savory *and* Winter Savory
Savory butter 122
Sawge (sage) 487—90 (with ill.)
Saxifragaceae 422
Scabwort (elecampane) 387—388
Scarlet Pimpernel 379
Scent of Roses (perfume essence) 161
Scented Geranium, *see* Geranium
Scotch Broom 341—42 (with ill.); companion planting 252, 256; in dyeing 188, 195 *see also* Broom
Scrophulariaceae 389, 394, 451, 501
Sea Holly 415—16 (with ill.)
Sea Hulver (sea holly) 415—16 (with ill.)
Sea Wormwood 528
Sedatives 79—80
Sedge, *see* Sweet Sedge
Seeds, growing herbs from 215—16; aftercare 216—21
Self-heal 73
Senna 496 (with ill.)
Sesame 104, 496—97
Seven Barks (hydrangea) 422
Shakers, The 27—30
Shakespeare, William 129 (on the rose); mentioned in his works: balm 325; bay 334; burdock 345; cowslip 380; garlic 399, 401; sweet marjoram 441; plantain 470; rosemary 481; rue 484; thyme 130
Shallots 245
Shelley, Percy Bysshe 330—31
Shen-nung, Chinese emperor 30
Shepherd's Needle (sweet cicely) 366—68 (with ill.)
Shepherd's Purse 70, 87
Sicklewort (bugle) 342—43 (with ill.)
Silver Birch 283, 337—38 with ill.) *see* Birch *and*